Retailing

PRINCIPLES AND PRACTICES
Fourth Edition

G. HENRY RICHERT
Professor of Marketing
Georgetown University
Washington, D.C.
formerly Program Specialist
for Distributive Education
U.S. Office of Education
Washington, D.C.

WARREN G. MEYER
Associate Professor of Education
University of Minnesota
Minneapolis, Minnesota

PETER G. HAINES
Chairman, Department of Business
and Distributive Teacher Education
Michigan State University
East Lansing, Michigan
State Teacher Trainer
for Distributive Education

GREGG PUBLISHING DIVISION
McGraw-Hill Book Company, Inc.
New York   Chicago   Dallas   Corte Madera, Calif.   Toronto   London

RETAILING, Principles and Practices, Fourth Edition

1 2 3 4 5 6 7 8 9 0 QB-62 9 8 7 6 5 4 3 2

Code Number 52608

Library of Congress Catalog Card No. 61-10138

PUBLISHED BY GREGG PUBLISHING DIVISION
McGraw-Hill Book Company, Inc.
Printed in the United States of America

Preface

Retailing, Principles and Practices, Fourth Edition, is a thorough revision of a book that has been widely used in its various editions throughout the country for nearly 25 years. The preceding editions have been popular in schools offering formal retailing instruction, in adult education classes, and in employee-training classes conducted by retail stores. The authors believe that the new features of this fourth edition will further enhance the book's usefulness in these training situations.

Organization and Features

The fourth edition of *Retailing, Principles and Practices* may be called a "progressive" approach to the study of retailing. By this is meant that the student starts his study of retailing as he would be likely to start a job in a retail establishment; that is, at the bottom and working up—progressing from the beginning jobs and techniques to the more advanced duties and concepts in retailing.

Section One. The book opens with a dramatic panoramic overview of retailing, emphasizing its ever-changing nature. The purpose of this overview is to show the scope of retailing and how it influences the lives of everyone. Then the student is shown where he can fit into this exciting retailing picture—the opportunities available and the educational and personal requirements needed for taking advantage of them.

Section Two. In this section, the student is introduced to the beginning jobs in retailing—jobs that he may expect to fill at the start—with emphasis on the importance of learning and doing these jobs well. The sequence is intended to parallel somewhat the student's own experience as a part-time employee or co-operative trainee. Great stress has been placed on human relations in dealing with customers, with fellow workers, and with supervisors.

Section Three. Here the student progresses to the "front-line" activities of retailing—selling, sales promotion, merchandising, and customer services.

Section Four. Finally, the student looks into the problems of retailing management, learning about such functions as store location, layout, buying, pricing, accounting, and personnel management—the top rung of the retailing ladder.

Emphasis

Retailing, Principles and Practices, Fourth Edition, covers all aspects of retailing. Most textbooks in the past have concentrated almost exclusively on department-store retailing. While this is a highly important type of retailing operation and deserves considerable emphasis, other types of retailing today are continually demanding attention: grocery stores, hardware stores, gasoline service stations, small service businesses, specialty shops, and so on. This book attempts to give the student a *total* picture of retailing as it takes place on Main Street, in suburban shopping centers, and on fashionable boulevards.

In this new edition, considerable stress is placed on the co-operative part-time student in retailing. Retailing textbooks have traditionally been general-information books without specific reference to those who are employed in a distributive education program. The authors feel that in making the book more appealing and helpful to the co-operative part-time student, it has also been made more appealing and helpful to all students, regardless of their reasons for studying retailing and the ways in which they carry on their studies.

Student-Activity Materials

The book is divided into twenty units, which are broken down into 70 parts. Each part contains an abundance of student activities—vocabulary lists, questions based on the text matter, problems and projects involving decision-making and problem-solving, and special activities for the co-operative part-time student under the heading "Learning Your Job." These "LYJ" activities help the student to relate the information in the textbook to that acquired on the job.

Illustrations

Again *Retailing, Principles and Practices, Fourth Edition,* claims distinction in the quantity and variety of illustrations, most of which were supplied by leading retail stores throughout the country. A special feature that has characterized this book for many years are the photographs of prominent pioneers and modern leaders in American retailing. The authors believe this feature will continue to provide inspiration and interest to students.

Supporting Materials

Objective Tests. A set of objective tests has been published to accompany this book. These tests are available at a nominal cost.

Manual and Key. The *Instructor's Manual and Key* contains a key to the student-activity material in the textbook, as well as helpful suggestions for organizing the course and teaching it effectively. It is available without cost to instructors.

Acknowledgments

A great many people assisted, both directly and indirectly, in the preparation of this book. Hundreds of retailing teachers and distributive education specialists responded to questionnaires concerning their preferences in retailing textbook content, organization, and emphasis. Many stores and organizations supplied valuable ideas as well as hundreds of photographs and drawings. It would be impossible, of course, to acknowledge individually the assistance given. The authors hope, however, that each person who contributed to this final product will consider this "Thank you" to be directed personally to him.

G. Henry Richert
Warren G. Meyer
Peter G. Haines

Contents

Section 3: Retailing: Basic Job Skills

Section 4: Merchandising Management

1. Retailing Is Dynamic

Unit 1

Part 1

The New Look in Retailing

Look around your town or city. Retail stores are everywhere—providing you, your family, and your friends with the goods you want. These wants are different today from what they were only ten years ago, because Americans are constantly changing their style of living. The modern retail store reflects these changes and continues to meet our new needs. New stores—shopping centers, discount houses, supermarkets—are springing up. Many stores are open one or more nights of the week. Many retailers now feature self-service. In addition, new merchandising techniques of display, packaging, and credit have been developed to attract and hold customers.

Retail stores are vital to the life of the community, bringing jobs and income to many families. For you personally, the modern retail store can be a thrilling, exciting center of activity, providing opportunities for an attractive career. By assembling products in many styles and fashions from all over the world, retailing provides a variety of work, a chance to meet people, stable employment, a rewarding income, and almost unlimited opportunities for advancement to executive positions. Before you choose your career, you will want to look into retailing, a dynamic world that is wearing a new look.

In grandmother's day, the corner grocery was just a small room with a potbellied stove, dusty shelves with assorted merchandise, a wooden counter, and open barrels of flour, crackers, apples, pickles, and salted fish. There was no meat department. Fresh produce in the winter months was rare. The store personnel often consisted of the owner, his wife, and possibly a delivery boy.

Today, the modern food store may be half the size of a football field. It may have cost nearly half a million dollars to build and equip and is probably staffed by a large number of specially trained men and women. It may have "magic-eye" door openers, a playroom for children, mirrored and muraled walls, chrome-trimmed shelves, piped-in music, and mechanized checkout lanes. It probably has air conditioning, refrigeration, special meat-processing rooms, and fresh fruits and vegetables the year round. At least $50,000 is needed to stock such a store with from 4,000 to 8,000 food and nonfood items.

1

The Changing Retail Scene

The startling changes in retail food stores are matched by similar changes in department stores, hardware stores, variety and specialty stores, service stations, and in other kinds of retailing establishments.

Department stores have modernized and enlarged their downtown establishments. They have installed escalators for customers who want to shop on upper or lower floors and express elevators for those who want to reach these floors quickly. They have added new customer services to make shopping more convenient and pleasurable. They have increased the number of merchandising departments and offer for sale goods from all parts of the world.

Hardware stores and variety stores have adopted visual merchandising as a principal means of attracting and selling to customers. Visual glass fronts, open counter displays, much forward stock (and little merchandise in the stock room), check-out counters—all these merchandising devices enable customers to see and handle the merchandise and to make purchases quickly and conveniently when the buying decision has been reached.

Specialty stores, such as dress shops and shoe stores, offer the customer with special needs an opportunity to make a selection from a variety of styles, sizes, and colors in the particular lines that the store carries. The modern specialty store is attractive, employs well-informed salespeople who serve as customer consultants, and offers specialized services adapted to the kinds of merchandise that the store sells.

Service stations are also emerging as a very important form of present-day retailing. Since a large majority of American families own automobiles, they require service stations conveniently located to supply not only fuel and oil but also a variety of services needed by the family car. Some service stations in metropolitan centers have become very elaborate with landscaped grounds, customer lounges, and well-equipped repair shops.

Our expanding population with larger family incomes is demanding many

Beautiful buildings with glass fronts, showing interior open displays, invite the customer to shop inside.

Courtesy Sears, Roebuck and Co.

A special service to shoppers—making shopping a pleasure by eliminating traffic in a central shopping area, planting trees and shrubs, and placing benches for the foot weary.

more services. Reaching out to meet this need are the service businesses that deal directly with consumers. These businesses may provide personal services, such as dry cleaning and appliance repairs; or they may sell intangibles, such as insurance. Technically, the service business is not a retail business, because it renders services and does not sell merchandise. However, since personal selling and other typical retail operating procedures, such as sales promotion, are involved, the service business can rightly be characterized as part of the new look in retailing.

Dynamic New Merchandising Techniques

In our rapidly expanding economy, some new merchandising techniques have had great impact on customer buying habits and retail practices.

Scrambled Merchandising. Not many years ago, most stores carried only one major line of merchandise. While this practice is still followed by some types of specialty stores, many stores have added greatly to the variety of merchandise they offer for sale. Today, some food supermarkets are small department stores, carrying profitable lines of hardware, housewares, garden supplies, toys, and even clothing. Many former 5-and-10-cent variety stores now have added lines of ready-to-wear and furniture. Some even sell power lawn mowers. This tendency among retailers to add profitable new merchandise lines that give the customer the advantage of "one-stop" shopping is called *scrambled merchandising*. This new concept in retailing calls for personnel who study customer buying habits and who can merchandise with imagination.

Night Openings. In many communities, some retail stores now remain open at least three evenings each week. This is particularly true in some shopping-center stores, which are open from 9 A.M. to 9 P.M. six days a week. One important effect of night openings is that stores now use at least two shifts of employees and need many more assistant managers and supervisors. These positions open up new opportunities for younger employees anxious for advancement.

A modern service station.

Visual Merchandising. Some of the most important changes that have taken place in retailing in recent years are those associated with the term *visual merchandising*—selling through display. Visual merchandising offers the customer the opportunity to see the goods plainly, frequently to examine them personally, and to obtain from show cards, manufacturers' labels, and price tags a description of the goods and information about prices. Through visual merchandising, the time and effort of the customer and salesperson are conserved. The customer can do her shopping more quickly and conveniently, and the salesperson can serve more customers and still perform additional store duties.

The development of visual merchandising has greatly changed the nature of store layout and equipment. Brick, stone, and wood store fronts have been replaced with all-glass doors and glass display windows reaching from ceiling to floor. The entire first floor of the store becomes a display window.

In the interior of the store, closed counters and shelves out-of-reach of the customer have been replaced with open-display counters, aisle-display tables and racks, and accessible shelving. On these are laid out most of the merchandise that the store or department has for sale. The amount of forward stock has been greatly increased; the merchandise back in the stock room, greatly decreased. Visual merchandising is of benefit to the customer because he can see and handle the merchandise and therefore understand better what he is buying; the benefit to the store is that it reduces selling costs and increases stock turnover and profit.

Automation in Stores. Mechanized and electronically controlled production is a reality in the modern factory. Retail stores are experimenting with ways to adapt these automated techniques to certain phases of store operation: (1) control of stock and stock maintenance, (2) mechanizing of check-out-counter operation, and (3) budgeting of sales and purchases, as well as control of expenses. Computers and calculators are destined to be important merchandising tools that will help retail-store executives gather figures and make computations to serve as a basis for decisions and store planning.

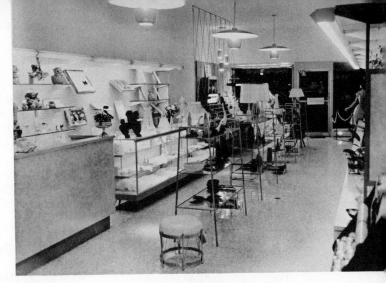

Everything out, displayed attractively, for the customer's inspection. That is the advantage of visual merchandising shown here.

Courtesy Fields Bridal Shoppe, Zion, Ill.

Selling by automation, that is by coin-operated vending machines, is gaining in popularity. Cold and hot drinks, candy, tobacco, toilet articles, dairy products, and even travel insurance are sold through vending machines. Experiments are being conducted to determine if items such as hosiery, cosmetics, notions, and toys can be sold in this manner. While it seems likely that most kinds of merchandise will not lend themselves to sale by vending machines, such machines may be used extensively to supplement personal selling and to make certain goods available after store closing hours.

Fabulous New Merchandise

New products are available today that no one dreamed possible a few years ago. New fibers are used to make fabrics that are crease resistant and that do not shrink. Instant foods and beverages, frozen foods, even packaged dinners, are found in most food stores. Customers by the thousands are demanding what used to be considered luxury goods—boats and motors, power tools, motion-picture cameras, projectors, and so on. New markets have opened up for garden supplies, toys, recreation equipment, do-it-yourself materials, and the like.

Today's retailer needs to know much more about his markets and about the vast array of merchandise he sells than formerly. Understanding the modern customer's needs and desires for goods is basic to sound merchandising in the progressive retail store.

Trade Talk

Successful retailers have a specialized vocabulary by means of which they effectively communicate ideas. The section called "Trade Talk" appears at the end of each part; it offers you a chance to build your retailing vocabulary. The following terms are part of the retailer's daily vocabulary. Define each one in your own words, then use it in a sentence.

automation   service retailer
scrambled   visual
    merchandising   merchandising

Can You Answer These?

1. If service businesses are not retail stores, why are they included in a study of retailing?

2. What major merchandising developments illustrate the dynamic nature of retailing?

3. How is the modern retailer affected by rapid changes in the variety of products available?

4. What are some of the physical changes that have taken place in retail food stores in recent years?

5. How have sources of store merchandise changed over the years?

6. What is one of the most important effects of store night openings? How might this affect your chances of getting part-time work?

Problems and Projects

1. To illustrate the new products on the market today, list at least five products that you know were not available five years ago. Compare your list with the lists of other class members and see how many new products you can list as a group.

2. Make a list of as many kinds of service businesses as you can. Do you agree with the statement that "service businesses are an important part of retailing service to the consumer"?

3. Prepare a paper giving arguments pro and con on the statement, "Merchandise vending machines will replace a majority of salespeople."

4. In order to understand better how widespread is the concept of scrambled merchandising, (a) make a chart of at least five different types of stores, such as hardware, apparel, and food stores; (b) for each type, name the lines of merchandise carried that are quite different from their main line.

Example:

Food store	Toys, cosmetics

Learning Your Job

If you have a part-time job in retailing, either as a DE co-operative trainee or just on your own, your job situation will help you really understand retailing. The activities throughout this book under the heading "Learning Your Job" are keyed to your job. Each activity helps you to apply the textbook principles to a store situation. In doing so, you will become a skilled retailer sooner.

1. Give examples of the ways in which your store has adopted the new merchandising techniques described on pages 3–5.

2. List articles sold in your store that have come on the market only within the last few years. In what ways does your list indicate the importance of your studying merchandise and acquiring product information?

3. In what phases of store operation has the store in which you are employed adopted automated techniques?

2 *A Store for Every Kind of Customer*

Many people think of retailing as the large store—the department store and the supermarket—for these are the stores used most often by consumers. Yet retailing includes stores of all sizes and types, each offering different products and services.

The *1958 U.S. Census of Business, Retail Distribution,* reveals that in that year there were 954,522 retail stores in the United States doing a business of less than $50,000 annually, some stores having annual sales of less than $5,000. These stores were owned and operated by 975,731 proprietors and employed 904,990 workers. You can deduce from these figures that retailing establishments are made up largely of small stores. When considering a career in retailing, remember that small stores offer good opportunities for an attractive income, either by going into business for yourself, or for gaining valuable experience for advanced positions in larger stores. They also provide a route of entry into other fields of distribution, such as wholesaling, insurance, and selling for manufacturers.

Developments and Trends in Retail Stores

While the number of retail stores in the country has remained fairly constant in the past few years (1,668,479 in 1948, 1,721,650 in 1954 and 1,788,325 in 1958), there have been marked changes in the field of retailing; and some types of stores have gained new prominence.

The Independent Store

Many stores, especially small ones, are classified as "independents" because they are independently owned and operated. An independent store is controlled

This specialty shop creates a harmonious atmosphere for its tweed clothing and accessories.

Courtesy The Tweed Shop, Fort Lauderdale, Fla.

by its own management. The management may consist of one person; a partnership of two or more persons; or in some cases, a corporation. Not only are the independent stores historically the oldest type, but they are also the most common and do a large share of all retail business. Independent stores do the major share of business in some fields (florists and automobile dealers, for example) but account for a relatively small share of the sales in other fields dominated by corporate chain stores, such as variety and foods. Many independent stores, particularly those dealing in specialty goods, have a substantial sales volume and earn a good profit; most of them offer opportunity to be one's own "boss."

The Rising Influence of the Corporate Chains

A corporate chain organization is owned and operated by one firm, which is organized as a corporation. Control, including buying, is centralized in the main office of the chain or, in the case of larger chains, in branch headquarters. A chain is said to be *local* if the majority of the stores are in or around one city; *sectional,* if its stores are confined to one section or region of the country; and *national,* if its stores are located throughout the country. For example, the Great Atlantic and Pacific Tea Company (A & P) is a national chain.

Although chain stores date back to before the turn of the century (the A & P to 1859 and Krogers to 1882), the chain-store movement did not become stabilized until the late 1930's. Corporate chain stores now account for over 30 per cent of the nation's total retail trade volume, and this percentage is growing. In some fields—food, variety, shoe, department, drug, and women's apparel lines—chain stores dominate the retailing picture.

Corporate chain-store merchandising methods are so successful today that they are an accepted part of the American system of distribution. These methods

GEORGE H. HARTFORD, 1833–1917
Founder of the Great Atlantic & Pacific Tea Company in 1859; pioneer in efficient low-cost mass distribution of food.

include: (1) closely controlled buying of merchandise, (2) effective visual display, (3) aggressive sales promotion, and (4) systematic bookkeeping. Although some independent stores have lost ground to the chains, many, individually or through their own co-operative organizations, have met the competition of the corporate chains by borrowing these merchandising techniques from them.

The Voluntary Chain Store

Some independent stores have banded together to form *voluntary chains* to enable them better to meet corporate chain-store competition. The voluntary chain organization is composed of a group of independent retailers who own and operate their own stores. They either own or are affiliated with a wholesale house or co-operative buying agency. The voluntary chain organization gives independents the advantages of joint buying and sales promotion. As is the practice with corporate chains, sales-promotion plans and advertising materials are centrally prepared and made available to the independent stores, helping them to meet corporate chain competition while retaining control of their own businesses. Voluntary chains or co-operative buying groups are very active in the grocery, drug, hardware, and dry-goods fields.

The Specialty Shop

A store carrying but one type of merchandise—such as hats, jewelry, hardware, furs, auto accessories, bakery items, and meats—is often called a *one-line* or *specialty shop*. The growing population in the United States, the automobile, and the customer demand for wider varieties and better selection of goods have brought about the growth of specialty or one-line stores. Such stores may be owned independently or may belong to a chain organization.

Because these shops specialize in a limited merchandising field, they are able to offer a wide assortment of the goods they carry, an extensive range in sizes, and the newest fashions. Specialty stores offer an opportunity to practice salesmanship of a high order. Salespeople frequently earn larger salaries in these stores than in other stores.

The Big Boys: Department Stores

A department store is a retail store that sells many different lines of merchandise, such as women's ready-to-wear and accessories, men's and boys' wear, piece goods, housewares, and furniture. It is, in effect, a combination of many specialty stores under one roof. The name "department" store comes from the fact that the store is organized into separate departments for purposes of merchandising, sales promotion, customer service, accounting, control, and personnel management.

Because the department store carries many lines of merchandise, it appeals to a large number of people. Through the various services offered, it seeks to attract customers who will return to the store often. The large department stores

Huge supermarkets are showplaces, offering everything from staple items to the fanciest of foods.

Courtesy Sunrise Shopping Center, Fort Lauderdale, Fla.

provide restaurants, reading and writing rooms, playrooms for children, lounges, and numerous other services. Most of them carry on excellent training programs for their employees. Thus, for the ambitious young person who likes merchandising, the department store offers an excellent opportunity for advancement.

Department stores play a prominent role in retailing, especially in large urban centers. Growing competition, however, has caused many independent department stores to affiliate with chain organizations or with co-operative buying groups. While the large department store will continue to play a major role in distribution, the smaller ones, faced with increased competition from other retailers—such as supermarkets, chains, specialty shops, and discount houses —are losing ground steadily.

A variation of the department store is the *departmentalized specialty store.* While departmentalized, this store usually restricts its merchandise lines to ready-to-wear and home furnishings. Unlike the department store, it does not carry lines such as appliances and hardware.

The Growing "Supers"

During the depression years of the 1930's, a remarkable change in food retailing occurred—the introduction of the supermarket we associate with self-service. A *supermarket* is a departmentalized retail establishment, having at least four basic food departments—grocery, meat, produce, and dairy. To be classified as a supermarket, a store must have a self-service grocery department and do a minimum annual business of $500,000. In the last few years, supermarkets have doubled in number. They now account for approximately two-thirds of all grocery sales.

The supermarket has had a marked influence on the other types of retailing. For example, drugstores, variety stores, and many department stores now feature open and accessible display, prepackaged items, and check-out counters, all pioneered by the "super." Self-service is also being used increasingly in hardware stores, lumber and building-supply stores, clothing stores, and gasoline stations. Many of the latest merchandising techniques are to be seen and learned in the modern "super."

The Newcomer: The Discount House

The discount house, which tempts customers with low prices, has become an accepted form of retailing in the United States. The number of discount houses has grown rapidly since the end of World War II. These stores offer nationally advertised merchandise, such as appliances, at prices substantially below those prevailing elsewhere. The discount house attempts to sell a large volume of merchandise at a small profit on each article. Usually, few services are offered; but some advertising is done. Much sales promotion results from word-of-mouth and through the use of "privilege" cards given to organized groups, such as union members and government employees. The discount house generally occupies an inexpensive building in a low-rent location.

Located chiefly in the larger cities, discount houses have enlarged their merchandise selection from appliances only to include housewares, toys, hardware, sporting goods, jewelry, and photographic equipment. In some cases they also sell ready-to-wear and home furnishings. Some have even increased their services, such as credit, delivery, adjustment, merchandise repair, and installation.

Discount houses have achieved substantial public acceptance, apparently showing that many customers are price-conscious and willing to forgo services that retailers had long thought necessary. Some regular retailers, particularly department stores and specialty stores selling appliances, have adopted discount-house policies in order to meet this form of competition. To customers who are willing to forgo their regular services, discount houses allow lower prices. The elimination of services reduces the servicing expense of the store and, to an extent, the overhead expense.

The Shopping Center

Not a store but a city of stores, the shopping center has mushroomed in recent years. In many modern shopping centers, the American customer can park his automobile in one of thousands of free parking places, enjoy family shopping in informal clothing, and purchase almost every product imaginable. Originally

Everything conveniently located in one shopping center.

designed to cater to the suburbanite, the large shopping center draws many customers from rural areas, small towns, and from the centers of cities themselves.

Shopping centers are of two main types. Small neighborhood centers, with from four to ten stores, are common. Such centers usually have as the main attraction, or anchor, a large food supermarket and often include gasoline stations, dry cleaners, drugstores, and hardware dealers. These "baby" shopping centers usually serve customers mainly from the immediate neighborhood.

On the fringes of many cities can be found the second type of shopping center—the new "retailing cities." These are the giant centers, often containing 25 to 75 stores surrounded by acres of parking space. The anchor of these retailing cities is often one or more large department stores. Clustered around them are the smaller shops providing almost every kind of merchandise and service the customer could wish for.

Mail-Order Retailers

Nearly everyone is familiar with the two largest mail-order houses—Sears, Roebuck and Company and Montgomery Ward & Company. And there are other well-known companies, too, such as Spiegel, Inc., and Aldens, Inc. Recently, discount mail-order firms have become prominent, offering merchandise at "wholesale prices" to "preferred" customers.

At one time, customers in rural areas did a substantial business volume with mail-order firms. However, good roads and better merchandising by retailers in smaller towns have contributed to the decline of mail-order sales. As a result, Sears and Ward have gone extensively into the chain-store business, operating hundreds of department stores of various sizes. Sears's retail stores account for over 75 per cent of the company's sales. Ward has stores in smaller cities and in shopping centers, while Sears has stores mainly in metropolitan areas. As an illustration of their widespread operations, Sears, the country's largest retail distributor of general merchandise, in 1959 operated 126 large department stores, 292 medium-sized department stores, 312 smaller units, as well as 883 catalogue sales offices.

The mail-order principle has been used extensively by department stores and larger specialty stores. However, as urban areas develop and shopping centers expand, it seems certain that mail-order retailing will not increase.

Even service stations are going co-op.

Courtesy Greenbelt Consumer Services, Inc., Greenbelt, Md.

Managed by Customers: The Consumer Co-operative

Consumer co-operative stores are owned and controlled by their customers. Members (customers) purchase shares of stock, vote on matters of management, and collect dividends on their investments. Usually sales are for cash (at regular retail prices); and, at the end of the year, the members receive back in cash a percentage of their total purchases.

Consumer co-operatives operate mostly in rural areas, selling feed, farm, and garden supplies and gasoline and petroleum products. Young people with farm backgrounds may find good opportunities for employment in farmer co-operative retail stores.

House-to-House Retailing: Direct Selling

A large volume of sales is done annually by *direct selling*. In direct selling, the producer or manufacturer sells to the consumer without going through intervening distributors, such as wholesalers and retailers. Usually, direct selling thrives best in medium-sized and smaller cities and in rural districts. Many companies, such as the Fuller Brush Company, Avon, the Aluminum Cooking Utensil Company, and the J. R. Watkins Co., distribute entirely by direct selling. In addition, there are thousands of small individual and family businesses in the direct-selling field. More than 4,000 firms sell food products direct to homes. Typical products sold direct are apparel, housewares, appliances, books, cosmetics, and general merchandise. Direct selling offers excellent sales training for young people. In fact, many successful businessmen have come from the ranks of direct salesmen.

Which Type of Retailing Is Best?

The final test of the various methods of serving consumers lies in how effective and efficient the method is. In the long run, that method of distributing goods is best that (1) offers to the customer the best possible merchandise at the lowest possible price, and (2) offers him the retail services he desires. There is no one best type or size of store.

Trade Talk

"super"   voluntary chain
direct selling   one-line store
independent store consumer
corporate chain co-operative

Can You Answer These?

1. How is a department store distinguished from a departmentalized specialty store?

2. In what way is a specialty shop similar to a one-line store?

3. Who owns the stores that are part of a voluntary chain?

4. What seem to be the major factors in the relative decline in importance of mail-order retailing?

5. In the American system of free enterprise, how does one determine which type of retailing is best?

6. In what fields of retailing have

the independent stores best resisted the inroads of chain stores?

7. What appears to have been the major influence of supermarket operation on other stores?

8. Which types of stores are recent additions to retailing?

9. What are the main differences between the giant shopping center and the baby shopping center in terms of (*a*) types of stores usually found, and (*b*) kinds of customers served?

10. In what ways do the merchandising practices of discount houses vary from those of other retail stores?

Problems and Projects

1. (*a*) Make a list of those chain stores operating in your community that are owned and operated by a corporation and a similar list of those chain stores that are conducted on a voluntary basis. (*b*) Indicate in your list whether voluntary chain stores are sponsored by a wholesaler or by the merchants themselves.

2. Interview the owners of several independent stores and the managers of several chain stores in your city. Find out what they consider the advantages of their type of store. Using this material and whatever you can obtain from other sources, prepare the arguments to be used on both sides of a brief debate on, "Resolved that the chain store is a better form of retailing than the independent retail store."

3. Compare the present classified telephone directory of your city with the same directory five years ago. What changes do you observe in the number of different types of retail stores?

Learning Your Job

1. Under which store type can your firm best be classified? List the characteristics of your store that support this classification.

2. Develop a brief list of reasons why your type of store seems to be an effective method of retailing goods.

3. If you are employed in a retail store, the preparation of a manual of store information will help you in your job and will also help you to understand the operation of the entire store. Such a manual will also keep you aware of your own responsibilities to your store and to your job. As a part of your retail training, make it a habit to put in your manual various facts and ideas that you collect in this course. Specifically, your manual should contain information on the following subjects: (*a*) basic facts about the store; (*b*) store rules and policies governing employees; (*c*) list of your duties in the store, both selling and nonselling; (*d*) layout of the store and of your department; (*e*) store policies governing merchandise lines carried, pricing, advertising, credit, and customer services; (*f*) system of sales-check writing; (*g*) store-employee training program; (*h*) relations of the store with the community—participation of the owner and employees in community affairs; (*i*) store housekeeping; (*j*) technical or trade terms you have had to learn.

Make a list of the duties you consider necessary to perform in order to do your job well in the store. Check this list periodically with your teacher and with your employer. Describe your job to the class, bringing out your duties and responsibilities as well as the advantages and disadvantages of your job.

3 *Goods and Services for All*

Almost every improvement in retailing comes from attempts to stimulate sales by providing better customer service. Sears, Roebuck and Company's policy, "Satisfaction or your money back" and the National Retail Merchants Association slogan, "Retailing—purchasing agent for the public" are evidence of the retailer's desire to serve the consumer. Since accepting this philosophy, retailing has made rapid progress in providing goods and services for all. But it has not always been so.

In the middle 1800's, Marshall Field of Chicago and John Wanamaker of Philadelphia were pioneers in the movement to emphasize what the *customer* needed and wanted, rather than what the merchant wanted to sell him. These merchants initiated the slogan, "The customer is always right." While not always true, the statement is better retailing policy than *caveat emptor* (Let the buyer beware), the policy in the early 1800's.

Retailers Help Distribute Goods

One of the wonderful results of our American system of free enterprise is the truly enormous selection of goods and services available to customers. In our country, one is not forced to buy what a few manufacturers (or the government) think one should have. Instead, everyone can use his own judgment in deciding what to purchase and how much he can afford to pay. The principal reason why we are privileged to select the merchandise we desire at the time and place we want it is the producers' competition for the consumer's dollar. By and large, producers and distributors survive and prosper if they make available the kinds of products and services consumers want. Those who are not able to do this—to compete—are eliminated.

Retailing Affects Everyone

Retailers, collectively, in the average American community affect every home and every individual. We work at the tasks that we can do best; and, with the money we earn, we buy from retailers the food and clothing we need to sustain life. In retail stores, we receive new ideas and see new merchandise that will make our homes and our living more enjoyable. Retailers help us in a variety of ways.

Raising the Standard of Living

"Build a better mousetrap, and the world will beat a path to your door" is a well-known saying, but certainly not a true one. Often "better mousetraps" have been met with indifference and skepticism. It requires effective merchandising to overcome consumer resistance to new products. Without mass consumption, the mass-production system breaks down. Without the stimulation of the retailer's resourcefulness and ingenuity, our standard of living would probably decline.

Serving the Community

Retail establishments serve our communities in many ways: (1) they serve as a center of civic pride, (2) they fill a social need, (3) they provide civic leadership, and (4) they serve as purchasing agents for the public.

Almost every community, large or small, takes civic pride in its business districts, and rightfully so; for the shopping areas—in the center city or in suburban shopping developments—are the parts of the community that everyone sees. When you visualize the typical town you have visited, chances are that you think of the retail stores.

To many people, the retail district is also the most interesting part of town. Colorful store fronts and neon signs command attention; store windows are filled with attractive displays. Many people love to spend time looking around and shopping. Friendly salespeople and pleasant surroundings create a congenial atmosphere. Because of this, retail stores may be said to help satisfy a social need.

Retailers also serve the community by providing civic leadership. Most retail executives are interested in projects that improve the community—parks, play-

The Thanksgiving Day parade passes right through the main retail district.

Retailers take an active part in projects that will help to improve their community.

Courtesy E. I. du Pont de Nemours and Co., Inc.

grounds, educational programs, cultural projects, better transportation facilities, better street lighting, and new industry. Retailers are members of local chambers of commerce and local retailers associations and civic clubs, whose purpose it is to improve the community. They assist in community drives to raise money for charitable purposes. They encourage school improvement and help student projects by advertising in local school papers and yearbooks. "It's good business for them," you say! Certainly, what is good for the community is good for business. Merchants, however, are actively engaged in civic improvement not only for business reasons but also because of their sense of civic responsibility.

Mr. Retailer renders an important service when he acts as purchasing agent for his customers. The wide assortment of merchandise from which his customers are able to choose represents the retailer's best judgment of what will satisfy their needs and wants. From manufacturers, wholesalers, and from the trade journals he reads, the retailer learns about the large variety of goods available from producers and distributors in this country. From import agents and brokers, he finds out about the many interesting articles produced in foreign countries. From these many sources, he selects the merchandise that will best serve his customers' needs. Collectively, retailers are the purchasing agents for the public, stimulating good taste that is reflected in the community.

The Retailer's Economic Importance

The American system of mass production and mass distribution has resulted in a great outpouring of goods and services. Just as a manufacturer specializes in producing one type of goods, each retail firm specializes in a particular kind of retailing. In this way, each retailer plays an important role in distributing America's goods and performs an important economic function.

Under our system of distribution in the United States, both wholesalers and retailers perform very important functions. The wholesaler assembles goods

A wholesaler in his warehouse pointing out items to the retail-store buyer.

Courtesy E. I. du Pont de Nemours and Co., Inc.

from many manufacturers in large quantities. He stores these in his warehouse and sells them in smaller quantities to the retailers in the territory he serves. The retailers, in turn, sell the goods in still smaller quantities to consumers at the time and in the place most convenient to them. The retailer, therefore, is an important link in the chain of distribution that stretches from the manufacturer or producer to the final consumer.

In the local community that he serves, the retailer also plays an important economic role. He employs department heads, salespeople, and nonselling workers, their number depending on the size of his store and the volume of business. He pays local taxes and, through his advertising, attracts people from outside the community who also patronize other local businesses. It can be truly said that the retailer makes a real economic contribution to his community.

Trade Talk

mass production   purchasing agent
caveat emptor

Can You Answer These?

1. In what respects are retail shopping districts centers of civic pride?
2. How do retailers serve the community?
3. What important change in merchandising did Marshall Field and John Wanamaker bring about?
4. How has the retailer helped to raise our standard of living? Is this true in other parts of the world? Discuss your answer.
5. Does the saying about building a better mousetrap apply to today's merchandising?

6. How does the retailer act as purchasing agent for his customers?

Problems and Projects

1. Discuss the things that the merchants of your community have done to improve the retail district. What additional improvements would you recommend?

2. List five products that are mass-produced and five that are not. How do they differ in their appeal to customers?

3. Obtain two copies of a popular magazine such as *The Saturday Evening Post*—one a recent issue and the other at least three years old. (*a*) Using one column on a sheet of paper for each issue, list at least ten products from each issue. (*b*) Circle those which are found in the recent issue, and not in the earlier issue. (*c*) Write out the conclusions you can draw from this little research project.

Learning Your Job

1. Make a list of products or lines of merchandise that your store has added or dropped in the past year. Do these changes reflect customer preferences?

2. Find out what civic activities your store participates in. Do these indicate a concern for civic improvements?

3. Be prepared to tell the class about window displays that your store has made in helping the community to play up special community events or affairs.

Retailing:
2. Opportunity Unlimited
Sale 9.99
GET IT AT
the costume
METAL MAGIC
NEW D
SAVE
NEW
s a rich girl.
ing goil to deny herself high fashion, when
e to the rescue with smart clothes at
s. If you're loaded with taste, but not wit,
nd walk out looking like a mi

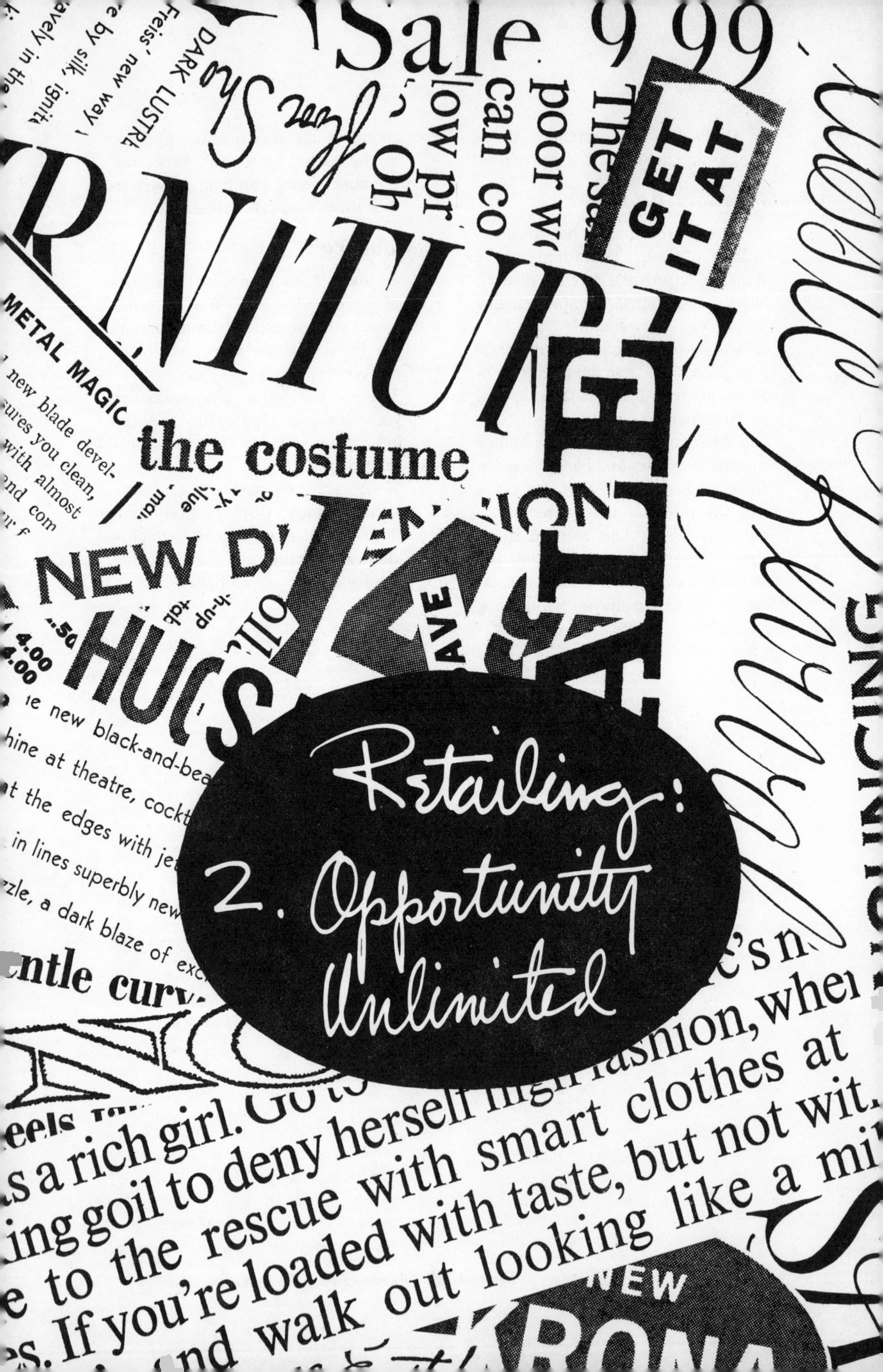

Unit 2

Part 4

The Customer in Retailing

While in school, you—and every young person—face an important decision—that of choosing a career. Although you may be uncertain of the type of work you should enter, you want to acquire some of the good things in life, to do something interesting, and to make the most of your abilities and talents.

But, where will you start? How many steps will lead to your future? Perhaps one step—from high school graduation into a full-time job. Perhaps several steps—from high school to business school, junior college, or college before taking a job. In any case, full-time employment may be supplemented by an additional step—evening-school courses or a company training program.

But regardless of the number of steps to your future, the first step is a giant one—it must be in the right direction. Before taking that step, carefully investigate retailing—a field of almost unlimited opportunity.

If a man-on-the-street interviewer asked various shoppers why they trade at a particular store, he would probably get several answers. A busy young housewife might say, "Oh, their service is so fast, and the goods are displayed so that I can find just what I want. Besides, their credit plans help stretch our income to cover the things we need for our new home." A man might answer, "The parking is great, and they keep their prices low." A career girl might take a different view, "They have a wonderful selection—all the latest fashions—and their advertising and show windows always tell me about the newest ideas." An older lady might reply, "Everyone's so friendly; they're interested in my problems, and they try to help me."

Each of these customers likes a particular store, and each for very different reasons. The opinions of customers determine whether the retailer succeeds or fails. The customer is in a very real sense the most important factor in re-

21

tailing. And it is for this reason that shopping habits and desires of customers have a strong impact on the career opportunities in retailing.

Retailing Is Many Things

The operation of a store, large or small, involves many different activities. Some, such as advertising, display, and sales promotion, require creative imagination and know-how with color, line, and design. Others, like managing, demand resourcefulness, a grasp of retail principles, good judgment, and the confidence to make decisions. Still others, like record keeping and stockkeeping, involve the ability to analyze records, keep details in mind, and work alone. These examples serve only to show that the many activities in a retail store provide job opportunities for people of different abilities.

Providing the Right Goods

There are two principal activities that provide customers with the right goods in the right quantity and at the right time and place. These activities are: (1) buying, and (2) receiving and marking, and stockkeeping.

Buying. It is customers who decide the kind and quantity of merchandise a store stocks. In buying stock, the store buyer must ask such questions as: Will customers buy it? When will they want it? How many will they need? What price will they be willing to pay? It is the buyer's job to know the answers to these questions. A buyer's position is challenging, pays well, and may lead to an executive position in merchandising management. Buyers are usually promoted from the ranks of assistant buyers, who in turn are chosen from among experienced salespeople.

How do stores determine what merchandise will please their customers? Many methods are used. In small stores, the manager or owner often does the buying. He and his salespeople are aware of customer needs through their indi-

Working on displays is one of many opportunities in retailing for young people.

Courtesy Macy's Kansas City

vidual contacts with them. Additional information is provided by wholesale salesmen who know about current retailer and consumer buying in other communities. While information from these sources is valuable, most stores require much more detailed knowledge—and this knowledge comes from records. Buyers must know how well articles are selling in each model, style, size, and color, and how many to reorder. They know that they must have the right goods at the right time. Most of the information they need is obtained from sales and stock-control records. A good buyer analyzes these data with judgment that comes from years of experience. Buying activities will be discussed in detail in Unit 17.

Receiving and Marking. Goods received from suppliers must be unpacked, checked for quantity and quality, price-ticketed, and stored in stock rooms or sent to the sales floor. All of these activities are part of the receiving and marking function. In small stores, these activities are often performed by the salespeople. In larger stores, specialized personnel are employed as receiving clerks, checkers, markers, and stockkeepers. These workers may be promoted to sales positions or to supervisory positions in the departments in which they work. Receiving, marking, and stockkeeping activities will be described more fully in Unit 6.

Making It Easy to Select Goods

The main purpose of sales promotion is to attract customers and make it easy for them to select merchandise. The store's major sales-promotion activities are (1) advertising, (2) visual merchandising, and (3) personal selling.

Advertising. As mentioned earlier, today's customer is faced with a vast array of goods from which to choose and a wide variety of stores offering these goods for sale. From the retailer's point of view, advertising helps him to bring in customers. But advertising is also a customer service: (1) It reminds him of his needs; (2) it describes the things available to fill these needs; (3) it tells him where he can buy what he needs; and (4) it advises him as to the time when he can purchase advantageously. Advertising is done through newspapers, radio and television, handbills, letter inserts, catalogues, and other media.

Personnel in stores, large and small, who work in or with the advertising department have many duties. They must plan space and time budgets with customers' buying and newspaper reading habits in mind, also their radio-listening and television-viewing habits. They must select the merchandise to be advertised, write the copy, and lay out the ads. The timing of ads is increasingly important, particularly in advertising high-fashion merchandise. Some retailers, therefore, engage in market research to find out when the customer reads and listens to advertisements and when he buys. Advertising-department personnel are sometimes selected from among salespeople but often are hired directly for their talent in copy writing or commercial art. Advertising will be discussed fully in Unit 12.

Friendly personal selling
at the service station will
bring back the customer
for future sales.

Courtesy National Cash
Register Co.

Visual Merchandising. As has already been pointed out, visual merchandising is a more recent merchandising technique that is becoming increasingly important in retail sales promotion. Merchandise is displayed in store windows and arranged on counters and racks in such a manner that articles related to the customer's shopping needs are skillfully brought to his attention. New packages are designed with customer eye appeal and shopping convenience in mind.

Salespeople participate in visual merchandising by suggesting items for display; in small stores, they may actually create displays and write signs and show cards. Larger stores hire specialized display personnel. Sometimes they are talented salespeople—often beginners—who have artistic talent. Visual merchandising is considered fully in Unit 11.

Although advertising and displays help to tell customers about the goods available, the shopper often needs help at the time of his purchase. He needs the salesperson's knowledge of merchandise, and he needs advice about credit terms and store services.

Personal Selling. Modern retail selling starts with the customer's buying problem. Its goal is a satisfied customer. Thus, a good salesperson must possess a service attitude. He must be able to apply his knowledge of merchandise and store services to the customer's specific needs. He must have the ability to recognize these needs and to communicate his knowledge effectively.

There are many different kinds of sales positions, each requiring its own knowledge and skills. The salesperson in a ready-to-wear shop must have a good knowledge of style, color, and fabrics as well as of sound selling techniques. The appliance salesman must know how to obtain prospects and meet them in their homes. The scope of such selling assignments is considerably greater than that of a salesclerk behind a tobacco or magazine counter. Simple selling assignments are, however, the training ground for promotion to more important and rewarding positions. You will find the study of salesmanship in Units 8, 9, and 10 challenging and interesting.

Making Customer Shopping Convenient

Some stores, department stores in particular, go to great lengths to make shopping easy and pleasant. They locate stores in convenient places, provide many services to shoppers, and plan store layouts so that customers can readily find the goods they want.

Credit. In their effort to accommodate customers, American businessmen have invented many devices that enable them to pay for their purchases while enjoying their use. Credit facilities have expanded greatly in response to customer demands. Retail charge-account privileges are very common. In recent years, the revolving charge account has become popular. Installment buying of large purchases is almost the rule rather than the exception. Retailers may also arrange credit for their customers through consumer credit agencies, such as banks. The retail credit field offers excellent career opportunities in positions as credit interviewers, supervisors, and managers. A detailed discussion of credit will be found in Units 13 and 19.

Accommodation Services. Retailers make shopping convenient by providing a variety of shopping services, such as parking, personal shoppers, telephone and mail-order services, interior-decorating consultants, and C.O.D. (collect on delivery) privileges. They also furnish such facilities as gift wrapping, check cashing, dining rooms, nurseries, and fur storage. They may also provide delivery service, though customers themselves determine whether or not they wish to use it. They are generally willing to take home small items, but demand delivery of heavy articles, such as furniture and electrical appliances. Service departments in large stores require many workers with different kinds of abilities. These departments offer promotional opportunities to positions as supervisors and managers. Store services are described more fully in Unit 13.

Store Location and Layout. Customers' desires are an important consideration in choosing a store location. Chain stores, perhaps better than any other type, have developed a good technique for choosing store locations. Days are spent "clocking" or counting the pedestrian and automobile traffic that passes the proposed site. The increase in the number of suburban shopping

Charge accounts make it easy for customers to buy the things they want.

Courtesy E. I. du Pont de Nemours and Co., Inc.

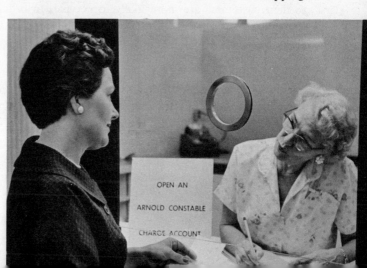

The shopping center with
its huge parking space is
a boon to suburbanites.

Courtesy National Steel
Corporation

centers has made it necessary to consider other factors in store location. Among these are the availability of large tracts of land for building sites and parking areas, accessibility to good roads, and the ability to estimate correctly future area development and population growth. Store layouts are based on the shopping habits of the customers to whom the appeal is made and on the merchandise and services offered.

Determining on store location and arranging store layout are very interesting occupations that, however, call for specialized training and experience. Chain-store organizations usually employ a staff of specialists in both fields, store location and store layout, or make use of outside consulting firms and experts employed by store-equipment manufacturers. Young people desiring to do this kind of work need to study practices in handling real estate, business law, and, in the case of store arrangement, some phases of architecture and merchandising principles as these relate to store layout. Unit 16 deals at greater length with store location and layout as a merchandising technique.

Keeping Costs Low

In the long run, retailers who can keep their costs down and pass on the savings to their customers are more likely to survive. In order to keep costs down, the modern retailer must have efficient financial records; a good accounting system is essential to sound management decisions. In this age of keen competition, it is necessary to know how much each department in the store earns and how much it costs to operate. The growing importance of finance and control means increasing opportunities for young people who aspire to positions in accounting, sales auditing, and merchandise control. Unit 19 contains many important facts on accounting and control.

Trade Talk

buying   accommodation
advertising   services
         retail credit

Can You Answer These?

1. What is meant by the statement, "Retailing revolves around the customer"? How does the customer bring about changes in store practices?
2. How does examining the activities of a retail store help a young person in choosing a career in retailing?
3. What is meant by the statement, "Providing customers with the right goods in the right quantity at the right time and place"?
4. Which sales-promotion activities are designed to make it easy for the customer to select merchandise?
5. In what ways does a store help its customers make buying decisions?
6. How do stores attempt to make shopping convenient?
7. Which store activities seem to be the best ones for a beginner to engage in? Why?

Problems and Projects

1. If customers are so influential in determining retail policies and practices, how do you account for the fact that they are often treated badly in retail stores?
2. Make a list of the things that influence a customer to purchase an item from a particular store. This list might be made by interviewing several adults. Explain how customer preferences affect the job opportunities offered by retailing.
3. Give evidence that the statement, "Retailing is more than selling," is true by explaining which retailing activities are nonselling in nature.
4. Make a chart showing the job opportunities in retailing. The following headings might be used:

Store Activity	Jobs in This Area
Buying	*Buyer, ass't buyer, etc.*

5. Of all the career opportunities discussed in this part, which groups appeal most to you: those dealing with sales promotion? those dealing with buying and selling? those dealing with nonselling activities, such as credit, accounting, stockkeeping, etc.? Give reasons for your choice.
6. Which of the store activities discussed offers the best long-range opportunity for a career? Why?

Learning Your Job

1. List the store activities as described in the text. Check those performed by your store. If any are not, try to find out the reason.
2. Prepare a brief report showing how your firm keeps the customer in mind when carrying out each of the store functions (buying, advertising, etc.).
3. Describe the opportunities you have, or will have, on your job to learn about the nature of the various store activities discussed in this part of the text.

5 *Advantages of Retailing*

You have observed that retailing is ever-changing—new types of stores are developing, new products are handled, and new merchandising techniques are adopted. And with this variety, you have discovered that retailing offers attractive careers to those who want satisfying, interesting work where there is room at the top.

Not everyone recognizes the fact that approximately 7,500,000 persons are engaged in some form of retailing—about one out of every ten workers in the country. There are about 1,800,000 retail stores—roughly one for every 100 people. The retail field is therefore diversified enough to provide employment for individuals with different abilities, interests, and training. The advantages of retail employment are many—employment opportunities everywhere, generally pleasant working conditions, financial benefits, and training plans in local stores and schools. This part of the text will tell you more about the advantages of retail jobs—then you will be ready for retailing.

Employment Opportunities Everywhere

Few persons looking for a job in a retail store need to travel very far to find a prospective employer. In every city, town, and village persons will find opportunities either as employees or as proprietors in retailing. Since the number of retail businesses in the United States is so large and the need for new and experienced employees so great, it is not difficult to obtain employment in this field. Retailing also offers great possibilities for business ownership to persons who have experience and moderate capital.

Plentiful Part-Time Work. Because of the daily, weekly, and seasonal sales fluctuations, retailing offers many opportunities to those desiring part-time work. Christmas, Easter, and other holiday seasons are peak sales periods and offer students and inexperienced persons employment for a few days, weeks, or possibly months. Many night openings also provide part-time employment. These opportunities for part-time employment enable students and workers to supplement their regular income and to acquire the experience so often essential to obtaining full-time employment.

Many Openings for Beginners. Earnest young men and women seldom have difficulty in obtaining a beginning job in retailing. The field offers beginners an opportunity, even though they have little or no specialized skill, technical training, or previous experience. This is true because many thousands

Many stores prefer to train beginners in their own specialties and methods.

Courtesy Kroger Co., Cincinnati

of new employees are required each year in the retail field to take the place of workers who are promoted or who, after securing good retail experience, enter other fields of distribution.

Steady Demand for Experienced Workers. Even during the great depression of the 1930's, newspapers carried "Help Wanted" ads for sales personnel and other retail positions. Expert salespeople are always in demand, because a high degree of persuasive skill is not easily achieved and the demand for those who possess it nearly always exceeds the supply. For similar reasons, a good display man seldom is without employment. The same may be said for numerous other retail occupations.

Opportunities for the Highly Trained. The field of retailing employs many specialists—merchandise managers, accountants, auditors, artists, research personnel, and a great many other technically trained personnel. These

Training for a job in retail display.

Courtesy Central High School, Evansville, Ind.

specialists are usually employed by the larger stores and chain organizations. The smaller stores also need technically trained people in such positions as store manager, bookkeeper, and head of special departments—such as medical prescriptions, building materials, furniture, meat, and produce. Insurance, real estate, and transportation services are rapidly approaching semiprofessional status.

Working Conditions

Working conditions in the retail field are apt to vary from store to store, even among stores of the same type. They also vary among different types of work within the same company and in different sections of the country.

Hours of Work. Most large department and specialty stores and the chain stores now maintain a strict 40-hour week for most employees. Managers and other executives may work longer hours. Stores usually open at 9 a.m. or later. Some smaller stores, in order to meet customer needs, may require longer working hours; but they, too, are trying to conform to accepted retailing practices.

Most stores are open on Saturday, and many are open at least one night a week. Employees, however, usually receive time off during the week to compensate for Saturday and evening work. Stores are open on Saturday and during evening hours in order to accommodate customers who have no other time to shop. Young, ambitious employees often welcome the opportunity to work the evening shifts in shopping centers, in order to have their mornings free to attend college courses in retailing.

Vacation privileges are comparable to those in other industries. It is usual for workers with at least one year's service to receive a week's vacation with pay. Most stores give two weeks' vacation with pay after three to five years of service.

Work Environment. Many people feel that one of the major advantages of retailing is the opportunity to work in clean, attractive surroundings. The retail-business atmosphere is usually one of courtesy and respect for individuals, perhaps because the business revolves around customers. Most retail work is not physically strenuous, nor is it hazardous to personal safety or health. Many stores are air-conditioned. Nearly all of them are well lighted and filled with attractive merchandise, fixtures, and decorations.

Working with People. For those who like working with other people, retailing provides many pleasant contacts—frequent association with interesting customers, with congenial co-workers, and with supervisors who usually are very understanding people. Salespeople experience genuine personal satisfaction when customers return to them time after time to be served. In fact, one study of department-store salespeople showed that helping customers with their problems was the most important satisfaction that salespeople receive from their jobs.

Retailing is based on good human relations. Employees are trained to be courteous and polite to customers. Constant emphasis on this quality tends to bring about better human relations between employer and supervisor and among employees. Of course, there are occasional disagreements as in any group; but usually human relations in retail stores are harmonious.

Remuneration

Wages. Retail salaries vary widely throughout the country, depending on the skill of the employee and his responsibilities. When comparing basic wages in retailing with those in other types of work, several points should be kept in mind.

First, many selling positions offer some kind of commission or bonus that enables salespeople to earn incomes well beyond their basic wages. Furniture and appliance salesmen, for example, usually receive a commission and sometimes a bonus. In fact, in many stores they must earn at least an average of

A pleasant place to eat lunch and meet your co-workers.

Courtesy Administrative Management

People like to work in stores in attractive neighborhoods.

Courtesy Louisville Central Area, Inc., Louisville, Ky.

$100 a week in order to be considered adequately productive by management. Salespeople in specialty shops, such as men's clothing stores, frequently earn in excess of $100 a week when working on a sales commission. (Commissions are paid on the basis of a percentage of sales.)

Second, retail employment is steady employment. Loss of pay due to strikes or lay-offs during times of production change-overs, recessions, or mechanical failures is rare in retailing.

Third, retailing offers an advantage over other fields because a college education is not required for advancement to higher income positions. Whereas wages are usually low for those without training while they are learning, the individual's income will rise sharply as he is advanced to a supervisory position or is placed on a sales commission plan.

Fourth, opportunities for higher incomes—exceptional ones in some cases—are more prevalent in retailing than in many other fields, because of the large numbers of supervisors, department managers, buyers, and executives needed in the business.

Advancement by Merit. In some occupations the beginning job—even though a well-paid one—is the ending job. Not so with retailing! Many stores, especially large department stores and chain organizations, expect to find future managers and executives within the ranks. To ferret out people with potentials for promotion, personnel departments objectively rate employees, test them for aptitudes, and seek out those who have both the ability and the will to advance. Systematic training and experience in various departments are part of the planned program of training for the future buyer, department head, manager, or merchandising executive.

Benefits. Profit-sharing plans are being used increasingly by larger stores. Sears, Roebuck and Company has an excellent and well-known plan, in which some veteran employees have accumulated more than $50,000. In smaller stores, a capable employee may be given an opportunity to become a partner. Most large retail organizations now offer some form of pension or retirement plan involving a contribution by the employer. Retail firms also contribute to the program of Federal Social Security (OASI—Old-Age, Survivors, and Disability Insurance).

Discounts of 10 to 20 per cent are commonly given to employees on merchandise purchased from the store. Such discounts can add up to a substantial amount in a year and should be considered by the employee as additional income.

Fringe benefits. Most progressive retailers offer *fringe benefits* comparable to those offered by industrial employers. Many large stores maintain a lunchroom or company cafeteria, offering meals at reasonable prices. Health care and employer contributions to medical insurance plans are common in large organizations. Many stores also make available low-cost group life insurance and sponsor employee credit unions. Some stores also furnish, and launder, work clothing, such as jackets and aprons.

Available Training

Interest in training for retail occupations has grown substantially in recent years. This has been brought about by a desire on the part of retail merchants to employ young people who are really interested in preparing themselves for retail careers. Parents have also become aware of the increasing opportunities for young people in retailing. As a result of this interest, the public high schools and vocational schools are offering additional courses in retailing, salesmanship, merchandise information, advertising, window display, and other distributive subjects.

L. T. WHITE
Manager of Research and Education for Cities Service Company.

Evening Classes. Distributive education courses for adults are offered by the public schools in many cities. Such courses cover a wide variety of subjects from retail arithmetic to store finance and from show-card writing to sales promotion. These courses are usually given in the evening, but they may be offered during working hours in co-sponsorship with a given store. A young person has ample opportunity to obtain specialized training through distributive education classes in his community or in a neighboring city.

College Training. Junior colleges, colleges, universities, and some business schools offer curriculums in retailing, food distribution, petroleum distribution, marketing, wholesaling, insurance, and real estate. The ambitious high school graduate, desiring college training, can find part-time employment in retailing to help finance his college education. Many colleges now offer work-study courses, combining classroom study and paid supervised training in local retail stores.

Company Training Programs. Large department and specialty stores and many chain organizations provide company training programs leading to supervisory and managerial positions. Some retailers now offer employees scholarships to attend colleges full time and study retailing and marketing. For example, several large food chains offer scholarships in food distribution; at least one oil company offers college scholarships in petroleum distribution.

The Value of Retail Training for Other Distributive Jobs. After getting a start in retailing, some young men and women choose to move to another field of distribution, such as insurance, real estate, wholesaling, direct selling, or selling as a representative for a manufacturer. Their retail training then pays off; they have experience and skill in getting along with others, in meeting customers' needs, and in understanding the management point of view.

Trade Talk

distributive OASI
  education profit sharing
fringe benefits sales commission

Can You Answer These?

1. In what ways does retailing provide a wide range of employment opportunities?
2. How many hours a week do most retail employees now work? What adjustments are made for evening and Saturday work?
3. When comparing wages in retailing with wages in other fields, what aspects, other than beginning wages, should be considered?
4. How do retailers go about advancing their employees on the basis of merit?
5. In addition to wages, what benefits are offered by retailers to their employees?
6. Where can a person interested in retailing obtain training before he begins work? after he is working and seeks advancement on the job?
7. For what other positions in distribution is retail training valuable?

Problems and Projects

1. Discuss the advantages and disadvantages of the hours of work in retailing compared with those in other fields of employment.

2. Be ready to debate the following statement: Even though beginning wages are higher in some other occupations, in the long run retailing offers greater total compensation.

3. Report to the class on the employee discount policies and profit-sharing plans offered as extra benefits by retail stores in your community.

4. Write to the registrars of colleges, junior colleges, and universities in your state for information about curriculums for retailing and other careers in marketing.

5. Report to the class on adult classes in distributive education offered by the public schools in your city.

6. Using the want-ad section of your local newspaper, or one from a nearby city, prepare a report concerning: (a) the number of retail job vacancies listed, (b) the wages offered, (c) the benefits mentioned in the ads.

7. If your area has a state employment service office, contact one of the staff members and secure infor-

mation about: (a) the going wages for beginners of your age and experience, (b) the current openings for both full- and part-time employment for a person like yourself.

8. Find out in your school whether there are any college scholarships available for the study of retailing or marketing. If there are, report to the class on the scholarships and how to qualify for them.

9. Prepare a solution to this problem: Which seems to be the wisest course for a young person eager to advance to a position of responsibility in retailing: (a) to enter retailing and enroll in evening classes in this field, (b) to go to college and secure a degree in retailing?

Learning Your Job

1. From your place of employment, obtain information concerning employee discounts, vacations, group insurance, and other benefits in addition to wages.

2. Prepare a paper showing the different wage-payment plans in your store and the departments in which they are used.

3. Ask your job sponsor for information about training programs and college scholarships offered by your employer. Prepare a brief report of your findings.

6 Wide Opportunities in Retailing

Now that you are acquainted with the different activities in retail-store operation, you are in a position to consider the job opportunities in the various kinds of stores. Imagine yourself standing in the middle of Main Street. On each side are dozens of stores—large department stores, units of chain organizations, and prosperous independent stores. Each offers a career in retailing. Which one will you choose?

Some firms offer an attractive job immediately at a fair salary. Others offer primarily an opportunity to learn many different phases of store operation. Some have complete training programs; others have none. Each store has its own advantages and opportunities. The fact, however, that there is a wide variety of types of stores means that there are many career opportunities for people of different talents and interests.

Store Organization and Job Opportunities

Part 4 described briefly the activities of a retail store and showed how these activities reflect customer needs. While every store performs functions that are common to all stores, each type of retail establishment has a somewhat different organizational pattern. Thus, the kinds of job opportunities in each store will be different.

Opportunities in Department Stores

The typical department store is a large, complex organization. For this reason, department stores offer many advantages to those interested in a retailing career. There are many beginning jobs for young people. At the same time, the variety of merchandise offered and the specialized services performed require people with many different interests and abilities. Large department stores provide well-defined routes of advancement to specialized positions in selling and other store work, as well as to supervisory and management positions.

Most department stores organize their operations into five major divisions: (1) merchandising, (2) sales promotion, (3) store operation, (4) finance and control, and (5) personnel management. Each division provides attractive job opportunities.

Merchandising. Merchandising is regarded by many people as the most important retail function, for every activity in a retail store revolves around the merchandising function—buying merchandise and selling it to customers.

DEPARTMENT STORES

·· offer employment in a wide variety of interesting jobs — only about half are in selling.

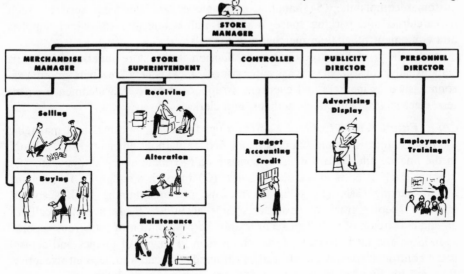

The merchandising division is responsible for purchasing the stock, setting the retail price, controlling inventories, forecasting fashion trends, and finally selling the goods.

Merchandising personnel include the general merchandise manager, divisional merchandise managers, buyers, assistant buyers, heads of stock, salespeople, stock clerks, fashionists, comparison shoppers, merchandise analysts, and research assistants. Furthermore, various office workers are required to keep accurate sales and stock-control records needed by the general merchandise manager and his staff.

Many stores not only sell goods but also change or alter them to customer requirements. The merchandising division, therefore, uses the services of tailors, pressers, fitters, jewelers, mechanics, refinishers, carpet layers, interior decorators, and other skilled workers.

Sales Promotion. It is the function of the sales-promotion division to attract and hold customers. This is done through attractive displays, self-service arrangements, advertising, and various public-relations activities.

Sales-promotion employees include the sales-promotion manager, art director, copy writers, proofreaders, advertising artists, window trimmers, and sign writers. Sales promotion also requires the services of skilled craftsmen, such as carpenters and electricians as well as office workers.

Store Operation. Those who work in store operation are responsible for the handling and moving of merchandise from the time it is received at the store until it is placed in the salesroom, and from the time it is sold until it is delivered to the customer. They are also concerned with (1) maintenance and appearance of the building, (2) protection of the physical property of the store and the employees, (3) safety of customers within the store, (4) adjustment of customer complaints, (5) handling of employee and customer services, such as cafeterias and parking space, and (6) purchasing and storing of supplies and equipment other than merchandise for sale.

At the head of the store-operations division is the store superintendent. His staff usually consists of service supervisors, stockkeepers, receiving-room personnel, such as markers and checkers, wrappers, detectives, watchmen, carpenters, electricians, painters, custodians, and clerks.

Finance and Control. Organizing, financing, housing, and managing the retail enterprise could scarcely be carried on without efficient records. Work in the finance and control division consists of (1) maintaining the payroll, (2) keeping track of costs in relation to sales, (3) preparing budgets, (4) receiving and disbursing cash, (5) filing tax returns, (6) maintaining bank accounts, and (7) keeping track of customer charge accounts. These activities call for an endless stream of well-kept records and the preparation of numerous reports.

In large and medium-sized stores, the person in charge of finance and control is the controller (comptroller), a highly trained financial and account executive. Working for him are bookkeepers, cashiers, ledger clerks, billing clerks, credit interviewers, receptionists, correspondence supervisors, calculating-machine operators, and other office workers—the largest group of retail workers engaged in nonselling activities.

Personnel Management. The personnel division recruits, interviews, employs, places, and directs the training of store personnel. Its function is to get the right person on the right job and to help him grow on that job. All this is no easy task when one realizes that in a large store, such as Macy's in New York City, over 10,000 people are employed in hundreds of different kinds of jobs.

In larger stores, the personnel division also carries on many other personnel activities—setting up and supervising merit-rating systems, job-evaluation programs, on-the-job training classes, and health and safety activities. They are also responsible for labor relations, profit-sharing and retirement plans, and other services contributing to employee welfare. Some of the job titles in this division are: employment manager, training director, assistant training directors, personnel interviewers, personnel clerks, stenographers, and various office workers.

Opportunities in Chain Stores

Because chain-store organizations operate differently from department stores (in reality they are complete systems of distribution, performing both retailing and wholesaling functions), they provide quite different job opportunities. Many corporate chain operations, such as buying, accounting, merchandising management, and sales promotion, are centered in the company's main office and in district headquarters. However, aside from this centralization, the individual stores in the chain operate under their managers much like independently owned stores. Many chain-store units—particularly in food, variety, and drug lines—are self-service operations

Knowing these facts about chain stores gives you some understanding of the unique career opportunities offered. First, chain stores, especially self-service operators, employ many nonselling personnel such as warehousemen, stock clerks, truck drivers, cashiers, and department supervisors. Assistant store managers are generally selected from workers employed in stores belonging to the chain. A second career opportunity offered by chain-store organizations is the chance for advancement into important positions. Jobs as chain-store managers are numerous; these managers are usually selected from the ranks of assistant managers. District supervisors and central-headquarters executives often are chosen from among those who are successful store managers. This "advancement from within" policy is typical of corporate chain retailing enterprises. A third unique career opportunity lies in the scope of activities of the modern chain. In addition to store-operating personnel, the chain seeks people for all its distributive functions—warehousing, transportation, selecting store locations, making layouts, sales promotion, buying, accounting, and so on.

Executives, supervisors, and store managers in chain organizations are paid well; and the size of a chain assures everyone with ability and initiative of a chance at many openings within the firm. Corporate chains usually require that personnel be willing to move from one city to another. Competition is keen; those who want to succeed must work hard or they will lose out to others who are just waiting for the right opportunity.

Opportunities in Small Independent Stores

Many beginners in retailing often find employment in small, independent stores. Because there are so many of these stores, numerous job opportunities exist. And often no experience is required.

The salesperson in a small independent store has many ways of serving his customers.

Courtesy E. I. du Pont de Nemours and Company, Inc.

An advantage of the small store, as far as the beginner is concerned, is that it offers him the chance to participate in many retailing functions. The beginner can serve customers, work with merchandise, perform stockkeeping activities, take inventory, create displays, and receive merchandise. Acquiring such a variety of experiences would require a long time in a large store with specialized departments. Another advantage of working in a small store is the opportunity to learn store operation thoroughly before going into business for oneself.

Smaller stores, especially in lines such as furniture and fashion apparel, offer sales positions that are challenging and remunerative. Some people like the intimacy of a small store where one gets to know well both customers and co-workers and where the opportunity to render personalized service is greater.

Opportunities for Women

In retailing, probably more than in any other type of business, women have opportunities for employment. In metropolitan stores, for example Filene's in Boston and Bullock's in Los Angeles, there are very few departments in which women are not employed. They are especially in demand in specialty shops, such as women's clothing and household furnishings.

Studies show that chances for women to reach higher positions are greater in retailing than in most other businesses. One study showed that over 45 per cent of the department heads and buyers in department stores are women. Many women own their own retail stores. Thus, while not strictly a "woman's field," retailing offers many opportunities for them to advance to responsible positions.

Retailing offers many opportunities to well-trained women.

Courtesy National Cash Register Co.

Trade Talk

merchandising   nonselling
store operation   personnel
sales promotion   personnel
finance and   division
    control

Can You Answer These?

1. Name the five divisions into which department-store work is divided.

2. (*a*) What activities are classified as "merchandising"? (*b*) What are some positions in this division?

3. What is the function of the sales-promotion division?

4. What do you understand by the term *controller?* What does he and his staff do?

5. What part does the personnel division play in the operation of a large store? What are its relations to the other divisions of the store?

6. In what phases of store activity do women find their greatest chance for advancement and remuneration?

7. What advantages in employment are offered by (*a*) a department store? (*b*) a chain organization? (*c*) a small specialty shop?

Problems and Projects

1. Compare the advantages from an experience standpoint of working in: (*a*) small, individually owned specialty stores, such as hardware, grocery, drug, clothing, and furniture, and (*b*) large retail businesses, such as department stores, chain variety stores, and supermarkets.

2. Bring to class newspaper "Help Wanted" ads. With a red pencil, circle all advertisements that refer to store employment. List the different job opportunities for young people. Check those for which you could qualify.

3. Prepare a list of discussion topics on (*a*) the advantages and disadvantages of retailing as compared with other principal occupations in your community, and (*b*) the long-range opportunities in retailing.

4. Describe the functions performed by each division of a large department or specialty store, as follows: (*a*) merchandising, (*b*) sales promotion, (*c*) store operation, (*d*) finance and control, (*e*) personnel. Must these functions be carried out in a small store?

5. If you were given your choice of work to do in a large retail store, which division of store activity would you choose? Why?

6. Select a retail-store job in which you think you would be interested. Using as many references as are available in your school or public library, list the requirements for the job you have selected. How do you expect this course in retailing to help you meet these requirements?

7. From the latest *U.S. Census of Business, Retail Trade,* find out the number of stores, total sales, total number of proprietors, and total number of employees in the following kinds of stores in your state and city: food stores of all kinds, furniture and household-appliance stores, restaurants, and men's and women's clothing stores.

Learning Your Job

1. Prepare a chart showing the organization of your store according to the five major divisions explained in this part. Show the position of your job on the chart. Include the chart in your manual of store information.

2. After conferring with your supervisor, prepare a brief report on the routes of advancement stemming from your present job.

Sale 9 99

GET IT AT

RNITURE

METAL MAGIC

the costume

NEW D'

HUG

 SALE

SAVE

the costume

new blade devel-
res you clean,
with almost
d com

4.00
00

e new black-and-bea
ine at theatre, cockt
the edges with je
n lines superbly new
le, a dark blaze of exc

entle curv

3. Qualities of the Successful Retailer

s a rich girl. Go
ng goil to deny herself high fashion, whe
to the rescue with smart clothes at
s. If you're loaded with taste, but not wit
and walk out looking like a mil

NEW
RONA

Unit 3

Part 7

Abilities Used in Retailing

The field of retailing makes use of a wide variety of abilities and talents—more so than many other fields. The successful retail-store employee today must possess many merchandising skills. For such jobs as constructing displays, wrapping gifts, and stocking shelves a certain amount of manual dexterity is needed. The current trend toward selling through display has placed a high premium on artistic abilities. The ability to figure accurately and to keep records is required in nearly every retail position. Those who sell, or are associated with merchandising in other ways, need skills in gathering information so that they can keep up to date on customer buying habits, markets, and merchandise.

There are positions in retailing for practically any kind of talent. Matching your knowledge and skills with the right job in the right store requires careful thought and planning.

Abilities used in retailing fall within six general categories: (1) customer relations, (2) manipulative, (3) artistic, (4) clerical, (5) occupational relations, and (6) study and research. Let us examine these abilities.

Customer-Relations Abilities

Customer-relations abilities are those required in dealing with the customer and call for the following:

Being courteous to customers
Understanding why and how people buy
Determining customers' needs and desires
Presenting merchandise to customers
Communicating effectively with customers
Answering customers' questions
Receiving and arranging for payments
Handling customer complaints
Following ethical sales practices

These abilities are put to use in selling, advertising, display, sales promotion, credit, and accommodation services. Even those who do not meet

43

customers face-to-face—such as display men, stockkeepers, and credit clerks—should have an appreciation of customer-relations abilities because they enter so largely into retail-store operation.

Manipulative Abilities

Manipulative abilities are those that require the use of one's hands, arms, and body. Examples of activities in which manipulative abilities are used are:

> Measuring and weighing merchandise
> Packaging and shipping merchandise
> Marking the price on merchandise
> Constructing displays
> Operating cash registers and adding machines
> Assembling merchandise for the sales floor
> Demonstrating merchandise

In some types of selling, manipulative abilities are highly essential. For example, selling power tools requires considerable manipulative skill when the salesman demonstrates his products. On the other hand, selling many other products—such as books, shoes, or domestics—requires a minimum of manipulative skill.

The ability to work skillfully with tools, machines, and materials is a valuable asset in obtaining and holding certain retail jobs, particularly in smaller stores where salespeople usually unpack merchandise shipments, stock the shelves, build displays, and help in store maintenance. A young worker who is handy with tools is a valuable asset to a store, because he can make minor repairs, recondition fixtures and merchandise, construct display props, and do small remodeling jobs.

Artistic Abilities

Artistic abilities are those that call for the use of the principles of color, line, and design. Among the most important are the following:

> Advising customers on texture and color in home furnishings
> Selecting color harmonies in personal apparel
> Arranging attractive displays
> Sketching advertising layouts
> Lettering and laying out copy for show cards
> Choosing appropriate gift-wrapping materials

Visual merchandising—using attractive packaging and well-designed displays to attract customers and sell merchandise—is continually increasing in importance, as you learned earlier. Customers are becoming more style and color conscious. Thus, a good retailer has command of color, line, and design and uses these talents in many ways; young retailers who plan on merchandising careers are encouraged to master them.

Presenting yard goods to a customer in a helpful manner is a necessary ability in that branch of retailing.

Courtesy National Cash Register Co.

Clerical Abilities

Clerical abilities are those involving the use of figures and records, such as:

>Keeping sales and stock records
>Computing, such as figuring discounts and sales taxes
>Making out shipping tickets and receiving records
>Handling customer communications by mail
>Making out credit contracts and other forms
>Helping maintain the company's financial records

Some people think of office work when the word "clerical" is mentioned. Yet, many retail employees must possess certain clerical abilities even though they are not office workers. Salespeople must make out sales slips, handle credit forms, take inventory, and keep sales records. Other retail personnel use clerical skills to maintain stock records, order merchandise, and make out shipping forms.

The ability to interpret records and use figures is indispensable to store managers, merchandise managers, buyers, and department heads. Perhaps this is why they so often criticize young people for their lack of skill with arithmetic and for their inaccurate records. Future retailers should pay heed to this criticism, because errors in records are serious, and their recurrence has an important bearing on advancement.

Occupational-Relations Abilities

Occupational-relations abilities are those that help a worker to get along well with others and aid him in his personal development. They are common to all workers regardless of their occupations and include the following:

>Working harmoniously with fellow employees and supervisors
>Participating intelligently in employee organizations
>Keeping physically fit for daily work
>Guarding one's personal safety and that of co-workers and customers
>Understanding laws, such as social security and income tax laws
>Planning for personal development in a chosen career

A friendly, cheerful manner is a necessary asset in all branches of retailing.

Courtesy National Cash Register Co.

Regardless of how skillful and hard-working a retailing employee is, he will be handicapped in his occupation if he cannot work smoothly and effectively with others; this, then, is one of the most important abilities for all young retailers.

Study-and-Research Abilities

Study-and-research abilities involve the gathering of information through observing, listening, examining, and reading. They include:

Studying merchandise labels, tags, and directions found on merchandise
Attending store meetings and training classes in schools or colleges
Observing the merchandising operations of the firm and its competitors
Gathering knowledge from trade-association literature and store manuals
Obtaining information from customers, buyers, and manufacturers' representatives
Reading newspapers and magazines for tips on style trends, economic conditions, and social changes

The successful retail worker must be a student of his field—one who knows where and how to get information, how to evaluate it, and when and how to use it well. He must study new products and the materials from which they are made, new selling and display techniques, and new ways of carrying out clerical and other store-system responsibilities. The worker who can find and use current retailing information usually is advanced ahead of his fellow workers.

Trade Talk

artistic abilities	customer-relations abilities	abilities occupational-relations abilities	study-and-research abilities
clerical abilities	manipulative abilities		

1. In which store would you expect to handle a greater number of tasks—in a large store or in a small one? Why?

2. In what positions are customer-relations abilities particularly important? Why should these abilities be understood by all workers?

3. How can manipulative abilities help one get and hold a job in retailing?

4. How does a retailer make use of a knowledge of color, line, and design? Why are these abilities more important today than ever before?

5. What retail occupations, if any, do not require clerical abilities? Why are these abilities more important today than formerly?

6. Why is it important for a beginner in retailing to cultivate study-and-research abilities?

7. Why are occupational-relations abilities so important in retailing?

Problems and Projects

1. Make a list of the ways in which retail employees must be creative.

2. Your textbook lists examples of six categories of abilities required by retailing. Give examples of your own for each of the categories.

3. What kinds of abilities characterize retailing as compared with industrial and clerical occupations? Are the occupations within the retail field as much alike as the occupations within the office field? Why?

4. List horizontally the six groups of abilities discussed in this unit. Then under each of your headings list as many duties as you can think of for one of the following occupations:

furniture salesman, sportswear buyer, gasoline service-station salesperson, food-supermarket stockkeeper, insurance salesman.

Learning Your Job

Place the name of a different group of abilities at the top of each of six sheets of paper. Under the proper heading, list the jobs you do while at work that require the use of these abilities. Then check your list with your training sponsor and with your teacher.

8 *Personal Qualities Important in Retailing*

Certainly no one expects to advance very far in his occupation unless he has the necessary skills. But many workers fail to realize that job skills are not enough for advancement. Employers will not hire—or they later dismiss—skilled workers who lack essential personal qualities. This fact was demonstrated in one study of 75 companies, which showed that of all the employees who lost their jobs, 90 per cent were discharged because of poor personality characteristics. While learning his specific job skills, the young retailer should, therefore, give a great deal of attention to developing desirable personal qualities.

Your personality is the sum total of all the mental and physical traits that set you apart from all other people. Your personality determines whether you are liked or disliked, your ability to obtain friendly co-operation from others, and how much success and enjoyment you get from life.

Good Impressions Are Important

The impression you make on others depends to a large extent on your appearance—grooming, posture, and choice of apparel. No matter how you feel about the nuisances of good-grooming chores, good posture habits, and care in selection of appropriate apparel, there is a level below which you cannot afford to slip. The clean, neat, and well-groomed person has a better chance of being respected, liked—and promoted. The slovenly, unkempt person is a source of annoyance to those with whom he associates.

Good Grooming Pays. Consistent carelessness in grooming and dress is likely to indicate to others a similar carelessness in work habits, as well as a lack of interest in other people. The advice of one large department store to its employees concerning the importance of grooming when meeting customers is summarized in the following paragraph:

WIN THE ADMIRATION OF CUSTOMERS . . . be well groomed. When you have that "scrubbed clean" look . . . when your hair is simply but neatly combed . . . when, if you are a man, your face is smoothly shaven; or if you are a woman, your make-up is artistically applied so as to look natural . . . when your teeth sparkle and your breath is sweetly scented . . . when your hands are clean and your nails conservatively manicured . . . when your suit or dress is spotless and well pressed . . . when your socks or stockings are neat and trim . . . when your shoes are polished and your heels in good repair. . . . in a word, when you are so clean and neat from head to toe as to have "eye-appeal," your customers will *admire* your well-groomed appearance . . . your customers will be *pleased* with you. COMMAND THE CONFIDENCE OF CUSTOMERS . . . be correctly attired.*

Posture Enhances Appearance. At the same time that a person is being judged as to his personal grooming, his posture is also being observed. Poor posture can detract from an otherwise pleasing appearance. One can make good posture a habit by being conscious of it, by refraining from slumping in a chair or leaning on a counter, and by standing and walking erect. Walk naturally, toes straight ahead. Good posture adds to the total impression that you make; at the same time, it helps you to avoid that tired, exhausted feeling.

Apparel Reflects Your Attitudes. Young women should choose clothes that are smart, feminine, and easy to care for. Simply designed suits and dresses,

---

* *Your Public Relations,* Sterling Lindner Davis, Cleveland, Ohio, pp. 17–18.

Customers prefer to deal with well-groomed salespersons.

to which can be added accessories for after-hour appointments, are practical and convey the impression of efficient service. Sweaters and bobby socks (or no hose at all) may be acceptable for school, but never for business.

Young men should choose a suit that is conservatively cut, in a fabric, such as a worsted, that will give good wear. Neckties and socks should harmonize and should not be so loud as to divert the customer's attention. If the young man follows the example of successful men supervisors and executives with whom he works, he will probably be safe. He will also feel more confident when he knows he is well groomed. Many stores, recognizing the value of correctly attired employees, issue dress regulations; some require that employees wear uniforms.

Cleanliness Is a "Must." The well-groomed person is, first of all, really clean. He bathes daily and always after physical exertion. Body odors may offend others, even though one may not be aware of them oneself. Perspiration increases with warm temperatures, exercise, excitement, embarrassment, worry, nervousness, or fatigue. If perspiration is a problem for you, it may be well to use a deodorant (this includes men, too!).

Bad breath is another serious offender and stems from a variety of oral, gastric, and emotional causes. Again, a person is not always aware that he is guilty of offensive breath. Be safe, wash your teeth regularly and keep a breath sweetener handy. If bad breath is a serious problem for you, see your doctor. You cannot afford to allow any hint of uncleanliness to establish a barrier between you and others.

Health Care Is Vital. In all retail jobs, but particularly on the sales floor, it is important to maintain a pleasant disposition, even if you don't feel well physically. A tired employee finds it difficult to give pleasant customer service. Many jobs in a retail store, especially selling, require much standing, often on hard floors. If you have good physical stamina, you can remain alert, enthusiastic, and courteous, even when tired. It is expected of you.

Regular sleep, balanced meals, and plenty of good exercise are essential to keeping in top physical condition.

Your Personality Counts, Too

Some people who create favorable physical impressions lack the personal qualities necessary for success. It is very important that the good physical impression you make is supported by deeper human qualities that make you a prized employee. Some of these qualities are discussed here.

Venturesome Spirit. A venturesome spirit—the courage to try new things—coupled with good judgment is very desirable. The majority of important retail executives possess this trait. The person who succeeds in retailing is almost always one who seeks to advance through his own efforts, rather than depending on breaks, "pull," or seniority. The person who is venturesome is always a self-starter; and he has an inquiring mind, resourcefulness, and an active imagination. He has the courage to stick with his convictions while remaining open-minded and willing to discard an unsound idea.

A venturesome spirit is acquired through experience. To develop it, a worker must take a constructive and optimistic attitude toward his work and the problems he encounters.

Loyalty. Loyalty has many meanings. An important one is being genuinely concerned about the store in which you work and protecting its interests. Loyal employees do not destructively criticize the store, its policies, its personnel, and its merchandise, especially to outsiders. The retail employee must be very careful not to disclose details of store operation; competitors are anxious for such information.

The loyal person does not habitually complain or gripe to his fellow workers. Nor does he gossip, spread rumors, or undercut the supervisory staff. Griping and gossiping can be very destructive, especially when it causes other employees to become unhappy or dissatisfied with their jobs.

Where money and merchandise are involved, honesty becomes an aspect of loyalty. Complete accuracy in handling money and credit transactions demonstrates a person's loyalty. In handling the store's money and merchandise, there is only one kind of honesty—complete honesty. For example, a worker must never take unfair advantage of his discount privilege by helping his friends obtain merchandise at less than the required price.

Giving 100 per cent effort is another form of loyalty. Wasting time on the job results in loss of profit to the store. An individual who is loyal to himself and his store does not take advantage of leniency in supervision, such as overstaying lunch hours, "cheating" on coffee breaks, or loafing on the job. The really loyal employee gives no less than his best effort at all times.

Loyalty also means being completely fair with fellow workers. Gossiping about associates, failing to keep one's word, betraying confidences, and shirking responsibilities are examples of being disloyal to fellow workers.

Initiative. A person is said to possess initiative when he has the ability to see a job that needs to be done and has the courage to go ahead and do it. Nobody has to tell him. Personnel directors frequently point out that initiative is a prime requisite in the selection of persons for supervisory and management training. Retailing is a field in which self-reliance and the willingness to do things without being told are extremely important. Especially in smaller stores, self-reliance and dependability are highly desired, because usually duties are less well defined than in large firms and there is less supervision.

Industriousness. Industriousness is steady, earnest, diligent effort. Besides willingness to put in a full day's work for a full day's pay, industriousness means keeping busy without being prodded. It is the opposite of clockwatching, stalling, "passing the buck," and other means of avoiding work—especially the less enjoyable tasks. An industrious worker attends strictly to business and is not distracted by noise or other disturbances. He will work as hard when he is alone as when someone is observing him, and his work will be so well done that no one will have to check on him.

Good Social Traits Make Friends

Desirable social traits—qualities necessary for working harmoniously with other people—are important to everyone in retailing. These traits are especially essential to those who occupy, or who hope to occupy, supervisory positions.

Courtesy. The courteous employee makes other people feel comfortable and at ease because he is always considerate, kind, and pleasant. Courtesy grows from an unselfish feeling toward others. Courteous people are usually friendly people. The importance attached to courteous treatment of customers by store employees is shown in the illustration on page 52, which appeared in the employee magazine published by a Milwaukee department store. The statements made during 1912 and 1918 are as timely today as they were when written.

Tact. The ability to say and do the right thing at the right time is called *tact*. Tact is particularly needed in dealing with people who have strong likes and dislikes, those who have grievances, and those who advocate principles that are in sharp disagreement with your own. To possess tact, a person must have good control of his emotions; he must think seriously about what he says in order to avoid hurting or embarrassing others.

Even the most courteous people once in a while inadvertently say or do untactful things. Tact is developed through study and much practice. Placing oneself mentally in the other person's shoes (empathy) is nearly always required when dealing with delicate subjects and with people who are a bit touchy.

Enthusiasm. Enthusiasm is the manifestation of eager interest or zeal a person has for an idea, person, or thing. Enthusiasm is contagious. It can be transmitted from one employee to another and from employees to customers where it may help to create buying desires.

Enthusiasm is largely dependent on knowledge. One can hardly be enthusiastic about something one knows little about. For example, you may not be very enthusiastic about your lead pencil. But undoubtedly the manufacturer's representative who sold it to a distributor is very enthusiastic about it and shows his enthusiasm. This is because he knows all about pencils.

Personal Qualities Can Be Cultivated

Now that you know some of the desirable personal qualities expected in retailing employees, you will want to know something about how they are developed. Personal qualities are formed through attitudes and habits. Good attitudes can be acquired and made habitual through practice. First, we must resolve that we *want* to possess the right attitude and then make this a part of ourselves through practice—that is, to make it a habit.

Forming a new habit is not particularly difficult. It requires just two essentials: a *genuine desire* and *constant repetition*. A desire, strong enough to give the habit a good start, is the beginning; keeping "everlastingly at it" will make this habit a permanent part of us. Benjamin Franklin, when a young man, wanted to acquire certain good habits. He soon found that he could not develop all these at one time. He discovered that forming *one habit at a time* was the best way in which he could improve his personality. He concentrated on one habit until it became natural and easy and a part of him. Then he began another. A good way in which the retail employee can acquire desirable new habits is to make this a game, with fellow employees and customers as "players," to help him test the effectiveness of his new habit.

Trade Talk

courtesy
loyalty
industriousness
initiative
personality

social trait
tact
venturesome
spirit

Can You Answer These?

1. Why must a young retailer give a great deal of attention to the development of favorable personal qualities?
2. What factors are largely responsible for the physical impression one makes?
3. What rules of good grooming should retail employees follow? Posture? Health?
4. What is venture-mindedness? How would you go about developing this quality?
5. What are the five aspects of loyalty discussed in the text? Which is the most important in retailing?
6. What are the characteristics of a person with initiative? of an in-

dustrious person? How can one develop these characteristics?
7. What are social traits? Describe several and tell how they may be cultivated.
8. What is the best way to form a new habit?

Problems and Projects

1. Construct a rating form on personal appearance that can be applied to retail personnel. Using the form, select the three members of your class who rank highest in personal appearance.
2. Make a list of the rules of health that a young person entering retailing should practice.
3. The statement is made that honesty and reliability in business dealings are just as much a factor in the success of a salesperson as they are in the success of a business firm. Discuss this statement.
4. Everyone has a few poor habits. Identify one of yours and describe your plan for correcting it.

5. Write a description of at least 200 words of the type of person who succeeds in retailing.

Learning Your Job

1. Obtain a list of the dress and grooming rules of your store, if one is available. If no such list exists, make up a list by discussing the question with your employer or sponsor. Include this list in your store manual.

2. Find out which qualities your employer desires most in employees. Rate yourself on each quality. Then make a list of specific ways by which you can eliminate your weaknesses.

3. Without revealing names, rate the persons you consider the poorest and the best workers in your department or store using the lists you obtained in problems 1 and 2 above.

9 *Finding the Right Job and Getting Started*

How does one begin to look for the right job? Wait for a friend's influence? Walk the streets? Read want ads? Any method is good if it gets results, but some methods are better than others. The right way to find the right job is to make a plan before you start. Taking the first available job that will put spending money in your pocket is likely to result at best in frustration and wasted years. Failure and an unstable employment record may result.

Reflect for a while, therefore, before you launch your hunt for the job that best meets your needs. A very important decision is that of choosing the type of store that will offer the opportunities you want. Stores are not alike; a person might be happy in one kind of store but not in another. One merchandise line may excite him, while others bore him. The wise job seeker selects his first employer very carefully.

Choosing the Type of Store

The job hunter should consider first the type of store that will give him the satisfaction he seeks and that best meets his present and future goals—a chain store, a department store, a specialty shop, or some other type of store. The merchandise line and the price ranges carried will be important factors, for they will determine in part the clientele he will serve and the type of people with whom he will work. How do you find out which type of store is best for you? Let us examine some of the factors that may influence your decision.

Past Work Experience. Previous retail experience on part-time or summer jobs helps a person to know the kind of store and selling or nonselling positions for which he is best suited. Working as a Christmas extra can be valuable try-out experience. The student who is seeking a part-time job naturally wishes to work in the type of store that meets his interest. Yet, certain stores have more part-time jobs than others. For example, stores in shopping centers need a number of part-time workers to staff night openings. Large chain outlets use many part-time employees to cover peak sales-volume periods. A recent study of midwestern states showed that food, variety, and drug stores have a larger proportion of part-time workers than other types of stores—at least 30 per cent of their personnel were part-time workers.

Supervised experience in a school work-study program is excellent, because the student-worker experiences balanced store activities and studies retailing practices in the classroom.

Interests, Hobbies, and Education. A young job seeker can use his interests, hobbies, and education as barometers of the kind of job that will give him the greatest satisfaction. A hobby often gives a young person special knowledge and skills that he can put to good use in retailing. An interest in fashion may lead to sales positions in ready-to-wear; an interest in children, in the children's wear department; an interest in mechanics, in an auto-accessories store. The boy who likes sports may use his knowledge in merchandising sporting goods. The girl who enjoys art or music may find satisfying employment in distributing products related to this interest. Those who raise animals, grow flowers, read books, or engage in any number of hobbies find interesting careers in stores that feature these goods and services.

Success in school courses often indicates success in various phases of retailing. Principles of color and design learned in an art course can be translated into employment in merchandise display, advertising, or selling. Bookkeeping and mathematics courses may bring out an aptitude for accounting and other office occupations.

Benefits Offered by Store. Wages, working conditions, and various employee benefits (such as vacations, pension plans, hospitalization, and life insurance) offered by various stores should be evaluated. While you should

This boy is learning stock keeping in a department store in his co-operative training program.

not choose a store strictly on the basis of the benefits it offers, if everything else is more or less equal, they may be a deciding influence. The opportunity to advance on the job, to learn, and to gain valuable experience should be considered ahead of employee benefits. Some stores offer excellent training courses and have definite employee-development and promotion programs. Accepting fewer benefits and a smaller salary in the beginning may be worthwhile if they can be traded for a wealth of experience that may be used later to obtain a better position or eventually to start one's own business.

Making the Employment Contact

There are many ways for the job seeker to locate the job he would like to have. Some suggestions are offered in the following paragraphs.

Apply at an Opportune Time. When is the best time of the year to apply for a position in retailing? Normally, stores seek extra help in September for the fall season; in November, for the Christmas season; and in March, for the Easter rush. However, any time may be a good time if the store needs employees. One young lady noted that a bridal shop was being built. Having an interest in such merchandise, she applied to the manager long before the store opened and obtained a satisfying job. Shopping centers under construction may also prove excellent sources of later employment.

Put Your Best Foot Forward in Person. In larger stores, application should be made to the personnel or employment office. In smaller stores, the applicant should seek an appointment with the manager or owner. In either case, the job seeker should appear in person rather than make a telephone call. Appearing in person gives the applicant an opportunity to make a good impression by his poise, dress, grooming, and self-confidence. Applying in person has another advantage: the applicant's name is more likely to be kept on file by the store for future vacancies—an important point when a specialized position in a prestige store is sought.

Check the Want Ads. The "Help Wanted" columns in the newspapers are excellent sources of information about retailing positions. Reading these ads is an excellent way for the job seeker to find out what qualifications are desired and whether or not he wants to apply. Many help-wanted ads are "blind ads." *Blind ads* are those that give only a post-office box number and do not identify the employer. They are often used by employers to obtain letters from numerous applicants. From these, only the most promising people are asked to apply in person. Such ads also protect the employer from having to interview many unqualified people. Blind ads are often used to fill better positions or to fill vacancies that the employer knows he will have in the near future.

The active job seeker should read the help-wanted ads in both morning and afternoon newspapers every day. It is wise to pick up an early edition from a newsstand rather than wait for a home delivery. This is especially true of morning

Various types of help-wanted ads can be found in a newspaper.

city papers, which can be obtained the previous evening. A prospective employer should not be telephoned in response to an advertisement, unless the ad specifically directs the applicants to do so. Following the directions in the ad is considered very important by the employer. If a letter is written in response to an advertisement, the job seeker should cover the points mentioned and state whether he has the qualifications asked for by the want ad. Advertisements often specify that the applicant should apply in his own handwriting.

Friends Can Help You. Is it unreasonable to ask friends or relatives to let you know about job openings? Some young people think so, feeling that they "don't need any help" or that using "pull" is wrong. Using friends to help you is not pull—most jobs are obtained only if the applicants merit them. It is, therefore, wise to let friends assist you in locating potential employers.

Retail-store managers often ask their best employees to be on the alert for

This student is learning to process merchandise in the warehouse of a department store during her co-operative training program.

future employees. They feel that good employees will want to suggest the names of good workers. In smaller towns where people know one another well, friends can be a valuable source of help. If you have been a good student in a distributive education class, your teacher-co-ordinator will be able to help you because he is well acquainted with the needs of local merchants.

An Employment Agency May Help You. There are several types of employment agencies that will help you find a job. Usually, the largest public agencies are operated by the state government. They are well informed on the employment picture both locally and throughout the state.

Other public employment agencies are operated by such organizations as the YWCA, YMCA, and B'nai B'rith. Also, many schools and colleges provide job-placement services for their graduates. Most public agencies charge no fee for their services.

Most cities have one or more private employment agencies that are good sources of jobs. Private agencies operate to make a profit. The job seeker pays the agency a fee, usually a percentage of his first month's salary. In some cases, the employer will pay the agency the employment fee. When dealing with a private agency, the inexperienced job seeker should be very sure that he understands thoroughly his obligations and the conditions under which the fee is to be charged.

Selling Your Services

After you have made contact with a prospective employer, you may have three opportunities to convince him of your merits. Often you will fill in an application blank; almost always you will be interviewed; sometimes you will take tests.

Don't Trip Over the Application Blank. In many stores, the application is the threshold to the interview. The personnel department tends to judge an applicant's qualifications by the quality of his application blank. Failure to follow directions or carelessness in completing the form often eliminates an applicant from further consideration.

Interviewers use the completed blank as a source of information from which to ask pertinent questions concerning education, experience, and family background. Thus, information on the blank should be complete and accurate. Falsifying any record, purposely or through carelessness, is a dangerous practice that can lead to a permanent black mark on a person's record.

The applicant is usually asked to provide names of people to serve as references. Courtesy demands that such people be asked in advance for permission to use their names. Although a friend can be listed as a character reference, it is better to list people who know and will say honestly *what you can do*. The person used as a reference who can only say, "Well, he's a nice young fellow," does the applicant little good.

The Interview. Interviewers note carefully how you are dressed and groomed, what you say, and how you act. Preparation for the interview is, therefore, important.

It is not necessary to carry along your high school diploma; however, appropriate awards of merit, for example, proficiency awards for skill in a business course, may be shown to the interviewer. Think about questions you will want to ask—questions regarding advancement opportunities and training offered by the store. But also be prepared to answer such questions as:

> Why do you want to work for this store?
> Why do you think you'll like retailing?
> What ambitions do you have for the future?
> Would you rather sell or be in a nonselling position?
> What can you do for us?
> How much salary would you expect?

When getting ready for the interview, dress your best—shoes shined, clothing freshly cleaned, hair and nails immaculately groomed—so that your whole appearance will have that "scrubbed clean" look.

The interviewer likes to see applicants walk confidently and alertly. A slouch is objectionable, just as much as a swagger. Sit comfortably, but upright without slumping. Do not distract from the conversation by fidgeting with your handkerchief, purse, keys, or other objects, and refrain from nervous mannerisms, such as wringing your hands or flexing your fingers.

Converse pleasantly and directly, answering questions in full rather than merely nodding or saying "Yes" or "No." Be patient, even though you have been waiting a long time. In small stores, particularly, the interview may be interrupted several times while the manager talks with customers or salesmen.

Prime qualities in every occupation are sincerity and earnestness, accompanied by confidence yet humbleness. It pays to:

Accompany your words with a smile.

Show that you are interested in learning and in a future in retailing.

Stress your strong points but do not hide your weaknesses.

Emphasize your reliability and dependability.

Ask for a specific position rather than merely say "you are willing to do anything."

Recognize when the interview is at an end, thank the interviewer, and leave promptly.

Tests May Be Given. Some larger stores provide tests that supplement the interview. Often tests of basic arithmetic are used to weed out those who are woefully weak in this skill. Tests of clerical ability, such as number-matching, may be given applicants for nonselling positions. Tests of manual dexterity are sometimes used in selecting people for positions as checkers, packers, and markers.

Where Should You Start?

Of course, you cannot expect to start at the top in retailing. In fact, many merchants believe that a worker who plans to make retailing his long-term career will do well to begin at the very bottom—sweeping, washing windows, and handling stock. Those who start at the bottom and work their way up know better than anyone else that every task, no matter how menial or seemingly insignificant, contributes to the success of a store.

Clean floors, well-organized stock, and sparkling windows impress customers. Merchandise arranged to best advantage and kept free from dust is easier to sell. It is the attention to these "little" details that adds up to success in retailing. This is one reason why many store executives like to start young people at the bottom. These merchants realize that only by performing menial tasks does the young worker learn to appreciate them. Performing the simple tasks provides an opportunity for you to get your feet on the ground floor; it helps you build confidence while you are learning how the store operates and getting acquainted with your fellow employees. The simple tasks offer you an opportunity to prove yourself worthy of advancement. If you were plunged directly into more complicated tasks, you probably would feel awkward, inadequate, and even frustrated.

When you advance in retailing, you will eventually supervise others; beginning supervisors who have been "through the mill" usually find their new assignments easier to learn than those who skip beginning jobs.

Simple tasks provide opportunities to develop good work habits, such as accuracy, thoroughness, neatness, and promptness. They also give you a chance to prove that you possess good job attitudes—co-operation, interest in your work, loyalty to the firm, willingness to accept responsibility, industriousness, and readiness to accept criticism.

Thus, as you approach your new job, accept the menial tasks cheerfully. Remember that the responsible jobs are reserved for experienced employees. As a beginner, you are likely to make many mistakes.

Trade Talk

blind ad
Christmas extra
employment
  agency

employment-
  agency fee
employee
  benefits

Can You Answer These?

1. Why is it so important to pick the right store in which to apply for a job?

2. In applying for a store position, what historical or background data should you be prepared to give?

3. Describe the three most common means by which the employer can obtain information about the applicant.

4. Why is a personal interview the most satisfactory way for one to apply for a position: (*a*) from the employee's standpoint? (*b*) from the employer's standpoint?

5. What reasons can you see for employers placing so much importance on the application blank?

6. In what ways are the type of store, merchandise lines, and clientele factors in the choice of the store in which you seek employment?

7. In what situations is it best to apply: (*a*) for a job in person? (*b*) by phoning or writing a letter?

8. What are the advantages in using the services of an employment agency to obtain a position?

9. Why do some employers believe new workers should start at the bottom?

10. What are the advantages to the beginning worker of starting a career by performing simple, menial tasks?

Problems and Projects

1. Assume that your father has friends who manage stores in which you would like to work. Would you want him to ask his friends to employ you? Would your answer be different if you only wanted part-time work?

2. Make a report to the class of the names and locations of private and public employment agencies in your community.

3. Obtain application blanks from several stores and compare them as to the amount and kind of information they ask for.

4. Interviewers often ask applicants many questions. Select a store where you would like to apply; and, assuming you will be asked the questions on page 59, prepare your answers.

5. Make a list of your hobbies, interests, and special abilities. For each item on the list, indicate whether or not it would be especially useful in retailing.

6. Look through the help-wanted ads in your local daily newspaper for several days. Do these show high or low store-employment opportunities? For what store positions does there seem to be the greatest demand? What qualities are asked for most often?

Learning Your Job

1. Suppose that you are your employer. Make a list of information you would like to know about a person to be hired for the job you now hold. How would you try to get this information?

2. List the menial jobs assigned to you. Why is each important, and what might happen if it were carelessly done?

10 *Breaking Down the Job*

Some people master their jobs much more quickly than others. Often, this is because they have established some excellent learning habits. For example, they are not satisfied with just knowing *how* things are done; they insist on knowing *why* they are done, and the reasons for doing them in a certain way. Usually, those who adjust quickly to a new job follow some kind of plan for mastering their jobs. The beginning of such a plan is the making of a job breakdown.

Make a Job Breakdown

Your first step in making a job breakdown is to make a list of your duties and responsibilities. A *duty* is a natural, legal, or moral obligation to do what is required. A *responsibility* is the accountability for a given task, whether done by you or someone else. You need not be concerned whether the activity is a duty or a responsibility—the important thing is that both are included. Also, it is unnecessary to follow any particular order or sequence at this point. The unorganized list of items as they come to mind is commonly referred to as a "laundry list." Each time you receive a new assignment, add it to your list until you are sure the list is complete.

Don't worry about how little or seemingly insignificant the duty seems to be. If there is doubt in your mind as to whether it is already recorded, write it down and make your decision later. Remember that all jobs need not include physical activity. For example, figuring or calculating is a duty; so is determining the proper color for a display.

There are several good sources of information about retail jobs that may be of help to you in making a complete job breakdown. Perhaps the best of these is your job supervisor. You will find that your fellow workers are also valuable sources of information about your work. You may also refer to your school and public libraries for copies of *Job Descriptions for the Retail Trade,* a U.S. Department of Labor publication that provides descriptions of many retail occupations.

Organize Your Duties and Responsibilities

Suppose that you have completed the laundry list of duties. Your next step will be to organize the list so that it is more meaningful. Just as a store is divided into departments where similar kinds of merchandise are kept together, so your job duties should be grouped into categories where similar kinds of work are listed.

For example, the broad categories of duties of a shoe salesperson might look like this:

✓ Assist customer in selection of shoes	✓ Take inventory
Fit shoes	Maintain stock controls
Suggest related merchandise	Make counter displays
Take special measurements	Build window displays
Stretch and make minor shoe repairs	Advertise shoes
	Perform clerical duties
Care for sales-floor stock	Do housekeeping duties
Stock-room duties	Receive and mark footwear

Under each category, several duties should be listed, similar to those found on the left-hand side of the chart given below. Note that some of the duties are physical, such as cleaning the counter; and some are mental, such as choosing the item to display.

Make a Job Study Plan

After you have made a job breakdown, your next step is to find out what you need to know in order to do each job well. Suppose that one of your jobs is to construct hosiery counter displays. You would list the steps in constructing a hosiery display, similar to those in the left-hand column entitled, "What Employee Does."

CONSTRUCT HOSIERY COUNTER DISPLAY

What Employee Does	What He Must Know
Choose kind of goods to display	Current fashions Seasonal demand
Choose items to display	Color harmony Customer needs and wants Features of the items
Select theme	Current vogue
Order show card	How to write show-card copy
Clean counter	Uses of cleaning materials How to clean counter
Assemble goods and props	Uses and location of props Location of stock
Prepare props	How to clean and adjust props
Place hosiery on form	How to dress forms
Place goods, props, and sign in position	Display selling principles

Your next task would be to list opposite each step the things that you would need to know in order to perform each step well. For example, in order to select the item to be displayed, you should know what the current fashions are in regard to hues, shades, and materials, so that the articles you display will be what your customers want. You would also take into account the kinds of hosiery that sell during the current season. In similar manner, you would list the things you should know in choosing the items to be displayed, selecting the theme for a display, and so on down the list.

Put Your Plan to Work

After you have completed your list of things that you should know, your next step is to select the information to be acquired first. In so doing, you may wish to consider what knowledge is essential immediately, what you already know, the logical order of learning, and how soon you will be called upon to create a display.

Study the Needed Information. Information may be learned from this book, from your teacher and classmates, and from references of various kinds. Your textbook and your instructor will be helpful in organizing your material. If you are employed in a retail store, even for a few hours a week, much essential information may be acquired from your supervisor and fellow workers.

Your co-workers' willingness to co-operate with you will depend on how tactfully you elicit the information. Careful timing of your requests is important. For example, pick a slack period for your questions. Stating the question in a manner that is easily understood and in a way that makes the person questioned feel glad to respond is an art that will carry you through many problems. Do not ask questions in front of others, if you can avoid doing so, because you may embarrass your superior if he is uncertain of the answer. Sometimes it may be necessary to view a demonstration and perhaps perform the job yourself under the observation of a person who can do it well.

Record Your Information. Recording information aids learning. You will find that a good test of your understanding comes when you try writing down your ideas. Also, recording is an aid to memory. Perhaps you have noticed that executives make many notes. None of us has a perfect memory. Thus, it is wise to form the habit early of jotting down facts and ideas.

Carry Through Your Study Plan. No plan is worth anything if it remains in a desk. It may take a great deal of self-discipline to put your plan to work consistently, but if you can carry it through to completion, you will have little reason to doubt that you will become a successful retailer.

It is quite likely that you will make several plans for learning a job during your lifetime. Most people change jobs several times, even though they remain with the same company. Your ability to plan the learning of a job and carry it out should improve with each experience.

Trade Talk

duty   responsibility
laundry list

Can You Answer These?

1. What is the procedure for making a job breakdown?
2. How should one go about organizing his list of job duties and responsibilities?
3. What are the steps in making a job study plan?
4. What things should be considered in deciding on a sequence in which the job in a study plan is to be learned?
5. Where can the beginning worker get help in finding sources of information about his job?
6. How should a beginner go about seeking help from his co-workers relative to learning his job?
7. How does writing down ideas help one to understand one's job better?

Problems and Projects

1. Following the recommended procedure in the text, the class may make a job breakdown for one or more of the following positions: (*a*) managing a football team, (*b*) president of a school club, (*c*) school-cafeteria cashier, (*d*) librarian's assistant, (*e*) an office on the staff of the school annual or newspaper, (*f*) committee chairman of a school committee.

2. Select a retail job that you might like to have. Using *Job Descriptions for the Retail Trade* or occupational literature available through your guidance department, list its job categories. Check them with a person who actually holds one of the positions listed.
3. How should a beginner go about soliciting the help of more experienced salespeople in acquiring product information and other information about his job? Demonstrate this using your teacher or a classmate to play the role of the fellow worker.

Learning Your Job

1. Make a job breakdown for your present job. List the categories of jobs. List the jobs that you would classify under as many of the categories as time permits.
2. In Part 2, you are asked to prepare a manual of store information in which you are to note important facts and place materials related to your store and to your job. Place the job breakdown and job study plan in this store manual. As you complete each unit in your retailing course, continue to record the facts about your store and job that apply to the unit.
3. Ask your employer for his opinion on what types of questions an employer likes and those he prefers not to answer. Ask him when is the best time to ask questions.

4. Retailing Is People

Unit 4

Part 11

Human Relations with Fellow Workers

In many occupations, workers deal primarily with machines, equipment, or paper work—that is, they work with *things*. In a retail store, however, most of the jobs involve close contact with others—with *people*. "Retailing is people" is a true saying; the people are customers, fellow workers, department managers, supervisors, and top executives. Thus, the ability to work harmoniously with people is a primary requirement for the ambitious young retailer. To succeed in retailing, you must succeed with people. You must like being around people and enjoy working as a team member. While store managers will tolerate a lack of some of the retailing skills and information while a person is learning, they cannot overlook failures in human relations. Actually, they cannot afford to, because poor relations with people affect not only the individual but all those with whom he works as well.

Although they have many similarities as a group, people are actually very different as individuals. Every worker has his own desires, ambitions, motives, and attitudes—each quite different from those of everyone else. The things that give one person pleasure may be painful to another, and vice versa. At the same time, an individual's attitude toward a given situation may not be the same on Tuesday as it was on Monday. Our attitudes vary with our moods.

What Do Workers Want?

Even though individuals are quite different as total personalities, most of them share in common the following rights and desires:

The right to work at the job of their own choice

The desire to get ahead—to be successful

The desire to be accepted and approved by fellow workers

The desire to feel important and to do work that is considered important

67

The desire to make a contribution
The right to have opinions and ideas heard and considered
The desire to be praised for a job well done
The right to think and act as individuals

How are these desires achieved? If we want to achieve our desires, we must first make sure that we practice the Golden Rule: "Do unto others as you would have others do unto you." In other words, if you want others to respect your opinions and ideas, you must first respect theirs; if you desire praise for a job well done, you must also be willing to praise the efforts of others; if you want to feel important, you must first make others feel important. And so on.

There is no magic formula that can be followed in achieving your desires. In addition to the general Golden Rule, however, there are two basic rules that the new worker must observe if he is to reach his goals:

Do the best work that it is possible for him to do on all jobs assigned, no matter how routine.
Take every opportunity he can find to learn about the company and about the various jobs in the company.

Opportunities come first to those who are ready for them, and the wise worker is constantly preparing himself to take advantage of these opportunities.

Desirable Traits of Retail Employees

We have already discussed in Unit 3 some of the desirable personality traits of the beginning worker. In thinking about developing good relationships with others, review this list of ten characteristics that supervisors rate most highly in sizing up a worker. How do you rate?

Enthusiasm	Industriousness
Honesty and dependability	Tact and courtesy
Initiative	Friendliness and
Sense of humor	cheerfulness
Loyalty (including the ability	Sense of fair play
to keep confidences)	Co-operativeness

Undesirable Traits of Retail Employees

Of course, some people are not willing to make the sacrifices necessary to achieve their goals. They try to take short cuts to success. When they do so, however, they usually wind up at the bottom rather than at the top. For example:

"Using" (exploiting) other people rather than making a genuine effort of their own
"Politicking"—currying favor with supervisors
Running down other people by gossip and tale bearing
Taking credit for ideas and achievements of other people

Methods such as these are the quickest route to failure that one could choose.

Friendliness and cheerfulness are important traits of the retail salesperson.

While they may seem to pay off temporarily, in the long run these techniques will spoil the worker's chances of success.

An undesirable worker can cause many difficulties in a retail store—bickering, resentment, and general friction, resulting in low morale for the entire staff. These characteristics (in addition to those just listed) mark the undesirable worker:

Is jealous of co-workers
Is indifferent to criticisms and suggestions
Shows little consideration for the rights of others
Is an "apple-polisher"
Gripes to everyone who will listen
Steals sales from fellow salespeople
Acts superior

Suggestions to the New Worker

The new worker in a retail store becomes a member of a new family. Within this family, some are, like himself, new on the job; others are old-timers—employees of long service in the firm. The job of the new worker is to fit in with this family and to be accepted as a welcome member as soon as possible. How does he go about gaining acceptance from those with whom he works? Here are some suggestions:

1. *Approach Your New Job with Enthusiasm.* Show people that you are glad to be on the team and that you are going to enjoy working with them.

2. *Be Friendly.* Don't be afraid to smile and show your eagerness to make friends.

3. *Don't Be Afraid to Ask Questions.* Mistakes may create problems for other employees; and getting information, in order to avoid mistakes, just

makes good sense. Of course, you should avoid incessant, foolish questions. But the general rule is: when in doubt, find out.

4. *Don't Join Cliques.* In some stores, as in any kind of organization, you may find cliques—little groups of people who organize against another group. Be nice to everyone, but don't become too friendly with any one of them or "join sides."

5. *Show That You Are Willing to Learn.* The new employee who acts as if he "knows it all" becomes very unpopular immediately. Show your respect for the know-how of experienced employees—they can help you.

6. *Show That You Are Not Afraid of Work.* If you recognize the opportunities to move up, show immediately that you are willing to do any job—even the dirty ones—because it will add to your knowledge and experience. Older employees will watch carefully to see if a new employee is a loafer. Be willing to tackle anything assigned.

7. *Look Sharp.* Follow the rules for good grooming and cleanliness discussed earlier. Everything about you—your attitudes, ambitions, and your personality—are reflected in your grooming habits.

8. *Show Appreciation for Help.* Experienced employees are usually eager to help a newcomer. Since beginners may add to the work load of those who are more experienced, the beginner should be grateful and show appreciation for help.

9. *Compliment Fellow Workers.* Experienced workers appreciate any indication that the new employee admires their knowledge and skills.

10. *Don't Be Too Eager.* Some young people who are ambitious to succeed show their eagerness too forcefully. You are not going to take over the store in your first month on the job. Take it easy.

11. *Learn the Names of Your Fellow Workers.* No sound in the language is so sweet to a person as his own name. Get names straight as quickly as you can. Do not be too quick to use first names, especially with older workers. Observe carefully the customs of the store in using first names.

12. *Learn About Your Fellow Workers.* Every successful retail employee is proud of his job and is pleased when someone shows an interest in it. Learn all you can about the jobs of your co-workers. And it is a good idea to learn something about the workers themselves—where they live, their social interests, and their families. Do not pry, but show genuine interest.

Practicing these rules will help you to gain acceptance by most of your fellow workers and will assure you of an important place on the team. There may be some people, of course, who will not accept you readily. Be friendly with them, but concentrate your efforts on those who show a genuine willingness to accept you. These are the ones from whom you can learn.

Maintaining Good Human Relations

Getting accepted on the team, of course, is only the first step. You must *keep* the confidence and respect of your fellow workers; and to do so, you must practice good human relationships constantly. They are not something you can put on and take off as the mood strikes you. Here are some suggestions for maintaining good relationships with your fellow workers on a day-by-day basis:

1. *Treat People as Individuals.* People differ in their attitudes, abilities, and backgrounds. They also face different problems at home and in the store. They, therefore, react differently to similar situations. The wise employee recognizes differences in individuals and treats them accordingly.

2. *Recognize That Human Behavior Is Unpredictable.* People's moods vary, because they face different problems. They may worry about money, their children, their health, or success on the job. Thus, a co-worker may have to be treated differently depending on how he feels on a given day.

3. *Don't Pass the Buck.* Blaming someone else and shifting responsibility to a co-worker is called *passing the buck*. Using excuses to cover up one's own unsatisfactory performance results in poor relations with fellow workers. A good worker feels secure enough to handle problems himself and is able to accept praise or blame equally graciously.

4. *Be Loyal to Others.* The person who is a loyal friend keeps confidences and respects his promises. He is dependable and refrains from gossiping about other workers.

5. *Seek Promotion on Your Merits.* Co-workers will respect promotions other employees earn by their good performances. On the other hand, promotions that come at the expense of others are certain to result in resentment and ill will.

6. *Help Build Department and Store Morale.* A new employee

You need a good sense of humor to handle some customers.

either adds to the problems of departmental operation or helps reduce them. Taking a full share of the load is expected. Giving a "little extra" helps build *esprit de corps,* group spirit, in the department. Co-workers appreciate a new employee who cheerfully becomes a part of the team.

Trade Talk

esprit de corps   passing the buck
initiative   industriousness
"apple-polishing" "politicking"

Can You Answer These?

1. What do most people really want to obtain from their work? Which of the desires given in the text do you feel is most important to achieve?

2. What does the phrase, "a desire to get ahead," mean to you?

3. By what kinds of behavior can a new employee fail to gain the acceptance of his co-workers?

4. List the foundations of building good co-worker relations. Which do you consider the most important? Why?

5. In what ways can a person show his loyalty to other employees? Explain whether this means that a person cannot be loyal to both his co-workers and the company at the same time.

6. What ways would you suggest to get to know and understand the people with whom you work?

7. For what reasons could experienced employees resent the new employee in the department?

Problems and Projects

1. Some desirable traits of co-workers are listed on page 68. Rate yourself on each trait, using as evidence your performance either on a part-time job or in school groups.

2. Make a list of examples of unacceptable ways to achieve one's goals. Explain: (*a*) why each method is unacceptable; (*b*) whether these methods are equally bad in one's social life as they are on one's job.

3. Assume that you are a retail-store manager. One of your salespeople, Jim Lark, sells far more merchandise than any person in the store. But Jim is not friendly to the other employees; he is cocky and is not willing to help the others. Can you afford to keep him on your payroll?

4. Do the foundations of good human relations discussed in this part apply in a classroom? How?

Learning Your Job

1. Observe carefully fellow employees as they work together. Report briefly on a situation showing how a co-worker either used (or failed to use) one or more of the foundations of good human relations.

2. The text lists some principles of gaining acceptance on a new job. Rate yourself as to how well you have used each principle in gaining acceptance on your job.

3. If you are a trainee in a co-operative distributive education program, prepare a brief report on the topic, "What a Co-operative Student Can Do To Gain Acceptance for Himself and the Distributive Education Program."

12 *Using Supervision to Advantage*

Learning to profit from supervision begins with your attitude toward your employer. What does he expect of you? What does he do for you in return? Good employer-employee relationships depend largely on mutual appreciation of each other's rights and responsibilities.

In Unit 2, you surveyed the world of retailing and learned of the career benefits that retailing offers. Then, in Unit 3, which was concerned with getting started on the job, you discussed the traits necessary for initial employment. At this point, you should review these topics, thinking about them from a different point of view—that of how management feels. Understanding what your supervisor expects of you is one of the keys to using supervision to advantage, that is, using it to help yourself to success!

What Employers Provide

A new employee often takes for granted the various benefits provided by his employer. But, the wise newcomer understands that management provides certain benefits and has a right to expect something in return. The following list reviews for you the employer's investment in his personnel:

1. *Space and Equipment.* Modern stores require large capital in-

JOHN RODMAN WANAMAKER, JR.
Chairman of the Board of Directors, Wanamakers, Philadelphia, Pa.

vestments in land, buildings, and fixtures, such as counters, display cases, lighting, and cash registers, and other office appliances. Your employer's capital investment provides thousands of dollars' worth of space and equipment for you to work with.

2. *Training.* Employers do not expect new workers to be fully productive immediately. They expect to lose money while the beginner is being trained. And, they invest many more dollars in advanced training—store classes, training by supervisors, and tuition for formal education in adult schools and colleges.

3. *Working Conditions.* Modern stores are pleasant places—clean, attractive, and comfortable. In addition, management often sponsors recreational activities, hobby clubs, and cafeterias.

4. *Financial Benefits.* Besides salaries, employers often provide other benefits that have monetary value—social security; medical, life, accident, and unemployment insurance; discounts on purchases; retirement plans.

What Employers Expect

In return for salaries and other benefits, managements feel that they have the right to expect certain things from their personnel. The following list reviews these expectations:

1. *Regular Attendance.* Supervisors expect punctual, dependable employees. Irregular attendance disrupts work schedules and places an unfair burden on both management and co-workers. Failure to return promptly from lunch and coke breaks not only annoys supervisors, but causes them to question an employee's initiative and co-operativeness.

2. *Adherence to Store Rules and Policies.* Employees who will not, or cannot, carry out assignments can create chaos in a store's organization. Most supervisors, however, encourage experienced employees to find out why things are done as they are. Usually management is willing to change rules that prove to be unworkable.

3. *Respect for Authority.* Management feels that it has a right to be treated with respect. Executives and supervisors want respect for their experience, their positions, and their responsibilities.

4. *Personal Characteristics.* Management constantly seeks employees with many desirable character traits; the most prized in retailing are initiative, creativity, and loyalty.

Understanding Your Supervisor

Employees who respect and get along well with their supervisors are happier on the job. They experience less wear and tear on their nervous systems and

Good relations between a supervisor and an employee are fundamental for good business, particularly in the buying of merchandise.

Courtesy J. L. Hudson Co., Detroit

consequently are less fatigued at the end of the day. A supervisor's attitude toward an employee is usually a reflection of the attitude of the worker toward his supervisor. Store personnel find it relatively easy to appreciate the position of the customer in relation to the success of a retail business. If they take the same attitude toward their supervisors that they take toward customers, much can be done toward establishing the friendly, co-operative spirit that is so essential to the operation of a successful retail business.

Supervisors are chosen by management because: (1) they know the jobs of the people they supervise, (2) they know store policies and rules, (3) they can handle people well, (4) they can improve job methods and increase production, and (5) they can teach the jobs they supervise. It is easy to see that supervision calls for a wide range of abilities. Much time is needed for a supervisor to develop all these abilities; but, because supervisors are human, not all of them possess all the skills and knowledge essential to excellent supervision. A worker who understands this and has a kindly feeling toward his supervisor and his position is likely to receive in return a friendly attitude of co-operation and understanding.

Foundations of Good Relations with Supervisors

There are a number of principles, or foundations, of building good relationships with supervisors. Understanding each one and practicing it in daily employment is the intelligent way of using supervision to advantage.

Foundation 1: Be Sold on the Aims of the Store. Retail management has three basic aims or purposes in its merchandising operation:

> To make a profit on the investment
> To attract and keep a satisfied clientele
> To develop and maintain a harmonious team of employees

The retail employee should be fully aware of these aims of management and be "sold" on them. If an employee cannot accept the purposes of his firm, he will find it very difficult to do his job well.

Foundation 2: Make Good Use of Constructive Criticism. A good supervisor often offers criticism by suggesting (or asking the worker to suggest) better methods of performing a job. A wise employee knows that constructive criticism helps him to see his weaknesses and alerts him to ways in which he can improve. Making best use of such criticism is achieved by:

Asking for suggestions as to better ways to perform the job
Requesting help from the supervisor in finding out how the job is best done
Accepting the criticism constructively—not defensively; that is, by profiting by the criticism and not resisting it.

Foundation 3: Be Loyal to Supervisors. In dealing with supervisors, the employee should practice these three rules of loyalty:

Uphold the decisions of the supervisor before others. If the decision is open to improvement, make such suggestions to the supervisor in private rather than gossiping with others.
Recognize the right and responsibility of a supervisor to direct activities and make decisions—even though the decision may seem to you to be improper.
Harbor no resentment toward the supervisor nor encourage resentment shown by fellow employees.

Foundation 4: Carry Out Responsibilities Assigned. It is the supervisor's job to direct the work of others. To do his job effectively, he must expect that workers will assume the responsibilities he assigns; and he has the right to expect these responsibilities to be carried out as perfectly as possible.

Foundation 5: Recognize the Supervisor as an Individual. Because supervisors are individuals, they are subject to varying moods. They have their own problems both in the store and in their private lives. As they react to such problems, their attitudes toward workers may vary from day to day. The wise employee recognizes that the mood of the supervisor will not always be consistent and adapts his own behavior accordingly.

Foundation 6: Contribute New Ideas. Retail management seeks creative ideas. If an employee has a new idea, he should discuss it with his supervisor; the supervisor's experience can result in making a good idea become a superior one. Caution: the newcomer to a store should become fully acquainted with the store policies and operation before suggesting new ideas or changes.

Profiting from Instruction

Although some supervisors are very good teachers of new workers, not all have had the benefit of training in how to instruct. Frequently they are so busy with other duties that they cannot devote the proper amount of time to training, and consequently new workers feel neglected. There are some things that an employee can do to ensure better learning on his part; therefore, the following tips will help you benefit from supervisory instruction: *

Step 1: Preparation

    Be at ease. You will have every opportunity to learn.

    Stand or sit where you can see clearly.

Step 2: Receive Instruction

    Repeat each step to yourself.

    Connect what you are learning with what you already know.

    Learn steps in logical order—not too many at once.

    Ask your instructor to repeat or explain doubtful points.

    Be sure you know what, why, when, where, and how you are to do the job.

Step 3: Perform the Job

    Do the job.

    Ask the instructor to watch you.

    Tell the instructor each step as you perform it.

    Ask questions—don't guess.

    Make new knowledge or skill a part of you by feeling, seeing, and talking about it.

Step 4: Get Out Production

    Work on your own.

    Strive for accuracy—speed will follow.

    Ask questions whenever necessary.

    Make a list of the steps in your job and refer to your list continually.

Trade Talk

capital   constructive
  investment   criticism
financial benefits   loyalty

Can You Answer These?

1. What benefits do retail employees receive other than salary?

2. Of what value to employees are company social and recreational activities?

3. If employees are expected to obey orders, why is "blind" obedience not desirable?

4. What does "using supervision to advantage" mean to you?

5. Why should a new employee delay suggesting changes in the store's operation until he has acquired experience in the store?

6. Is it disloyal to question the orders of a supervisor? Give reasons for your answer.

7. The statement is sometimes made, "An employee is a mirror of his supervisor." What does this statement mean to you?

8. What benefits for the worker can you see if he builds a satisfying relationship with his supervisors?

* Adapted from *Job Instruction Training for Supervisory Personnel in Sales and Merchandising Organizations*, U.S. Office of Education, Washington, D.C.

9. Explain how you will benefit from the use of the four steps in learning from the supervisor's instruction.

Problems and Projects

1. Based on any job experience you have had, make a list (in addition to the ideas in the textbook) of what employers expect of employees.

2. Make a collection of employee manuals or any other store pamphlets that describe what the store expects of its employees. Perhaps this literature can be displayed on a bulletin board.

3. Prepare a list of points you would cover in discussing the question, "What constitutes a full day's work for a full day's pay?"

4. Interview several store managers or supervisors and prepare a report to the class on the topic, "The most common faults of beginning employees," or invite a retail-store executive to talk to your class on this topic.

5. Almost everyone has supervised others at some time, either at work, at school, or in organizations. Write a short description of the traits you most dislike in people you have supervised.

Learning Your Job

1. Ask your supervisor what he thinks your store expects of its employees. Ask some of your co-workers the same question. List their answers and compare them.

2. Review your experiences in working with others on a job, in school, or in some group, such as the YMCA. Write a brief statement about outstanding traits of the person for whom you most like to work.

3. Find out what services and facilities your employer provides for you that are beyond those that are essential to your welfare.

4. Make a list of the things you *have done* at work that showed that you possess initiative. Be specific. Now make a list of the things you *could* do to demonstrate initiative.

5. Make a list of the things the best liked co-worker in your department or store does to cause him or her to be well liked by fellow workers.

6. List the foundations of building sound relationships with supervisors. Rate yourself on how well you are now putting each into action. Give evidence for each rating. For each poor rating, suggest a plan for overcoming it.

13 Solving Human-Relations Problems

Thus far in this unit we have discussed the importance in retailing of maintaining sound human relationships. We have found that a new retail employee must develop satisfying relationships with his co-workers, with his supervisors, and with management. We have learned, too, some of the principles of building good human relationships. At this point, we shall study the application of these principles in solving human-relations problems.

A Typical Human-Relations Case Problem

Irene had been employed in the cosmetics department for only three days when Ruth drew her aside one morning and said, "Let's have lunch together today. I've got some real news I want to tell you." Later, as the two were seated in a small sandwich shop, Ruth blurted out, "I wouldn't want you to repeat this, but I've been told that Mr. Curtiss is going to make Cathy the new assistant manager of our department."

"That's a pretty nice promotion, isn't it?" Irene replied. "Cathy seems to be such a good salesperson. She's done a lot to help me since I've been here."

"Oh, Cathy's not as good as she tries to make everyone think she is," said Ruth. "She just flirts with the boss. She's always asking his advice about how to do things, so's he'll notice her. Why, Verna has been in the department lots longer than Cathy, and if anyone deserves a promotion, it's Verna."

"I don't know very much about the situation," Irene ventured, "but I suppose Mr. Curtiss had a good reason for choosing Cathy."

Sensing Irene's feelings, Ruth responded, "Well, anyway, the rest of us in the department don't like it, and we're not going to exert ourselves too much to co-operate with Cathy. Since you're new in the department, I thought I'd better talk to you. I know you'd like to go along with the rest of the gang."

At this point the following questions summarize the nature of Irene's problem:

Is Irene in any way responsible for what is happening in the department? Is Verna?

Can Irene do anything to improve the situation?

Before finding out how Irene should answer, it is necessary to determine how a problem can best be solved. An individual who is faced with a problem has two choices: (1) He can decide immediately on the course of action he should take; or (2) he can think logically through his problem, getting all the facts and weighing several solutions before deciding what to do. Experience has

Many human-relations problems are solved in the personnel department.

A. Devaney, Inc.

shown that the second course of action is better. This action involves the four-step method of solving human-relations problems.

Problem Solving: The Four-Step Method

To see how the four-step method works, let's apply it to the case problem of "Irene and the Gossiper."

Step 1: Get the Facts. Sometimes what appears to be a fact actually is not, for people often see in a situation only what appears to be true, or what they want to see. They are sometimes blinded by prejudice and emotion. Thus, the first step in solving a problem is to check carefully to be sure one has all the necessary, *actual* facts. For example, in the case of Irene a few of the actual facts are:

> Irene has been in the department only three days.
> Ruth *thinks* she knows that Mr. Curtiss is going to promote Cathy.
> Ruth *seems* to be jealous of Cathy.
> Irene is asked not to co-operate with Cathy.

Only after *all* the facts pertinent to the situation have been gathered, is it possible to determine the *real* problem rather than the imagined one.

Step 2: State the Problem. The second step is to state the actual problem as shown by the facts gathered in Step 1. This is very necessary, because sometimes an apparent problem obscures the significant one. A person who is skilled in solving human-relations problems knows how to perceive the important problem. He has the ability to cast the others aside.

In the case of Irene, one *apparent* problem is how to help Cathy get her promotion. Yet, a second look at the facts reveals that the real problem for Irene is how to deal with the gossiper, Ruth.

Step 3: Determine Possible Solutions. After the real problem has been determined, it is then wise to decide on the courses of action that are possible. Of course, all courses of action may not turn out to be good ones. It is important, however, to review many of these solutions in order not to overlook the best ones. In the case under consideration, Irene has at least the following possible courses of action:

Tell Cathy what is happening.
Discuss the situation with the supervisor, Mr. Curtiss.
Go along with Ruth and make it "tough" for Cathy.
Refuse to discuss the situation further.
Help Ruth and the others see that it is to their advantage to get along with Cathy.

Each of these solutions is a possible one. Yet each must be analyzed to decide which will produce the best results.

Step 4: Weigh and Decide.   The final step is to weigh the advantages and disadvantages of each of the possible solutions to the problem. One must consider the effects of each decision on one's own relations with other workers and with the management. It is important, however, also to consider the effect of a solution on the morale and efficiency of the department and the store. Before deciding on a single solution for the case of "Irene and the Gossiper," it will be wise to review (on page 71) the principles of building good relationships with others.

In the case under study, Irene's going along with Ruth would violate almost all principles of building good relationships. The other possible solutions have merit, but each violates one principle. The solution is best in which Irene attempts to help the others see the advantages of getting along with Cathy. Of

LINCOLN FILENE

Founder of the Retail Research Association and the Associated Merchandise Corporation, as well as of Filene's in Boston, Mass.

course, since Irene has worked in the department only three days, she will have to consider this fact when carrying out her decision.

Practice Makes Perfect

Developing skill in solving human-relations problems requires practice. The newcomer to retailing will do well to study the four-step method of problem solving and practice applying the steps to his daily situations.

A person who can get along successfully with his co-workers and with management has a valuable asset. This skill is acquired only as an individual is able to gather facts carefully, see a problem clearly, and weigh solutions intelligently.

Trade Talk

human relations in retailing

apparent problem

real problem

prejudice

emotion

Can You Answer These?

1. When a retail employee is considering a solution to a problem, what groups may be affected by his decisions?
2. For what reasons are the *real* problems likely to differ from the ones a person *imagines to be real?*
3. Why is it necessary to state the problem after determining the facts of a situation?
4. Why is it a good idea to consider *all* possible solutions to a problem when some solutions are not desirable ones?
5. When a person with long experience is faced with a problem, is it a good idea to use the first solution that he thinks of? Why, or why not?
6. How are the foundations of good human relations used in the four-step method?
7. Can the four-step method be used in solving problems other than those of human relations?

Problems and Projects

In this unit, the four-step method

of solving human-relations problems has been discussed and illustrated; however, the best way to learn to use this method is to try the steps in the classroom. Following are some case problems. For each one: (*a*) Write out your solutions, following the four-step method. (*b*) Prepare to play the role of each person in each case. To do this, try to place yourself in the same position as the characters in the case problems. Then try to think of how each person might act. With several other students, put on a skit, acting out the case problem to a desirable solution. Then, be prepared to discuss why your solution is a good one.

CASE 1

Bob Mason has sold men's wear for several years. He's a fairly good salesperson and he knows his merchandise well. Late one afternoon, he walked over to Mr. Bronson, an older salesperson in the department, and said, "Did you see that latest shipment of sport shirts? I've seen some bad merchandise in my time, but never anything like that . . . How does Mr. Wurtz expect us to sell stuff like that?"

"They're going to have to be mighty strong selling points," he continued. "You know, Bronson, I've quit buying my shirts and ties here. Discount or no discount, no one is going to get me to buy anything in this department. I want high-quality merchandise. I think Mr. Wurtz is making a mistake not to stock the better lines."

CASE 2

Mr. Carpenter, the buyer of domestics, was well liked by his salespeople. He greeted them each morning, and he kept them well informed on new merchandise. He discussed department plans with them and often asked for their reactions to merchandise before buying it.

At noon yesterday, an incident occurred which has Muriel, one of the salesgirls, a little concerned. She was walking hurriedly down the block when she sighted Mr. Carpenter coming toward her. As they passed she smiled and said, "Hello," but Mr. Carpenter did not return the greeting.

Muriel began to wonder what she had done to make him ignore her. Was he angry about something? Her lunch hour was spoiled, because of the incident. "Maybe he just didn't see me," she said to herself. But during the afternoon, Mr. Carpenter walked through the department twice and paid no attention to Muriel. This convinced her that he was annoyed with her personally. She thought she ought to talk to one of the other girls about it. But she decided to put it off until morning.

Learning Your Job

1. As you perform your work activities, you will invariably see some human-relations problems develop. An observant employee is able to get the facts about an incident and report them accurately. Describe briefly one or more human-relations problems that have occurred where you work. Use fictitious names and: (a) give the facts; (b) state the problem; (c) suggest possible solutions; (d) decide on the best course of action and explain your decision.

2. Tell your supervisor about the four-step method of solving human-relations problems. Ask him what he thinks of it. Then ask him how he attempts to solve such problems. Report to the class on his opinion.

3. Ask your supervisor what he considered to be his most difficult human-relations problem when he first started to work in retailing and how he overcame it. If he is willing, have him cite a particular incident in which the problem arose and how he faced it.

5. Learning Store Policies and Store System

the costume

METAL MAGIC

FURNITURE

SALE

GET IT AT

NEW D'

HUG

Part 14

Interpreting Store Policies and Services

There are many things to learn about a new retailing job—company policies and rules, store services, how to take care of and merchandise your stock, how to write sales checks and operate the cash register, what is expected of you, and so on. Usually, you will have a great deal of help from your fellow workers and supervisors. Even so, you will need to give considerable time and effort to individual study. Regardless of whether you hope to rise to an executive position or prefer a job with less responsibility, you will need a well-rounded understanding of retailing—a "balanced knowledge" of the field. While retailing needs specialists, every specialist needs a balanced knowledge of all phases of retail-store operation—not just his own specialty. In this unit, you will learn first about the store policies and the customer services. Then, you will learn about store system—how to write a sales check, operate the cash register, make change, and wrap packages. These beginning skills are among the most important in retailing, for you are in direct contact with the store's most priceless assets—its customers.

What is the personality of the leading store in your city? Perhaps you have not thought of stores as having personalities—but they do. Just as a person has distinctive, individual qualities, a store creates a general impression on customers and business associates.

Progressive stores are very much interested in developing a personality that will attract the kind of customers they choose to serve. They, therefore, offer customer services and establish company policies that are aimed toward pleasing their clientele. As a present or future retailer, it is important that you understand the policies and customer services of your store, so that you may fit into its personality.

The Store Image

The *store image* is the impression, personality, or mental picture generally called to mind when the firm's name is mentioned. A store image is much more complex than the personality of an individual, because it is the result of the sum total of impressions made by all the firm's employees either directly or indirectly. Each time a salesperson serves a customer, each time the store runs an advertisement, each window or interior display, each assortment of goods, each remark about the store made by an employee (or anyone else)—all contribute to the store image. In order to bring about the desired consistency in store operation and treatment of customers, management establishes store policies to guide employees in making judgments in their daily work. Thus, all can work together in creating a favorable store image.

Factors Influencing the Store Image

While management has a great deal to say about its services, policies, and the resulting store image it tries to create, it is not entirely free to do what it likes. Store policies and services evolve from several sources: (1) from within the company, (2) from government regulations, (3) from merchant groups, and (4) from the necessity to meet competition.

Company Policies.　Major policies originating within a corporation are formulated by the board of directors; in a small business, by the owner or owners. An example of a major company policy is deciding to sell on credit. A second level of policy formation in the large company is that determined by major division heads, such as the personnel director. Regulation of employee vacations is an example of the kind of policy he might make. The third level occurs within the department. An example on this level might be the decision that the assistant buyer must approve all merchandise returns. In a small firm, all these decisions may be made by the owner or manager.

Legal Policies.　Policies stemming from federal, state, and local laws are usually referred to as *mandatory policies*. The store is compelled to enforce government regulations, such as one requiring stores to refrain from selling certain products to minors, or the one requiring the labeling of wool as "virgin," "reworked," or "reprocessed."

Intertrade Policies.　Some policies and services originate from agreements with trade associations, local merchant groups, and labor organizations. Examples of this kind of policy are meeting the price competition of discount houses, agreeing to close at a certain hour, and paying employees according to an accepted wage scale.

Meeting Competition.　Competition sometimes forces a store to change its policy in order to retain its share of business. For example, many merchants are compelled to give out trading stamps against their will.

The Store Image and the Size of the Firm

In a one-man business, the store's personality is that of the operator. As the business grows and help is added, the owner-manager finds it necessary to talk

The store owner himself can advise the boy on the fine points of the bat—possible only in a one-man business.

over operating policies with his employees, so that everyone with whom the business deals will be given similar treatment. When the number of employees grows to the point where the owner cannot personally supervise each worker, communicating his thoughts becomes difficult. Policies need to be clearly defined and explained, so that they can be passed along to employees through their supervisors.

Managements of large firms spend a great deal of money to communicate their policies to their own personnel, to customers, and to business firms with whom they deal. Brochures, manuals, meetings, company newspapers and magazines, advertisements, and letters are used for this purpose. In addition to achieving uniformity in customer treatment, sound company policies (1) reduce confusion, wrangling, and argument among employees, (2) maintain employee morale, (3) build good will on the part of vendors, customers, government, and the public, and (4) reduce friction with competitors. In the absence of established policy, personal considerations often play a part in the action taken; and the resulting inconsistencies in operating practices cause difficult human-relations problems.

Sometimes employees encounter a problem for which there is no established policy. If you are employed in a store and face this situation, it may be wise to report the problem to your supervisor rather than to make an independent decision.

Types of Store Policies

There are five types of store policies: (1) merchandise policies, (2) sales-promotion policies, (3) customer-service policies, (4) personnel policies, and (5) general policies. All should be consistent with the character of the company and the image the firm is attempting to create.

Merchandise Policies

What kind of merchandise should be carried? How wide should be the variety of brands and prices? What stress should be given to fashion? The answers to these questions represent the *merchandise policies* of the store.

Types of Goods. Stores must decide what types of goods are to be handled. Some stores are highly specialized and carry only a few types of merchandise, such as millinery and purses or men's shoes and belts. A large department store, on the other hand, may have more than a hundred departments, each with several kinds of merchandise. The store's location and the kind of customers it seeks are important factors in determining the types of goods to stock.

Lines. The number of lines to be handled is another merchandise policy to be determined. Some stores will decide on a single line. This is sometimes done by electrical-appliance shops, men's apparel stores, or paint stores, which agree with the manufacturer to carry only one brand. Others may carry several lines or offer to get any brand the customer wants.

Assortments. Size of assortments is another factor of merchandise policy. Assortments refer to the number and variety of sizes, styles, colors, brands, and prices to be carried in each line. Some firms carry very complete assortments, while others stock only fast-selling merchandise.

Quality. The quality of the merchandise to be handled is another part of this policy. One generally thinks of stores as being exclusive, medium priced, or popularly priced, depending on the quality of merchandise handled. In some kinds of merchandise, such as apparel and jewelry, the quality range is great. Of course, this is not so true of hardware and many drugs.

Retailers who handle fashion merchandise must decide whether to follow the practice of handling new styles that are just appearing on the market or dealing only with accepted popular fashions. Many retailers merely follow their competition and carry an assortment of goods that meets the average taste. This places competition on the basis of convenience, service, and price.

Price. Price policies are also necessary. In some kinds of goods, like many food items, competition brings about nearly uniform prices in a given locality; and there is little a merchant can do about it. In other goods, such as women's apparel, the price is largely determined by the cost of the business operation. Thus, a store that offers many free customer services is compelled to charge more than one that offers very few services. Some companies have a policy of consistently selling at prices below those of competition in order to build large sales volume.

Most retailers have a *one-price policy*—the same price to all customers except for those buying in quantity. Some types of goods, such as automobiles and electrical appliances, are not always sold under the one-price policy, but are bargained for. Sometimes manufacturers and retailers agree that the merchandise will be sold at a stated price.

Convenience Goods. To understand merchandise policies, the retailer needs to distinguish between classes of products. One common classification of merchandise places goods into two general categories: convenience goods and shopping goods. *Convenience items* are those that customers usually buy with a minimum of effort, at an accessible location, and without shopping from store to store for the best buy. Such articles usually are low priced. This category includes gasoline, foods, hardware, magazines, tobacco items, dairy products, and many articles sold in drugstores. Some convenience goods are purchased as *impulse items* (goods purchased on the spur of the moment). Examples of impulse purchases are candy and soft drinks from vending machines, garden plants from food markets, and some toys for children.

Shopping Goods. Customers, however, plan their purchases of some products quite deliberately and compare articles for price and quality in a number of stores. Items on which customers spend such effort are classed as *shopping goods.* Examples are: furniture, appliances, ready-to-wear, jewelry, power tools, and chinaware. Among shopping goods are certain types known as *specialty goods.* The consumer will go out of his way to purchase these. Examples are furs, expensive perfumes, and fine watches.

Hard Lines or Soft Lines? Retailers often classify merchandise as either hard lines or soft lines. *Durable goods*—such as hardware, appliances, furniture, paints, and electrical supplies—are classed as *hard lines.* Textile merchandise—such as ready-to-wear, fabrics, domestics, and shoes—is known as *soft lines.* Groceries, meats, dairy and bakery products are examples of *food lines.* Soft lines and food lines are classified as *nondurable goods.*

Retailers must utilize these merchandise classifications constantly when they determine types of sales promotion, methods of display, types of stock control,

No service here, but good buys for your money.

Courtesy S. Klein on the Square, New York

and selling techniques. The beginner in retailing finds that definitions such as these are part of the vocabulary he must learn—his "trade talk."

Sales-Promotion Policies

Some stores are known as promotional type businesses. They spend large amounts of money on advertising, feature many sales, and encourage their salespeople to use forceful methods of selling. Many stores do promotional work of a different nature. They seek to build good will through *institutional advertising*—advertising that stresses the store's name, its reputation, and civic-mindedness. Price appeals and special promotions are held to a minimum, and sales training emphasizes service to the customer. Some stores follow the policy of not advertising on Sunday.

Personnel Policies

Personnel policies are established to bring about consistent fair dealing with employees. They involve such things as: (1) selection of personnel, (2) amount and kind of training, (3) lines of job promotion, (4) wages, (5) hours, (6) employee recreation activities, (7) vacations, (8) employee discounts, and (9) retirement. Personnel policies are very important; the morale of the store employee is reflected in the way he treats the store's customers.

General Policies

The store's relationships with the community and its suppliers, as well as with competition, are extremely important. Definite policies should exist in regard to paying the store's bills, treatment of vendors' representatives, comparative shopping, participation in civic organization activities, and other matters.

The chart in Part 47, page 317, lists a number of services offered in various combinations in retail stores. At this point in your study of retailing, it is necessary only to be alert to the services offered by the store in which you may work; a more detailed study of store services will be found in Unit 13.

Learning About Customer Services

The newcomer to retailing discovers very early that helping a customer means providing him with information about the services offered. The salesperson who understands customer services offered by his store is at a distinct advantage over less well-informed fellow workers. Knowledge about services such as lay-away, gift wrapping, and credit clinches sales. Even cashiers, stockkeepers, and deliverymen must answer questions about such things as credit, alterations, and delivery schedules.

Why Services Are Offered. Many small independent merchants, as well as large department stores, attempt to meet competition through better

The sky's no longer the limit

When you and I were growing up, we called it the sky. And it was far away. Now it's space... and yesterday Commander Alan B. Shepard Jr., USN brought it down to earth for us. He was there and he came back...an achievement of the human spirit and the human mind almost beyond imagination. Commander Alan B. Shepard Jr., USN and all the men behind the Project Mercury flight have given us new horizons...and new heroes.

Boys and girls growing up today accept astronauts and spacemen and rockets as part of the world they live in. They may very well grow up to take space for granted, just as we take electricity...which was revolutionary to our grandparents...for granted. Some of these children may ride rockets, some may design them, and most of them will know what the inside of a spaceship looks like. They will all look back on May 5, 1961, as an historic day and will tell *their* grandchildren about it.

Their life will be a different life than ours, just as ours is different from life a century ago. Ultrasonics, astrophysics...the changes are already apparent. But some things, happily, remain constant. Cherry blossoms will still herald Spring, the shad will still swim upstream in the Hudson, the city skyline will still reach towards the sky...as man reaches further and further into outer space. And today's children and their children and their children's children will be shopping at Macy's. Because people will always want lovely things for their homes, beautiful clothes to wear. The sky may no longer be the limit of adventure and exploration... but generation after generation will discover that it's smart to be thrifty.

What will the future be like? We can only guess. But there's one prediction you can safely make: just as Macy's had more bustles to choose from when women wore bustles, we'll have more spacesuits when there's a spacesuit in every wardrobe...and everything else for the bright new world of tomorrow...in and out of space.

Macy's, the world's largest store

An institutional advertisement that made good use of a historic event.

Courtesy Macy's New York

customer services. They find that, even when prices are slightly higher, many customers will still patronize the store in order to take advantage of good customer services. In recent years, many chain stores have added services in an effort to court the customer's favor. Even discount houses have found it necessary to offer some customer services, such as credit.

Customer-Service Policies. The service policy should specify which customer services the store will offer. Service policies depend on the policies of competitors, the kinds of merchandise carried, the type of clientele, the location of the store, and the costs of the service. Food supermarkets, drugstores, variety stores, and discount houses usually offer few services; department stores and large specialty shops usually offer many.

Trade Talk

company policy
institutional
  advertising
convenience
  goods
shopping goods
mandatory policy
specialty goods

one-price
  policy
impulse item
merchandise
  policy
hard lines
store image
soft lines

Can You Answer These?

1. What is the relationship of company policies to the store image?
2. What causes customers to form a store image?
3. What factors must the store consider in trying to create a store image?
4. What are the purposes of company policies?
5. From what sources do company policies originate?
6. What are the personal advantages to employees of mastering company policies?
7. What course of action should be taken when a problem arises for which there is no established company policy?
8. What are some examples of sales-promotion policies? personnel policies? general policies?
9. What are the different kinds of merchandise policies? Give an ex-

ample of each.
10. What factors determine what services a store should offer?

Problems and Projects

1. Describe on paper the personalities of three stores in your city. Compare these with your classmates' descriptions. How do you account for the differences?
2. Does giving uniform treatment to customers mean saying the same thing and acting in the same way each time you contact a customer?
3. List three examples of store policies originating with a board of directors, three with store management, and three within a department.
4. What customer services are offered by the following retailers in your community: (*a*) grocery supermarkets, (*b*) automobile service stations, (*c*) independent hardware stores, (*d*) women's apparel shops, (*e*) restaurants, (*f*) department stores?
5. Make a list of at least five items for each of the following classifications of goods: convenience, shopping, impulse, and specialty.

Learning Your Job

1. Describe, in writing, the image

you believe your store tries to convey to the public. Have your supervisor check it.

2. List the merchandising, sales-promotion, customer-service, and general policies of your store. After your supervisor has checked it, compare it with that of your classmates who work in the same or related kinds of stores.

3. Make a list of the customer services your store offers. Which three of these do you believe are most valuable to your store? Explain.

Add the above information to your store manual.

15 *Sales Recording Requires Accuracy*

Have you ever been given the wrong change or found an error in a sales check when you made a purchase? If you have had this experience, you were probably annoyed; perhaps you even ceased to be a customer of the store. Millions of dollars and thousands of customers are lost annually because of errors in handling money and making out sales checks. Most of these errors are due to carelessness in the routine handling of sales transactions.

Much thought has gone into store systems, and everything that you are asked to do has good sound reasoning behind it. In small businesses, sales records are simple. In large firms, where many different people handle the merchandise and more services are offered, more information is needed and forms are more numerous and complicated. If you will accept your responsibility and follow directions, you will contribute to the better functioning of your department and to larger profits for the store.

Basic Types of Sales Transactions

Basically, there are two kinds of sales transactions—cash and charge. Some stores, however, also sell merchandise C.O.D. (collect on delivery), and some accept partial payment, withholding delivery of the goods until full payment is made. This latter practice is called "will-call" or the "lay-away" sale.

Cash-Take. In the cash-take transaction, the customer pays *cash* for her purchase with money or check and *takes* the merchandise with her. The sale is rung up on the cash register, which records the transaction on a roll of tape inside the machine and usually also issues a receipt. If the customer desires to return the merchandise, she uses this receipt as evidence of the purchase.

In some stores, *sales checks* are written for the cash-take sales. These serve the same purpose as the cash-register receipts but give more information about the merchandise purchased. The sales check serves other purposes as described on pages 94–96. In some apparel stores, price tags are substituted for sales checks.

Cash-Send. In the *cash-send* sale, the customer pays for the merchandise and has it delivered by the store. The sales check is used to provide the deliveryman with the customer's name and address. In some systems, the sales check may be stamped by the register. As evidence of his purchase, the customer is given a copy of one portion of the sales check, known as the *stub;* the remainder is placed with the merchandise.

Charge-Take. In the charge-take sale, the customer charges the merchandise to his account and takes it with him. Charge transactions are more expensive to the store because of additional record keeping, billing, and the interest on the money tied up in the charge accounts. Credit sales, however, are an important part of modern merchandising.

A most important step in handling charge transactions is the identification of customers to make certain that they are who they claim to be. Usually, charge sales must be authorized by the credit department, which checks to make certain that the account is not overextended and that the customer is not delinquent in his payments.

In many cities, stores give credit customers some token of identification and authorization—a numbered coin, a small metal plate, or a card. This identification device must be presented by the person authorized to use the charge account when charge purchases are made in the store. A commonly used identification device or charge plate is shown here. In stores where these plates are used, customers are permitted to charge purchases up to a certain amount, such as $20 or $25, without the salesperson having to secure the authorization of the credit department. The salesperson uses the plate to stamp the customer's name

The charge plate is an effective customer identification tag.

and address on the sales check by inserting the plate into a device provided for that purpose.

This type of charge plate facilitates the handling of difficult names, gives the delivery department legible addresses, and reduces authorization expense because the customer has already been given the privilege of charging a definite amount.

Charge-Send. In the charge-send sale, the customer has the purchase charged to his account and delivered. Since the customer is not taking the merchandise with him, he does not need to wait while the charge-send sale is being authorized. The authorization, however, is made before the merchandise is delivered. A common practice is to attach the sales check to the goods that are sent to the delivery department. The package is held there until the credit department approves the charge. In some stores, the sales check is sent directly to the credit department for authorization while the package goes to the delivery department. In either case, if credit is denied, the merchandise is returned to the department from which it was charged.

C.O.D. (Collect on Delivery). In the C.O.D. sale, the customer has the merchandise sent and pays for it when it is delivered. To call special attention to C.O.D. sales, some stores use specially colored sales checks; others use regular sales checks imprinted with a special rubber stamp, or they use special labels. This is done to remind the deliveryman to collect for the merchandise. Some firms require a deposit on C.O.D. sales for certain kinds of merchandise to insure the customer's acceptance of the goods when they are delivered. Such goods are referred to as *part-paid C.O.D.* transactions.

Will-Call or Lay-Away. In the will-call or lay-away transactions, the customer makes a partial payment. The merchandise is withdrawn from stock but is retained by the store until it is completely paid for. This permits a customer without a charge account to take advantage of special offers or to avoid the risk of a particular item being out of stock when he wants it.

A sales check is made out for the cash collected, and a lay-away or a will-call tag is attached to the merchandise that is placed in the will-call department. A time limit is set, after which the merchandise is returned to stock if the customer has not made the payments agreed upon.

Exchange. Sometimes the customer for one of many reasons returns an article and selects another in its place. If the price of both articles is the same, it is called an *even-exchange transaction.* In some stores, all the salesperson has to do is to make the exchange without making out a new sales check; in others, the exchange must be approved by a floor manager or assistant buyer; and a new sales check is made out for the even-exchange transaction.

If the price of the goods returned and of those given in exchange is not the same, the operation is called an *uneven-exchange transaction.* When the price of the merchandise purchased is more than that of the goods returned, a new sales check is written; and the price of the returned merchandise is subtracted from the new price on the sales check. If the new merchandise selected costs less than the returned goods, a refund must be made and a new sales check is written for the new merchandise. In both kinds of uneven-exchange transactions, approval of a floor manager or assistant buyer is usually needed.

Discount. Many stores offer discounts to employees; some give them to members of the clergy and other special classes of customers. In this type of transaction, the salesperson makes out a sales check in the regular manner and subtracts the discount from the regular price. Such transactions generally require the approval of the floor manager or assistant buyer.

Other Kinds of Transactions

Some stores offer special payment arrangements, such as revolving charge accounts, time payments, and depositor's accounts. Since these are handled in ways that are individual to the particular store, it will be necessary for the salesperson to receive special training from the store training personnel on handling that type of transaction.

Writing Sales Checks

When you write out a sales check, you are performing one of the most important procedures in store operation and control. Your accuracy helps in many ways: (1) you are contributing to the good reputation of the store among customers; (2) the buyer uses information recorded on sales checks when ordering merchandise; (3) the delivery department depends on the information you record for accurate delivery; (4) the credit department uses the information for billing charge accounts; and (5) the accounting department uses sales checks in determining sales volume. Sales checks differ widely among stores; however, the most common items of information required on sales checks are:

1. Date of purchase, needed for billing and for accepting returns.
2. Description of merchandise purchased, needed to identify the purchase, to help the store in ordering, and for accepting returned goods.
3. Price of merchandise purchased, needed for verifying the charge to the customer, for billing, and for returned merchandise.
4. Department, needed for cost control and returns.
5. Purchaser's name and address, needed for delivery, credit, returns and adjustments.
6. Salesperson's number, needed for sale date, returns and adjustments, also to credit the salesperson with the sale.
7. Kind of sale, needed to identify the transaction as cash, charge, C.O.D., etc.
8. Amount of money received from customer, needed where more than one person is involved in handling the amount tendered.
9. Customer's signature, needed to identify the purchaser in charge transactions.

10. Identification space, needed where special kinds of charge identifications are used.
11. Instructions, needed for delivery directions.

Tips on Writing Sales Checks. In large stores, four copies of the sales check are generally made: (1) original, (2) duplicate, (3) customer's copy, and (4) the tissue. There are usually three parts: (*a*) the address label or top, (*b*) the body or middle, and (*c*) the voucher or bottom. A charge sales check is illustrated below.

Each sales check is numbered. Sales checks must be used in sequence and each one must be accounted for. If you make a mistake in writing up the sale, have the check voided by an authorized person. Place it with your tally card when you turn in your money at the end of the day. A sales check must never be destroyed! If a customer purchases in more than one department, a separate check is used for each department.

Filling in the Tally. The *tally,* shown on page 98, is also called an "index," a "score card," or a "summary." Start each day with a new tally. If

CASHIER'S STAMP — TOTAL SALE 41 15

94780-45

CA | SOLD BY 8005 | DATE 11/25 | LORD & TAYLOR

DEPT.	QUAN.	ARTICLE		
32	1	dress 2581-X	39	95

APPLIED CREDIT NO. - SPECIAL ORDER NO., ETC. | GIFT WRAP | Sales Tax 1 20
CARD | TOTAL 41 15

CHARGE TO — FIRST / MIDDLE / LAST: Mrs. Charles A. Thompson
NO. / STREET: 65 East 65 Street
CITY / STATE: New York N.Y. 94780-45
SERVICE MGR. AUTHORIZATION — PURCHASER x Alice Thompson

FILL THIS SECTION IN IF CHARGE AND SEND TO ADDRESSES ARE DIFFERENT
SEND TO
M
ADDRESS

SOLD BY | DATE / | HOW SOLD | CHGE. AUTH. OR AMT. RECD.

SOLD BY | DA / | HOW SOLD | PROMISED DATE

SEND TO — Mrs. Charles A. Thompson
NO. / STREET: 65 East 65 Street
CITY / STATE: New York
APT. 12A ROOM | INSTRUCTIONS

Lord & Taylor FIFTH AVENUE, NEW YORK 94780-45

ENCLOSE IN WHITE ORIGINAL SALESCHECK ENVELOPE

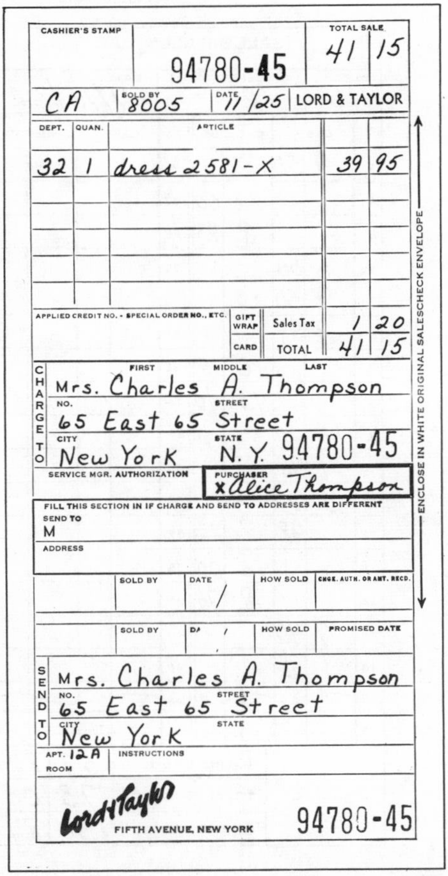

Notice how clearly this charge-sales check has been written. This becomes important if any adjustments must be made later.

Courtesy Lord & Taylor, New York

you use more than one book, use the same tally. Enter each sale on the tally in the proper column and opposite the number corresponding to the number of the sales check. Always circle on the tally the number on which you write your first sale each day. C.O.D.'s and lay-aways are entered in the cash column with C.O.D. or L.A. written before the amount. Total the tally at the end of the day, and give it to your department manager. The tally serves as an index to find a missing or incomplete sales check. It is also used in determining whether or not a department has sold as much as expected. The tally may be used in the accounting department as a check list in determining whether all your sales checks have been received.

MERCHANDISE RETURN TALLY BAG

DEPT. 46   SALES NO. 12   DATE 7/15/62

REFUNDS		CREDITS		REFUNDS		CREDITS	
6	00						
4	50						
		3	50				
		2	75				
8	50						
	REFUND TOTAL	19	00				
	CREDIT TOTAL	6	25				
	GRAND TOTAL	25	25				

FORM 821-24

The front of a sales tally.

The back of a sales tally.

SALES TALLY BAG

DEPT. 46   SALESPERSON 12   DATE 7/15/62

	CASH		CHG&COD			CASH		CHG&COD	
1	9	50			26				
2			12	00	27				
3			8	75	28				
4	6	00			29				
5	9	50			30				
6	3	98			31				
7			10	15	32				
8			15	40	33				
9	11	20			34				
10	1	98			35				
11	5	30			36				
12		98			37				
13			18	00	38				
14			8	75	39				
15	7	40			40				
16	1	98			41				
25					50				
	TOTAL CASH		57	82					
	TOTAL CHG&COD		73	05					
	GRAND TOTAL		130.	87					

Trade Talk

credit   charge plate
   authorization   tally
C.O.D.

Can You Answer These?

1. What kinds of sales transactions require (*a*) the customer's name and address, (*b*) his signature, (*c*) a deposit, (*d*) approval of supervisory personnel? Explain why these are necessary.

2. What are the advantages of the C.O.D. sales transaction? of the will-call or lay-away purchase?

3. Are the transactions in Question 2 of disadvantage to the customer and to the store?

4. Explain why each item of information on the sales check on page 97, is needed.

5. Why is a separate sales check needed for each department of a department store? Why isn't it needed in a small specialty shop?

6. What is the purpose of the tally? Why is a new one needed each day? How does the tally help the salesperson keep track of his selling costs?

Problems and Projects

1. Collect as many address labels and parts of sales slips from your home as you can. Compare them as to the printing or writing of the name and address. What other information is on the address label?

2. Compare the sales-recording procedures of two of the following businesses: dry cleaning, restaurant, women's ready-to-wear, mail-order house, service station, men's specialty shop, department store, hardware store. Explain the reasons for the differences in forms and procedures.

3. Accompany someone on a shopping trip. Be aware of any errors the salespeople make in getting the name and address of the customer. Tell what you particularly liked about the way they handled sales recording.

Learning Your Job

1. Bring to class a voided copy of a sales check used in your store. Mount it and compare it part by part with other sales slips brought in by other class members. Note the similarities and the differences.

2. An error in writing a sales check may result in a loss to the store. Based on your experience, what are some of the errors made in writing sales checks?

3. Describe the procedure used in your store for exchanges, will-calls or lay-aways, and discounts of various kinds.

4. Describe briefly the procedure used in your store for identifying a customer and for authorizing credit.

16 *Handling Money Correctly*

Pleasing, efficient service in making change and operating the cash register helps build a following of repeat customers. It also brings personal satisfactions that make a job worthwhile. Many able salespeople have suffered embarrassment because of mechanical errors at the close of the sale. In addition, it takes more effort to unlearn bad money-handling habits than to learn correct ones.

How to Check Your Change Fund

Your first job in preparing for the day's sales is to obtain a supply of change for your cash-register drawer. This money is called a "change fund" or "bank." The amount of money in the salesperson's bank varies, depending on the type of merchandise sold and the amount of business expected. In any case, you should count your change. The person who placed the money in the fund may have made a mistake, which would result in your being charged with a shortage or overage of money at the end of the day.

Ring up a "No Sale" on the cash register to open the cash drawer. If you are using a receipt-printing machine, a "No Sale" receipt will be issued, which you are generally required to keep in your cash drawer.

A simple, convenient way of counting your change is to place it on a stiff piece of cardboard over the till, so that it covers the paper-money compartments but leaves the coin compartments uncovered. The *till* is the metal compartmentalized tray that fits into the cash drawer; see illustration below. Empty

Use cardboard cover when counting change into cash drawer.

Courtesy National Cash Register Co.

Count each denomination of coins separately and slide them into their proper compartment.

Courtesy National Cash Register Co.

your change-fund bag on the cardboard. Do not count your change on glass counter tops, because coins scratch the surface.

Note that there is a compartment for each kind of coin: from left to right—pennies, nickels, dimes, and quarters. Half dollars are placed in the small compartment back of the pennies. Paper money is placed in the larger compartments in the back row according to the amount of the bill.

Count the coins, one denomination at a time, sliding them from the card into the correct compartment; see illustration on page 100. List each denomination on the back of the "No Sale" receipt or on a slip of paper. Then count the paper money and list it in a similar fashion. Total your figures to make sure the amount of your fund is correct. If your change fund is correct, close the cash drawer. If not, follow the procedure that you were taught to use by your store.

How to Make Change

Always follow the basic rule of "ring the sale—then wrap" because: (1) it will prevent giving out merchandise without getting the money for it; (2) you will save time and embarrassment in case your customer does not have enough money to pay for the purchase; and (3) unless you ring first—then wrap—you cannot put the cash-register receipt in the package.

1. *State the Amount of the Sale and the Amount Tendered by the Customer.* Here is an example of what you might say and do when you receive money from the customer: Hold the money so that the customer can see it and say, "That is $1.98 out of $5." This practice helps you remember the amount of the sale and the amount of money the customer gave you. It gives the customer an opportunity to correct you before the sale is rung, and you are able to correct the customer if he is confused. It also shows the short-change artist that you are well trained.

2. *Place the Money Received on the Change Plate.* The reason for placing the money on the cash-register change plate, which is sometimes called a "slab," is that it prevents you from forgetting the amount given you by the customer (amount tendered). It also leaves both hands free to operate the register, and the customer can see his money; see illustration on page 103. Do not put the bill in the drawer until after the change has been made. Always keep the change plate or ledge clean and clear of paper or other articles.

3. *Ring the Sale.* Punch the keys for the amount of the sale. Press the department key and your salesperson's key if the register has such keys. Check to see that you have depressed the right keys. If you have made an error, you can correct it by operating the release key or lever and then punch the correct amount. Then crank the register or press the control key or bar—the one that operates the drawer.

As the cash drawer comes out, catch it with your hand because the speed of the opening drawer may cause the coins to bounce into wrong compartments.

The cash register indication shows amount of sale and, perhaps, other details of the transaction.

Courtesy National Cash Register Co.

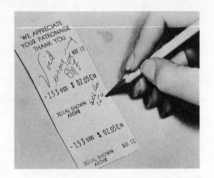

"Voiding" a cash register receipt. The number of the correct receipt is copied on the incorrect receipt.

Courtesy National Cash Register Co.

4. *Check the Cash-Register Signals.* Check the signals or indicators at the top of the register, which change as the sale is rung. This is done to make certain that you have the correct amount of the sale and the correct department and salesperson's drawer. Discipline yourself on this point, and you will make fewer errors. If you have rung the wrong amount, follow store procedure in correcting it; see illustration above right.

5. *Place the Receipt on the Change Plate.* This helps you remember to place in it the customer's package, because it is in plain sight; see illustration on page 103.

6. *Count the Change to Yourself.* Start counting with the amount of the sale shown on the receipt and on the signals or indicators, and build up to the amount received. This method is faster, safer, and makes it unnecessary to add or subtract.

Always use the largest denomination coins you can, because your change in your till lasts longer, you will have fewer mistakes, and the customer will have less small change. For example, use a dime instead of two nickels, a quarter instead of two dimes and a nickel, and a half dollar rather than two quarters. A typical situation is as follows: if the purchase is $2.58 out of $5, start counting with $2.58 plus 2 cents is $2.60, plus 5 cents is $2.65, plus 10 cents is $2.75, plus 25 cents is $3, plus $1 is $4, plus $1 is $5.

7. *Place the Customer's Money in the Cash Drawer and Close It.* Put the coins in the proper compartments. Place the bills face up and with the tops on one side. The change may be placed on the slab. The salesperson may then wrap the merchandise, taking the package and the change to the customer at the same time. Never leave your cash drawer open.

8. *Count the Change Back to the Customer.* Count the change back to the customer coin by coin and bill by bill starting with the amount of

Place the cash register receipt on the change plate beside the customer's money.

Courtesy National Cash Register Co.

the sale and adding up to the amount he gave you, in the same manner you did when you counted it to yourself. Counting the change to the customer provides a three-way check on accuracy—first, when you counted it to yourself; second, when you counted it for the customer; and third, the customer counts it with you as you count it back.

How to Finish the Sale

After you have completed the eight steps given above, two things remain to be done that are of importance to the store and also leave a good impression with the customer.

Enclose the Receipt with the Merchandise. This is good practice, because the receipt may serve as a basis for later exchange of merchandise; and it protects the store against accepting returned goods purchased elsewhere. Place the printed side of the receipt up, so that there will be no danger of wet ink damaging the goods. Be certain to ring up the sale immediately, even if the customer will not wait for a receipt. Do not serve another customer before registering the sale. Destroy any receipts left by the customer to prevent their being used by other customers.

Thank the Customer. No sale is complete without a sincere "Thank you," looking at the customer with a smile. Make sure that the customer will want to return to the store and to you.

End-of-Day Activities

At the close of the day when you are sure that no more customers are to be served and you will not be interrupted, you count your money and fill in the needed report forms.

Total the Tally, or "Index." Total your tally and attach the required "No Sale" and voided register receipts, voided sales checks, and other forms called for by your firm.

Turn in Your Cash. Following the same practices used in checking your change fund in the morning, count the necessary coins and paper money for the next day's cash fund and place it in the bag used for this purpose. Now count the remainder of the money, which is usually placed in another bag of larger size. Leave your cash drawer open as a protection against damage by thieves in the event someone breaks into the store during the night and tries to open it.

The difference between the amount of money in the cash drawer at closing time and the amount you placed in it from your change fund in the morning is your cash sales and deposits for the day. This amount is usually recorded on a cash-record form (sometimes a special envelope). The cash-record form usually lists the coins and paper money that you fill in and total.

In many firms, the change fund and money received are taken to the cashier's office where the salesperson is given a receipt or brass coin on which is stamped the register number. Never permit anyone to turn in your money for you.

Tips on Money Handling

Keep Your Cash Drawer Closed. An open drawer is an invitation to theft. The purpose of the bell, which rings when a cash drawer is opened, is to attract the attention of the salesperson. Registers that have more than one drawer have bells with different sounds for each drawer. Even separate registers usually have different bell tones. Form the habit of listening to register bells and learn to recognize the sound of your bell, so you will know if someone opens the drawer.

Don't Run Out of Change. Running out of change while a customer is being served leads to delay, embarrassment, and errors. Obtain your change from an authorized source, rather than make change from your own pocketbook, which may arouse suspicion. Never "buy" change from another salesperson or another cash register, unless authorized by a supervisor to do so.

Give Care to Paper Money. New paper bills may stick together. To make certain that you do not give a customer two bills instead of one by mistake, crumple new bills and then straighten them out again. Always keep one-dollar bills separate from larger bills in your cash drawer. Keep all bills face up in the same direction.

Don't Bunch Sales. Always ring each sale separately, no matter how busy you are. Bunching sales destroys the accuracy of store records, because it shows that only one customer was served instead of several. It also may result in suspicion of dishonesty on the salesperson's part. In a store using receipt-printing registers, bunching sales prevents giving each customer a receipt.

Correct "Over-Rings" and "Under-Rings" Immediately. If you ring up too much, you should re-ring the sale correctly and then void the incorrect cash-register receipt, which should be okayed by a supervisor and kept in the cash drawer. It is turned in with your cash at the close of the day. If the register does not issue a receipt, it is necessary for the supervisor to mark the tape instead of the receipt. In some cases, he may okay both of them. You should never attempt to correct an error by making up the difference on the next sale.

Mistakes in Making Change. When a customer questions the correctness of the change, always be polite. Ask him to give back all the change; then start counting over again. If you find that you were wrong and you are *positive* of the error, ring a "No Sale" and make the necessary correction in the amount of change.

If you are doubtful of the error, have your cash drawer checked by an authorized person. This is usually done in the customer's presence, but it may be necessary to wait until the close of the day's business. Explanations to the customer should be made tactfully and politely. If the customer is argumentative, let someone in authority take charge of the situation. Never argue with the customer!

Take Good Care of the Cash Register. Cash registers are expensive machines. They protect you as well as the store by recording transactions on tape. The register should be dusted each morning. Never put pins or paper on the register because they may work their way into the machine and cause damage. Any mechanical defect, such as illegible printing of receipts, should be reported immediately. When the receipt roll is near the end, you will note that the receipts are colored in a characteristic manner. This should be reported to the proper authorities and a new roll obtained.

F. W. WOOLWORTH, 1852–1919
The originator of the idea of the 5- and 10-cent store.

Trade Talk

salesperson's   till
bank   index
change fund   (salesperson's)
cash-register   change plate
   signals

Can You Answer These?

1. Explain the purpose of the change fund. Why is it necessary to count your bank at the beginning of each day or work period?

2. List the eight major steps in making change from the cash register. Give the minor steps, precautions, and key points. Justify each step.

3. One reason for cash-register signals is to permit the salesperson to see what has been registered. Can you think of another purpose?

4. Prove that the best way to make change is by building up to the amount tendered.

5. Identify the three checks in the three-way check on accuracy in making change.

Problems and Projects

1. Each member will bring to class several cash-register receipts for family purchases. Compare and tabulate the information on the receipts.

2. Accompany one of your parents or a friend on a shopping trip. Watch closely the cash-register procedure. Make a record of the ways in which the salespeople depart from the procedure described in this part.

3. Make a survey of customers to determine whether or not they have encountered mistakes in change making by salespeople. Try to find out in whose favor the mistakes were made. Find out how they felt about the errors.

4. Purchase several articles for yourself or someone else. Rate each salesperson on money-handling techniques and record your findings.

Learning Your Job

1. Observe three of your co-workers to see what steps in money-handling procedure are followed and which are violated. Write them down for your future guidance.

2. After completing each sale during an afternoon, tabulate the number and kind of errors you make in handling money.

17 *Protecting the Firm's Money*

Checking accounts are widely used today by customers. For this reason, the salesperson and cashier will often be asked to accept a check, and it is their responsibility to be sure the check is valid.

Usually, checks received in payment of purchases must be approved by a supervisor. The customer is asked to show identification on which his signature appears—such as a driver's license. Check-acceptance procedure differs among firms; it will therefore be necessary for you to learn the practices of the store in which you work. You can save much time for the supervisor, however, if you will learn to look for certain mechanical things that must be correct before a check is acceptable.

What to Look for in Accepting Checks

A check should be written in ink, indelible pencil, or typed. There should be no erasure or alteration.

The *date* should be the current date. Predated checks, those dated in the future, are not acceptable by most firms.

The name of the *payee,* the person to whom the check is addressed, should be legible; otherwise, the check may not be valid. It is better to have checks made out to the store, rather than merely to cash. If checks are made payable to cash, however, they should be endorsed by the *maker,* the person who writes the check.

A personal check. Note how close to the dollar sign the amount is written; likewise, the spelled-out amount starts at the beginning of the line.

No. *158*

May 7 19 —   00-791
                    831

PAY TO THE ORDER OF *Karen Sands* $ *18.⁹⁸*

Eighteen and ⁹⁸/₁₀₀   DOLLARS

PRAIRIE NATIONAL BANK
ST. LOUIS 6, MISSOURI

Rose Allen

The amount stated in figures should correspond to the amount written in words. If there is a difference, however, the bank will pay the amount written in words.

The *signature* should be legible and must be written in ink. As a further safeguard, some firms require the signer to write his address and telephone number below his signature.

An *endorsement* is required on the back of all checks not made out to the store. If the payee's name is misspelled on the face of the check, he must write the endorsement with the same spelling, endorsing it again correctly. If the check is made out to someone else, and there is no endorsement, the check cannot be cashed by the store.

While checks endorsed only with a name are valid, they are not so safe as checks endorsed with the words "Pay to (name of store)" and then signed by the endorser. Checks endorsed "For deposit only" should not be accepted. In case a check form is used in which the name of the bank must be filled in, be sure the correct bank or branch of that bank is given.

Though the salesperson must use caution in accepting checks, he should not act as though he were suspicious of the customer. Most checks are good, and the customer presenting a check should be treated as courteously as one who pays cash.

Traveler's checks or United States postal money orders are usually safe to accept. The salesperson, however, should be sure to check the policy of his store regarding these money substitutes.

Safeguarding and Protecting Your Store's Money

Short-change artists, check forgers, and counterfeit money passers are more

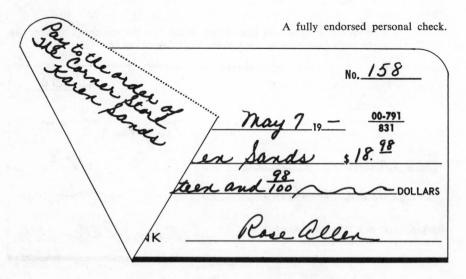

A fully endorsed personal check.

common than most people think. You should know something about the way they operate, so that you may help reduce losses due to this cause.

Protecting Yourself from Short-Change Artists

The professional short-change artist is a good actor. He may be well dressed or poorly dressed depending on the tricks he uses. He makes it a point to look honest. Usually he is well dressed to give the impression that he is a person of means, of whom the salesperson need not be suspicious. Short-change artists are nearly always drifters, who move from one section of the state or country to another, frequently traveling in pairs. They are most likely to try their wiles on inexperienced salespeople.

One kind of short-change artist will try to confuse you while you are counting change, hoping to get you to make a mistake in the amount of money you give him. For example, he may interrupt you while you are counting change and ask that you change a large bill; he may suddenly "remember" some small item that he wants you to add to his purchase; or he may ask you to exchange one item for another. He is always willing to be "helpful" in suggesting the easiest way out of your confusion which, of course, results in some advantage to him.

Another trick is to interrupt you before you finish counting change to yourself, by asking you to give him five ones for a five-dollar bill. Frequently the salesperson will give the five one-dollar bills to the "customer" and forget to take his five-dollar bill.

To avoid being deceived by the short-change artist, do not allow yourself to be interrupted. Ignore the request or question until you have finished counting the change and then give him the attention he requests. Finish making change before adding another item to the purchase or making an exchange. Consider additional items as separate transactions. Do not let the customer do your thinking for you.

Sometimes pairs of short-change artists use the marked-bill trick. The first customer buys an article and pays the salesperson with a $5 bill that has some unusual marking on it, such as an ink blot or writing. A short time later the second "customer" buys some article for a small amount, paying for it with a $1 bill. After the salesperson has placed the dollar bill in the register, the "customer," as he turns to leave, says, "I gave you a $5 bill and you gave me change for a one." When you disagree, he calls attention to the marked bill that the first "customer" gave you saying, "I remember the $5 bill because someone had spilled ink on it." You examine your till and find the marked bill, which convinces you he is right.

The best way to avert this trick is to observe both sides of each large bill you take in. If you notice any unusual marking or tear and you are suspicious, call the customer's attention to it. If the customer is a short-change artist, he will know that you are not a novice and will warn his partner not to complete the trick.

The split-bill trick is only rarely practiced, but salespeople are still fooled by it. New bills of large denominations are split into two pieces. The thin halves are pasted to $1 bills which, in the case of a twenty-dollar bill, would result in nineteen dollars profit to the deceitful person. These bills are usually passed at times when the department is busy. They are presented with the large denomination side facing the salesperson. Always look at both sides of large bills, and you will not be fooled by this trick.

To protect yourself against short-change artists, be alert, but do not act suspicious or make accusations. If you are quite certain the person is a short-change artist, observe his appearance carefully and report him to your employer or to the police. Let them take the responsibility of apprehending the criminal. If you practice good money-handling techniques, the chance of a short-change artist trying his tricks on you is small because he chooses his victims carefully.

Protection Services

Many stores operate a protection service or employ an outside company to perform certain police services. Large department stores and chain stores find it profitable to use specially trained personnel who are familiar with the ways of thieves, short-change artists, counterfeiters, and other dishonest people, who may be either customers or employees of the firm. Protection personnel may or may not be known to the salesperson.

Dishonest people have devised many clever ways to cheat their employers, and in some cases, losses through this source have been high. While store-protection personnel observe salespeople as well as customers, they should be regarded as friends. They prove the salesperson's honesty, inasmuch as every favorable report is a mark to his credit.

Trade Talk

endorsement	postal money
predating	order
traveler's check	counterfeit

Can You Answer These?

1. Explain each part of a personal check and the proper way to fill in the blank spaces. Illustrate three ways of endorsing a check.
2. Which is preferable, a check made out to cash or one made out to the store?
3. Tell how you would handle the situation if you encountered (*a*) what you thought to be a short-change artist who interrupted you while counting change, (*b*) a person using the marked-bill trick.

Problems and Projects

1. Your instructor may want to appoint a committee to contact the police-department officer responsible for investigating forgery cases, asking him to speak to the class on the procedure to follow when forged checks and counterfeit money are presented by a customer to the cashier.
2. Interview a local banker on the method used to clear and process checks.
3. Make a list of the names of persons whose pictures are found on each denomination of paper money. Memorize the names, faces, and denominations. Explain why it is important to know them.

1. Make a list of the steps used in handling checks at your store.
2. Interview your employer regarding his experience with forged checks and counterfeit money.
3. Describe the "protection services" that to your knowledge are used in your store.

18 *The Appeal of Well-Wrapped Packages*

Suppose that you are going to buy a gift for a friend and that you can buy the identical article from several stores. Will you choose the store where merchandise is crammed into a sack or the one that wraps packages attractively? Obviously, the latter will get your business. This is what is meant by the statement, "Wrapping is a part of merchandising."

After the merchandise leaves the store, the package becomes the showcase for the customer's purchase. A well-wrapped package says in effect, "The firm I represent admires and respects this merchandise and the customer who purchased it," rather than, "The person who sold you this article was in a hurry to get rid of you." Action in the form of well-wrapped packages confirms the store's claim of giving good customer service.

Wrapping Requires Knowledge and Skill

Wrapping is like arithmetic—the mistakes are easy to see. Have you ever encountered a salesperson who seemed to know very little about wrapping? If you suspected earlier that he was new on the job, you became certain of it when he wrapped your package. Experienced workers, on the other hand, know where the wrapping supplies are kept; they use the correct size bag or paper; the package is quickly but securely wrapped and taped or tied; the result is a pleased customer.

Wrapping know-how consists of making packages that are: (1) appropriate—ones that serve their purpose; (2) durable—packages that will not come undone prematurely; (3) attractive—ones that are neat and can be carried proudly; (4) economical—packages that require a minimum of material in accomplishing their purpose; and (5) timesaving—they are wrapped quickly, so the customer is not kept waiting.

Keys to Well-Wrapped Packages

Here are keys to success in wrapping. All of them will not apply to a particular wrapping problem, but most of them will.

1. *Appropriateness*

a. Assemble carefully articles to be wrapped in one package, making sure that heavy articles are on the bottom.

b. Select the kind of wrap suited to the package: bag, box, square sheet-wrap, cornerwise sheet-wrap, inner wrap.

c. Select suitable materials—paper, bags, or boxes of the right weight and size. (Use special paper for holidays when possible.)

d. Make the bundle no larger than necessary.

e. Be sure that the articles are fully covered to avoid embarrassment to the customer. (Fold soft merchandise, so that it can be inserted completely into the bag.)

f. Make flat packages when possible.

g. Use appropriate binding: gummed tape, scotch tape, twine, or ribbon.

h. Use square tie for large boxes; corner tie for small boxes.

i. Use enough twine of sufficient strength for carrying packages.

2. *Durability*

a. Use paper and twine that are strong enough for the goods being wrapped. (Use double paper if necessary.)

b. Prepare merchandise carefully before wrapping.

    (1) If possible, fold so that it protects itself to some extent.

    (2) Place perishable merchandise on top.

    (3) Protect breakable merchandise with corrugated board or padding.

c. Fold edges and ends well to make a stronger package.

d. Put cord around package in enough places and often enough to give maximum support without waste.

3. *Appearance*

a. Use the correct amount of paper and binder (break or cut the twine close to the package).

b. Fold in all edges and ends.

c. Adapt wrapping to special occasions: holidays, birthdays, gifts, child's package, mailing.

d. Strive for original and distinctive methods of wrapping that will appeal to the customer.

e. Bags should not be left open. Fold the flap securely.

4. *Economy*

a. Wrap the parcel correctly the *first* time.

    (1) Inspect the goods to make sure they are in perfect condition.

    (2) Check the price tickets or tags.

    (3) Remove price tickets on gift merchandise.

b. Wrap as much as you can in one package consistent with good judgment.

c. Differentiate between packages that are to be carried and those that are to be sent.

5. *Speed*

a. Work for accuracy in the beginning: speed will follow naturally.

b. Take time to judge the kind and amount of wrapping material needed.

c. Arrange articles to be wrapped, so that you need not start over.

d. Have wrapping materials placed conveniently at hand to avoid waste motion.

e. Keep wrapping area clear, so that there is plenty of free space to work.

f. Perfect the method for severing twine and tape, so that it is done correctly and quickly.

Tie large bags of soft merchandise so customers can carry them by the string. Be sure the string is tied securely. Of course, an item easily crushed should be put in a sturdy box.

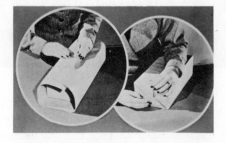

To wrap a square-cornered item, center it on a sheet of paper and draw the ends of the paper together smoothly. Fold into neat triangles over the ends of the item and tape or tie.

To wrap cans, glasses, or similar items, place the item across one corner of the sheet and roll it to the center. Turn in the ends of the sheet and finish rolling. Secure with tape or string.

Protect fragile merchandise with an inner wrap of soft paper. If several such items are to be packed together, wrap each individually and then protect the assembled items with corrugated paper.

All wrapping illustrations courtesy of National Cash Register Co.

He's proud of those beautifully wrapped packages, even if he is taking up too much space.

Courtesy Eastman Kodak Co.

Displaying a willingness to wrap packages can sometimes reduce delivery costs for your firm. A pleasantly offered suggestion by the salesperson may encourage the purchaser to take the merchandise with him. Statements such as: "Would you like your other packages wrapped together with your new purchase?" or "Do you want to take it with you, so that you can use it this evening?" frequently appeal to the customer and save delivery cost.

There are three basic wrapping systems: salesperson wrap, department wrap, and central wrapping.

In most small stores and in some departments of large stores, each salesperson wraps the merchandise he sells. To save the time of salespeople and to economize on space, wrapping may be done at a special desk on the floor (department wrap) where the sale is made. In many large stores, articles that are to be delivered are put in bags or containers, which are placed on conveyors leading to a central wrapping room. The actual wrapping is done in this room, which is usually located in the basement or subbasement of the store. Wrapped parcels are then sorted according to localities and are either delivered direct to customers or sent to outlying stations for distribution.

Wrapping Requires Study

The correct and economical use of wrapping paper, cartons, and twine is a matter of much importance in the wrapping process. Indeed, the adoption of suitable wrapping and packaging methods is considered so important by retailers that they conduct packing clinics at some of their conventions. Trade publications in the retail field often devote space to a discussion of better wrapping practices and illustrate these practices.

Gift wrapping has become a major service in the better type of stores throughout the country, and customers are increasingly being given year-round gift-wrapping service that formerly they received only in December or in a small part of June. For a small charge, many stores place articles in special gift boxes, wrap them in attractive paper, then tie them with ribbon. This practice has become popular to such an extent that the Dennison Manufacturing Company, manufacturer of crepe paper and special wrapping paper, decided to send instructors to stores and to retailing classes in public schools to teach present and prospective salespeople how to wrap gift merchandise attractively.

Trade Talk

department   salesperson
   wrapping   wrap
central
   wrapping

Can You Answer These?

1. Explain why wrapping may be considered a merchandising activity.
2. In this part of the text, five keys or rules for success in package wrapping are described. Write down all you can recall about each rule.
3. List as many reasons as you can for each of the different kinds of wrapping procedures used by stores.

Problems and Projects

1. Justify the offering of a gift-wrapping service in various kinds of stores—such as department stores, hardware stores, and supermarkets.
2. Now that you know the requirements of a good package, criticize the packages of merchandise received in your home recently.
3. Observe the way in which pur-chases are packed at a number of supermarket check-out counters. Report your observations to the class.
4. From the Dennison Manufacturing Company, or some other firm issuing publications on wrapping, obtain all the information you can on good wrapping practices. Be prepared to give a wrapping demonstration making use of this information.

Learning Your Job

1. Make a sketch of the wrapping counter which you use at work. Explain its good features. Make suggestions for its improvement if you can.
2. Make a list of the different ways of wrapping or packaging goods that are used in your department or store. Do you feel that you are proficient in using these various methods of wrapping goods?
3. Observe your fellow workers on the job while they wrap packages. Note whether or not they use good wrapping procedures as explained in the text.

Readying 6. Merchandise for Sale

Sale 9 99

GET IT AT

METAL MAGIC

the costume

NEW D

HUGS

4.00
4.00

ne new black-and-bea

hine at theatre, cockt

at the edges with je

in lines superbly new

zzle, a dark blaze of exc

entle curv

eels

s a rich girl. Go

ing goil to deny herself high fashion, when

to the rescue with smart clothes at

e. If you're loaded with taste, but not wit

s. and walk out looking like a mi

NEW
RONA

Learning to Merchandise Your Stock

Even the best efforts of salespeople cannot satisfy the customer when the merchandise he wants is out of stock, when goods are not fresh and clean, or when full size and color ranges are not available. On the other hand, stocking too much merchandise can tie up the retailer's money and curtail profit.

Selecting merchandise in the right quantity and of the most salable type is the buyer's job and requires advanced merchandising know-how. The salesperson and stock clerk, however, play important parts in preparing this merchandise for sale. Shipments of merchandise must be opened and the articles counted and marked with the retail price. Then, the merchandise must be placed in the reserve stock room or in the forward stock. Salespeople must keep it fresh and clean. Shelves must be kept full and inventories taken periodically.

A person who is anxious to learn retailing will find many opportunities to learn by observing the work of receiving-department supervisors, of buyers, and of merchandise managers. Here is an opportunity to gain knowledge about many types of merchandise and the sources from which they are purchased. Getting goods ready for sale and maintaining the floor stock is an excellent way to learn retailing "from the ground up."

In every store, large or small, someone must care for the stock, keeping it clean and in good condition, arranging it properly, and having it on hand in salable quantities. In small stores, salespeople often perform all the stock work. In large stores, some of the departmental duties of salespeople include caring for the forward stock. In this case, department stores often designate in each selling department a person known as a *head of stock* to supervise the other salespeople.

Some department stores employ specialized personnel, known as *stockkeepers,* to care for reserve stock and move merchandise from reserve stock to the forward stock. Stores—such as drug, variety and grocery—operating by simplified selling methods (self-service) also have stockkeepers to care for and replenish shelf and counter stock. Stores that sell big-ticket items—high-value items such as furniture and appliances—by floor sample, do not expect salespeople to care for the stock; but employ special stockkeepers.

117

Improper Care Hurts Everybody

There is an old saying in retailing, "Merchandise is money." Improper care of merchandise hurts the customers, the salespeople, and the management.

Customers like to buy stock that looks, and is, fresh and clean. They look for merchandise that is in style, rather than out-of-season models or leftovers. They want to select their purchases from well-filled displays and full shelves. If they do not find such an assortment, customers look elsewhere.

Salespeople reap benefits when stock is properly cared for. Even the best salespeople find soiled and worn stock difficult to sell. They also benefit from well-arranged displays and full assortments. If customers can see the merchandise and in a full assortment, they are more tempted to buy. Profitable "suggestion selling" is made easier when related items are displayed together, an important factor in arranging merchandise for sale. Also, customers return fewer goods when they can select the proper size, color, and model the first time.

Store management is particularly concerned with good stockkeeping practices, for merchandise represents invested capital—the investment of the owner or stockholders. Stock in good condition has a better chance of quick turnover. This rapid turnover of stock stretches capital in three ways: (1) Money from sales can be reinvested in additional merchandise to replenish stock. (2) With cash on hand, the store can buy fashion merchandise or novelties that customers suddenly decide they want. (3) Ready cash can be used to buy merchandise when the market price suddenly dips, thereby bringing higher profits.

Different Types of Stockkeeping

Stockkeeping procedures vary with the type of merchandise sold. For example, ready-to-wear must be carefully protected from soiling and careless handling. Tools must be protected from rust. Grocery stocks must be checked daily and shelves filled. The important factor, however, that determines stockkeeping needs and procedures for the type of service the store offers—self-service or salesperson service.

Self-Service Stores. Keeping stock fresh and clean and on display in correct amounts is particularly important in self-service stores, since such stores depend on point-of-sale display to sell the merchandise. Usually these stores operate on a low-profit margin and a high volume of sales. Stock must be checked constantly to keep sizes, colors, and models arranged in the proper bin, rack, or section of shelves and counters. Merchandise on open display must be cleaned and dusted on a regular schedule, often daily and always when the stock is replenished.

Stock must always be rotated when shelves are restocked. *Rotating* the *stock* means that older merchandise is always brought to the front of the shelf or to the top of a stack. Rotating the stock prevents older stock from becoming shopworn or stale, thus reducing losses from unsalable merchandise.

In self-service stores, replenishing shelf, counter, bin, and rack displays is a

He's learning to keep his vegetables looking fresh and tidy during his part-time co-operative training.

Courtesy School District of Philadelphia

daily activity. During peak, high-volume days, stock may have to be brought forward from reserve stock to the point of display. A key to self-service stockkeeping is the *basic stock list,* which shows for each item the minimum number that must be on the shelf. This minimum is equal to the sales for an average period of time, usually a day, several days, or a week. When shelf stocks are replenished, the merchandise should be arranged with labels to the front or on top. Also, prices should be checked to insure that articles are still correctly price marked.

Salesperson Service Stores. In salesperson service stores, sales personnel have several stockkeeping duties that occur frequently:

1. Returning merchandise to its proper place after each transaction
2. Keeping the stock neatly arranged and in the proper order
3. Dusting and cleaning stock before the store opens and during slack sales periods
4. Replenishing the assortment on the floor using a basic stock list or an average week's sales as a guide
5. Helping customers avoid damage to the stock by such carelessness as placing wet umbrellas on displayed merchandise or staining ready-to-wear with lipstick when trying on a garment
6. Carefully handling merchandise when demonstrating its use
7. Refraining from handling goods with hands soiled from sales-book carbons, etc.

Salespeople also have other major responsibilities in helping to maintain an adequate merchandise assortment. Each will be discussed briefly in the following paragraphs.

Becoming a Good Stockkeeper

The best way to learn your stock well is to take care of it physically—in other words, to be a good stockkeeper. In performing these duties, one may compare features of different items while handling them, learn their strong and weak points, and their appeal to customers.

Protecting the Goods. Markdowns can be reduced considerably by protective measures, such as covering textile merchandise at night to reduce damage caused by dust. In some cases, metal products must be brought inside or covered to prevent rusting. Stock to be carried over to the next year may be wrapped. Dusting is another protective measure.

Locate Stock Quickly. In order to locate stock quickly, one must understand the department layout and know what kinds of items are found in different sections of the department and on certain counters and shelves. A good stockkeeper knows what is carried in the *forward stock,* the merchandise on display. He knows the exact location of the *under stock,* forward stock concealed in drawers, cabinets, and boxes. He is also familiar with the *reserve stock,* the merchandise located in the stock room or in a warehouse.

Good stock knowledge includes knowing the location of damaged goods and articles that have been marked down. It also includes a knowledge of what goods are advertised and where these are located, as well as what merchandise is in the display windows.

Replenishing and Arranging Stock. Replenishing stock on counters and in display cases, keeping the stock orderly, well arranged, and displayed in proper amounts are distinguishing marks of the successful salesperson.

Reconditioning the Merchandise. The retail salesperson can learn much from refreshing and reconditioning merchandise. In this work, he finds out which colors soil readily, which goods are most perishable, which articles are most durable. Information about cleaning and repairing methods and about materials used in the manufacture of merchandise may become valuable information to relay to customers. Reconditioning also includes replacement of price tickets and returning the refreshed goods to stock.

Helping Reduce Stock Shrinkage. Another way to assist your firm

A stockkeeper is placing reserve stock in the storeroom of a newly opened drugstore.

Courtesy Drug Fair, Arlington, Va.

A salesperson is placing forward stock on the display shelves of a drugstore getting ready for opening day.

Courtesy Drug Fair, Arlington, Va.

in making a profit is to reduce *stock shrinkage,* the difference between the amount of the stock on the inventory records and what is really on hand when it is physically counted. For example, suppose that the retail value of stock when purchased is $1,000. During a given period, sales records show sales of $800. Thus, the inventory shows a stock of $200. A physical count of the stock reveals a retail value of $175. The stock shrinkage is $200 minus $175, or $25. Any employee associated with stock work can reduce stock shrinkage by guarding against pilferage, and by counting, weighing, and measuring accurately.

Reporting Damaged Goods. Salespeople and others who have contact with stock can help make larger profits by reporting damaged goods to their superiors. Defective or damaged goods are nearly always returned by customers, which is a costly operation for the retailer.

Helping Determine What to Buy. Salespeople can help the buyer determine what to buy by reporting items requested by customers that the store does not carry. Many stores use special forms, called *want slips,* for this purpose. Salespeople fill in the necessary information and give the form to the buyer or the department head. Another way salespeople help is to observe what people are wearing or using and report their findings to the buyer. When time permits, much information may be obtained by talking to customers about their wants and needs.

Behind-the-Scenes Stockkeeping. Keeping stock in good condition begins in the receiving area. It must reach the sales floor undamaged and fresh-looking; therefore, markers should avoid handling merchandise with soiled hands; and stockkeepers, when moving merchandise from reserve stock to forward stock, must handle and arrange it properly. Goods in reserve stock rooms must be regularly dusted, cleaned, and inspected for deterioration. Stock first to be moved to the sales floor should always be that which has been on hand the longest. Above all, merchandise cannot be sold that is not on the sales floor or

```
                    WANT SLIP


    DATE 7/15/62   DEPT. 46    SALESPERSON 12

    MERCHANDISE CALLED FOR, GIVE SIZE
    COLOR, PRICE AND STYLE
                                ORDER   SUBST  SALE
                                TAKEN   SOLD   LOST

    1 Dress L 482 BLue A          ✓




    WRITE PLAINLY       TO THE SALESPERSON
                        PUT ONE COPY IN INDEX
                        GIVE ONE COPY TO MANAGER
```

A want slip.

Courtesy The Dayton Co.,
Minneapolis

that is not known by salespeople to be in reserve. Speedy processing in receiving and marking will put goods where they are wanted in the forward stock where they can be sold.

Trade Talk

want slip
basic stock list
head of stock
reserve stock

stock shrinkage
rotate stock
under stock

Can You Answer These?

1. What steps can a salesperson take in helping customers prevent damage to merchandise on display or while handling goods during the sales transaction?

2. Self-service arrangements have increased the need for keeping stock in good order. What are some reasons for this increased need?

3. What can salespeople do to protect the merchandise? to recondition the stock?

4. How does a basic stock list aid in replenishing stock?

5. What stockkeeping activities must be performed at least weekly in a self-service operation?

6. In what ways is proper stockkeeping of value to customers, to salespeople, and to the store management?

7. In what ways can a salesperson help determine what stock should be bought to maintain an adequate assortment?

Problems and Projects

1. Select some item of merchandise you would like to sell. What precautions should you take, or help the customer to take, to keep the merchandise assortment fresh and in good condition?

2. Visit several stores during busy sales periods. Report to the class your observations of how well the salespeople keep the stock neat and well arranged and whether or not they return merchandise promptly to its proper place.

3. Debate the statement, "Well-trained salespeople should not waste valuable time on stockkeeping duties. Instead, special stockkeepers should be employed to care for stock."

Learning Your Job

1. List your duties in keeping stock fresh and in good order. Classify each duty as daily, weekly, or monthly.
2. Bring in a basic stock list used in replacing floor stocks. Explain how it is used. If your store does not use such a list, explain how you determine how much merchandise to bring forward.
3. List the specific activities that are performed in your department or store that: (a) keep merchandise in salable condition; (b) keep the racks, tables, bins, and shelves full; (c) help sell slow-moving merchandise; (d) aid in maintaining the stock-control system; (e) reduce stock shrinkage.

20 *Receiving Merchandise*

In a retail-store operation, goods are bought, placed in stock, and finally purchased by customers, who are attracted by advertising, by window displays, or by previous satisfactory experiences with the firm. A store may have an attractive interior, good accounting records, satisfactory credit practices, and good employee relations; but it will fail if all employees do not do their part in carrying out the merchandising function. You have learned in the previous part of this unit how to keep your stock. Now you are ready for the merchandising functions of receiving, marking, and inventory control.

Maintaining an Adequate Assortment of Goods

Our study of the merchandising process begins when a quantity of goods is ordered from the *vendor* (seller), the manufacturer, or wholesaler.

The type of goods offered for sale by the store is an important factor in determining whether a merchandise assortment is adequate. Fashion goods, such as sportswear and blouses, must be carried in forward stock in many combinations of sizes, colors, styles, and prices. This is also true of some shopping goods, such as men's clothing, china, linens, and children's clothing. For both classes of merchandise, an adequate assortment means an extensive stock and one that is fresh and up-to-date. On the other hand, in lines like furniture and appliances, an adequate forward stock may consist only of samples of the merchandise, the major stock being carried in the warehouse.

The Receiving Function

Maintaining an adequate assortment of merchandise means having immediately available the goods customers want. Of course, an inventory of merchandise cannot be considered salable until it is received and put into stock.

Receiving stock is an activity that must be done promptly, accurately, and safely. It is an important cog in the wheel of merchandising operations.

Store personnel assigned to receiving stock must have "know-how" in the following operations:

> Receiving goods delivered to the store
> Checking and inspecting shipments for quality and quantity
> Routing shipments from suppliers
> Arranging returns to vendors
> Marking merchandise with price and stock-control information
> Moving merchandise to reserve and forward stock rooms

Receiving the Goods

Merchandise may be delivered to the store's receiving dock by truck freight, express, parcel post, or messenger. In some cases, it is shipped by rail in carload lots. The receiving room is usually near the dock area, so that heavy cartons need not be carried far. Receiving rooms are usually close also to the areas where goods are price marked as well as to the reserve stock rooms.

The receiving clerk is responsible for one or more of the following activities:

1. Helping to unload shipments and stack cartons and crates. It is important that he know how to handle and stack shipments safely, in order to protect himself from injury and to prevent damage to the merchandise.
2. Counting the number of containers and checking the condition of packages. Since the deliveryman usually must obtain a receipt for safe delivery, careful counting and checking is necessary in case a claim is to be made later for damaged shipments.
3. Sometimes, receiving personnel pay the shipping charges to the deliveryman. At other times, they approve the shipping receipt; and the store's office pays the delivery charges.
4. Keeping accurate records of each incoming shipment. This is a major responsibility of receiving personnel. These records serve as evidence (*a*) when making claims for incomplete or damaged shipments, and (*b*) when making payments to the vendor for the merchandise that has been accepted.

Receiving Records. In small stores, the receiving records may be only simple notations in a small notebook or on delivery receipts (later "filed" on a spindle). In larger stores, more complete receiving records are kept. Usually a

The receiving and loading facilities in this department store are large, efficient, and up to date.

receiving book is used in which is "logged" (recorded) such information as number of packages in the shipment, condition of goods, date and time of receipt, vendor's name, shipping charges, and the name of the delivery firm.

Larger stores may use a form called a *receiving apron,* which takes the place of the receiving book. The receiving apron, however, is not just a record of receipts—it is also used in marking and storing goods. Copies of the transportation receipt, the store's original order, and the vendor's invoice are usually attached to the apron. When a shipment has been completely processed, the completed apron serves as a permanent record of the shipment. It is used later as a primary source of information to (*a*) authorize payment for the shipment, (*b*) return incorrect merchandise, and (*c*) make claims for shortages in the shipment.

Checking and Inspecting Shipments

The packages in a shipment may be opened by the persons who received them or by another group of specialized workers called *checkers*. Checkers must know how to open containers in such a way as to avoid personal injury and to protect valuable merchandise. For example, a good checker will not use a razor blade to slit open a box, since it may tear or rip fabrics inside or scratch furniture and appliances, or he may injure himself.

After a shipment is opened, it must be checked and inspected carefully for shortages and damages and to make sure that styles, models, grades, sizes, and colors are as ordered. For example, meat and produce must be inspected for freshness and conformity to a grade or other standard of quality. Ready-to-wear must be of the color and style ordered and must meet certain tailoring specifications. Appliances must be inspected to make sure all attachments and accessories

SHIPPER		RECEIVED FROM	REC-VIA	CARRIER'S NO.	PCS.	WT.	CHGS.	DEPT.	LOC.	KEY-REC NO.		RECEIVED DATE	TIME
Jack Feit Co.	DATE	N.Y.C.	X	110215	1	12		300	11	U 23672 SHORT = .NY MARKED = YK		7/10	3

VENDOR-NUMBER	Doc.Code	INVOICE NUMBER	INV. DATE MO. DAY	DEPT. OR ACCT.	CLASS	Store	RETAIL		COST		DUE DATE MONTH DAY YEAR		DISCOUNT	ANTICIPAT.
6.E. FACTOR		4567	6 15	300	A	M	26		15	13	8-10-61		0%	0%

DEPT. MGR'S O.K.	NUMBER OF EXTENSIONS						ORDER NUMBER
S.J.	1						687548
COUNTER SIGNATURE	JOB NO.	CHARGE BACK NO.					ROUTING Pool Car
CHECKER D.E.R.	DATE	CHARGE BACK AMT.					F.O.B. POINT Mpls
COMMENTS		C. B. DATE				TICKET CODE	MFG. NO.

CODE	CLASS	DESCRIPTION	STYLE	SIZE ▶ COLOR ▼		10	12								TOTAL	RETAIL
A	A	Dress	780	09		1	1								2	26.00

ORIGINAL INVOICE APRON

▲ ATTACH INVOICE BELOW THIS LINE ▲
DO NOT DESTROY! ACCOUNTING MADE FOR EACH KEY-REC

This receiving apron is made out in four copies: the original is attached to the vendor's invoice and goes to Accounts Payable; the Buyer's Record is the control from the receiving area to the buyer's area; the Marking Record is kept in the marking area; the last copy is the stock-control record.

Courtesy The Dayton Co., Minneapolis

are included. Sheets must be inspected for thread count; and china, checked for the quality of the glazing process. The checker may or may not be given the *invoice,* a list of items and prices of merchandise sent by the vendor to the purchaser, or the original order to use in the checking process. The invoice may accompany the merchandise; it may be sent to the store before the delivery is made; or it may arrive after the merchandise reaches the store. Invoices and copies of the original order, if on hand, are usually filed in the store offices or are temporarily filed in the receiving room, depending on the store's system. Whether these forms are made available to the checker also depends on whether the store uses an open check or a blind check.

Open Check. An *open check* occurs when a checker has a copy of the order or invoice and can compare his count with the amount that is supposed to be received.

Blind Check. A *blind check* occurs when the checker has no order or invoice or knows only what was ordered but not how much. Supervisors often insist on a blind check first, then comparing it with the original order or with the invoice. This double check makes for greater accuracy. Accuracy is so important that checkers may be offered bonuses for discovering shortages or overages in orders and for spotting mistakes, such as merchandise that is of the wrong size, model, or color.

Spot Check. *Spot checks* are often used on large shipments, especially those containing many small, inexpensive items. For example, one box of hand tools may be selected at random from a shipment of ten boxes, and the contents counted. If the count of one box is correct, the entire shipment is approved. If errors are found in the box checked, the entire shipment may be opened and counted. Since the spot check is not so accurate as a complete check, it is usually used only on shipments from suppliers who have been reliable in the past.

While inspecting merchandise for its condition is usually done by receiving personnel, inspection for quality and conformity to samples or vendor descriptions is usually done by other personnel. In small stores, the manager or experienced salespeople usually inspect goods. In large stores, it is done by buyers or merchandise managers, usually at the time they decide on the retail price. Some large stores maintain laboratories or merchandise-standard departments to check on quality.

Routing Shipments from Suppliers

In larger stores, receiving personnel are sometimes responsible for selecting the type of carrier—truck, rail, or air—and the company that is to haul the shipment. This choice usually depends on the costs of each method in relation to desired speed of delivery, convenience of the unloading point, value of the goods, and size of the shipment. Small shipments cost more per pound than larger ones. For example, shipping by rail in less-than-carload (LCL) lots is more expensive than using a full carload. Shipments sometimes can be combined to obtain lower freight rates.

Arranging Returns to Vendors

There are three instances when merchandise is returned to the vendor: (1) when merchandise arrives in damaged condition, (2) when goods are not of the kind ordered, and (3) when unsold merchandise is to be returned for credit. In

In this department, goods are received and marked.

each instance, receiving personnel are often asked to pack the return shipment, arrange for transportation, and notify the vendor of the return.

Usually, merchandise cannot be returned to the vendor just because it does not sell. A return privilege is granted, however, under the following contractual conditions: (1) Unsold merchandise that was ordered on consignment—that is, the title remains with the vendor until it is sold at retail—may be returned. (2) Some vendors, such as shoe manufacturers, sell merchandise to retailers under so-called "Fair-Trade Agreements" in which merchandise unsold at the end of a season may not be reduced from the accepted price. These goods must be returned to the vendor. (3) Some kinds of merchandise—books, for example—can be returned for partial credit under conditions agreed on at the time of purchase.

All the receiving functions discussed so far are conveniently grouped, in larger stores, in a department called "Receiving and Marking." However, because of its importance, the marking function will be discussed separately in the next part.

Trade Talk

blind check
checker
consignment goods
invoice
LCL shipment
log
open check
receiving apron
receiving dock
spot check
vendor

Can You Answer These?

1. Why should the young person who wants to make a career of retailing begin in the receiving department of a store?

2. Why must shipments of merchandise be checked accurately and promptly?

3. Under what circumstances should merchandise that is received in the store be checked for quality as well as quantity?

4. When is it of advantage to spot-check incoming merchandise?

5. What is meant by maintaining an adequate merchandise assortment?

6. Why do stores need to keep records of incoming shipments?

7. Why do some stores use a blind-check system?

8. Under what conditions may a store have the privilege of returning unsold goods?

Problems and Projects

1. From a store manager or owner in your community, find out how merchandise in his store reaches the sales floor from the receiving dock or area. Draw a chart showing how the merchandise goes through the various steps of this process.

2. If you were a vendor of hardware, would you give retailers the privilege of returning unsold stock? If so, under what conditions would you do so? Would your answer be the same if the product were bread? if it were women's ready-to-wear?

3. Choose an item of merchandise with which you are familiar as a consumer. If you were responsible for inspecting incoming goods, what features of the item would you instruct your men to look for?

4. Discuss the advantages and disadvantages of paying bonuses to checkers for discovering and reporting shortages and overages in shipments.

5. Obtain from a local retail, wholesale, or industrial firm a copy of an invoice. Explain to the class what an invoice is and what information it provides.

Learning Your Job

1. Select two items of merchandise sold by your store. For each item list the safety precautions that must be observed in receiving and unpacking (a) to prevent damaging the goods; (b) to prevent personal injury to yourself.

2. Find out whether some types of goods in your store are spot checked and if so, what they are. Explain why they are spot checked and also why full checking is necessary for other goods.

3. Obtain samples of receiving and inspection forms used by your store. Describe on paper how the forms are used and why the information on the form is necessary.

Add the forms to your store manual.

21 *Marking Merchandise*

As a consumer, you already know that most items of merchandise have price tickets attached or the price written on the container. You may also have noticed that, in addition to the retail price, the price ticket contained other information, usually appearing in code—stock numbers, cost price, and the name of the manufacturer. Marking is a very important function in the merchandising process.

Why Mark Goods?

An important reason for marking goods is that the customer wishes to see the established price. The policy of "one price to all customers" is common in retailing in the United States today. (In a few stores, the retail price is marked on the merchandise only to show the customer at what point price bargaining is to begin!)

There are many other good reasons why a store desires accurate and legible marking of goods:

1. To help self-service cashiers in speedy and accurate cash-register operation
2. To prevent merchandise from being sold at the wrong price, reducing the store's profit
3. To guard against customer complaints of having been overcharged
4. To provide information for inventory and stock-control purposes
5. To give the salesperson information about the manufacturer of the product and when it was put into stock

Price-Ticket Information Helps Everyone

The amount and kind of information placed on price tickets varies by stores. But, in general, some or all of the following are given:

1. The original cost, usually expressed in code. Most stores adopt a code sentence or word containing ten letters, assigning each letter in order to the numbers 1 to 0; for example:

YOU	CAN	LIVE		RESUMPTION
123	456	7890		1234567890

2. The name of the manufacturer or wholesaler from whom the purchase was made. This information may be indicated by a number.

3. Season letter, so that the length of time goods are in stock may be determined. The National Cash Register Co. (Merchants Service Bureau) suggests the following code:

Month	Code	Month	Code
January	A or 1	July	G or 7
February	B or 2	August	H or 8
March	C or 3	September	I or 9
April	D or 4	October	J or 10
May	E or 5	November	K or 11
June	F or 6	December	L or 12

The years may be designated by letters starting at the end of the alphabet, as 1960, "Y"; 1961, "X"; 1962, "W." An article stocked in December, 1961, would be marked "LX" or "12-X." When goods are marked in this way, it is easy to know how long they have been in the store.

4. Store name, department name or number

5. Classification letter, indicating the particular class of merchandise into which the article falls

6. The retail price, plainly indicated in figures, so that it may be easily read by customers

7. Size, color, style, or other particular items of information necessary for some kinds of merchandise

Special tags may be used when desired for marked-down goods, for non-returnable merchandise, or for any other articles that are different from regular stock.

Tickets, Tags, or Hand Marking?

Prices and other information are often hand marked with a grease pencil, ink, or a rubber stamp on the containers of merchandise, such as groceries, hardware, and some drug items. Hand marking, especially with rubber-stamp sets like those used in food supermarkets, is very useful for items sold through self-service checkout stands and saves time when many small items must be marked.

How to Mark Merchandise

In order that all Ben Franklin Stores will have uniformity in ticketing merchandise, a recommended marking procedure is outlined below. One important precaution in ticketing merchandise is to make sure that all pins on pin tickets are crossed. Very often these pins become straightened out, and they may cause an injury to a customer.

Item	Type ticket	Position	Remarks
Rayon hose	Snagless ticket	On welt	Hose and anklets should be ticketed so that ticket holds pair together.
Cotton	" "	" "	
5/8 hose	Pin ticket	" "	
Campus	" "	" "	
Knicker	" "	" "	
Anklets	" "	" "	
Crew Socks	" "	" "	
Men's Work Hose	" "	" "	
Men's Dress Hose	" "	" "	
Belts	Gummed labels	On back of belt	
Collar and Cuffs	Pin ticket	In back of neck	
Dickies	" "	In back of neck	
Wool Gloves	" "	On wrist	
Fabric Gloves	" "	" "	Pin should hold pair together
Leather Gloves	Gummed labels	Inside cuff	
Scarfs	Pin tickets	On edge	
Headkerchiefs	" "	" "	
Handbags	String ticket	On handle or zipper ring	
Handkerchiefs	Gummed labels	On corner/on box	
Rayon Panties	Pinless ticket	On waist band	
Slips	" "	Back of shoulder strap	
Gowns	" "	Back of neck	
Pajamas	" "	" " "	
Brassieres	Pin ticket	On band	
Girdles	" "	Middle of back	
Corselettes	" "	" " "	
Corsets	String ticket	' " "	
Vests	Pin ticket	Back of neck	
Panties	" "	Back of waistband	
Union Suits	" "	Back of neck	
Dresses	String ticket	Left sleeve	Attach with crochet hook
Coats	" "	" "	
Jackets	" "	" "	
Sweaters	Pin ticket	Back of neck	
Skirts	String ticket	At waist button	
Blouses	Pin ticket	Back of neck	
House Frocks	" "	" "	
Slacks	" "	Above knee fold on pants leg showing	
Shorts	" "	Bottom of pants	
Robes	String ticket	Left sleeve	
Housecoats	" "	" "	
Smocks	Pin ticket	Back of neck	
Felt Hats	String ticket	In band	
Soft Millinery	Pin or string	" "	

Courtesy Butler Bros.

Price tickets and tags are usually printed by machine. The machine can be set for required information, such as that on the list above, so that it will print an exact number of tickets and will count the tickets as they are attached to the merchandise.

What Kinds of Price Tickets Are Best? The merchandise or its container, and the way it is displayed make a difference. A large wholesaler, Butler Brothers, issues the above instructions to employees of its affiliated Ben Franklin Variety Stores, which are individually-owned stores.

Who Determines the Retail Price?

On some merchandise, prepackaged by the manufacturer or supplier, suggested retail prices are printed on the carton, wrapper, or tag. This is especially true of so-called "Fair-Trade" items that are sold by retailers at a price agreed upon with the manufacturer. In chain organizations, the central buying office often pretickets articles before shipment from the central or branch warehouse.

The marker in the retail store gets his information for price marking from several sources. Often smaller stores, carrying standard merchandise, use *markup* charts that show the retail prices corresponding to known cost prices. The marker who has the cost price on the invoice can find the correct retail price on his chart. In some stores, the manager, department head, or store buyer may *pre-retail* the shipment before it arrives by writing the retail price on the duplicate purchase order that he sends to the receiving room. A common practice, however, is to write the retail price on the invoice after inspecting the merchandise for quality when it arrives. Another method used in chain stores, especially food supermarkets and variety stores, is to provide for the markers a retail price list supplied by the central office. Such lists are commonly used where goods on the sales floor must be remarked because of frequent price changes.

The Salesperson's Responsibilities

In smaller stores, salespeople often assist in preparing price tickets and in marking prices on merchandise that has been received. Salespeople in large stores usually do not make price tickets except in preparation for a sales promotion when price tickets must be remarked or new price tickets attached to sale items. In this case, legible printing, using the proper color tag or ink, is important in aiding both salespeople and customers in identifying sale-priced items.

All salespeople have, however, a major responsibility connected with checking the prices marked on merchandise. During a sales transaction, the salesperson must always check the price ticket to be sure the ticket is correct and that no

Here a co-operative part-time student is marking prices by hand. In many stores, prices are stamped on goods by means of inked stampers shown on tray below.

Courtesy Gary High School, Gary, Ind., and National Cash Register Co.

discrepancy exists between the price on the ticket and the usual or advertised price. If an article has no price ticket, the supervisor should be consulted about the correct price before the sale is made. Merchandise sold for the wrong price has serious consequences. If the customer has been overcharged, both the salesperson and the store suffer a loss of good will and the loss of potential sales not only to the angry customer but also to his friends. When a customer is undercharged, the retail price of the article certainly will not yield a profit and may not even cover the expenses of making the sale.

Stock Turnover Is Desirable

Frank W. Woolworth, founder of the Woolworth chain of stores, once said "Small profits on an article will become big if you sell enough of the article." Most chain stores, especially variety, drug, and food outlets, adopted early the principle of limited stocks and rapid sales. Although their margin of profit per item is not large, they sell in sufficient quantity to make the total profit substantial. Many independent store operators, especially large ones, have adopted this principle of rapid turnover at small profit margins.

What Is Turnover? If you were a newsboy, you would buy a stock of papers each day. Assuming you sell all of them that day, you will have your money (capital) back, ready to invest in a new stock (inventory) the next day. You have in one day turned over your stock; that is, you sold all your inventory and achieved one stock turn. If you did this every day for a year, you would have an annual stock turnover of 365. Thus, the disposal and replacement of a given stock of merchandise constitutes a *stock turnover*. In most retail stores, of course, the inventory never sells out completely; additional merchandise must constantly be ordered and put into stock. The calculation of turnover involves advanced techniques and will be discussed later. At this point, a definition of turnover is important, since each employee has certain responsibilities for achieving turnover.

Why Is Turnover Important? When stock turns are increased to a desired number, certain advantages are obtained that bear heavily on the success of the store:

1. Stocks are kept fresher; and since fresh stock sells better, less stock will have to be marked down to clear it out.
2. Turnover provides valuable space needed for new stock. No store wants this space occupied by hard-to-sell stock.
3. Sales are increased because the merchandise is up-to-the-minute in style.
4. Profit is increased as sales volume rises.
5. Capital is used more efficiently, since it is not tied up in inventories.

The desired turnover can be obtained by making sure that (1) merchandise is put into stock promptly, (2) merchandise is well cared for and is fresh, (3) proper stock-control information is available to the buyer, and (4) sales skills are improved to help move merchandise.

Trade Talk

cost code   stock turnover
fair-trade item   markup chart
price ticket   preretailed
preticketed goods

Can You Answer These?

1. In what ways does legible price marking of goods help the customer, the salesperson, and the store?
2. What information besides the retail price is often included on price tickets? Why is this information necessary?
3. What advantages or disadvantages can you see in the practice of manufacturers printing suggested retail prices on the containers, cartons, or labels on merchandise?
4. How does a store employee know what retail price to mark on merchandise that has just been received?
5. What kind of price-marking method would be best for: hosiery, lipstick, sweaters, hand tools, and auto accessories?
6. Why are specially colored price tickets often used for sale-priced articles?
7. What are some causes of slow stock turnover? How can these be eliminated?

Problems and Projects

1. Make up two easily remembered words that could serve as cost codes used on price tickets to show the cost price of the merchandise.

2. Collect samples of the different kinds of price tickets used on various kinds of merchandise. How does the information given on these tickets compare with that suggested in the text?
3. The next time you visit a supermarket observe the various ways in which goods are price marked. Be prepared to report your observations to the class.

Learning Your Job

1. As you have the opportunity, make a study of the price tags used in your store. Note especially the different kinds of information given for different kinds of merchandise. If you are unable to interpret the information given in code, perhaps your supervisor will be willing to help you.
2. Do your store duties include marking price tickets? If so, what information and store forms are given to you to use for that purpose?
3. Does your store use different colored price tags for different occasions, such as special sales? If you are selling at such a time, note how these special tags help the customer and the salesperson.
4. Stock turnover varies with different kinds of merchandise and in different types of stores. Find out from your job sponsor what the desired turnover is for several kinds of merchandise in your store. Report on what is done to increase turnover.

22 *Stock Control*

In the past, many store owners and buyers believed that they could remember those items that sold well and those that did not. They thought that, by watching the activities on the sales floor and talking with the salespeople, they could acquire enough information to buy wisely and to keep a balanced stock. Most retailers today, however, do not rely on their memories but accumulate the information necessary for intelligent buying through an efficient stock-control (sometimes called *merchandise control*) system.

The owners of a large furniture store that had installed a merchandise-control system in the rug department made the following comment:

> Our rug buyer said that the largest number of rugs were sold in the 9-by-12-foot size. We made a careful check of past sales and found that although we had formerly sold the most rugs in the 9-by-12-foot size, the greatest volume now was in the 7½-by-9-foot size. After we learned the facts, it was clear that the change was due to the increasing number of small apartments being built in our city. Accordingly, we increased our assortments in the smaller sizes, advertised them, and received a very substantial increase in business.

In a large business, the stock-control system is a complex operation. However, at this point in our study of retailing, it is necessary only to learn some of

MARSHALL FIELD, 1835–1906

Founder of Marshall Field & Co., Chicago, known for its high quality merchandise.

Here physical inventory is being taken by hand.

Courtesy National Cash Register Co.

the basic principles of stock control. In a later unit, the management aspects of stock control will be studied.

What Is Stock Control?

Stock-control procedures tell the merchandiser what is selling and what is not, what should be reordered, and what should be marked down for clearance. Some firms—such as grocery, drug, hardware, and variety stores—use a basic stock list in controlling the stock to be ordered. Some stores also use a re-order system based on reorder reminder slips, which are placed on shelves or in the boxes of goods, such as hosiery. Such a slip appears at the point in which experience has proved that merchandise should be reordered, thus the term "reminder."

There are two major types of stock-control systems in common use in stores: dollar control and unit control.

Dollar Control

The *dollar-control* system tells the retailer how much money, based on the retail price, he has invested in goods on hand. A physical inventory (actual count) is made. For example, a departmental inventory reveals a stock of ten hammers, each retailing at $3. The dollar-control inventory will show a stock of $30 at retail. This system provides information for regulating the stock by showing the amount invested. It does not provide detailed information, such as the models or sizes of the merchandise on hand.

Unit Control

The *unit-control* system provides considerable information about each item in stock rather than showing only the total amount invested. A physical inventory

Here inventory is being taken by stub control by a machine.

Courtesy National Cash Register Co.

(actual count) need not be made to find the amount of stock on hand. Using the hammers again as an illustration, a unit-control system tells the retailer (1) how many units (hammers) are in stock, (2) weight and model of the hammers, (3) where he bought them and when, (4) how many he has on order, and (5) how many have been sold.

Unit-control records give information about merchandise in terms of individual items carried in stock rather than in terms of their dollar value. They are particularly useful for high-unit-price items—such as refrigerators—and for items, such as ready-to-wear clothing, that differ in details, such as color, size, or model. Unit control is particularly useful in stores where merchandise is sold by floor samples, representative of the stock in the warehouse. Furniture and appliances are good examples of this.

How Stock-Control Information Is Obtained

There are three basic methods of supplying sales information for merchandise-control systems. The salesperson is usually involved in all three.

Sales-Slip Control. Sales-slip control uses stock information written on the sales slip by the salesperson. This requires accurate and legible sales recording. In this system, copies of the sales slip are forwarded to the unit-control office. There clerical workers transfer the stock information from the sales slips to unit-control records.

Stub Control. Stub control depends on tags attached to the merchandise. The tag usually is perforated into two parts, with identical information appearing on each half. At the close of the sale, the salesperson detaches half of the tag and deposits it in a container. Unit-control clerical workers use these tags to record sales information on stock records.

Inventory Control. Inventory control gathers sales information by periodic physical inventories that show the goods on hand. Inventories and

BASIC OR "NEVER-OUT" ITEM STOCK CONTROL

DEPARTMENT NUMBER *S 20*

~~ᴵᴼᴺ~~ *Marlin White Shirts*

SUPPLIER *Acme Supply Co*   MAILING ADDRESS *St. Louis, Mo.*

UNIT COST *$2.75*   RETAIL *$3.95*   TERMS *2/10/net 30*   MINIMUM PACKAGE *4*

CHECK DATES	Sleeve Length	32	33	32	33	34	32	33	34	35	32	33	34	35	32	33	34	35	32	33
	Sizes	14	14	14½	14½	14½	15	15	15	15	15½	15½	15½	15½	16	16	16	16	16½	16½
	Ideal or Basic Stock	4	4	8	8	4	16	16	4	4	12	16	4	4	4	8	4	4	4	4
5-1-	On Hand	2	3	9	3	6	9	11	3	2	8	6	3	6	2	3	1	4	4	0
5-1-	On Order	4	0	0	4	0	8	8	4	4	12	12	0	4	4	4	4	0	4	4
5-15-	Received	4	0	0	4	0	8	8	4	4	12	12	0	4	4	4	4	0	4	4
	On Hand	4	1	3	7	3	11	10	4	4	7	10	1	6	4	5	4	2	4	3
	Sold	2	2	6	0	3	6	9	3	2	13	8	2	4	2	2	1	2	4	1
	On Order / Received																			
	On Hand																			
	Sold																			
	On Order / Received																			
	On Hand																			
	Sold																			
	On Order / Received																			

purchase-record figures are combined to determine what items have been sold.

A stock-record form for use in a men's-clothing department or store is shown above. This form has been filled out to show its use in stock control of men's white dress shirts.*

The information contained in the headings of the form is self-explanatory. At the top of the 19 vertical columns are shown the sleeve lengths carried, with the collar sizes appearing immediately below. In the line below this, entitled "Ideal or Basic Stock," are entered those amounts that are considered necessary for proper selection by customers.

On a given date, the amount of each particular size on hand is entered on the "On Hand" line. It is assumed that the first physical inventory was taken on May 1. By comparing the "On Hand" line with the "Ideal or Basic Stock" line, it can be seen, for example, that 7 shirts in size 15 collar with a 32

* U.S. Small Business Administration, *Basic Stock Control for Small Stores,* Small Marketers Aids Number 5, 1955, p. 3.

sleeve length are needed in order to bring this stock up to the proper level.

On the lines below appears information concerning the number of shirts on order May 1, those received by May 15, and the shirts sold during the period, and the number on hand. After each successive physical inventory has been taken, it is possible to determine quickly how many shirts in each size have been sold since the preceding period. This is done by adding the amount in the "On Hand" line to the amount in the "Received" line and subtracting the amount found in the "On Hand" line for the second period.

Supplying Information About Orders

Stock-control systems require not only sales information, but also data concerning merchandise that is on order. A record is made when merchandise is ordered and when merchandise is received. For this reason, careful handling of merchandise order forms, invoices, and receiving-room reports is important for sound stock control.

Who Benefits from Stock Control?

Brown eggs are popular in Boston, white cars are popular in California, and button-down-collar shirts are popular in the East. Regional preferences are but one reason why merchants must have what customers want—in the size, style, color, model, and price range. Thus, stock-control systems are very important in maintaining an adequate merchandise assortment.

Everyone benefits when inventories are controlled. The customer finds that the merchandise assortment meets his needs and is fresh and clean. The sales-

J. C. PENNEY
Leader in the chain-store movement in the United States.

person benefits because wanted merchandise is easier to sell. The store gains in a number of ways: (1) Intelligent buying helps prevent loss of sales or customer ill will over substitute articles. (2) The right stock results in greater turnover on a smaller invested capital. (3) Salable stock lessens the need to take markdowns on unwanted items. (4) Inventory control gives the buyer enough information to enable him to buy without guesswork. (5) Stock control makes for effective sales planning, as well as for effective purchasing.

In simplified selling and self-service arrangements, the retailer depends on effective visual presentation of well-assorted merchandise. The ready availability of a complete stock of merchandise wanted by customers is the store's form of salesmanship; unit stock control is a necessity for successful self-service operation.

Beginning Responsibilities for Stock Control

If you work in a nonselling department, you may be assigned periodically to take inventory. You may be given responsibility for the unit-control cards or books, transferring sales information from sales slips or stubs.

If you are a salesperson, you may also help with inventories monthly or at longer intervals. During sales transactions, you play an important role in maintaining an accurate merchandise-control system. If stock-control stubs are attached to the goods, you must always detach the stub and deposit it in a container to be collected and audited. Where stubs are not used, you must copy stock information on the sales slip accurately and legibly.

When merchandise is returned, stock-control records must be corrected. If the merchandise is returned to the department, the salesperson can co-operate by notifying the person responsible for stock records of the return, by checking the merchandise to see that it is in good condition, by seeing that price tags are replaced promptly, and by making certain that goods are returned to stock promptly.

Salespeople can co-operate with control systems by reporting out-of-stock items and dangerously low stock, instances that sometimes occur when items sell faster than expected.

Trade Talk

stock-control system
stub control
sales-slip control
dollar control
physical inventory
unit control
inventory control

Can You Answer These?

1. Discuss some of the advantages that the installation of a suitable unit-control system should bring to a store.

2. What is the difference between dollar control and unit control of merchandise?

3. From what sources does the stock-control clerk obtain the information he enters on his control records?

4. What kind of information is provided by unit control?

5. Why is unit control often used for appliances but not for fresh fruits and vegetables?

6. What kind of information is necessary for stock-control systems?

7. Why is unit stock control especially important in self-service operation?

Problems and Projects

1. Select some type of merchandise that you have sold or would like to sell, which comes in different sizes, colors, and styles, such as hosiery, shoes, or suits. Make a list of information about the merchandise that would be important to know when deciding on a reorder. Draw up a simple stock-control form that you believe would be suitable for use in a store carrying this merchandise.

2. Find out and report to the class on the kinds of clerical workers employed by stores to keep stock-control records.

3. The upper half of the stock-control tag is often left attached to merchandise when it is delivered. Bring to class such a tag. Explain what each symbol means and why it is necessary to efficient merchandising.

Learning Your Job

1. Most progressive stores maintain efficient stock-control systems. From such a store, obtain specimen copies of the printed forms used in maintaining stock control. Request the store manager or the head of the department in which these forms are used to explain their advantages. Compare these forms with the ones used in your store.

2. In your job notebook, record your responsibilities for maintaining the control of stock.

7. Knowing Your Merchandise

Product Information Needed by Customers

Mrs. Jones went shopping for a birthday gift for her husband. She decided to surprise him by giving him an electrically operated tool that would give him greater enjoyment in his woodworking hobby of building simple pieces of furniture and other articles for the home. Her problem was that of deciding on the tool to buy and where to make the purchase.

The hardware store in the suburban shopping center that Mrs. Jones patronized had made a special window display of woodworking tools. Mrs. Jones saw the display and entered the store. From the well-informed salesman she learned that a power saw was a basic piece of woodworking equipment. The salesman emphasized the features of the power saw carried by the store and demonstrated its use. He pointed out that the store was prepared to provide parts and service for this tool. The price for the saw was reasonable, and Mrs. Jones purchased it.

Mrs. Jones was helped by the store window display and by the salesman in a number of ways. The window display suggested that home mechanics could use power equipment; the salesman pointed out the good features of the power saw, the store service policies, and the reasonable price. Mrs. Jones was given full product information and helped through the steps of the sale to her final decision to give her husband a power saw for a birthday gift.

While store services are very important, sales are not made on the basis of services alone—the customer wants facts about the merchandise. It is impossible for the average customer to make a study of all merchandise he purchases. His time and facilities for obtaining facts are too limited to do so. He must rely largely on the information and advice he receives from salespeople, labels, and advertisements. This means that the retailer must assume a large share of the responsibility for helping consumers get the right product information to make wise purchases.

What Customers Want to Know About a Product

Basic product knowledge is helpful to all retail personnel, but it is particularly essential to those engaged in selling, advertising, and display work. It is knowledge about the product from the customer's viewpoint. It is knowledge of the services or satisfactions the

143

product can give the customer. These include such things as appearance, fashion, suitability, durability, coupled with information about the materials used, the workmanship, the color and design, the style, the size, necessary care, and the reputation of the manufacturer. These and other facts about the product convince the customer that he will get the satisfaction for which he is looking.

Customer Values and Technical Information. The customer usually refers to the satisfactions or services he seeks from his purchase as "values." Technical information given to the customer concerning materials, workmanship, and manufacturing processes serves to prove that the values he seeks can be enjoyed through the purchase.

The particular value a customer seeks when purchasing a product depends largely on the use to which he intends to put it. One customer is primarily interested in fashion, while another is concerned more with economy or comfort.

The fact that customers are interested primarily in values in no way lessens the need for technical information on the part of retail personnel. Idle claims about values are not enough to convince today's well-educated customers—they want facts. Also, technical information provides salespeople with convincing evidence that builds their confidence in the products they sell. Without this confidence, merchandising activities tend to be weak and ineffective. Let us now look at an appropriate means of organizing product information that will help us develop a merchandising point of view.

The Merchandising Approach to Product Information

If we are sincere in our belief that the purpose of retailing is to serve customers as they want to be served, we should practice thinking from the customer's point of view. In order to do so, we must organize our product information according to the customer's probable thinking when making buying decisions. While the particular values being considered vary with the customer and the merchandise, product information can be organized under the following major questions:

1. Who uses the product?
2. What do customers need and want from it?
3. How well will it fill the customer's needs and wants?
4. Where should it be purchased?
5. When should it be bought?
6. How much should be paid for it?
7. How should it be used?
8. How should it be cared for?

This co-operative part-time student is finding out the selling features of the camera.

Courtesy Virginia Association, Distributive Education Clubs of America

1. *Who Uses the Product?* Information that answers this question is fundamental to good merchandising. Placing oneself in the customer's shoes requires objective study of consumers and their problems. Here are the major categories under which the information falls:

Age, sex, and marital status of users
Income level of users
Occupational, social, and cultural background of users
Fashion consciousness of users

2. *What Do Customers Need and Want from It?* (Need Decision) Each item the store carries provides certain values that are important to some customer. Most of the values concerning needs and wants of consumers may be classified under the following headings. They are used as basic appeals in advertising and personal selling.

Appearance	Prestige	Sentiment
Comfort	Protection	Serviceability
Convenience	Recreation	Suitability
Distinctiveness	Seasonability	Trade name
Economy	Security	

3. *How Well Will It Fill the Customer's Needs and Wants?* (Things-to-Fill-the-Need Decision) Information concerning the thing to fill the customer's needs and satisfy his wants has to do with the properties or characteristics of the product. It is this information that gives the customer the assurance that the article will provide the values he desires. Such knowledge includes the following:

Effectiveness of the product
Its advantages over other products
Methods used in its manufacture
Materials used in its manufacture
Quality of workmanship and construction
Special processes and finishes that give it value
Where it comes from and its history
Cost of upkeep
What makes it particularly suitable for the customer

4. *Where Should It Be Purchased?* (Source Decision) From the retailer's viewpoint, this is the customer's most important decision; hence, product information, bearing on the source from which the purchase is to be made, needs to be included in the total pattern of product information. These are the major classifications of product information relating to source decisions:

Adequacy of the assortment from which to choose—sizes, colors, styles, models, materials
Accessibility to the customer—properly displayed
Speed of sales service

Availability of replacements
Demonstration facilities
Guaranty by the manufacturer and retailer
Alteration, repair, and parts service
Trained sales and service personnel

5. *How Much Should Be Paid for It?* (Price Decision) In our competitive economy, prices are sometimes confusing to purchasers. They need information to justify prices asked and help in making price comparisons.

Some of the more important considerations concerning the prices are:

Relative values of differently priced goods to the purchaser
Savings through quantity purchases
Savings through cash purchases
Value of free customer services
Convenience of different payment arrangements
Prices charged for the product by competitors
Cost of maintaining the product

6. *When Should It Be Bought?* (Time Decision) Information that helps customers decide when to buy is essential to completing a sale. Many customers need help in making this decision. Many sales are lost because salespeople and other members of the merchandising team fail to give helpful information concerning the time to buy. Following are some of the kinds of information the customer needs:

How seasonability affects quality, appropriateness, comfort
Off-season price advantage
Sale-price time limit
Delivery-time advantage
Availability at a given time
Fashion timeliness

7. *How Should It Be Used?* (Use Decision) Knowledge of the intelligent use of the product is essential to helping prospective customers with their buying problems. Suggestions regarding consumer use are particularly welcome to new users of the product. They are very important in merchandising new products. Information regarding product use may be grouped under:

What should be used with the product
How to prepare it for use
How to operate it
When and how to wear it
When and how to serve and eat it
When and how to apply it
How to arrange it
How to assemble it
How to adjust it
How to display it
Where to place it

8. *How Should It Be Cared For?* (Care Decision) Knowledge of how the product should be cared for is valuable in building customer satisfaction. It is also helpful when making adjustments. Much of the information pertaining to the care of the product may be classified as follows:

How to handle the product
How to clean it
How to store it
How to repair it
How to lubricate it
How to refrigerate it

Need for Product Information Determined by the Kind of Goods

What a particular customer wants to know about an item depends largely on the kind of merchandise under consideration. Usually a customer wants much less information from a salesperson about *convenience goods,* items that he does not shop for and buys wherever and whenever it is convenient, than he does about *shopping goods,* merchandise that customers usually compare with similar goods and shop for before purchasing. Certainly, an experienced housewife wants little help in buying coffee, a buying decision she has been making for years. But she may need a great deal of information and assistance in purchasing a fur coat or refrigerator.

To the two basic classes of goods—convenience goods and shopping goods —may be added a third, specialty goods. *Specialty goods* are those that attract the customer for some reason other than price. They induce him to put forth special effort to visit a store where this merchandise is sold and to make his purchase without shopping. Specialty goods are usually branded and highly advertised. They usually require considerable investment by the consumer. Some typical specialty goods are: high-grade watches, men's better-grade suits, and fine china.

Customers Determine Merchandise Classifications. Individuals differ in methods used in purchasing articles. Some buy automobiles only after shopping carefully for them. Under these conditions automobiles are shopping goods. Others decide upon the make or brand they want and go directly to the retail outlet that sells it. Under these conditions automobiles are specialty goods. It will be seen that classification of goods really varies with a particular customer. Retailers are, however, concerned primarily with the majority of customers when classifying goods for merchandising purposes.

Conveying Product Information to Customers

For convenience goods—bread, tobacco, bobby pins, and lead pencils—product information is transmitted to customers largely through national advertising and sales-counter displays. This does not lessen the necessity for retail merchandisers having product information, for it requires even more skill to sell goods when

Auto accessories are big business for modern service stations, as this attendant shows with a purchase suggestion to his customer.

Courtesy Firestone News Service

limited to these visual means of presentation. In other words, it is much easier to talk about an item than it is to write advertising copy, make an effective display, or write a good show card.

Shopping goods demand very complete product information on the part of those who sell them. Competition in this field is based largely on sales appeals through personal salesmanship, local advertising, and store displays. Merchandisers using any of these media must thoroughly understand the product they sell in order to compete for the shopper's favor. Those who are unable to make the proper appeals convincingly soon lose out in this highly competitive field.

Merchandising specialty goods usually requires even better command of product information than the sale of shopping goods. In order to maintain the status of specialty goods, it is necessary that those who merchandise these products continuously make their clientele conscious of the product's superior features.

New articles on the market, regardless of kind, require a great deal of product information on the part of those who merchandise them. This is why manufacturers frequently employ specially trained personnel to demonstrate their product in retail stores. Beginners in retailing can profit much from studying the consumer values and technical information explained by sales demonstrators in describing the merchandise they are selling.

Trade Talk

convenience   shopping goods
   goods   customer values
specialty goods

Can You Answer These?

1. How does a thorough knowledge of product information help the salesperson? the stock-room personnel?

2. What is the relationship of customer values to technical information?

3. What should a retail merchandiser know about the kind of people who patronize his store?

4. Name as many as you can of the values customers seek when purchasing products.

5. What product information should members of the merchandising team have about: (*a*) how the merchandise will fill customer's needs and wants; (*b*) how to help the customer determine where to buy the product; (*c*) how to help the customer determine when to buy the product; (*d*) how to help the customer determine the price to pay; (*e*) how to care for the product?

6. Why is it important to know the differences between convenience goods, shopping goods, and specialty goods?

7. What are the differences in the need for product information relating to (*a*) convenience goods, (*b*) shopping goods, (*c*) specialty goods, (*d*) newness of the product?

Problems and Projects

1. Make a list of the differences in the ways convenience goods and shopping goods are displayed, advertised, and sold.

2. Classify the products advertised in one issue of a popular magazine as to convenience, shopping, and specialty goods. What differences can you find in the copy and illustrations for the three kinds of goods?

3. Clip a large advertisement from a local newspaper. List the customer values described and technical information found in it.

4. Select an item of merchandise. List the values the customer seeks in that item. To what extent are these values to be found in the item?

5. Select a shopping-goods article. Now select the items of product information that apply to it from among those listed under the eight product-information questions in this part.

Learning Your Job

1. From the standpoint of possession of product knowledge, how would you rank the people in your department, including the supervisors? What evidence do you have to back up your opinion?

2. Give five illustrations of convenience goods and five illustrations of shopping goods sold in your department. Are specialty goods carried in the department?

3. List the customer values and technical information (proofs) given in a newspaper or magazine advertisement for one of the products that your store handles. Try using this information on at least three customers who are interested in this product.

4. Select from your stock an article you would like to know more about. Make a list of the questions you would ask concerning this article.

24 Sources of Product Information

There are many rich sources of product information available to those who are merchandising minded. To the successful merchandiser, gathering product information is a habit. He is continuously on the alert for information that can be used to increase sales. He is well aware of good sources and makes it his business to utilize them. Such sources may be divided into four groups: (1) direct experiences, (2) other people, (3) literature, and (4) incidental sources.

Direct Experiences

Direct experiences are those gained through direct contact with the product and with the customer. They are the most accessible sources of information and are very productive for those who use them well.

Studying the Merchandise Itself. Merchandising personnel can learn a great deal from the merchandise itself. They can capitalize on this source while carrying on regular sales and stock duties and during lulls in business. It is advisable to make mental and written notes on materials, construction, and workmanship at each opportunity. Comparisons among several grades of merchandise may be made. In some instances, such as piece goods, the materials can be tested. The habit of intelligent observation pays good dividends.

A high school graduate, who had never sold before, started to work in one of the departments of a large department store in his community. To everyone's surprise, in about sixty days he was selling as much merchandise as the best of the older, more experienced salespeople. When asked how he accomplished this, he replied that he looked carefully at each article of merchandise in his stock and memorized every pattern. He listened to the conversation of the most successful salespeople and encouraged them to talk about their sales and how they made them. He asked questions when he was in doubt. By these methods, he established his reputation as a salesperson.

Studying Labels and Attached Descriptive Materials. The label is a modern merchandising tool. By giving the essential facts about the product quickly, clearly, and authoritatively, the time of both the salesperson and the customer is saved. A study of labels gives the salesperson a knowledge of facts that he can use in his sales presentations. The National Consumer-Retailer Council provides a Master Label Outline, shown on page 151. This outline contains the essential information that should appear on a label.

MASTER LABEL OUTLINE

PURPOSE OF AN INFORMATIVE LABEL

The purpose of an informative label is to enable the consumer to buy wisely and the store to sell intelligently, to the end that the consumer gets the maximum satisfaction for the money expended and the store handles the transaction with the minimum possibility for returns and adjustment. An informative label should give the consumer a *definite* idea of the quality of the product by telling its composition and construction, what it will do, how to use it, and how to care for it — as a basis for intelligent choice, and to enable her to compare qualities. A definite idea can only be conveyed by *specific* facts. It is suggested that these facts be grouped under the six headings listed below. *The order and the form used here are not significant.*

OUTLINE FOR INFORMATIVE LABELS

It is understood, of course, that labels should conform to local, State or Federal regulations where such exist.

WHAT IT WILL DO (Performance)
Degree of color permanence; shrinkage or stretchage; breaking strength; seam slippage; resistance to water, perspiration, wind, wear; light, heat and power tests; power consumption; cost of upkeep; etc.

WHAT IT IS MADE OF (Composition)
Kind and quality of fiber, metal, wood, leather, ceramics, cement, rock, fur, plastics, petroleum products, rubber, paper, bone, chemicals, drugs; ingredients of food products; etc.

HOW IT IS MADE (Construction)
Size, weight, number of yarns per inch, weave, number of stitches per inch, finish, ply, cut, hand or machine made, pressed, molded, stamped, inlaid; etc.

HOW TO CARE FOR IT
Detailed instructions for washing and/or cleaning; precautions to be observed in cleaning or in storage; refrigeration; oiling and greasing; polishing; etc.

RECOMMENDED USES
Purposes for which it is most suitable; recipes; etc.

BRAND NAME OF PRODUCT AND NAME OF MANUFACTURER OR DISTRIBUTOR
Brand name of product and name and address of the manufacturer or distributor

This master label outline, prepared by the National Consumer-Retailer Council, has proved helpful in organizing copy to be printed on informative labels.

Personal Experiences with the Product. When salespeople personally buy such items as food, clothing, recreational items, and automotive supplies, they obtain product information through firsthand experiences. One reason for employee discounts is to make this experience possible. While personal-use testimonials in selling must be discreetly used, the information gained and enthusiasm generated are conducive to good merchandising practices.

Personal Shopping Experiences. Some firms engage in *comparison shopping,* the practice of keeping track of competitors through shopping their stores. Comparison window and advertising shopping is very common. Good retailers continuously study the activities of other firms, borrowing and modifying competitors' ideas to suit their own organizations. When you are in the market for a product, it may be wise for you to engage in comparison shopping on your own.

Visiting Factories and Wholesale Houses. Visits to manufacturers' plants and wholesale distributing firms offer many contacts that provide valuable product information. While on such visits, one should observe the manufacturing and distribution processes going on, ask questions concerning products, obtain sales literature, and be generally observant.

Other People as Sources of Information

A wise man profits from the experiences of others, and the smart merchandiser uses these experiences to his advantage. Customers, salesmen, and training classes are good sources of information.

Training Classes. Large department stores and chain stores usually offer classes in various kinds of product information that are attended by salespeople from the departments concerned. The public schools conduct similar classes. Both sources employ well-qualified teachers and tailor the course content to meet the needs of class members. Such classes are a short cut to learning product information.

Talking to Customers. Perhaps the most valuable sources of product information are customers themselves, when selling to them and making exchanges for them. Good salespeople and adjustment personnel are alert to customer comments that give clues to the needs and wants of customers and make use of the information in succeeding sales.

A good salesperson encourages customers to talk about their buying problems and finds out why they prefer certain brands, models, and colors. This information can be obtained after a sales transaction has been completed or when goods are returned.

Talking with Wholesale or Manufacturers' Salesmen. In small establishments, the salesperson is usually in a position to learn much from the sales representatives of manufacturers and distributors. Because these representatives observe the selling practices of many retail establishments, they can pass on valuable ideas for increasing sales. And they are eager to do so, because it helps the sale of their products. Owners of small stores sometimes find it advantageous to ask the representative to instruct salespeople in how to sell his products. A Chicago manufacturer of baked goods requests his salesmen

This young couple believes in careful inspection of labels and merchandise before buying.

Courtesy E. I. du Pont de Nemours and Co., Inc.

Employees in this department store are receiving instructions on the selling points of the fabrics shown.

Courtesy Woodward & Lothrop, Washington, D.C.

to spend their Saturdays behind the retail-store counters, so that they will be better able to offer advice to the retail stores to whom they sell.

Listening to Department Buyers. In large department stores, the buyers for the various lines of goods arrange for product demonstrations to merchandising personnel. In such demonstrations, the merchandise is fully described, its uses and advantages explained, and the best ways of selling it are dramatized.

Talking to Fellow Salespeople. You will recall the story of the high school graduate who made such an enviable sales record by listening to the conversations of successful salespeople and encouraging them to talk about their sales. Most salespeople, if properly approached, are willing to talk about their successful sales. They realize that it is to everyone's advantage to have each member of the sales staff perform good customer service.

Visiting with Good Home Managers and Friends. We can learn a great deal about merchandising from discussing buying problems with friends, particularly those who are good household managers. From them we can discover variations in taste, their expectations of store services, criticisms of store policies, new uses for products, and ways of caring for goods. Discussing buying problems is a very acceptable topic of conversation and a profitable one. Frequently, information gained from friends may be used as a testimonial when selling.

Literature on Product Information

There is an abundance of literature dealing with products and related retail subjects. Much is available free of charge or at a moderate cost. Up-and-coming young retailers make it their business to become familiar with as many sources as possible.

Manuals. Excellent sources of information for merchants and sales-people are the numerous manuals produced by business firms, magazine publishers, and educational institutions. Fairchild Publications, publisher of *Women's Wear Daily,* 7 East 12 Street, New York 3, New York, produces a series of know-how handbooks. Household Finance Corporation, Prudential Plaza, Chicago 1, Illinois, a consumer credit organization, is an example of a rich source of information. Consumer education publications of the National Association of Secondary School Principals, a department of the National Education Association, 1201 16 Street NW, Washington 6, D.C., are of value to consumers and to salespeople who sell to them.

Sales Literature. Literature published by manufacturers to describe their products to merchants ranges from leaflets to expensive books. Circulars and pamphlets are sent freely to merchants and store employees upon request. Some companies supply samples as well as literature.

Trade-Association Publications. A group of manufacturers or retailers, who are engaged in making or marketing similar products and who have combined to further their interests, study their markets, and generally improve conditions in their own lines of business, is known as a *trade association.* Most retailers belong to some kind of trade association. Many trade associations publish bulletins, books, and other kinds of literature on the products and problems of their members. One of the outstanding examples of this type of service is that of the National Retail Merchants Association. It collects and correlates information on merchandise practices, methods of accounting, personnel training, and other matters.

Trade Journals. Besides numerous association publications, a large number of trade magazines are published by private firms especially for operators of specialized kinds of businesses. Dealers in automobiles, furs, meats, drugs, hats, ice cream, and hundreds of other articles are provided with facts and items of interest through journals published exclusively for them and their salespeople.

Government Publications. Several U.S. government departments publish information of value to consumers, retail merchants, and salespeople. Most of these publications are distributed at a very small price; some are free. Requests for government publications should be sent to the Superintendent of Documents, Government Printing Office, Washington, D.C. This office sends out lists (including price and description) of literature prepared by different government departments.

Mail-Order Catalogues. Mail-order houses and retail stores offering mail-order service distribute catalogues that provide excellent basic product information. This source is particularly valuable to beginners as an aid in getting acquainted with product lines.

General Consumer Magazines.   Merchandising personnel should make good use of general consumer magazines, because customers read them and obtain from them facts concerning the merchandise. Advertisements and feature articles contain helpful information. The consumer magazines that reach the average American home provide some excellent information about products.

Make Good Use of Your Library.   The public library in your town or city frequently has available books, pamphlets, and magazines on consumer products. The student who has learned to use the library card catalogue intelligently saves himself much time.

Incidental Sources of Product Information

Sources of product information are nearly everywhere. At the movies, one can often pick up ideas on merchandising during the feature picture and from the newsreel. At the county or state fair, talking with exhibitors and viewing the displays will present new product information; likewise, just watching people on the street will produce hints that can be used in selling.

At home, the merchandiser reads the newspaper, section by section—front page, sports, home and hobby, editorial, financial, even the comics. If he has a receptive mind, he finds new ideas for merchandising. Radio, TV, even the record player can be sources of product information. Truly, product information is nearly every place you look for it.

Trade Talk

comparison	sales literature
shopper	testimonial
merchandise	trade association
manual	trade journal

Can You Answer These?

1. What does an intelligent observer do when studying the merchandise itself?
2. What information does a good label contain?
3. Explain the different ways in which a salesperson can get good product information from customers.
4. What kinds of merchandise information may be procured from comparison shopping? What precautions need to be considered in using this source?
5. How can a retailer take advantage of his contacts with other people, both within and outside the company, to obtain product information? Which of the persons he contacts is of greatest value to the beginning salesperson?
6. What product information can the wholesale salesman give to the retail merchant and his salespeople?
7. Name as many incidental sources of product information as you can.

Problems and Projects

1. Choose an article in your classroom. Study it carefully and list as many customer values as you can. Opposite each, place the technical information that proves the value.
2. Collect at least three labels or tags and evaluate them according to the master-label outline on page 151.

3. Under what conditions would you tell a customer about your experience in using a product? Give examples of the kinds of merchandise with which you would use your own experience as a testimonial.

4. From the standpoint of obtaining merchandise information, what are the advantages in buying from a mail-order house? What are the disadvantages?

5. Bring to class an article from a popular magazine that contains good product information.

Learning Your Job

1. From your stock, choose two articles of the same kind that sell at different prices. Compare them, value for value, listing the values and the technical information that justifies the difference in price.

2. Bring to class three labels on merchandise you sell or copy the information from them. Rank the labels according to the criteria in the master-label outline on page 151.

3. List ten items of information that customers have given you which you would consider helpful in selling. Ask three customers why they like a particular product they buy from you.

4. Bring to class at least three pieces of sales literature. List the customer values given in this literature and opposite each value the technical information that proves the value.

5. List the names and addresses of trade-association publications to which your firm subscribes. List the trade journals also.

25 Textiles and Nontextiles— Examples of Merchandise Study

In the preceding parts of this unit, the importance of a thorough knowledge of merchandise and its uses has been pointed out and numerous sources of merchandise information have been given. In this part, specific merchandise will be described, illustrating the kinds of information desired by customers.

The retail salesperson who hopes to make progress is, or will have to become, a student. As such, he will gather facts, organize them, and make use of them in his daily work. He will not trust to memory alone, but he will make notes of pertinent information. Keeping a record of questions that customers ask is one of the best ways to learn the selling points of different kinds of merchandise.

Kinds of Merchandise—Textile and Nontextile

The retailer may sell one or both of the two kinds of merchandise (1) textile merchandise or (2) nontextile merchandise. Included in the classification of textile merchandise are articles made of wool, cotton, linen, silk, and rayon, or other materials made from man-made or synthetic fibers. These have been woven, knitted, felted, or braided into cloth. Illustrations of textile goods are yard goods, sheets and pillowcases, handkerchiefs, neckwear, and hosiery.

Merchandise that is not made by weaving, knitting, or felting, but by some other means, is called *nontextile merchandise*. Canned goods, tools, and writing paper are all illustrations of nontextile goods.

Information About Nontextile Goods

Information customers desire about textiles will be described and illustrated later in this unit. Since nontextile merchandise is also important to consumers, descriptions of several kinds will be given, as illustrations of the kind of information the salesperson should possess concerning them.

Furniture. Even though furniture is important in the lives of individuals and to families, little is known by the average person about the materials used and about the construction of the furniture purchased for his home. The salesperson in a furniture store or department has to be particularly well informed. Customers of the store, selecting furniture for a lifetime of use, want to be sure of the workmanship and of the suitability of materials of the pieces they are buying.

Does the wood have beauty of grain pattern, does it take and hold an attrac-

Here is the famous story of Dr. Paul Ivey, lecturer in salesmanship, who visited two hardware stores in search of a hammer. In one store, he was simply handed a hammer; in the other, the good points of the hammer were explained:

1. Head of crucible cast steel
2. Completely nickel plated
3. Handle of second growth of hickory
4. A mahoganized finish
5. The head wedged on in such a way it couldn't fly off
6. The prongs so shaped they would grip a tiny brad

Ewing Galloway

tive finish, is it durable—these are questions to which the buyer desires answers. After the customer has given the article of furniture its rightful place in his home and has begun to enjoy it, he will need to begin caring for it. It will need to be dusted, cleaned, and polished. The salesperson who advises the customer on the best methods of caring for the new article of furniture will help him keep his home beautiful.

Household Utensils. In departments where customers often have little background knowledge, for example the household-utensils department, the salesperson can be of real service as an advisor. The selection of pots and pans and other kitchen utensils often is an important matter from the standpoint of fuel consumption, the preservation of food values, and—what is most important—the promotion of family health. The salesperson should be able to analyze the customer's needs and assist him in the selection of household utensils. Since proper care is essential to the long-time use of a utensil, the salesperson should likewise explain how the utensil is to be cared for.

Jewelry. Jewelry is divided into two large classifications—novelty, or fashion, jewelry and fine jewelry.

The novelty, or fashion, jewelry classification is made up of such items as imitation pearls, glass stones, plastic costume jewelry, wood ornaments, and articles made of metal with platings of silver, gold, or chromium. Sterling silver jewelry may be included in this classification.

Fine jewelry includes such items as watches, cuff links, necklaces, rings, bracelets, and earrings made of solid gold or platinum set with precious stones. Fine jewelry is displayed and sold in a different manner than that used in the sale of novelty, or fashion, jewelry. The purchaser of fine jewelry is interested in its durability, its style importance, its intrinsic worth, and its appropriateness for the individual and for the occasion for which it is selected.

Since the average customer does not buy fine jewelry often, he considers such a purchase a real occasion. He appreciates particularly the help of the salesperson in pointing out the qualities of the different pieces of fine jewelry that he is examining.

Leather Goods. Leather is a natural body covering. It is available in quantities needed and is relatively inexpensive for the comfort, service, and beauty it gives. No other material serves our footwear needs so well as leather, but it is also well suited to other needs.

A knowledge of the qualities of the leather used and the construction of the shoe enables the shoe salesman to intelligently sell shoes to his customers. Shoes are made for different purposes—for dress wear, for work, and for use in sports activities. The interested shoe salesman will know the qualities of each kind of shoe and describe these to his customers. He will remember that he is selling more than the shoes—he is selling comfort and enjoyment in the use of the shoes.

Customers expect the salesperson to advise them on the fashion importance and color harmony of clothing accessories, such as gloves and handbags. They want to know about the materials used and the workmanship and how these factors account for a difference in prices.

The luggage salesman should be an expert on leather, fabric, and construction of cases. He should be able to intelligently advise the customer about the kind of luggage best suited for specific travel needs. He should know about railroad, plane, and boat regulations as these apply to luggage.

Information About Textile Goods

Textile fibers have been useful to mankind for many centuries. They have provided material for clothing, for home furnishings, and have served a wide variety of other personal uses. As consumers of textile materials, we soon learn the value of knowing something about them. A knowledge of how to buy textiles wisely and how to use them intelligently earns dividends for the consumer in the qualities of long wear and satisfactory service. The retailer must be thoroughly familiar with this merchandise, in order to give full information to his customers about it and to lessen mistakes in buying and selling. Salespeople who know textiles have an unusual opportunity to render personal service to customers.

Kinds of Fibers Used

All fibers are divided into two classes—natural fibers and man-made fibers. We are all familiar with the natural fibers. Two of these are vegetable fibers, cotton and linen; and two are animal fibers, wool and silk. The humble silkworm really contributed the idea for producing synthetic fibers. For centuries, he has manufactured silk by chewing up mulberry leaves, mixing them with chemicals he carries around in his body, and then squirting a continuous silk filament through his "spinneret." In 1884, a French nobleman made a mulberry-leaf stew and, in imitation of the silkworm, squirted an extract of this through a homemade spinneret.

During the later years of the nineteenth century, scientists began to experiment with new man-made fibers created to supplement those of mother nature. The first patent for the making of an artificial fiber from a solution of cellulose was granted in 1884. This invention was generally known as *artificial silk* and aroused considerable interest. Commercial productions of these fibers in the United States began in 1911 and within a few years this country produced a substantial part of the total world output. Because the new artificial silk was beginning to enter into competition with real silk, it became necessary to invent a new name for these artificially produced fibers. The name finally agreed upon was *rayon,* and in most English-speaking countries, including the United States, this name is still used. *Rayon* is now only one of numerous man-made fibers woven into cloth.

Fibers Are Made Into Cloth

A textile fabric is a cloth made up of textile fibers. If the quality of these fibers is good, the fabric is likely to be strong. The strength of fabrics, however, depends not only on the qualities of the fibers, but also on the strength of the yarns (strands of twisted fibers), the method of construction (weaving, knitting, or felting), and on the way in which the fabric is finished. The processes performed after the fabric is constructed are called *finishes*. These may be of different types, for example, coloring, bleaching, or stiffening.

Finishes. Finishing processes are used to change unattractive gray cloth into fabrics that are useful and attractive to customers. They not only make a fabric more attractive but may change its texture, cover its defects, or make it more suitable for its intended use.

Cloth may have a finish applied to it either by chemical or mechanical means. The use for which a cloth is intended, the degree of permanency of finish expected, and the care the cloth will probably receive while in use determine the type of finish needed. Dyeing and printing, which are the methods used in the coloring of cloths, are not considered finishes in the textile field. A dye may be applied to a cloth at different stages in the fabric's manufacture—in the fiber stage, in the yarn stage, or after weaving.

Printing of fabrics may be done by machine or by hand. Machine methods include photographic, direct, resist, and discharge printing. Hand-printing methods include block printing, stencil printing, air brushing, and other methods.

Fabrics should be colorfast to the elements to which they will be exposed. Such elements are: sunlight, perspiration, washing, spotting, or dry cleaning. Salespeople should understand the meaning of the term "colorfast" on a label. They should read labels carefully, so that they can advise customers intelligently about the care of the fabrics they purchase.

What the Customer Needs to Know About Fibers

In recent years, the number of man-made and synthetic fibers has greatly increased. It will require systematic study over a period of time for the salesperson to learn the characteristics of all these fibers. The salesperson of textile fabrics and of clothing and other articles made of textiles should, however, know well the qualities of the natural and principal man-made fibers. This knowledge will help him give customers the information they need to know about fibers and fabrics.

Wool. Before selling a woolen garment, the salesperson should find out the use for which the garment is intended. Woolen cloths have characteristics that are quite different from those of worsted cloths, and the salesperson needs to point this out to the customer. For example:

Woolen cloth is generally

1. Soft because woolens have short, elastic wool fibers, slack twisted, carded yarn, fuzzy or hairy surface

2. Comfortable because of the quality of wool fibers to retain heat, the elastic quality of the fabric, the ease in tailoring, which makes the garment fit well
3. Attractive because of its soft texture, its adaptability to coloring, its draping quality

Worsted cloth is generally

1. Firm because worsteds have longer fibers, tighter twisted yarn, harder surfaces
2. Well wearing because of its tightly twisted combed yarn, its close weave, its clear surface
3. Easy to keep pressed because of tightly twisted yarn, close weave, hard surface

Cotton. The principal selling points of cotton are:

1. Versatility—suitable for various occasions
2. Easy to care for—launders well
3. Durable—when the right kind of fibers, yarns, weave and finish are used
4. Attractive—particularly in fancy weaves, colors, and textures
5. Comfortable—in all seasons
6. Moderate in cost—as compared to other fibers

Linen. The limited production of linen and its high production cost make linen higher priced than some of the other fibers. The customer, however, who appreciates the beauty of linen and its serviceability also recognizes its worth. Linen is made into beautiful garments of long-wearing quality. Home-makers who use linen sheets, tablecloths, and other household articles made of linen cherish them because they are a symbol of luxury.

Silk. Some interesting facts to know about silk are:

1. Silk is the finest of the natural fibers—so fine that a garment or other article made of silk weighs very little when packed for traveling.
2. Silk takes dye readily, and silk colors are varied and beautiful.
3. The silk fiber is elastic. Cloth made of silk drapes gracefully, and a silk garment that is wrinkled will regain its shape when hung out overnight.
4. Silk is an animal fiber, it keeps the heat near the body and is warm in proportion to its weight.
5. Silk is durable, because the silk fiber is the strongest natural fiber in commercial use. Illustrative of the lasting quality of silk are the silk gowns and suits worn by kings and queens of earlier days, now to be seen in museums.

Nylon. Nylon is a synthetic fiber that is widely used. Its principal characteristics are:

1. Nylon is very elastic, a factor that is important in knitted goods.
2. Nylon fibers, when dry, are stronger than any other fiber. They are wear and tear resistant. This becomes an important factor when choosing articles of clothing, such as women's stockings.
3. Nylon does not mildew and is not attacked by moths.

Fiber	Composition	Structure	Length	Luster	Strength *	Elasticity	Heat Conductivity
Acetate	Cellulose acetate (synthetic)	Striated due to irregular trilobed shape	Any length	Bright, semidull, dull	17	Stretch greater than rayon. More resilient than rayon	Medium
Acrilan	Acrylic (synthetic)	Round to bean-shape, speckled	1 to 6 inches	Semidull	11	Little stretch; excellent resilience	Very low
Arnel	Cellulose triacetate (synthetic)	Irregularly shaped solid	Any length	Bright; dull	19	Stretch similar to acetate; more resilient than acetate	Medium
Cotton	Cellulose (natural)	Flat, twisted, ribbon-like, with a wide inner canal	1/2 to 2 1/2 inches	Generally none. High quality has good sheen	6	Very little stretch. Wrinkles very easily but can be treated	High (Cool)
Creslan	Acrylic (synthetic)	Substantially round, speckled	1 to 6 inches	Semidull	10	Little stretch; excellent resilience	Very low
Dacron	Polyester (synthetic)	Substantially round, speckled	Any length	High	3	Practically no stretch; excellent resilience	Medium for filament, Low for staple
Darvan	Dinitrile (synthetic)	Irregular ribbon	1 1/2 to 4 1/2 inches	Bright, semidull, dull	16	Little stretch; excellent resilience	Low
Dynel	Acrylic (synthetic)	Irregular ribbon	1 1/4 to 5 inches	Semidull	8	Little stretch; excellent resilience	Very low
Fiberglas	Glass (synthetic)	Cylindrical translucent rod	Any length	High	1 (strongest)	No stretch; flexible	High for filament. Low for staple
Linen	Cellulose (natural)	Bamboolike	12 to 20 inches	High	5	Practically no stretch. Wrinkles very easily but can be treated	Higher than cotton (Cool)
Nylon	Polyamide (synthetic)	Fine, smooth, solid, round rod	Any length	Bright, semidull, dull	2	High stretch; excellent resilience	High for filament. Low for staple
Orlon	Acrylic (synthetic)	Dog-bone shape, speckled	1 1/2 to 4 inches	Semidull	12	Little stretch; excellent resilience	Very low
Rayon, Cuprammonium	Cellulose (man-made)	Fine, smooth, solid rod	Any length	Bright, semidull, dull	14	Little stretch. Wrinkles easily but can be treated	High
Rayon, Viscose	Cellulose (man-made)	Threadlike longitudinal lines; uneven, very irregular surface	Any length	Bright, semidull, dull	15	Little stretch. Wrinkles easily but can be treated	High
Saran	Vinylidene chloride (synthetic)	Cylindrical translucent rod	Any length	Soft luster	13	Fair stretch, returns to shape slowly; good resilience	Medium (melts easily)
Silk	Protein (natural)	Smooth solid, slightly uneven diameter	1,200 to 4,000 feet	High	4	Has good stretch; very resilient	Low (Warm)
Verel	Acrylic (synthetic)	Dog-bone shape, speckled	1 1/2 to 2 1/2 inches	Semidull	9	Little stretch; excellent resilience	Very low
Vicara	Protein (man-made)	Cylindrical rod	1 to 6 inches	Semidull	20 (weakest)	High stretch; excellent resilience	Very low
Wool	Protein (natural)	Roughly cylindrical solid, covered with overlapping scales, crimpy	1 to 8 inches	Generally none. Poor quality has luster	18	Stretches readily, tends to return to size; very resilient	Very low (Very warm)
Zefran	Nitrile-acylic alloy (synthetic)	Almost round, dark, solid rod	1 1/2 to 4 1/2 inches	Bright, semidull	7	Fair stretch; resilience almost that of wool	Low

* Numbers run from 1–20 (strongest to weakest); † 1–19 (most absorbent to least absorbent).

Absorbency	Cleanliness and Washability	Reaction to Bleaches	Effect of Heat	Effect of Mildew	Effect of Light	Reaction to Alkalies	Reaction to Acids	Affinity to Dyes
7	Use mild soap, warm water; shrinks	Deteriorates; use hypochlorite or peroxide with care	Melts and burns; use cooler iron than for rayons	Highly resistant	More resistant than rayons	Weakened by strong solutions	More resistant than rayons; damaged by concentrated strong acids	Fair, but can be solution dyed
15	Retains shape; does not shrink; may pill	Resistant	Melts; reacts like nylon	Wholly resistant	Highly resistant	Fair resistance to weak alkalies	Good resistance	Good
8	Retains shape; does not shrink; dries quickly	Deteriorates; use hypochlorite or peroxide with care	Melts at higher temperature than acetate	Very highly resistant	Loses some strength	Weakened by very strong solutions	Like acetate	Fair, limited solution dyeing possible
6	Gets dirty easily; will shrink	Weakens; may be used with care	Will scorch and burn	Damaged	Loses strength; yellows	Not damaged (strengthened with caustic soda)	Easily affected	Excellent
13	Retains shape; does not shrink	Resistant	Melts at higher temperature than Arnel	Wholly resistant	Highly resistant	Fair resistance to weak alkalies	Excellent resistance	Good
17	Most stains wash out readily; dries quickly; does not shrink; retains shape	Resistant	Melts; reacts like nylon	Wholly resistant	Loses some strength over prolonged period	Good resistance to weak alkalies; fair resistance to strong alkalies	Good resistance except to sulfuric acid	Good
12	Good shape retention; must use warm water, warm iron	Resistant to hypochlorite; damaged by peroxide	Melts at fairly high (340° F) temperature	Wholly resistant	Highly resistant	Fair resistance to weak alkalies	Good resistance	Fair
16	Retains shape; does not shrink; may pill	Resistant	Will not support combustion, but will melt	Wholly resistant	Darkens somewhat; loses some strength	Highly resistant	Extremely resistant	Good; limited solution dyeing possible
19 (Least absorbent)	Dirt wipes off	Resistant	Incombustible; melts above 1,500° F	Wholly resistant	No effect	Damaged by hot solutions of weak alkalies and cold solutions of strong alkalies	Damaged by hydrofluoric, hot phosphoric, concentrated hydrochloric and sulfuric acids	None; requires special technique to apply color to surface
5	Will shrink	Weakens; use with care	Will scorch and burn	Damaged	More resistant than cotton	Not damaged (strengthened with caustic soda)	Easily affected	Fair
9	Retains shape; filament dries quickly; does not shrink	Fairly good resistance	Quickly damaged by cigarette sparks; use warm iron	Wholly resistant	Bright is more resistant than most fibers; semidull, dull, good resistance	Unaffected	Weakened	Good
14	Retains shape; does not shrink; may pill	Resistant	Melts; reacts like nylon	Wholly resistant	Extremely resistant	Fair resistance to weak alkalies	Good resistance	Good
3	May shrink; weakens when wet	Deteriorates; use hypochlorite or peroxide with care	Reacts like cotton but at lower temperature	Damaged	Loses strength over prolonged period	Weakened by strong solutions	Easily affected; like cotton	Very good
3	May shrink; weakens when wet	Deteriorates; use hypochlorite or peroxide with care	Reacts like cotton but at lower temperature	Damaged	Loses strength over prolonged period	Weakened by strong solutions	Easily affected; like cotton	Very good; can be solution dyed
18	Use warm or cold water; washes readily	Resistant	Self-extinguishing; melts at 167° F	Wholly resistant	Darkens slightly, no strength loss	Affected by ammonium hydroxide	Good resistance	Poor, generally requires solution dyeing
2	Some silk fabrics can be washed with care	Deteriorates; use peroxide with great care	Less resistant than wool; reacts similarly	Good resistance	Less resistant than cotton or wool	Destroyed by strong alkalies; damaged by weak alkalies	Somewhat affected	Excellent
10	Retains shape; shrinkage varies with type	Discolors	Will not support combustion; will become stiff and discolored	Wholly resistant	Highly resistant	Not damaged; some discoloration	Excellent resistance	Good
4	Will not pill, felt, or shrink	Resistant	Melts; should be ironed like acetate	Good resistance	Slow deterioration	Not damaged except by strong, hot solutions	Excellent resistance	Excellent
1 (Most absorbent)	Weakens when wet; will shrink, pill, felt	Deteriorates; use peroxide with care	Does not flame; will char	Good resistance	Weakens	Destroyed by strong alkalies; damaged by weak alkalies	Generally resistant except to hot sulfuric acid	Excellent
11	Retains shape; practically no shrinkage; washes easily; little pilling	Resistant to hypochlorite; damaged by peroxide	Melts at very high (490° F) temperature	Wholly resistant	Highly resistant	Resistant to weak alkalies	Excellent resistance	Very good

163

4. Nylon dries quickly. This is important for clothing articles such as hosiery, blouses, underwear, and bathing suits.

Rayon and Acetate. Rayon and acetate are man-made fibers because they are made of natural materials. There are two kinds of rayon on the market today. Viscose and cuprammonium, although made by different processes, are both made of pure regenerated cellulose. Acetate fiber is different chemically from viscose and cupra rayons and possesses characteristics different from these rayons. The Federal Trade Commission, under a ruling effective February 9, 1952, requires that rayon and acetate be labeled as two separate fibers. Rayon includes all fabrics made by the regenerated cellulose process; while acetate includes fabrics made by the cellulose acetate process. The following table compares the qualities of viscose, cuprammonium, and nitrocellulose acetate.

Characteristic	Viscose	Cuprammonium	Nitrocellulose Acetate
Absorbency of moisture	Very good	Very good	Medium. Does not absorb much moisture
Effect of heat	Will scorch and burn	Will scorch and burn	Melts and burns; use cooler iron than for Viscose or Cupra
Heat conductivity	High. Not as cool as Cupra as it is heavier	High. Cool to wear	Medium. Warm and clammy on warm days
Strength when wet	Temporarily loses 40–70% of strength when wet but regains it when dry	Temporarily loses 40–70% of strength when wet but regains it when dry	Temporarily loses 45% of strength when wet. Weak fiber
Effect of light	Loses strength over prolonged period	Loses strength over prolonged period	More resistant than Viscose or Cupra

Dacron. This synthetic fiber (made from chemical elements) is used alone in cloth making or blended with other fibers, both natural and man-made. Its advantages are that it holds creases and pleats; washes easily and dries quickly; resists wrinkling, moths, and mildew; is strong, and feels crisp. Dacron has the tendency to melt at high temperatures and should not be washed in hot water or ironed with too hot an iron. It is susceptible to static electricity.

Dacron is combined with wool in the making of men's suits. A man buying such a suit will have a garment possessing the advantages of wool and which, at the same time, will hold creases and require less pressing.

Acrilan. This is one of the newer synthetic fibers. It holds creases and pleats, washes easily, and dries quickly; resists wrinkling, sunlight, moths, and mildew; provides bulk without weight; is strong and feels warm. Acrilan, like Dacron, is weakened by the use of too hot an iron and builds up static electricity unless specially treated.

Acrilan is blended with other fibers in the making of woven fabrics and knitted goods. It is used in women's suits and dresses, playsuits, sport shirts, and infants' wear.

The table on pages 162–163 will give you a summary of the comparative qualities of all textile fibers—natural, man-made, and synthetic— in use at present.

Trade Talk

textiles   nontextiles
worsteds   synthetic fiber

Can You Answer These?

1. What should the salesperson's attitude be toward acquiring product information?

2. It has been said that the retailer is a purchasing agent for his customers. In this capacity, what are his responsibilities for giving them product information?

3. Why is it especially important that customers be given full information before purchasing articles of furniture and fine jewelry?

4. Why is it important for us to know about textile fibers, their qualities, and the care required: (*a*) as consumers? (*b*) as salespeople?

5. In your opinion, will synthetic and man-made fibers eventually replace the natural fibers?

6. What printed specifications are attached to woven goods that help the consumer judge them?

Problems and Projects

1. Make a list of the sources from which a salesperson can obtain product information about furniture, household utensils, jewelry, and leather goods.

2. From your family and friends find out how much time they spend as consumers in obtaining product information. From what sources do they get this information?

3. Bring to class advertisements from newspapers and magazines describing merchandise made from the fibers referred to in this unit. Note particularly the claims made for the merchandise and the selling appeals used.

4. As a means of showing the general use made of the different fibers, make a list of all articles of clothing you are wearing today. Opposite each article, indicate the kind of fibers used in its manufacture.

5. Using samples of materials made of the principal fibers, perform some of the simple tests given in this unit. Compare your results with those given in the tables.

Learning Your Job

1. Find out what efforts are being made in your store to help salespeople acquire product information. Prepare a report for your class.

2. Interview one or more salespeople in your store and ascertain from them how useful their knowledge of fibers has been in selling. Prepare a brief class report.

3. Cut out three advertisements from a newspaper and circle all textile terms that have taken on new meaning for you since you started to study textiles. Explain how your familiarity with these textile terms proves helpful to you in your store work.

8. Basic Requirements for Successful Selling

Unit 8 Part 26

Surveying Retail Selling

The list of successful merchants who began their careers by selling back of the retail counter is very long. Included in this list are such names as Marshall Field, J. C. Penney, Aaron Montgomery Ward, John Wanamaker, Adam Gimbel, and W. T. Grant.

Like these men, every successful retail salesperson must quickly learn to know his customers, their buying motives, and how to make the appeals to which customers will respond. He must learn to know his goods, their qualities, and their usefulness to his customers. Also, he must learn about the sales policies and practices of the firms that make and distribute the products he sells. Mastery of these fundamentals is especially important to the person who expects to own and operate his own business.

The Nature of Sales Work

Selling is an occupation that attracts men and women who like activity and variety. As one career salesman explained, "I couldn't sit at a desk all day and do the same kind of job over and over. I want to talk to people, to move around, and to get to know the people with whom I work." This statement bears out, in part, the findings of *Glamour Magazine* researchers who found that the main satisfactions from retail selling are (1) the enjoyment of meeting and helping people, and (2) the opportunity to handle attractive merchandise.

Good salespeople enjoy the opportunity provided for self-expression through giving information and advice to their customers. To them, selling is not a matter of trying to "outwit" customers, but rather an opportunity to be of service to them. Particularly in neighborhood stores and small communities, customers and salespeople often learn to know each other quite well. Occasionally, personal friendships develop from these store associations.

The great challenge in retail selling arises largely out of the differences among customers—no two are exactly alike. Most are pleasant, some are disagreeable, some are critical, while others may be indifferent. Salespeople learn to adjust quickly to a variety of personalities; they soon learn that to succeed they must become students of human nature. As they gain in knowledge and practical experience with customers, they learn to adjust to many kinds of customer behavior. Gradually they develop a sensitivity for their customer's wishes which helps them to know such things as when to let a customer look around leisurely, or when to give prompt personal attention to his wants.

Grade Levels of Sales Occupations

There are three recognized grade levels in the sales occupations. In order of prestige, a *salesman* ranks first; a *salesperson,* second; and the *salesclerk,* third. These are official classifications made by the U.S. Department of Labor.

Salesclerks. *Salesclerks* are people whose duties are to accept primarily the customer's payment and write out sales checks. They have little to do with solving customer buying problems. Some examples of salesclerks are found in tobacco and candy stores and at soda fountains.

Salespersons. A *salesperson* is characterized as one who helps his customers solve their buying problems by giving information and guidance. Unlike the salesclerk who is responsible only for filling orders, the salesperson provides needed technical information about products to customers and advises them about such merchandise problems as appropriateness, fashion, and special use. Examples are found in millinery shops and paint, china, and furniture stores.

Salesmen. A *salesman,* like the salesperson, helps customers solve their buying problems. The difference is that the salesman seeks out his customers rather than merely serving them in a store. In other words, he calls on prospective purchasers whom he hopes to convert into customers. This is called *prospecting.* Another kind of salesman is one who sells products from house to house, taking orders for later delivery. His method of selling is called *canvassing.* Some examples of salesman occupations are: automobile, roofing, and electrical-appliance selling.

Knowing the difference between these three grade levels—salesclerk, salesperson, salesman—is important because in each of these kinds of selling one finds very different applications of sales skills. Once you understand the three grade levels, you will realize that, if you were a salesclerk in a notions department or variety store, you would not be expected to give customers many detailed technical points of information about the material used in the construction of products. On the other hand, if you become an electrical-appliance salesman, you will be expected to know a great deal about motors, construction, and other technical information regarding your merchandise.

Here a salesperson is helping a bride-to-be select her china.

Courtesy Woodward & Lothrop, Washington, D.C.

The Study of Salesmanship

Good sales personnel are made, not born. An individual may possess many of the inherent qualities necessary for good salesmanship, but he will still have to learn his trade if he is to become a productive, well-paid salesclerk, salesperson, or salesman.

Hundreds of successful salespeople will admit that they had to learn to like selling. Perhaps you have heard someone say, "I'd never make a salesman; I just couldn't ask people to buy anything." This attitude is fairly common, and beginning salespeople frequently approach their first selling experience with some hesitation. However, as soon as they learn that good salesmanship is not a matter of asking favors but rather that it is helping people solve their buying problems, they start to enjoy their work and want to learn more about the vocation of selling.

The Science and the Art of Selling

Salesmanship is both a science and an art. The science of selling is based on psychology and a knowledge of human nature. The art rests in the technique of applying sales skills to sales situations. Thus, a knowledge of what to do or say in selling to a particular customer may be based on scientific understanding; but the judgment used in applying the knowledge is an art. The art of selling is usually enhanced by good grammar and speech. Some sales positions may require familiarity with chemistry, physics, and agriculture.

The Dynamic Nature of Selling

Salesmanship is a field also in which there is continuous change. Technical developments bring about constant changes in merchandise and services; sales methods must be changed to meet new economic conditions; and selling techniques change with new marketing methods. This is why many companies carry on a continuous sales-training program. The dynamic nature of selling is one

This saleswoman, or can-
vasser, is selling cosmetics
to a housewife in her
home.

Courtesy Avon Products, New York

of the primary reasons why selling is fascinating work for those who are intel-
lectually curious.

The Modern Definition of Retail Selling

Every good student of retailing should develop for himself a practical definition
of personal selling that can be used as a guide in making judgments on the sales
floor. Experience has shown that the most useful definition of retail selling is
helping customers make satisfactory purchases. This definition implies that
selling consists of finding the customer's needs and desires and putting oneself
in the customer's place. It further implies helping him find a satisfactory solution
to his buying problems. Also, if this definition is accepted, the sale is not considered completed until the customer has used the merchandise with satisfaction.
Unsatisfactory goods returned by the customer would not be considered sold.

The Basic Steps of a Retail Sale

Some sales are very simple to handle, while others are quite difficult and con-
sume a great deal of time. The sales procedure is simple when the customer
has already made up his mind to buy a particular article before entering the
store and all that needs to be done is to write up the sale. Such sales are called
wrap-ups. In a situation where the customer has only a vague idea of what he
wants, the sale may prove difficult. In either case, the salesperson performs a
series of duties. For the purpose of studying salesmanship, these duties can
be divided into six basic steps, usually referred to as the "steps" of a sale:

1. The approach
2. Finding the customer's needs and desires
3. Helping customers examine the goods
4. Answering customer questions and objections
5. Completing the sale
6. Suggesting additional merchandise

The salesperson is showing the fine points of the car to the prospective buyer.

Obviously, the approach takes place at the beginning of the sale; and completing the sale occurs at the end. Usually, suggesting additional merchandise also comes at the end of the sale. Steps 2, 3, and 4, however, nearly always overlap or occur simultaneously. The study of personal selling in this unit will consist of a discussion of the relatively simple techniques for carrying out the above basic procedures.

Trade Talk

canvass   salesman
prospecting   salesperson
salesclerk   wrap-up sale

Can You Answer These?

1. How does retail selling experience pay off for the manufacturer's or wholesaler's salesman?
2. In what ways does retail selling experience provide a good work background for retail-store management personnel?
3. Why is it important to know the difference between the three classifications of sales occupations?
4. What are the differences between the duties of salesclerks and salespersons? between salespersons and salesmen?
5. In what respect is salesmanship a science? an art?
6. What areas of study might be included in the study of salesmanship?
7. Why is it necessary to study salesmanship continuously?
8. What are the steps in a sale?
9. What causes some sales to be simple, while others are difficult?

Problems and Projects

1. Describe your experiences with the retail salesperson who has served you best within the past two months. Do the same for the one who has given you the poorest service.
2. List the high school courses you believe to be of value in the training of a retail salesperson, and explain why you chose them.
3. Describe what is meant by the statement that selling contributes to success in life. Specifically how

might one apply salesmanship in one's relationship with members of one's family? in school? in other activities?

4. In observing a sale on your next shopping trip, see if you can identify the "six steps" of a sale mentioned in the text. Report your findings orally to the class.

Learning Your Job

1. Select the salesperson in your department or store whom you con-sider most successful. In your opinion what are the reasons for his success in selling?

2. Interview your supervisor or a member of the personnel depart-ment on the question, "What quali-ties do you look for when hiring a salesperson? How do you identify these qualities?"

3. Ask the salesperson whom you select in Activity 1 to give you his definition of salesmanship. Report his answer to the class.

27 *Starting the Sale Off on the Right Foot*

As a customer, you probably have been served by a salesperson whom you liked immediately because of his or her friendly greeting, alertness, congenial manner, and interest in your buying problem. On the other hand, it would be unusual if you had not been "waited on" by a salesclerk who, through his dis-interested, listless attitude, antagonized you from the start. Thus, from your own shopping experiences you may have discovered that what the salesperson does and says during the first two minutes of a sale sets the stage and often makes or breaks the sale.

A good sales approach will make the customer feel confident in his sales-person's willingness and ability to help solve his buying problems. On the other hand, a negative initial impression increases the possibility of sales resistance. It makes good sense for the salesperson to make things easier for himself by giving careful attention to his sales approach.

How Customers Like to Be Approached

A customer usually goes into a store because he wants to purchase something, though sometimes he is only interested in getting ideas or information regard-ing a possible future purchase. Occasionally, he is just looking around with the thought in mind that he may discover a bargain. Whatever his reason for coming in, your job as a salesperson is to get in tune with his thinking and help him achieve his purpose.

Customers Like to Feel Welcome. Abraham Lincoln said, "If you would win a man to your cause, first convince him that you are his good friend." Every good salesperson has learned from experience the wisdom of Mr. Lincoln's suggestion. Even when everything seems to go wrong and he does not feel like being friendly, a good salesperson makes his customer feel that he is glad to see him.

Customers Like to Feel Important. Nearly all customers think of themselves as being important, at least when shopping. When they have money to spend, they like to think that they are appreciated. Regardless of the customer's appearance, his manner, or the quality of merchandise he asks for, the seasoned salesperson treats his customers respectfully and makes them feel important from the very start with a courteous sales approach. He applies this practice to children as well as adults.

Customers Like to Have Confidence in a Salesperson. Most customers feel that they work hard for their money and want to get as much as possible for their dollars. For this reason, they prefer a salesperson who takes a genuine interest in their problems. They like to believe that he is competent and willing to help them select the merchandise that, within the limits of their pocketbooks, will best meet their needs.

Customers Like Prompt Attention. Even though they are just looking around, customers like to feel that their presence is known and appreciated. Attention is a subtle form of flattery. Even a slight delay in acknowledging a customer's presence is irritating, particularly when the customer is in a hurry.

How to Start a Sale with Good Customer Relations

The ability to build warm, sincere initial relationships with customers is an art that is acquired through constant practice. Some retail executives feel that it takes a beginner considerable time to learn *how* and *when* to approach a customer properly; and they stress the approach in their sales-training programs.

Customers like to feel that the salesperson is interested in their problems.

Courtesy Eastman Kodak Co.

In this unit, we shall start with simple, practical sales approaches and leave the more advanced techniques for a succeeding unit.

The Greeting Approach. When someone calls at your home, what do you say and do to make him feel welcome? Do you immediately ask him what he wants? Likely not. Usually, you greet him by name in a friendly manner. Likewise, when a customer calls at your store, you should greet him by name, if you can, and make him feel welcome with a friendly smile that shows you are pleased to see him. This is called a *greeting approach.* If you do not know the customer's name, you may use an appropriate title such as "Sir," "Madam," "Doctor," or "Lieutenant" as the case may be; or you may omit the salutation entirely, depending on the situation.

Passing the time of day is an old American custom that usually brings some kind of response from a customer. If he has some definite article in mind, he will usually return your greeting and follow with some remark that indicates what merchandise he is interested in.

The Service Approach. There are times when the department is very busy, and you may find it expedient to omit the greeting and use a *service approach,* such as "May I help you?" or some other polite question that indicates your willingness to be of service. Some firms that distribute convenience goods insist on a service approach, though they do not discourage the use of a greeting along with it. A word of caution is appropriate here—constant repetition of a stereotyped service approach is very monotonous to customers and frequently ineffective, particularly in a shopping-goods department. Be careful that the "May I help you" approach does not become a lazy habit.

Words are only part of making your customer feel welcome and important. The tone of your voice, your inflections and gestures, and the look in your eyes also convey your attitude. Thus a sincere greeting must include a smile, good eye contact, and perhaps a slight advance toward your customer. A little experience will soon teach you how to transmit your feelings and enable you to make a natural, friendly approach.

How to Create Customer Confidence in You

You can command the confidence of customers through acceptable personal appearance, through the attractiveness of your department, and through the things you do and say. All three are within your control.

Win Confidence Through Your Appearance. In Unit 3, you learned that the first impression we make on people depends on our appearance. This is particularly important in sales work. Before you can use your knowledge of merchandise or sales skills effectively, you must have made a favorable impression on your customers. If your appearance is not acceptable, you may lose many opportunities to give the valuable information you possess to people who approach your sales counter.

Win Confidence Through the Appearance of Your Department. An orderly department means that the salespeople in it have prepared for the customer's arrival. It also indicates systematic businesslike practices, and implies good customer service. An attractive and orderly department silently says, "We have tried to make this a pleasant place for you, and we wish to make it easy for you to shop."

Win Confidence Through Your Words and Actions. Words make a much stronger impression if they are backed up with actions. Give your customer your undivided attention after you offer to serve him, and this will help instill in him the belief that you have his interest at heart. Listen carefully as he speaks and follow through on his suggestions at your earliest opportunity, so that he knows you are sincere. Eye contact is important too, because some people will judge your honesty by your ability to look them in the eye.

Many successful salespeople visibly register their agreement or disagreement in a way that inspires confidence. They nod or shake their heads and use little words to express approval, such as "Yes," "Surely," and "Certainly."

How to Convey the Feeling of Prompt Attention

The best way to make a customer feel that he is being given prompt attention is to give it to him. Drop what you are doing, and make your sales approach without hesitation. It takes practice to keep an eye on customers entering the department while performing stock work or other duties at the same time, but you will learn to do it.

Time Your Greeting. Beginners, especially, may profit from the fol-

STANLEY MARCUS
President of Neiman-Marcus,
Dallas, Houston, Texas.

lowing advice: If your customer is some distance away from you when you greet him, you are apt to give the impression that you are overly aggressive. Greet the customer when he is near your counter or sales station. Catch his eye as you greet him.

Recognize Waiting Customers. When the department is busy, beginning salespeople frequently are confused as to who is being served and who is not. Experienced workers have a knack for observing customers as they approach their sales stations and are able to acknowledge them without appearing to be inattentive to the customer they are serving. You will form a habit of recognizing customers with a word, a smile, or perhaps an appropriate remark that tells them you know of their presence.

Encourage Customers to Look Around. Sometimes it is quite obvious that a customer is just looking. When this is the case, it usually is a good idea to greet him anyway and encourage him to continue looking. He will then feel free to take his time. When he is ready for assistance, he will be inclined to come to you. In the meantime, you should be on the alert for any indication of his readiness for assistance.

What to Avoid When Approaching Customers

Some opening statements, even though they are serious approaches, are less effective than others, especially when overused. Here are some examples:

May I help you?   Have you been waited on?
What can I do for you?   Do you wish attention?
Something for you today?

Such approaches may become routine, impersonal, or ineffective. They solicit a negative response—"No thank you," or "No, I'm just looking." The moment a customer refuses your offer of service, you are at a distinct disadvantage, because persistence in the face of a flat refusal may be annoying. Remember that very often the customer is not ready to buy immediately and does not wish to accept service too quickly, thus putting himself under an obligation to buy. He may not wish to commit himself or to allow himself to be hurried. That is why the answer to the question, "May I help you?" is easily answered negatively.

Opening remarks that almost surely will result in a negative impression are the curt, impersonal questions such as, "Something?"; "Yes ma'am?"; "Sir?"; "What's yours?"; and "What will it be?" These remarks show lack of interest in the customer and border on rudeness. At best, they are brusque and careless questions that should not be risked when there are so many courteous, helpful, and effective ways of starting the sale off on the right foot.

How to Custom-Tailor Your Greetings

There are many ways of varying a greeting approach. You may say "Good Evening," or even "Hello" in certain situations. If you know the customer's name, be sure to use it as a part of your greeting—"Good morning, Mrs. Donner." Very likely the way you say "Good morning" will have a slightly different ring each time you use it depending on what you think of your customer. Two precautions—guard against overfamiliarity and also against haughtiness. You can further individualize your greeting by making a friendly pertinent remark or by an understanding smile.

Trade Talk

greeting   service
  approach   approach

Can You Answer These?

1. Why does the approach have such an important influence on the sale?
2. For what reasons do customers enter a retail store?
3. Describe how a customer should feel when he is properly approached by a salesperson.
4. Under what conditions should a service approach be used?
5. How can a salesperson make a customer feel welcome?
6. What can a salesperson do in his approach to make his customer feel that he will get good service?
7. How does the appearance of the department contribute to the approach?
8. Why is it so important that customers be given prompt attention?
9. What can a salesperson do to acknowledge a customer who has not been served?
10. What procedure is recommended in dealing with customers who say they wish to look around?

Problems and Projects

1. Make a list of the opening sentences you have heard retail salespeople use. Indicate the kind of store or department in which each was made. Now rate them as good, fair, or poor and justify your rating.
2. In an open department where there are no counters, how can a salesperson approach customers promptly without being accused of being a sales grabber?
3. Criticize the following advice:

Some customers just want to look around and prefer to be alone. Let them have their wish but show that you are interested in their being served by passing near them casually once in a while. If they ask a question, that is your cue. You can make a remark that will lead into a conversation about what they need and what you think they would like. Never let a customer drift out of the department without a smile or a suggestion.

4. Make a check list for rating a retail selling approach based on the information in this part of the text. Use your check list in rating three retail salespeople and make a report.

Learning Your Job

1. List five opening remarks used by one of the most successful salespeople in your department or store. Do the same for one of the least productive salespeople. Now list five of the opening remarks you most often use. What conclusions can you draw from the differences?
2. List your own opening remarks to five successive customers. After each one, describe the customer and state your reason for using the opening words.
3. Observe how the salespeople in your store recognize waiting customers. Rate and describe five of your observations.

28 *Finding Your Customer's Needs and Desires*

Now that you know how to establish good relationships with your customers, you are ready to study a very crucial part of the sale—finding customers' needs and desires. The importance of this phase of the retail sale is dramatically illustrated by the following incident which was observed by one of the authors on his first sales job.

A woman asked to be shown some black four-in-hand neckties. Assuming that the requested item was to be worn with a work uniform, the young salesperson went into great detail regarding the merits of a high-quality tie as compared to an inexpensive one favored by the customer. After listening patiently to his sales talk, the customer courteously said, "I appreciate the information, young man, and normally I'd buy the better tie; but I'll take the inexpensive one. You see, for my purpose it will serve just as well—I want it for a corpse." This incident illustrates the necessity for a salesperson's understanding his customer's needs and desires before launching into a sales talk.

When you are able to detect your customer's needs and desires quickly and satisfactorily, you will shorten the time spent on a sale; and probably your customers will be better satisfied with your service. Also, it is likely that they will be more receptive to your suggestions during the remainder of the sale, and you can proceed smoothly.

Recognizing the Strength of Customer Desires

Customers may be classified according to their awareness of their needs and the strength of their desires as follows: (1) customers who know exactly what they need and desire—for example, a customer who knows that he needs a new tire to match the others on his car; (2) customers who are aware of their needs but have only a general idea of their desires—for example, the man who knows he wants to change to another brand of tire because he is dissatisfied with the service from those he now owns, but does not know what type or brand to buy; (3) customers who are unaware of their needs and consequently have no desires. In this category is the customer whose tires are badly worn but who is unaware that he needs new ones and does not realize the danger of driving on worn tires. Understanding the classification of customers according to the strength of their needs and desires will help you in planning your sales procedure.

Worn brake linings can spell trouble to motorists, and this service-station attendant is showing his customer an unsafe condition that exists in his car.

Courtesy Firestone News Service

Serving Those Who Know Exactly What They Desire

Those who know exactly what they desire are easy to serve if the requested merchandise is in stock. Then you can quickly get the article for your customer and find out whether he needs anything else. But if your store does not stock the requested article, you are faced with the problem of determining whether some other brand or a different kind of product will meet his needs as well or possibly better. Selling a product or brand other than that which the customer asks for is called *substitute selling*.

When engaging in substitute selling, observe the following cautions:

1. Be sure that the article you suggest as a substitute will serve the customer's needs as well or better than the article requested.
2. Be very careful not to "talk down" the article originally requested. (Talking down means knocking or belittling a product—for example, telling a customer that the requested brand of shoes is made of inferior leather. Any inference that the product the customer calls for is inferior might be interpreted as an insult to the customer's judgment.)

Serving Those Who Have Only a General Idea of What They Desire

Most shopping-goods customers have only a general idea of what they desire. Success in selling to this kind of customer depends largely on how well you can uncover his needs and desires.

Determining the Use of the Merchandise. Don't be like the necktie salesperson and fail to determine your customer's intended use of the requested merchandise. A customer who has a general idea of what he wants may say, "I'd like to look at some typewriters" (or dresses, or some other product). At this point, the salesperson should ask a question regarding the intended use of the merchandise such as "Something for the office?"; or in the case of dresses, "Something for sportswear?" This will enable the salesperson to show several styles any one of which may serve the customer's needs.

Avoid a Cross-Examination. Too many direct questions regarding your customer's desires endanger the sale. Suppose that in response to the customer's request to look at some dresses, the salesperson had asked several specific questions such as "What color?"; "What kind of material?"; "About how much would you like to spend?" This kind of procedure gives rise to several possible dangers:

1. It might force the customer into making decisions concerning which he has given little thought.
2. The answers to specific questions of this type usually restrict the variety of merchandise that may be shown without disregarding his answer.
3. Numerous direct questions increase the danger of being out of stock or the store's not carrying the merchandise.
4. The customer may justly feel that the salesperson is not much interested in showing a broad selection.

On the other hand, questions about the use of the product create the impression that the salesperson is interested in his customer's problems, rather than trying to get rid of his customer as quickly as possible.

Serving Customers Who Are Unaware of Their Needs

The customer who is unaware of his needs or has not clearly defined them presents an interesting challenge, even for experienced salespeople. This kind of customer does not really plan to buy. He is, however, usually open to suggestions and becomes aware of his needs when they are brought to his attention. For example, a customer who has a tire repaired may be shown that he has

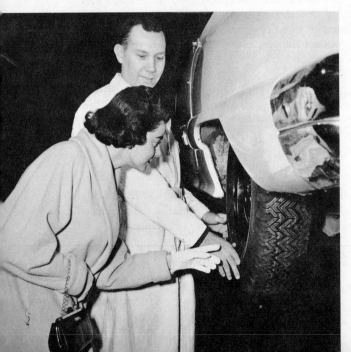

A service-station attendant is suggesting that the customer buy new snow tires for her car.

a damaged place on the casing and advised about the seriousness of the damage. In a situation such as this, the salesperson usually can easily prove to his customer that a new tire is needed—that the purchase of a new tire may prevent an accident or even loss of life.

Suppose that you as a salesperson are talking to a customer who is browsing around looking at various garden tools. You learn that gardening is his hobby, but that he obviously does not like to pull weeds. Showing this customer how a new tool on the market will reduce weeding time may make him aware of his need for the new device. Thus, by showing concern for the customer's interests, you are able to help him define his needs.

Sizing Up Your Customers

Listen with your eyes as well as with your ears! Many experienced salespeople know full well the soundness of this rule.

Observing Your Customer's Reactions. Many times you will be able to appraise your customer's needs and desires by listening carefully to what he says and by closely observing how he reacts to different items as they are shown. If a customer were to say, "I want a stemmed goblet that is practical for everyday use and won't cost too much," the salesperson would have a good idea of his needs. Then, if the customer were to smile when shown a goblet of a particular style, the salesperson would know that he was on the right track. If, on the other hand, the customer's facial expression registered dissatisfaction, he might ask another question such as, "Would a shorter stemmed goblet look better with your other dishes?" Quite likely this question about the use of the merchandise would draw from the customer some description of the dishes with which the goblets were to be used. Then the salesperson would listen carefully again for further indications of the customer's desires.

Studying Your Customer's Habits. The way a customer is dressed is not necessarily an indication of how much he or she is willing to spend. There are those who dress up to go shopping, those who dress for comfort, and those who dress indifferently. All three kinds may belong to any income group. Thus, it does not pay to draw hasty conclusions from your customer's dress habits alone. But a customer's choice of clothing and grooming habits may provide clues to tastes in merchandise. The colors and style of the clothing a person wears, the way a woman wears her hair, and the condition of a person's clothing may be clues that will help determine a customer's taste and what merchandise will appeal to him.

A customer's mannerisms may also provide additional clues to the things he likes. The speed of your customer's speech, the tone of his voice, the inflection he gives certain words, and even his accent are meaningful to the alert salesperson. So is the speed or casualness of his approach to the department. They are clues used by professional sales personnel in sizing up their customers in order to do an intelligent job of finding their needs and desires.

Trade Talk

customer   merchandise
desires   size up the
customer   customer
needs   substitute
talk down the   selling

Can You Answer These?

1. Why is finding the customer's needs and desires a crucial part of the sale?
2. As to needs and desires, what are the differences between the three classifications of customers?
3. What should the salesperson do when serving a customer who knows exactly what he needs when the merchandise is in stock?
4. Give two rules to follow in practicing substitute selling. Explain why these rules are important.
5. What kind of questions should salespeople ask customers who have only a general idea of what they desire? What kind of questions should be avoided? When is an exception made to the latter?
6. What procedure should a salesperson follow in serving a customer who is not aware of his needs?
7. What should be done about customers who reveal vaguely defined needs?
8. What activities are included in sizing up customers?
9. Why does a competent salesperson refrain from doing too much talking?

Problems and Projects

1. What is your reaction to the following statement? "If you do not have what the customer asks for, he will be glad to have you suggest something that will take the place of what he had in mind.

Many times customers aren't sure what they want anyway."
2. Develop a list of statements and descriptions of salespeople's actions that illustrate how salespeople talk down a product.
3. Make a list of salespeople's questions that may restrict the assortment of merchandise to be shown. Make a second list of questions about the use of the merchandise that permit the showing of a good selection.
4. List the various ways in which a salesperson can tell how a customer is reacting to the merchandise shown him.

Learning Your Job

1. On a 5x3 card, rule a 4-column form similar to the one shown below. Throughout one day place a check mark in the proper box for each customer you serve. Figure the percentage of successful sales for each classification. This will be of some help in dealing with similar situations in the future.

	Customer Knows Exactly	Has General Idea	Is Not Aware
Sale Made	√		
Sale Missed			√

2. List five items in your department or store. Then list three questions you might ask a customer to determine his intended use of each. Decide which of the three is the best and try it out on the job.

29 *Helping Customers Examine the Goods*

Merchandise cannot speak for itself; its story must be told by merchandising personnel. There are two basic ways of telling people about the store's products: (1) through personal selling and (2) through impersonal media—newspapers, radio, television, window displays, displays inside the store, show cards, and other advertising devices. Sometimes the impersonal media have "sold" the product before the customer enters the store. Sometimes these same media have confused a customer so much that it is difficult for the salesperson to help him out of his dilemma.

Many customers need help with their purchasing problems, particularly in buying shopping goods. They need a salesperson (1) who knows what merchandise is available, (2) who will point up the advantages and disadvantages of the many products and brands, and (3) who will give sound advice about the suitability of the merchandise for their purposes.

Make Use of the Five Senses

Competent salespeople help their customers make use of as many of the five senses as possible. Studies show that people receive ideas from their senses in the following proportions: Sight, 87 per cent; hearing, 7 per cent; touch, 3 per cent; smell, 2 per cent; taste, 1 per cent.

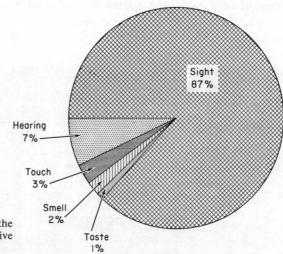

A pie chart showing the proportions of the five senses.

Sight

Sight is 27 times faster than hearing and has 22 times more impact; therefore, skillful salespeople take particular pains in showing their goods in an interesting, effective way. You may have noticed how a person selling diamonds uses soft, black velvet to display the stones. He utilizes this contrast between the hard, sparkling gem and the soft, rich, black velvet to appeal to the sense of sight and thus impress the customer with the beauty of the diamond.

Hearing

Customers use their ears to hear facts that point up the application of the product to their needs. Realizing this, salespeople carefully describe their products with stimulating adjectives and phrases. They avoid vague, general words, adjectives, such as "nice," "pretty," "wonderful," and "fine," and try to use specific and appealing words and statements that carry conviction. How much more effective it is to say "See how smoothly and attractively this garment fits across your shoulders," than to say, "It is a nice fit!"

Competent salespeople use correct language, even when serving a customer who does not. And they avoid the use of slang, because not only does it make a poor impression on the customer but it also conveys a vague, inaccurate meaning. They do not switch their vocabularies for different kinds of customers, other than perhaps small children, because they realize that every customer understands many words that he does not use himself. In other words, simple, correct, accurate communication is appropriate for nearly all customers.

Touch

The sense of touch complements sight and hearing. Perhaps you have noticed how a good salesperson gets his customer to try on a garment, sit behind the wheel of a car, or feel the balance of a golf club. Some characteristics of a product are not effectively communicated by sound or sight, whereas the sense of touch conveys a definite meaning. For example, feeling a fabric tells one much about

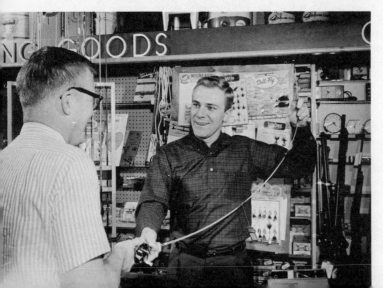

Various senses come into play in the sale of a fishing rod: sight, touch, and imagination.

A sense of touch—feeling the softness of the towels—is an important aid in making this sale.

Courtesy New York Life Insurance Co.

whether it is soft or hard, smooth or rough, cool or warm, lightweight or heavy. Thus, the customer's handling, lifting, operating and other ways of using the sense of touch add to selling effectiveness.

Smell

Obviously, the sense of smell is very important in selling products such as cosmetics, tobacco, and food. But we often do not realize that aroma plays an important part in creating a pleasant shopping environment for any product. This is the main reason why retailers are concerned about eliminating a musty warehouse odor, the fumes of gasoline and oil, the odorous smell of decaying fruit, and of course offensive breath and body odors among employees.

Taste

For hundreds of years, merchants have made use of the appeal to the sense of taste in selling foods and beverages. Only recently, however, has the importance of this sense been recognized in merchandising drugs, tooth paste, and similar products. In selling orally consumed goods, the salesperson should describe or at least refer to taste. When practical, it may be advisable to give the customer a taste or a sample of the product.

The Combined Use of the Senses

As a salesperson, the more senses you can appeal to, the stronger your impression on the customer will be. The minor senses of touch, smell, and taste provide the interesting accent that will help tell the story of the product.

Show the Right Merchandise in the Right Amount

A good salesperson quickly gets the merchandise his customer wants. He realizes that hesitancy may put his customer in a poor frame of mind and cause him to lose confidence in him. He has an advantage over other salespeople who do not keep up with what is in stock and often take too much time looking for things to show their customers. Because of his superior knowledge of stock, he is able to show his customer a more suitable selection of merchandise. As a result, he usually completes a larger percentage of his sales.

What to Show First

In determining what to show first, we can look to five guides used by expert salespeople:

1. Show what the customer asks for—style, color, price, and other features.
2. If the customer expresses no definite desire, show something you think he will like after you have mentally sized him up.
3. If the customer provides no clues as to price, usually show him the medium-price line first.
4. If the customer shows no preference, show articles that are being advertised or have some unusual value.
5. Show goods in the department, and after that, goods from the reserve stock.

How Much Merchandise to Show

The amount of merchandise that needs to be shown will vary with the kind of goods and with different customers. The following suggestions from experienced salespeople will help you with your judgments regarding this problem. (1) Show enough merchandise to allow the customer a sufficient choice—when buying some products he should be shown several articles. (2) Indicate that you are interested in your customer's buying problem and will cheerfully show him all he needs to see—a broad selection gives you a better chance of finding something he will like. (3) Try to avoid unnecessary steps in getting more goods from stock. Bear in mind that your effectiveness in displaying and describing your merchandise has a bearing on the amount of stock you will be called upon to show.

Successful salespeople agree that a customer should be shown only a few articles at one time, even though he ultimately has to be shown nearly everything in stock. Thus they avoid confusing and discouraging the customer with too large an assortment.

Display Your Goods Effectively

Customers seek out salespeople who can display their goods in an interesting, attractive manner; it makes shopping much easier and much more fun. To many customers, the hundreds of items competing for attention are confusing. Reducing the distractions and helping customers visualize how a certain product will answer his buying problem usually brings repeat business for the salesperson.

Isolate the Goods You Are Showing

A contrasting background in a display window makes the merchandise on display stand out and command attention. In similar fashion, isolating the goods you are showing from competing products will attract and hold your customer's attention. If the article is small, it is advisable to pick it up and hand it to your customer—not just point to it. In selling clothing, the salesperson should ask his customer to try on the garment or at least hold it up to himself. Likewise, folding a necktie and laying it on a shirt is an excellent way to isolate and display it.

Handle Merchandise Meaningfully

Have you noticed how some salespeople convey their feelings toward merchandise through the manner in which they handle it? One can see from the special care they take in showing an item that they respect and admire it. In today's selling, even canned foods are handled meaningfully—witness the way a good check-out boy in a progressive supermarket packs your groceries when he fills a bag for you.

Strengthen Your Talk with Gestures

A good salesperson does not deliver his sales message with his words alone; he communicates with his hands, his arms, his face—with his whole body. Each movement reinforces his words. This unspoken communication through movements and facial expression is known as the *language of gestures*. Gestures will help make a sales presentation interesting. They express enthusiasm that usually is transferred to the customer. Note how expert salespeople hold their customer's interest without detracting from the merchandise.

Help Your Customer Visualize the Product in Use

Whenever possible, creative salespeople show their customers how the mer-

Here the salesperson is selling his paint by helping the customer visualize the beauty of the newly painted kitchen.

Courtesy National Cash Register Co.

chandise will look in actual use—a towel folded over a towel bar, a rug spread on the floor, a hi-fi record player played by the salesperson or customer. With a similar objective in mind, the salesman of combination windows takes his prospect to see the windows on the home of a user. These devices aid customers in making up their minds concerning the application of the merchandise to their buying problems.

Get Your Customer to Participate

Customers usually like to taste the fruit cake, sit in the chair, try on the garment, open the refrigerator door, or turn the electric-range controls. The customer should also be encouraged to participate in the figuring of costs and savings in relation to his purchase. Customer participation in the sales presentation helps develop the customer's desire to possess the merchandise. It also helps the salesperson understand his customers' desires, because he can watch reactions while his customer examines and tests the merchandise.

What the customer does during a sale is easy for him to remember. It has been reported that most people remember: 10 per cent of what they *hear;* 50 per cent of what they *see;* 90 per cent of what they *do*.

Make Full Use of Your Hands

The best display fixtures in a store are the hands of its retail salespeople. These live "display props" serve many purposes: (1) they direct the customer's attention to the merchandise; (2) they point out its outstanding features; (3) they frequently give action or movement to the merchandise; and (4) they help express the salesperson's ideas about the product. Your hands are your trademark and your best friends, so let them help you make sales. Keep them active and attractive—never hide them in your pockets.

Point Up Consumer Values

Customers want to know what a product will do for them. They think about the features of a product in terms of values to them. In this text, we shall try to tune in on the customer's point of view on *consumer values*. Salespeople often refer to consumer values as selling points.

Hardly any two customers attach the same importance to each consumer value. One customer may be interested in such things as serviceability and economy, while another is looking for appearance and prestige. Some other consumer values are comfort, safety, fashion, and security. It is your job as a salesperson to find out just which consumer values are important and how important they are.

Explain Consumer Values

Salespeople with large customer followings offer the advice below in dealing with consumer values:

1. **Be Concrete.** General statements are not nearly so effective a[s defi]nite, specific ones. To say that a garment looks well does not mean half so m[uch to] a customer as to say that it helps him keep a neat appearance because it is [made] of virgin, long-staple, crush-resistant wool.

2. **Prove the Consumer Value to Your Customer.** Use facts to prove the values you claim for your products. Merchandise purchased on the basis of facts usually stays sold because the customer has confidence in it.

3. **Emphasize the Most Suitable Consumer Values.** Stress the values that seem most appropriate to the customer's situation. Compare or contrast the advantages with those of other merchandise.

4. **Follow Your Customer's Lead.** Listen closely to every word your customer says and watch every movement he makes. These indicators let you know what to stress.

5. **Speak with Confidence.** Confidence is catching. State accurate facts in a positive manner without giving the impression that you think you know it all.

6. **Do the Right Amount of Talking.** Not enough talking may cause your customer to think that you lack interest in the sale; too much talking can make him feel that you are more concerned about making a sale than you are in his problem. After pointing up a consumer value, stop and let your customer ask a question. If he does not respond in some way, mention a point in a questioning way. For example, "Did you notice the neat way the trim is tacked on this chair?"

How to Answer Your Customers' Questions

Always answer customers' questions honestly and pleasantly. Questions about your merchandise or store service are indications that your customer is interested and sincere. They enable you to help him reason his way through his buying problem. For this reason you should welcome customer questions and express your appreciation for them. For example, you might say, "I'm glad you mentioned that point," or, "Thank you for calling that to my attention."

Trade Talk

    consumer value   language of
    selling point   gesture

Can You Answer These?

1. What customer services can salespeople perform that impersonal sales media are not able to accomplish satisfactorily?

2. How are each of the five senses used by superior salespeople?

3. Why do some salespeople take too much time in selecting the first merchandise to show their customers?

4. What suggestions can you make for determining what merchandise to show a customer first?

5. Why should a salesperson show only a limited number of articles at one time?

6. What general rules do experienced salespeople follow in deter-

mining what merchandise to show a customer?

7. What can salespeople do to isolate the article being shown from the rest of the merchandise?

8. How does a good salesperson create the impression of value through the way he handles the merchandise?

9. What is the function of the language of gesture in selling?

10. Why should a salesperson get his customer to participate in demonstrating merchandise?

11. How does a good salesperson make use of his hands?

12. How does a good salesperson explain consumer values?

13. What attitude should the salesperson take toward his customers' questions?

Problems and Projects

1. Select an item of merchandise that you sell or would like to sell. Write the name of the item at the top of a sheet of paper. Under the item name, write, equally spaced, the names of the five senses. Now list as many ways of appealing to each of the senses as you can. As each member reports his appeals to the class, add new ideas to your list.

2. For the same item, make a list of consumer values. After each value, give the facts that prove it.

3. By means of class demonstrations, illustrate how the following merchandise can be handled appreciatively by a retail salesperson: (a) jewelry, (b) fine fabrics, (c) books, (d) any other items of your choice.

4. Based on recent shopping experience, tell exactly how you would feel and what you would do as a customer in the following situations: (a) too little merchandise is shown to you; (b) too much merchandise is shown to you; (c) the salesperson brings out merchandise that is too expensive; (d) the salesperson brings out merchandise that is too cheap; (e) the salesperson gives you information that you know is not true.

5. Describe in detail how the best salesman you know demonstrates his product.

Learning Your Job

1. What phase of helping the customer examine the goods is most difficult for you? Describe on paper a specific case in which you were puzzled regarding what to do. Place your problem along with those of your classmates in a hat or box and conduct a man-on-the-street quiz program.

2. Interview the top salesman in your department or store to find out how he or she judges the amount of merchandise to show a customer. Exchange your findings with those of your classmates.

3. Ask permission to listen in on a sale made by your on-the-job trainer or sponsor or by another co-worker. After making notes on his talk, analyze the number and kind of adjectives used and then substitute better words for the weak ones.

30 *Completing the Sale*

Steve Wilson knew his stock better than anyone in the department. He understood the consumer values of his merchandise, and he charmed customers with his fascinating sales presentations. He was patient, understanding, and well liked by those he served. Steve had all these traits and abilities; but in spite of them, he had a serious problem. Customers whom he thought he "sold" frequently seemed to buy from someone else. It appeared that they could not make up their minds at the time Steve waited on them, and they left saying that they would be back later. Although some of them did return, Steve frequently would see another salesperson closing a sale on which he had spent a great deal of time and effort.

Steve's trouble was that he could not close his sales—and a salesman who cannot close sales is not a salesman at all; he is merely a conversationalist. There are vast differences among salespeople in the percentage of sales completed per customer contact; and the ability to close sales is a major factor affecting this index of sales efficiency.

How to Help Customers Make Decisions

Helping the customer reach a decision to buy is called *closing the sale*. The customer's decision to buy is simply the climax to a series of favorable small decisions concerning the merchandise. When you have skillfully paved the way by helping the customer with minor choices, the decision to buy will not be difficult to obtain.

How to Detect Customer Readiness for a Decision

When the merchandise has been favorably presented, usually your customer will take the article with little hesitation. Some people, however, need help in making decisions. If your customer has shown signs of his approval of a particular article and appears disinterested in further information, the time for you to suggest making the final choice has arrived. You should try to close the sale when you feel that: (1) sufficient merchandise has been shown to enable your customer to make a satisfactory selection; (2) all serious objections have been met to the customer's satisfaction; and (3) the customer's frame of mind is one of approval.

Don't be afraid to ask your customer for his final choice. Many sales have been lost because salespeople continue to talk when they should have closed the sale.

When to Stop Showing Additional Merchandise

Learning to watch customers, rather than the merchandise, will help you acquire a sort of intuition about when a customer is ready to make up his mind. Here are some of the clues to watch for that will help you determine when to stop showing additional merchandise.

1. When the customer looks pleased with some article and does not seem to be looking for more, ask for a decision.
2. When your customer keeps looking about and lets his eyes wander over the counters as if he hoped to see something more suitable, show additional merchandise.
3. When your customer appears restless and annoyed if anything else is brought out after he has shown interest in an article, try for a decision.
4. The instant that your customer begins to show signs of confusion, it is time to stop bringing out goods.
5. After all suitable styles or models have been shown, it is wise to tell the customer so. He may then become interested in something that he has already been shown, because he feels that he has seen everything.

How to Help Customers Narrow Their Choices

A knowledge of how to help customers narrow their choices of articles would have helped one high school part-time salesperson. One day while selling men's sweaters, he had spent 45 minutes showing many styles to a customer and finally the choices had been narrowed to two sweaters. At this point, the young salesman suggested in desperation that the customer buy both of them. The customer agreed that this was a good idea and decided that he would like to take one with him and place the other on a lay-a-way order. At this point, the young salesman asked the customer which sweater he wanted to take with him; and the customer took another 20 minutes to make up his mind.

Situations such as the above can be avoided by following procedures recommended by leading salespeople:

1. *Focus Attention on Suitable Articles.* When you see that the customer is inclined even slightly toward a suitable article, it is time to begin to call his attention to its advantages for his particular need.

2. *Remove Articles in Which Little Interest Is Shown.* Articles that have not seemed to interest the customer should be put away quietly or laid to one side. If one that interests the customer has been removed, he will probably ask to see it again. Putting away merchandise must be done carefully, however, to avoid seeming to hurry your customer.

3. *Offer Your Opinion.* When the customer asks for your opinion, give it without hesitation and state your reason from the customer's point of view. For example, the young sweater salesman might have said, "I think that this one is more suitable because it brings out the color in your complexion." Sometimes it is wise to ask permission to give an opinion. The customer should always feel that he is making his own decisions.

4. *Review the Consumer Values.* When it appears that any of several articles will meet your customer's need equally well, point up the consumer values of the article the customer seems to prefer and prove your points. For example, say, "You might like the wider lawn mower better because it reduces the time needed to cut a lawn." Reminding a customer in this way of the benefits he will receive from a particular product aids him in recalling the facts about it and helps him to organize them in his mind so that he can come to a decision.

How to Build Good Will After the Sale Is Made

The first few moments after the customer receives his goods or change usually offer the salesperson one of the best opportunities to build good will. Even though making the sale may have been hard work and the temptation is to relax or to hurry on with other work, high-producing salespeople keep right on selling. They make certain that they leave favorable lasting impressions on their customers. Here are some postsale activities they carry out:

Show Sincere Gratitude

Expressing appreciation for a sale is one activity that beginners can perform as well as experienced workers. When a salesperson says sincerely, "I enjoyed serving you," or "I appreciate your business," the customer usually feels that his business is appreciated. Continued interest in a customer and his buying problems, after there is no longer any apparent personal gain for you, testifies that you are sincerely interested in your customer's welfare.

Give Extra Service

Do little things beyond the call of duty, such as wrapping small packages into a convenient bundle, or escorting the customer to another department where he wants to shop. These extras take little time and contribute to the development of repeat sales.

Inquire About Previous Purchases

When you ask a customer about a previous purchase, it shows you are interested in your customer's satisfaction with the merchandise. For example, a question such as, "Is your daughter pleased with the sweater you bought her last month?" indicates genuine interest in the customer's welfare. In addition, your customer's answer may result in your getting some excellent product information for use in future sales.

Use Friendly Conversation

Casual conversation, sometimes referred to as *small talk,* is a characteristic of American congeniality. Weather may be a trite subject, but it is customary to

Friendly conversation and interest help to make a sale.

Courtesy Eastman Kodak Co.

talk about it. In effect, what you are saying when you talk about the weather is, "Feel at home. We are glad to have you with us." Other matters of local interest sometimes make good casual conversation too—for example, sports, school, and holidays.

Pay Discreet Compliments

Everyone appreciates a compliment. Even though you are a beginning salesperson, do not hesitate to express your admiration for something pertaining to your customer. People like to hear genuine compliments about their children, their property, their tastes, their judgment, their thoughtfulness, and a hundred other things that concern them. If you are willing to try, you will soon learn how to compliment your customer gracefully.

How to Treat the Customer Who Does Not Buy

It pays to be courteous, even though your customer does not buy. He might return to you if he is unable to purchase goods elsewhere that will meet his needs more adequately than the merchandise you have shown him. A second reason is that courteous treatment of nonpurchasers builds good will for future sales. Successful salespeople offer the following sound advice regarding the treatment of customers who do not buy:

> Tell your customer that you are glad to show him your merchandise and if he doesn't find elsewhere what he wants, you'll be pleased to help him when he returns. Do not leave or turn away too quickly. It may be appropriate to give the customer your name or sales number and ask him to inquire for you. Tell him that you'll be glad to attend to him personally when he returns.

Trade Talk

closing the sale   postsale activities
good will   small talk

Can You Answer These?

1. What conditions should be met before a salesperson tries to close a sale?

2. What clues signal a salesperson to stop displaying additional merchandise?

3. Specifically, what can a salesperson do to help a customer reach the final decision to buy?

4. Why are the things that transpire after the customer makes a decision to buy so important in building good will?

5. In what ways can a salesperson show appreciation for the sale?

6. What extra services can a salesperson provide for his customer after the transaction is completed?

7. Give an illustration of an appropriate compliment.

8. What procedure is recommended for treating customers who do not buy?

Problems and Projects

1. What kind of impression did the salesperson who served you last leave with you? What did he do and say to cause you to feel the way you do?

2. Have you ever experienced difficulty in making a final choice when purchasing something? Name the merchandise and describe the incident. To what do you attribute your difficulty in making up your mind?

3. Using books, notebooks, pencils, or some other articles available in several styles or models, demonstrate how you would help a customer reach a decision. Following the demonstration, discuss your technique with the class.

4. Make a list of two ways of doing each of the following activities without duplicating the examples given in the text. (*a*) Show appreciation for a sale. (*b*) Compliment a customer. (*c*) Show interest in the customer. (*d*) Inquire about a previous purchase. (*e*) Perform an extra service. (*f*) Start some casual conversation.

Learning Your Job

1. Prepare a rating form or check list for closing the sale that is based on the material in this textbook. Arrange to have your on-the-job trainer, co-ordinator, or someone else use the form in rating you while at work.

2. After studying Part 30, write a description of closing and postsale activities for three sales you or one of your co-workers make.

3. Select a postsale activity that appeals to you. Try it out on five customers when appropriate. Report your experiences to your class members.

9. Moving Up the Sales Ladder

Unit 9

Part 31

The Buying Motives

Sales are made in the minds of customers; therefore as a salesperson, you will need to give much thought to how your customers think and why they act as they do. A good salesperson is no mere order taker. He understands people and their desires. He can, therefore, guide them through buying decisions.

Your first step in becoming a salesperson is to learn about buying motives—the desires that cause people to buy. Appealing correctly to customer buying motives is basic to all merchandising, including advertising, display, and all forms of personal selling. Thus, if you are planning on a merchandising career, you will want to give buying motives special attention. Understanding them will enable you to use to better advantage such sales skills as the merchandise approach and suggestion selling; it will also bring to mind additional ways of presenting merchandise to customers and ways of meeting objections and closing sales.

The story is told that Emerson, the great author, and a hired hand were trying to get a year-old calf into a shed. Several times they succeeded in getting the calf up to the door where Emerson would pull on the halter while his helper pushed from behind. Each time the calf would bolt and free itself. The two men were about to give up the task when a milkmaid approached. "Shame on you both for handling that beautiful animal in such a manner," she chided them. "Now if you men will step aside, I'll get the calf into the shed without such rough treatment." And sure enough, she did. She placed her finger in the calf's mouth and, as she backed through the door, the animal began to follow her.

The maid in this story was successful because she understood motivation. She made the calf want to do what she wanted it to do. In similar manner, salespeople must appeal to their customers' buying motives. Thus, an understanding of the real reasons why

197

people buy enables retailers to improve their effectiveness and efficiency in serving customers.

The Basic Motivating Forces

Many forces motivate people—that is, cause them to act as they do. Customer motivation is achieved through the right appeal to buying motives that may be divided into three groups: (1) biological, (2) psychological, and (3) economic.

Biological Motives

Man needs air, food, shelter, and clothing to satisfy his biological needs. Actually man needs very little to keep himself alive, but he wants a great deal. Retailers, therefore, realize that their job is not merely to sell food, clothing, and houses, but rather to sell these on the basis of taste, appearance, comfort, convenience, prestige, and other appeals of a psychological nature.

Psychological Motives

Human beings are social creatures who live and grow and work together. They possess psychological wants that must be satisfied. While the stimulus for biological wants stems from within the body, the stimulus for psychological wants arises from contact with other people. The following grouping of psychological motives is useful to retailers.

1. The desire to be *respected*
2. The desire for *affection*
3. The desire for *security* and *safety*
4. The desire for *convenience* and *pleasure*

The Desire to Be Respected. All of us want to think well of ourselves and would like others to think well of us too. Most of us like to receive special recognition from our associates. There are some who desire to be leaders, and

The salesman, a co-operative student, in trying to make a sale, is appealing to the customer's desire to be respected.

Courtesy Lincoln, Nebraska, Board of Education

a few choose to dominate others. In each case, the basic motivation is the desire to be respected. This is one of the most important buying motives. Making the customer feel important is, therefore, not only good manners and good psychology, but good business practice.

Their desire for respect influences the type of merchandise people purchase. For example, people often select their clothes, automobiles, homes, and recreational equipment to show their good standing. The desire for respect also influences customers' decisions as to whether or not to buy; for, unless they receive courteous, considerate treatment from tactful, interested salespeople, many people will take their business elsewhere.

The desire to be respected is the root of fashion. Many people want the prestige of being "in style." Some want the distinction of being among the first to introduce a new fashion to their social group. Others believe that they might lose the respect of their associates if they fall behind the current fashion.

Dual Nature of the Desire to Be Respected. There are two ways in which people attempt to satisfy their desires for respect—through being distinctive and through imitating others. The method a customer chooses depends on his relationship to the people with whom he associates. Generally speaking, customers are desirous of imitating those whom they consider superior to themselves in wealth, social position, or accomplishment. For example, a young woman may be induced to purchase a certain gown because her favorite movie actress is depicted wearing a similar one. On the other hand, to tell her that another member of her social set has purchased a similar gown would very likely cause her not to buy it.

Expressions such as the following may be used as appeals to the want to be respected.

> "This garment is going to be the outstanding high fashion of the season."
> "Only people who appreciate fine furniture will purchase this table."
> "A study of these books will give you information that few persons possess."
> "As a man, you will be interested in these new mechanical features."
> "This is the kind Mrs. —————— buys."

The Desire for Affection. Throughout the year, people of all ages buy things because of their warm feelings toward others and because they want others to love them. This desire for affection is particularly strong during the Christmas shopping season. Affection for their children influences fathers and mothers to make purchases—often at a sacrifice that they would not be willing to make under any other circumstances. The salesperson of children's books, clothing, toys, or nursery furniture has an excellent opportunity to appeal to the buying motive of affection—an appeal that will bring buying responses limited only by the financial means of the customer. Moreover, if the customer is accompanied by a child, the salesperson can, by showing sincere interest in the child, gain good will for himself and the store. What parent is not flattered by attention shown his children?

The desire for affection also includes the desire to be loved by members of the opposite sex. This buying motive underlies most appeals concerning beauty and youthfulness. Thus, the salesperson who emphasizes the alluring aspects of a garment is attempting to appeal to the desire for affection from the opposite sex.

There are many ways of appealing to the want for affection as illustrated below:

"Here are some cuff links that will make your husband appreciate you more."
"A lasting gift will be remembered for a lifetime."
"This building set will help develop mechanical ability in your boy."
"This dress is very youthful and slenderizing."

The Desire for Safety and Security. The desire to protect life and to be secure is more psychological than biological. People of all ages have this desire, but it is more pronounced after the age of thirty. Most people are vitally concerned about extending their lives and increasing their leisure time. They want to be protected against possible dangers to their physical, domestic, or financial security, and that of their loved ones.

Salespeople who appreciate the importance of the desire for safety and security emphasize health and protection. They are alert to the customer's desire to make life fuller and more enjoyable through freedom from worry. The motive of protection and safety is largely responsible for the demand for sanitary qualities in merchandise, safety devices, and insurance. Some examples of appeals to the want for safety and security are:

"This safety glass will protect you and your family from injury caused by flying glass."
"Smart new luggage provides you with peace of mind."
"This provides the extra margin of safety in an emergency."
"Toys like this keep your little girl off the dangerous streets."
"Being properly dressed frees you from worry and enhances your opportunities to enjoy yourself."

Desire for convenience and ease of operation are important motives in the selection of a vacuum cleaner.

Courtesy E. I. du Pont de Nemours and Co., Inc.

The Desire for Convenience and Pleasure. The desire for convenience and pleasure has intensified since World War II. Among the apparent reasons are: (1) our general prosperity, (2) the disappearance of domestic servants, (3) the increase in the number of women who combine working and keeping house, (4) a decline in the moral feeling that pleasure is a sin, and (5) an increase in the opportunities for pleasure and recreation.

The desire for convenience and the desire for pleasure are so closely related that they cannot be separated satisfactorily. People seek convenience so that they can have more time for pleasure. Actually, pleasure is indirectly the basis of almost all other wants, but here it will be thought of as a simple desire embracing play, comfort, and luxury.

Pleasure and convenience now rank high among the wants of women. Recognizing this is a key to success in today's highly competitive market. For example, women want help in performing their everyday duties; and they demand such things as packaged food mixes, the "instants," frozen foods, many electrical appliances, and detergent laundry products.

The desire for convenience, comfort, and pleasure has stimulated the production of many new products—softer, warmer fabrics of lighter weight, and comfortable clothing, furniture, mattresses, and automobiles. It has caused the creation of drive-ins, shopping centers, banking by mail, and a host of innovations in the operation of businesses. As a salesperson, you will want to know how to make good use of this desire. Here are some sample statements that may be used in retail selling. They are similar in nature to those appearing in the advertisements of household magazines.

> "The richest, longest lasting luster you've ever seen on furniture accomplished without rubbing."
> "Get through with those dishes faster with _____."
> "Note that bite-size piece of candy within the large size candy package."
> "This clothes dryer will free you to have more time with your children."

Economic Motives

Most women like to pride themselves on their thrift and shrewd buying. They give evidence of this in a number of ways. Customers who grew up during the years of the great depression, customers with European cultural patterns, and certain religious and ethnic groups usually are much concerned with thrift; and many of them will shop for hours to locate the best values.

Striking a Bargain. Women still love to find a bargain at a bargain sale. They watch specials and are attracted by markdowns. Many are enticed by premiums and will change stores in order to get trading stamps. Buying things on sale gives some women a sense of satisfaction and pride in their ability to manage a household. It frequently earns for them the approval of husbands and friends.

This housewife checks prices in order to get the most for her money.

Courtesy E. I. du Pont de Nemours and Co., Inc.

Getting the Most for One's Money. Appeals to economy are so often made that they have become commonplace. People no longer accept them at their face value unless the appeals are obviously sincere. Nevertheless, an appeal to the desire to economize is one of the strongest sales weapons. If the salesperson can persuade his customer that he is giving him a good value for his money, the customer is almost certain to purchase the goods being considered. Frequently, women will buy the large-sized package or three cans at one time at a special price in order to get the best value for their money.

You can appeal to economic buying motives in several ways. For example:

This golf bag is a better buy because it will last a lifetime; even if you are caught in the rain it won't be injured." (save money)

"A rug mat will save you money because it makes your rug wear longer." (protect money)

"This shoe polish not only makes your shoes look better but actually makes them wear longer because it keeps the leather pliable." (protect money)

"The large size really gives you three ounces free." (save money)

"You can increase your production of vegetables up to 25 per cent by applying this fertilizer." (make money)

Motives and the Individual

If you would sell Bill Jones
What Bill Jones buys
Then you must see Bill Jones
Through Bill Jones's eyes.

Buying motives are a part of the make-up of people. The important thing is to recognize what they are and be able to effectively appeal to them.

Each Customer's Motives Differ. Buying motives differ as to (1) their presence or absence in an individual, (2) their strength or intensity, (3) their persistence, and (4) the kind of appeal that stimulates them. Thus, the salesperson's job is to find the motives that influence a given customer to buy and then to do his best in interpreting information about the product in terms of these motives. A salesperson should not use the same appeals indiscriminately on all customers. For example, he should not conclude that every customer is economy-minded and is interested in price appeals. Before the salesperson introduces the price appeal, he should try to find out whether some other buying motive has brought the customer to the store. Though price appeal may be important to some customers, it is a secondary motive in many cases.

Human needs and desires vary with geographical location. Perhaps you have noticed the differences in living conditions as you have traveled from city to farm or from one section of a large city to another.

Family attitudes also play an important part in the formation of needs and desires. What is more, even within the same family two members may live by two very different standards. Thus, their motives will differ.

Buying Motives Are Changeable. There are forces at work that exert a strong influence on the formation of our buying motives—forces such as ideals, desires, sentiments and duties. Thus at any given time there is much similarity in our desires. But the social pressures that mold our motives change through the decades. For example, today's thinking is a far cry from the prudish Victorian times and even from the mid-thirties during the great economic depression.

Motives change also with the age and maturity of the individual. Witness the contrast of opinions of your grandparents on thrift with your own, and you will become aware of the differences in values brought about by time.

DONALD C. DAYTON
President of Dayton's, Minneapolis, Minn.

Trade Talk

biological motives

buying motives

economic motives

psychological motives

Can You Answer These?

1. What are the kinds of merchandising activities in which a correct appeal to buying motives is essential?

2. What motive or desire did the maid appeal to in the story of Emerson and the calf?

3. What are the differences in the three kinds of motives?

4. What are the various ways in which a salesperson can appeal to a recognized desire or want of the customer?

5. In what way is fashion based on the "want to be respected"?

6. What appeals can be used to satisfy the want for affection?

7. In what ways can a salesperson appeal to the "desire for safety and security"?

8. What is the relationship between the "want for convenience" and the "want for pleasure"?

9. For what reasons has the desire for convenience and pleasure become very important since World War II?

10. What causes the differences in wants or buying motives among customers?

Problems and Projects

1. Describe how buying motives have changed during the past ten years.

2. Clip ten advertisements at random from magazines of your choice. Underscore with black crayon the appeals to buying motives in each advertisement. Classify the appeal according to buying motives described in this unit.

3. The desire for respect can be satisfied by appeals to be distinctive and appeals to be like others. List at least ten selling sentences that appeal to the desire for respect and indicate which of the two facets of the motive are appealed to.

4. Construct three good questions to ask women shoppers about their opinions on bargain sales. Ask at least four women the questions you have constructed, and report your findings to the class.

5. Debate the proposition: Resolved that customers are primarily interested in price.

Learning Your Job

1. Choose a product sold in your department or in your store. Clip as many different advertisements dealing with this product from magazines, newspapers, catalogues, and brochures as you can find. Underscore with a black crayon the appeals to buying motives. Make a list of good selling sentences that appeal to these motives.

2. Make a collection of clippings of advertisements as in the activity above. Make a list of the appeals used in each advertisement. How do you account for the differences in the appeals used in the different advertisements?

3. Make a list of appeals used in selling a product carried by your store. Ask your training sponsor or supervisor to check the appeals he thinks are most effective in selling this product. Then ask him which kinds of customers he thinks would respond to the chosen appeals.

32 Making the Merchandise Approach Work for You

"May I help you?" "May I help you?" "May I help you?" This is what Mrs. Thompson heard all afternoon, and her answers were always the same, "No thank you, I'm just looking." She was about to call it a day when a display of new fall purses caught her eye. She hesitated, picked up an attractive black calf-skin bag, opened it, and looked inside. At this point she heard a genial voice say, "Isn't that a clever side pocket? It's just the thing for your compact and lipstick. Little things like that certainly help one maintain order, and they also reduce loose-powder damage." "They certainly do," thought Mrs. Thompson, and right after that she purchased one that was just what she had been looking for. Her shopping trip was a success after all.

This shopper, the efficient salesperson who served her, and the store benefited from this experience largely because the sale started with a merchandise approach. Bear in mind that the overworked service approach had failed all afternoon. The *merchandise approach* is the sales technique of addressing a customer, who is already looking at merchandise, with an interesting remark about the product. It capitalizes on the customer's interest in the merchandise.

How the Merchandise Approach Works

One way to learn about how the merchandise approach works is to read and analyze the following anecdote told by a customer. It shows how the characteristics of a good merchandise approach were present in the sale of a hat.

Selling in a bridal salon takes for granted customer interest, but good salesmanship is still required.

Courtesy L. S. Ayres and Co., Indianapolis

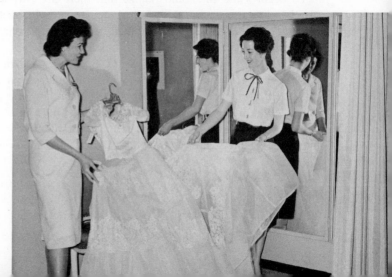

It was late in the afternoon of a hot, sultry August day and the store I was shopping in was closing in a few minutes, said Mrs. Wright * . . . The millinery division was fairly busy with customers picking up last-minute purchases for vacation use, but (1) as I stood looking at a white fabric hat on display (2 & 3) I heard almost immediately a pleasant voice saying, "That hat would be most becoming to you (4) as you are tall enough to wear it well." "Yes, I believe it would," I thought to myself, but aloud I said, "Oh, it's so late—I don't believe I'll try it on today."

(5) "It will take only a minute and it is so obviously your hat, why risk losing the pleasure of wearing it? These summer hats are going very fast." Her manner was courteously interested; there seemed to be no closing-time hurry, no feeling that I would be inconveniencing her by staying. The hat was mine. The salesperson had made it so.

Characteristics of the Merchandise Approach

(1) The customer was showing interest at the time the approach was made.

(2) The salesperson selected a remark that did not disturb the customer's trend of thought.

(3) The salesperson appealed to a buying motive.

(4) The appeal was appropriately individualized.

(5) The remark led directly into the sale.

How to Select Opening Remarks

As much meaning is conveyed by the manner in which words are spoken as by the words themselves. Even the most carefully chosen opening remarks will be ineffective unless the salesperson, through his manner and tone of voice, expresses courtesy and interest in the customer. Keeping these thoughts in mind, we shall examine the selection of opening words for merchandise approaches.

To begin with, we should realize that there are two situations that call for a merchandise approach: (1) when the customer's interest in the merchandise is evident, and (2) when the customer is a *shopper*—one who hunts for values, bargains, and ideas. Each will be discussed separately.

When Customer Interest Is Evident. When a customer shows interest in a specific item, it is wise to use a remark that follows up clues to his interest. For example, a customer who is examining the price tag is likely to be interested in prices; one who is reading a label may be interested in brand names or materials or construction; one who is handling the merchandise probably is interested in the quality of the workmanship and materials. Such clues help the

* Mary F. Wright, *Bloomington Evening World*, Bloomington, Indiana.

This customer is checking the special feature of the collar pointed out by the salesman.

Courtesy E. I. du Pont de Nemours and Co., Inc.

salesperson to choose an interesting bit of information about the merchandise that will fall in line with the customer's thoughts—something that will justify and support his interest in the merchandise. A salesperson might say to a customer who has picked up a hammer and is weighing it, "The built-in balance of that hammer helps reduce fatigue." Note that this remark is simple, directed specifically at the merchandise, and that it appeals to a buying motive.

When the Customer Is a Shopper. Sometimes, when a customer is looking around but seemingly showing no specific interest in any particular merchandise, you may surmise that he is looking for ideas on things to buy, comparing values, or is bargain-hunting. The merchandise approach is appropriate for any of these situations. When serving the "shopper," it is highly important that your remarks arouse curiosity and hold attention, for you do not have the advantage of knowing his specific interests as you do when customer interest is evident. Your opening words should contain a special appeal to a buying motive, and you should quickly transfer your customer's attention from yourself to the merchandise. The customer's attention may be directed to three kinds of merchandise: (1) *popular items*—those that sell faster than other merchandise; (2) *specials*—items designated as outstanding values by your store; and (3) *items with unusual appeals*—new merchandise, products with new features, articles likely to be especially appealing because of style, color, or some other feature.

For example, assume that a building contractor finally pauses at the hammer rack after looking around the department for several minutes. An effective approach would be to unobtrusively take a particular hammer from the rack, hand it to the customer, and say, "The face of this hammer isn't likely to mushroom or chip." Then if the customer shows interest, the salesperson might say, "Note that it is absolutely round, uniformly beveled, and accurately crowned." Very likely this approach would arouse curiosity and hold attention. It would appeal to a buying motive and transfer attention immediately to the merchandise.

To a shopper who pauses at a display of dresses, the salesperson might say, "Did you notice that the new dresses have a higher waistline?" at the same time, taking one from the rack to illustrate the point.

To a "looker" in the swimming-goods section, the salesperson might say, "Our special today is Liberian gum rubber flippers—they're fully serrated."

Sometimes your customer may be interested in the merchandise you mention; other times, he may not. But in either case, your merchandise approach will probably avoid an unfavorable response and often will prompt the customer to tell you what merchandise he wants to see.

What to Avoid in Opening Remarks. Effective opening remarks avoid statements of personal opinion by salespeople. The reason for this is that, if the customer should happen to disagree with an opinion, his attention would be directed to the salesperson instead of to the merchandise. This would create a negative feeling on the part of the customer that would retard the progress of the sale. Neither should an opening remark carry any hint of forcing or soliciting a buying decision from the customer. Instead, the comments or remarks of the salesperson should be based on appeals to buying motives—as the examples given show—and also should be supported with merchandise facts if possible. If questions are used, they should require no commitment from the customer.

Proper Timing of the Merchandise Approach. Proficient salespeople time their approach to the customer's actions. If a customer enters a department hurriedly and seems anxious to buy, he should be approached

The customer looks to the salesperson as the selling expert in the department. One valuable source of merchandise information is the hangtag on the garment. This and other informative labels contain many specific selling points.

briskly as though the salesperson's sole desire is to satisfy him quickly. On the other hand, if a customer comes in and leisurely wanders around, he should be approached in an easy, tranquil way, but with deliberate and unmistakable interest. Conversation with this type of customer should be opened by degrees, so as not to seem to be rushing him.

Why Stores Encourage Use of the Merchandise Approach

Retail management favors the use of the merchandise approach for three reasons:

1. *It Results in Good Will.* Good will is built up because a skillfully executed merchandise approach does not make the customer feel that he must either buy something or leave, as other approaches do. It does not put the customer in a position where he needs to think of some reply to give the salesperson unless he wishes to do so.

2. *It Saves Time.* The merchandise approach saves time for both the salesperson and the customer, because attention is focused immediately on the merchandise. Other approaches often direct attention first to the salesperson (who may be a positive or a negative influence on the sale) rather than to the merchandise.

3. *It Results in a Larger Percentage of Sales per Customer Contact.* Larger sales per customer contact usually result when the merchandise approach is used, because the salesperson is able to pick up valuable sales information early that can be used in helping the customer make a quick and intelligent selection. Almost before the customer is aware of it, he finds himself making buying decisions.

Because retail management recognizes these favorable factors in this selling technique and because the modern open-display method of putting merchandise in bins, on racks, counters, and shelves creates many opportunities to use it, the merchandise approach seems destined for wide use.

Trade Talk

merchandise   shopper
approach   specials
popular item

Can You Answer These?

1. What are the essential elements of a merchandise approach?
2. What clues tell a salesperson about the nature of a customer's interest in merchandise?
3. How do the customer's opening remarks give a clue to his thoughts? Illustrate your answer.

4. What are the three kinds of merchandise that may be the subject of a merchandise approach when the customer is a shopper? Illustrate your answers.
5. What are the things to avoid in making a merchandise approach?
6. How does a good salesperson time the merchandise approach under the various conditions mentioned in the text?
7. How does a good salesperson pace his approach?
8. In what ways does the merchandise approach result in good will?

9. How does the merchandise approach save time for the salesperson and his customers?

10. Why does the merchandise approach result in a larger percentage of sales per customer contact than other approaches?

Problems and Projects

1. Write a description of the opening of a sale in which the merchandise approach is used (*a*) when the customer shows that he is interested in merchandise and, (*b*) when the salesperson judges the customer to be a shopper. Justify your opening statements in the light of each situation.

2. Make a complete check list of factors to be considered in judging the effectiveness of a merchandise approach. Test the check list on a demonstration sale in which the merchandise approach is used.

3. Explain briefly the psychology of the merchandise approach.

4. Using magazine or newspaper advertisements as a source, construct five good opening remarks for merchandise approaches. Repeat the assignment using mail-order catalogue advertising copy as a source.

5. Record three radio or TV commercials and analyze the opening remarks in the light of the discussion of the merchandise approach.

Learning Your Job

1. Ask permission to observe a sale of your sponsor or of a co-worker who uses the merchandise approach. Record the opening sentence. Ask your sponsor or co-worker how he selects opening sentences.

2. Test your ability to use the merchandise approach in your store. Try a merchandise approach on five customers who are looking at merchandise. Record your opening words. Analyze these opening remarks to see what buying motives were appealed to. Reconstruct the remarks in class to obtain the advice of your class members, and repeat the experiment on the job.

3. Clip your store ads dealing with merchandise sold in your department. From them construct merchandise approaches and try these out on your job.

33 *Assisting Your Customers with Suggestions*

Some salespeople are primarily order takers—they wrap packages, take the customer's money, and give him an appreciative smile. Many of them are good customer servants—they are well informed about their stock, know the merits of their products, understand store services, and respectfully and willingly share their knowledge with their customers when called upon to do so. But the real salespeople, those who help raise the American standard of living, who run high sales books and advance to high-paying sales positions, are those who master the power of suggestion. They understand how the human mind works and are able to get in tune with their customers' thoughts. They make appealing, timely suggestions that are gratefully received.

Now that you have been introduced to buying motives, you are ready to explore the fascinating art of suggestion selling. In this part of the unit we shall concern ourselves with three uses of suggestion selling: (1) suggesting additional merchandise, (2) suggesting better quality merchandise, and (3) suggesting substitute merchandise.

The Nature of Suggestion

The Psychology of Suggestion

According to Webster, *suggestion* is "the mental process by which one thought leads to another, especially through association of ideas." In personal selling then, suggestion is the customer's acceptance of an idea from a salesperson that is associated with an idea he already has. Thus, one idea leads to another, forming a link in the thinking process. Conclusions derived from a salesperson's good suggestions frequently are as strong and firm as those made after thoughtful consideration.

There are very good reasons why customers often welcome appropriate suggestions. Many purchases do not warrant the time and effort it takes to think through the buying problem step by step. When a customer reasons his way through a buying problem, it usually takes longer and is more laborious than taking a salesperson's suggestion. Thus, it will be seen that if customers had to think through each purchase, many needs would remain unfilled.

The Acceptability of Suggestions

Sometimes customers accept salespeople's suggestions with enthusiasm, while at other times they resent them. It is important to understand the nature of a suggestion and how it should be presented, so that the percentage of successful ones can be increased. The effectiveness of a suggestion may be attributed to four factors:

1. *The Customer's Need for the Items Suggested.* Unless the customer needs the merchandise, the salesperson's suggestion will be rejected; and he will be better off not to have made it. Because of his training and experience, usually the salesperson is in a position to see clearly what is best suited to his customer's needs. Thus, he can make timely, effective suggestions almost intuitively.

2. *The Customer's Attitude Toward the Salesperson.* If the customer suspects that the salesperson is primarily interested in a sale rather than in the customer's welfare, the suggestion is not likely to be accepted. On the other hand, if the customer believes that the salesperson is sincere and competent,

This customer looks quite pleased with the sales-man's suggestion.

A. Devaney, Inc.

he will accept a reasonable suggestion. Thus, before the salesperson makes a suggestion, he should first gain the customer's confidence.

3. The Amount of Time the Customer Can Spend. When the customer is in a hurry, he is unlikely to accept any suggestion about merchandise that will delay him. Under these circumstances, suggesting anything other than necessities, impulse goods, and staples should not be attempted. Staple items are those for which there is an active, steady demand—such as sugar, nails, and sandpaper.

4. The Way in Which the Suggestion Is Made. It is important that the suggested item be introduced at the appropriate time and that opposing ideas be excluded, so that only one course of action is suggested. For example, a good salesperson would not say, "Would you like some shoe polish?" because the customer might have the opposing idea that he has some on hand. On the other hand, the salesperson might say, "This is the polish that was prepared for these shoes. If you polish them before you wear them, you will be assured of their long-lasting well-groomed appearance."

Suggesting Additional Merchandise (Suggestion Selling)

You will recall that suggesting additional merchandise is really only one form of suggestion selling—other common forms are the suggestion of better quality merchandise and the suggestion of substitutes. In retail circles, however, *suggestion selling* is more commonly identified with selling additional merchandise only.

Benefits from Suggesting Additional Merchandise

Most stores encourage the practice of suggesting additional merchandise for two reasons: (1) it builds good will through improved service to customers; (2) it increases sales and the percentage of profit. Very few stores operate at maximum capacity. Costs, such as rent, heat, light, and advertising, remain the same even though sales volume is increased. Thus, suggestion selling that increases sales volume increases profit. The percentage of profit on the sale of additional items is, in effect, several times greater than on the original purchase as shown in the following example.

Sale 1		Sale 2	
Selling price of item	$1.00	Selling price of 2 items	$2.00
Cost of item	.65	Cost of 2 items	1.30
Gross profit	$ .35	Gross profit	$ .70
Expenses	.30	Expenses	.30
Net profit	$ .05	Net profit	$ .40

This illustration is slightly exaggerated, because it may actually cost the store somewhat more to transact sale number two. Doubling the sale, however, often increases the profit substantially.

Not only does management profit from suggestion sales—so do customers. Most people need merchandise in addition to that for which they came into the store. They appreciate suggestions that will save them from making unnecessary shopping trips and telephone calls to the store. Usually, they are grateful if they are informed about items that are needed for use with the products they purchase. Frequently, they like to know about new products and about opportunities to save money; as a salesperson you should therefore not hesitate to make appropriate suggestions.

How to Choose Suggestion Items

Several of the more important sources from which good salespeople get their ideas on appropriate items to suggest to customers are: (1) listening to and observing customers, (2) mentioning related merchandise, (3) mentioning items that provide savings or economy, (4) mentioning items that provide comfort and convenience, and (5) mentioning items for gifts and special occasions.

Listening to and Observing Your Customer for Clues. You learned in Unit 8 how to find out about a customer's needs and desires by observing him and listening carefully to what he says. Now you should train yourself to look and listen for leads to items for suggestion selling. During the original sale, your customer is likely to reveal additional needs. For example, he may intimate that he is planning a trip, that he plans to have company, or that he has a daughter in high school—all of which might call to your mind his need for additional merchandise. Friendly conversation also frequently reveals customer interests that prove to be leads to suggestible articles. If you sell clothing, you may get clues from observing the style, color, and texture of the garments your customer wears.

Mentioning Related Merchandise. The term, *related merchandise,* sometimes called *companion merchandise,* refers to items logically related to the article originally purchased in any of several ways:

1. They may improve the appearance of the original item—costume jewelry, a scarf, or belt to go with a dress.
2. They may be used with the original article—brushes, turpentine, and sandpaper that are usually sold with paint.
3. They may enhance the value of the original purchase—shoe polish for protecting shoes and a rug mat for adding to the life of a rug.

Perhaps you have noticed that in each kind of related merchandise the relationship resulted in an advantage to the customer. Related merchandise makes a relatively safe suggestion article because the reason for calling it to the customer's attention is obvious.

Mentioning Items That Provide Comfort and Convenience. Buying in larger quantities, such as when purchasing foods, hosiery, and drug items, offers the convenience of having a supply on hand. Salespeople who sell such items usually increase the size of their sales by quoting the price for a quantity of the article, rather than for just one. They make certain to include an appeal to convenience or economy in soliciting a larger order. Some sample sentences are: "You can save time and money by ordering a half dozen." "It's convenient to have a reserve supply and economical too." "Taking several will eliminate that last-minute bridge-prize problem. Would you care for three or four?"

Mentioning Items for Gifts and Special Occasions. Giving of gifts for Christmas, Mother's Day, Valentine's Day, and Easter is based on the desire for affection. Birthdays, weddings, and showers are special occasions that give rise to the same buying motive. Wide-awake salespeople suggest appropriate gifts for these events throughout the year. They use appeals such as, "It's never too early to buy for Christmas" and "Do you have a son who might like to have one of these _____?"

When to Suggest Additional Items

Authorities agree that, except for foods and inexpensive merchandise, it is wise to satisfy the customer's request before suggesting additional items. To suggest the purchase of additional items before the decision to buy is reached may confuse your customer and lose the sale for you. The preferred time to suggest additional goods is just before the purchase is wrapped and paid for while the customer is still in a spending mood. A few minutes after completing a buying chore the customer has a tendency to relax and may not give much attention to further needs.

The salesperson need not always wait until the first sale is completed before introducing the suggestion item. When the suggested article might increase the customer's desire for the original merchandise, it is advisable to introduce it at an appropriate time during the sale. For example, suppose that a customer is examining men's dress shirts. An attractive, appropriate necktie, knotted and laid in position on the shirt, might enrich its appearance and help the customer visualize the shirt in use. In this case, if the customer does not ask for the tie along with the shirt, the salesperson might say, "Buying a shirt and a tie at the same time saves one the trouble of picking out a good combination later on."

How to Suggest Additional Merchandise

Here are three rules that will help you in making suggestions for additional merchandise.

Rule 1. *Give Your Reason Ahead of the Suggestion.* Customers are willing to look at additional merchandise provided there is some advantage for them in doing so. In order to gain a receptive ear, the salesperson should, therefore, give the reason first to pave the way for the introduction of the merchandise. This creates an impression of helpfulness and a willingness to satisfy the customer's needs. For example, in suggesting rug mats, the salesperson might say, "Do you want this rug to last longer and feel softer?"; or in selling flash bulbs, he might say, "Do you like to take pictures indoors?"

Rule 2. *Suggest a Specific Item.* Always suggest a specific article to individualize your suggestion. For example, in calling attention to the need for typewriter cleaning fluid, the salesperson might say, "This cleaning fluid is recommended by the manufacturer for cleaning the type face of the typewriter you have just purchased."—not, "Do you need any type cleaning fluid?" "Will there be anything else?" These are not good suggestion-selling statements.

Rule 3. *Show and Demonstrate the Article.* Often the merchandise will speak for itself. If the article is handed to the customer, his attention is assured and you will have appealed to additional senses. It is usually better to describe the article and state the reason for the suggestion as you are handing it to the customer.

As you are learning the best ways of suggesting additional merchandise, you should be reminded that even the most successful salespeople are unable to close all their suggestion-sales attempts. Many times the customer is not in a position to make a purchase at the time, but returns later for the suggested merchandise. And, of course, the suggestion sometimes does not appeal to the customer.

Suggesting Better Quality Merchandise (Trading-up)

Many customers are willing to buy higher priced merchandise if they believe that the additional value received warrants their doing so. Better quality merchandise is usually a better value for the customer than low-priced goods and can be recommended sincerely. Store management encourages the practice of

-up, because higher priced merchandise usually results in larger profits
ter satisfied customers. The following four keys to trading-up successfully
will help you master this technique.

1. Do not belittle the lower priced merchandise. Remember that your customer may not want the higher priced goods, and you may jeopardize your chances of making any sale at all. Furthermore, disparaging remarks about the requested product imply somewhat that your customer lacks judgment or good taste.
2. Determine the customer's intended use of the product before trying to trade-up. When this is done, you are in a position to help your customer find the best value for his money; also, you reduce the possibility of misjudging the consumer value he seeks.
3. Point out similar features in both products of interest to the customer. This reinforces his judgment and supports his ego.
4. Call your customer's attention to additional features and prove that the merchandise will provide the desired consumer values. (Note that use of the term "additional" does not disparage the lower priced goods, while using the term "superior" does.)

An example of an introductory statement in selling hosiery might be, "Many of my customers believe that this line of _____ is a better buy, dollar for dollar. It has this feature in addition to those in the other brand."

Substitution Selling

Customers usually like to be served quickly, and if you do not have what they ask for, they are often glad to take your suggestion for something to take its place. It is quite possible that you have something in stock that will meet their needs as well as or better than the article called for. Also, there are many times when customers are not sure of what they want. It has been found that salespeople who succeed in making a large percentage of substitute sales follow procedures similar to these:

1. They make a sincere attempt to locate the requested article if the store carries the line of merchandise.
2. They bring out the substitute merchandise.
3. They tell the customer that it is not the requested brand.
4. They inquire about the intended use of the product.
5. They point out the features that are similar to those in the requested article.
6. They point out additional features if the substituted merchandise is of a better grade.

Trade Talk

Can You Answer These?

1. Why is an understanding of the psychology of suggestion so very important in modern merchandising?

2. How does the association of ideas take place in making a suggestion? Give an example.

3. Why do customers welcome appropriate suggestions?

4. In what ways does suggestion selling benefit the customer, the store, and the salesperson?

5. How do proficient salespeople choose items to suggest to their customers?

6. How does a good salesperson choose the proper time to suggest additional merchandise?

7. How would you go about trading-up?

8. How would you go about making a substitution sale?

Problems and Projects

1. Rank in order of importance the factors that determine the effectiveness of a suggestion. Justify your rankings and compare them with those of other members of your class.

2. In the two sales on page 213: (*a*) What is the percentage of increase in net profit? (*b*) In what respect is the case for larger sales overstated? (*c*) What do you estimate to be the actual increase in profit?

3. Make a list of reasons why attempts to suggest additional merchandise fail. Place this list on the chalkboard. Suggest remedies for each cause of failure listed.

4. Prepare demonstrations before the class of the different kinds of selling discussed in this part.

5. Interview your speech, debate, or English teacher on the value and techniques of suggestion. If possible, have a teacher of one of those subjects talk to the class on the power of suggestion.

Learning Your Job

1. Make a list of questions regarding the use of suggestions in personal selling that you would like clarified. Arrange with your job sponsor for a time to get his opinions on these questions. Report your findings to the class.

2. Make suggestions to five customers to purchase additional merchandise and record the following information: (If you do not sell, observe a salesperson.) (*a*) what the customer purchased originally; (*b*) what merchandise you suggested; (*c*) why you chose to suggest that article; (*d*) what you said to introduce the suggested article; (*e*) whether or not the customer purchased the suggested item; (*f*) why you believe the suggestion succeeded or failed.

3. Record and report your specific activities in one sale in which you attempted to trade-up and one sale when you attempted to do substitute selling. Have your fellow class members criticize your activities in the light of the recommendations made in the text.

34 *How Customers Buy*

Few people today have not shopped in a self-service store where they are required to make independent buying decisions—a far cry from the days when the customer expressed a wish and relied on his favorite salesperson to come up with the answer to his buying problem. Being forced to think independently has changed most customers. They have become more self-sufficient and independent. This caused salespeople to change their tactics too. They found it to their advantage to get "in tune" with their customer—determine which buying decisions had already been made and help him with the remaining ones. Thus, today there is more interest than ever before in how customers buy.

The Five Buying Decisions

In studying Unit 7, "Knowing Your Merchandise," we learned that salespeople can be most helpful to customers if they organize their product information according to the customer's probable thinking when making buying decisions. In this unit, we learn that professional salespeople must have a practical understanding of how people buy. They must be able to "talk the customer's language" and to help him with the five major buying decisions that he must make during the course of every purchase.

It will be easy for you to master the five major buying decisions because they are the same decisions you have made many times—perhaps without realizing it. You may wonder why you haven't thought of them before. They are the decisions that answer the following questions:

> *What* do I need? (need decisions)
> *When* shall I buy it? (time decisions)
> *Where* should I get it? (place decisions)
> *Which* one should I choose? (item decisions)
> *How much* should I pay? (price decisions)

Examples of the Five Buying Decisions

The five buying decisions can be illustrated by tracing them through an imaginary buying situation. Suppose that you notice that only a few pages are left in your notebook. Your first thought will probably be, "I need a new notebook." You will then have made your first buying decision—the *need* decision.

Suppose that you then count the pages left in your present notebook and find that there are only three pages left. You reason that they will hardly be enough for tomorrow's class, so you think, "I'll get one after school." You have then made your second buying decision—the *time* decision.

Suppose further that on your way home you will pass through a shopping district where there is a drugstore, a variety store, and a bookstore, all of which sell notebooks. You think, "I'll stop at Gray's Drug Store," because you like to go there. You will then have made your third decision—the *place* decision.

Now suppose that you like the kind of notebook you are presently using, so you make another decision, "I'll get another one like the old one." You then have made the fourth decision—the *item* decision.

Your only remaining decision is easy. The price is the same, so you think, "That'll cost me 35 cents." You will then have made the fifth decision—the *price* decision. Sounds simple, doesn't it?

Omnipresence of the Five Buying Decisions

The imaginary purchase of a notebook is a simple clerk-level transaction, and quite likely you would hardly be aware of making any decisions. Now imagine that you are confronted with buying a class ring. The buying problem probably will be somewhat more complex, but you will need to make the same buying decisions. Failure to make any one of them will result in your not buying the ring. Most of the buying decisions will be more difficult to make, and likely you will be well aware of them.

In buying a ring, the reasoning might be like this:

1. **Need (What?)**	It would look well on my finger, identify me before and after graduation, and my friends would admire it.
2. **Time (When?)**	The sooner I buy it, the more use I'll get from it. Besides I have the money now.
3. **Place (Where?)**	The "X" Company has been selected by a committee, and everyone else is getting rings from them.
4. **Item (Which?)**	Of the three types, the middle size is most becoming to my hand and personality.
5. **Price (How much?)**	I can afford the middle-price ring. It won't cause me financial embarrassment.

Buying an automobile, an insurance policy, or a home is much more difficult because of the greater need for technical information about the product and the market, and because of the consequences of spending a large sum of money.

From these illustrations, you may be safe in concluding that, regardless of the kind of merchandise or service purchased, whether the item is trivial or expensive, and notwithstanding who purchases it, the five buying decisions are always present.

Variations in Buying Procedure

You already realize that the customer's needs for technical information and the size of the expenditure make a great deal of difference in how difficult it is for him to make buying decisions. Two other factors influence buying decisions that concern you as a salesperson: (1) the difference in the sequence in which the decisions are made, and (2) the number of buying decisions the customer has made before you met him.

Variety of Sequences. Nearly always, the need decision is made first; but the other buying decisions are not made in any definite order. For example, a teen-age girl decides that she needs a sweater. She may next decide that she will get it at her favorite specialty shop (place decision); or that she will get one like the style she saw in the window display (item decision); or that she will spend ten dollars for a sweater (price decision); or that she will shop for sweaters on Saturday morning (time decision). The sequence of the buying decisions is partly a matter of habit and partly a matter of circumstances, as you will discover if you reflect on your recent buying experiences.

Variety of Presale Buying Decisions. The number of buying decisions a customer makes before entering the store has much to do with the size of the sales task at hand. For example, in the imaginary sale of a notebook on page 219, all the buying decisions were made before the customer entered the store—the sale was a wrap-up, and the task was easy. Examples of a more difficult sale might be serving a shopper who is "just looking" and in making a suggestion sale. Selling positions that require training and real selling ability involve sales that require the salesman to lead his customer through all five buying decisions.

Usually, all five buying decisions in convenience-goods purchases have been made before the customer enters the store. Most of the buying decisions for shopping goods are made at the point of sale. The fact that salespeople selling shopping goods usually are called upon to help customers with more buying decisions than those selling convenience goods partly explains the difference in pay for different kinds of retail sales occupations.

Directing Your Selling at Missing Decisions

It makes good sense to gear your sales presentation to missing buying decisions and not waste your time—or the customer's—on rehashing old information. Besides, you can easily talk yourself out of a sale by repeating information the customer already knows. Skilled salespeople, therefore, find out as soon as possible which of the five decisions the customer still must make and proceed to help him with them.

Locating Missing Decisions

How do you detect the missing decisions? Either by watching and listening or by asking questions. Usually you will be able to tell from the customer's questions and remarks what major decisions need attention. For example:

Customer's Question or Remark	Missing Decision
I'd like to look at sweaters, but I want to shop around before I buy.	Place
That's a little more than I wanted to spend.	Price
Perhaps I should wait until after payday.	Time
My present car gets me there and back.	Need
Will synthetics wear as long as the natural fibers?	Item

These customer objections provide obvious clues to missing buying decisions. Of course, customers usually reveal other clues to missing decisions through the remarks they make, their actions, and facial expressions throughout the sale. This was discussed in connection with "Finding Your Customer's Needs and Desires" on pages 178 to 182.

Occasionally there are customers who fail to indicate which buying decisions have been made or which questions remain to be answered. Then, a skillful salesperson tactfully asks questions to get clues on decisions needing attention. Examples of such questions are:

Salesperson's Questions	Missing Decision
It would be difficult to get along without a _____, wouldn't it?	Need
Do you think that these shoes would be suitable for your kind of work?	Item
Do you think that this price line offers the best value for the use you have in mind?	Price
Wouldn't it be a good idea to make your selection while there is an adequate assortment from which to choose?	Time
Are you familiar with the (name of store) policy of backing its merchandise with a guarantee of satisfaction?	Place

Satisfying the Missing Buying Decisions

Now that you understand the major buying decisions, you can avoid the usual hit-or-miss sales presentation and concentrate on definite goals—the missing decisions. In applying the buying-decision technique, you will soon find that it is not always possible to deal with one decision exclusively at a time, particularly if your customer likes to dominate. When two or more decisions remain to be made, there is apt to be interplay among them. You will soon learn to cope with several decisions at the same time. When you master the system, you

RICHARD W. SEARS, 1863–1914
Founder of the mail-order house Sears, Roebuck and Co., Chicago, Ill.

will be able to help your customer concentrate on missing decisions one at a time.

Henceforth, your customers' remarks will carry new significance for you. Form the habit of weighing each comment in terms of missing or completed buying decisions. A single comment, particularly one that is made early in the sale, cannot always be considered a safe and certain indication of a buying decision. Sometimes customers' remarks are merely excuses that cover up real reasons. Occasionally, customers waver in their thinking; and a buying decision you thought was clinched must be approached again. The customer's remarks, however, are usually sincere and accurate, and you will want to concentrate on missing decisions. In so doing, you will save the time wasted by untrained salespeople in trying to win decisions the customer has already made. Each action you take will be a step forward.

Trade Talk

item decision   price decision
need decision   time decision
place decision

Can You Answer These?

1. What is the reason for the current interest in how customers buy?
2. What customer questions do the five buying decisions answer?
3. Explain the fact that buying decisions are present in all completed sales.
4. How do customer buying procedures differ?
5. How do customers reveal missing buying decisions?
6. What should the salesperson do if the customer fails to reveal the missing buying decisions?
7. What sales procedure should a salesperson follow in applying the five buying decisions?

Problems and Projects

1. Analyze the purchase of a sweater similar to the way your textbook analyzes the sale of a ring on page 219. Under each of the five buying decisions, list the questions you would need to answer before the purchase was made.

2. From the standpoint of the five buying decisions, compare the amount of assistance needed by the average customer in purchasing the following items. Place them in three categories: little assistance, average assistance, and much assistance. (*a*) groceries, (*b*) men's clothing, (*c*) cosmetics, (*d*) insurance, (*e*) electrical appliances, (*f*) lingerie, (*g*) auto accessories, (*h*) tobacco, (*i*) watches, (*j*) furniture, (*k*) notions, (*l*) sporting goods.

3. List at least three objections customers commonly make for each of the five buying decisions. State how you would answer each objection. See customer questions on page 221.

4. For each of the five buying decisions, list at least three questions you might ask customers to determine whether or not the decision has been made. See salesperson's questions on page 221.

5. Demonstrate the selling of an item of your choice. Have your classmates criticize the way in which you used the five buying decisions.

Learning Your Job

1. Make a written report on a sale in which you use the five buying decisions technique. State how you located the missing decisions and what you did and said to help your customer with the missing decisions.

2. For each of the five buying decisions, make a list of the questions you might ask customers in order to locate the missing decisions for items in your department.

10. Becoming a Consumer Consultant

Sale 9.99

GET IT AT

the costume

METAL MAGIC

NEW D'

HUG

s a rich girl. Go to the rescue with smart clothes at ng goil to deny herself high fashion, when to the rescue with smart clothes at if you're loaded with taste, but not wit, s. If you're loaded with taste, and walk out looking like a mil

NEW RONA

Customers are people who
Come to buy their needs from you.
They are fair to see or plain
Not like links within a chain,
All alike, but different very,
Some are solemn, some are merry,
Some with sorrows great are freighted,
Some are quickly irritated.
But the cross ones and the sunny
Come to you to spend their money.

Looking at them as they come,
Happy face or visage glum,
As before your wares they tarry
You can't tell what hurts they carry,
What makes this one seem so swanky,
Or why that one is so cranky,
Or from cut of coat or tie
Just how much they want to buy
Sometimes those who look the poorest
Are the ones whose pay is surest.

Customers are people who
Long remember what you do.
If a sneer your face has crossed,
As a salesman you have lost,
If you think you have a right to
Pick the ones you'll be polite to,
Soon you'll find to your dismay
You've let business get away.
Never mind your whims and fancies,
Give your best and take no chances.

EDGAR A. GUEST

In this poem, the poet Edgar Guest expresses the point of view of professional salespeople—those who believe that salesmanship is an important personal service, custom-tailored to the needs and desires of customers, no two of whom are alike. In order to deliver professional customer service, the salesperson must continuously study customer similarities and differences.

Part 35

Analyzing the Sales Load— The Sales Variables

Ted Smith's first selling job was in a drugstore as a soda-fountain clerk. He was soon permitted to sell throughout the store. After about a year, his family moved to a large city and because of his sales experience Ted was offered a position in a department store selling men's furnishings—shirts, ties, underwear, and the like. Within six months, he was elevated to the sportswear department where he sold slacks, robes, and swim wear. Some time later, young Smith was promoted to the men's clothing department.

This sketch of Ted Smith's progress illustrates a point. Each position was a step up the ladder, because it called for more sales responsibility. Why are some kinds of sales more difficult than others? Why are some sales difficult, while others are easy? Is it the customer? the merchandise? the way you feel? Even in selling the same item on the same day, there may be striking differences.

Factors in the Sales Load

Many factors enter into what may be called the *sales load,* the amount of selling effort required to make a sale. The amount of customer assistance required for a given sale depends on many things called "sales variables" which may be grouped under (1) the product, (2) the store, (3) the competition, (4) the salesperson, and (5) the customer. Understanding the *sales variables,* factors contributing to the difficulty of a sale, helps the salesperson in adapting his sales presentation to his customer.

Benefits from Understanding the Sales Variables. When you understand the sales variables, you will be in a good position to size up a sales load. As a result, you should: (1) be able to do a better job of planning sales presentations, (2) have a clearer idea of the relative position of the various occupations in the retail sales hierarchy, (3) know what kinds of jobs may be considered advancements over others, (4) have a better understanding of the relationship of your job to other sales positions, (5) be able to decide what sales practices are best suited to the kind of selling you do, and (6) have a better understanding of the reasons for differences in remuneration for sales occupations.

Variable Group 1: The Product

The first sales variable is the nature of the product. Obviously, it is more difficult to sell an adding machine than a box of breakfast cereal. The adding machine is an example of *business goods,* products usually used in the operation of a business. Breakfast cereal is an example of *consumer goods,* products used by ultimate consumers. The purchasers of these two kinds of goods buy for entirely different reasons—one to improve business efficiency, the other for personal satisfaction. Business goods are usually purchased by trained, cautious buyers who, as compared to consumer-purchasers, strike a hard bargain.

Within the consumer-goods classification, there are convenience goods, shopping goods, and specialty goods. The nature of these goods was described in Unit 7 on pages 147–148 along with the need for the salesperson's having product information about them.

Another consideration in exploring the sales variables as these relate to the product is the classification of merchandise lines into "hard lines, soft lines, and foods." Durable goods—such as hardware, appliances, furniture, and electrical supplies—make up the *hard lines.* Textile merchandise—such as ready-to-wear, fabrics and domestics, along with shoes—is known as *soft-lines* merchandise. Dry groceries, produce, meats, dairy and bakery products are examples of *food-line* merchandise. Soft lines and foods are considered to be nondurable goods. Each kind of merchandise has its characteristic sales practices that influence the weight of the sales load.

In retailing, the need for technical product information plays an important part in determining the sales load. For example, the electric-appliance salesman needs a great deal more technical product knowledge than does the person selling hand tools; and consequently he usually receives more remuneration. Another product variable closely associated with technical information is the amount of knowledge needed concerning the product's installation—floor tile, for example—and servicing of the product, such as the maintenance of office machines.

Thus, it will be seen that the product is a variable in the sales load and that the factors in this variable are whether it is (1) consumer or business goods, (2) convenience, shopping, or specialty goods, (3) a hard line, soft line, or food product, and (4) the amount of technical information required about the product, its installation, and service needed.

Variable Group 2: The Store

The second sales variable is the store management's concepts of what constitutes good salesmanship. Management's beliefs are far from uniform—and for good reasons. Each store management advocates the sales practices that it believes appeal most to its clientele. Some favor an appeal to the customer's reason or common sense, while others prefer an emotional sales appeal. There are those who believe in *hard sell,* the use of strong persuasion. Others advocate *soft sell,* limiting sales effort to furnishing requested information. In actual practice, there are a number of points of view between these positions.

In promotional-type stores, selling costs are usually held to a bare minimum. Rapid sales and large volume per salesperson are strongly encouraged. On the contrary, in prestige-type stores and neighborhood stores, salespeople are usually expected to spend more time with customers, thus increasing selling costs.

Methods of compensating sales personnel have a bearing on sales practices. Salaries, commissions, quotas, and bonuses have a direct influence on customer treatment. They may encourage or discourage the development of a salesperson's personal customer following. This factor is particularly important when all persons in the department are not paid on the same basis.

There is considerable difference among stores in the amount of assistance salespeople get from other sales media, such as advertising and display. For example, sometimes good advertising and display do the entire selling job with the exception of making the actual sales transaction. On the other hand, in some situations the salesperson must introduce the product to a prospective customer for the first time.

It may be concluded that the policies of the store with regard to merchandising practices, management's concept of salesmanship, methods of compensation, and allocation of selling functions, all have an important bearing on sales techniques and on the sales load.

Variable Group 3: The Competition

Another important variable in the sales load is the type of competition the store and the salesperson face. For example, when competition is keen, sales efforts are intensified and innovations in sales practices appear. Competitors feel forced to match their sales practices with those of other stores, and a sort of duel develops. On the other hand, when there is little or weak competition, selling is much easier.

Some trade associations have developed codes of ethics in an effort to upgrade sales practices. Some groups have succeeded in getting legislation to control competitive practices. Better Business Bureaus have used various means to protect merchant and consumer alike. Still, great differences exist in sales policies and practices. The closer the competitive stores are to each other, and the greater their number, the heavier the sales load is likely to be.

The demand for the goods on the part of the customers is a sales variable that influences the sales load. In times of scarcity of goods, such as during war periods, we experience a *sellers market,* one in which goods are scarce and demand is high. Normally, however, there is a *buyers market,* one in which the supply of goods is adequate for the demand. During a sellers market, little salesmanship seems necessary. It was said of the period beginning with World War II and extending to the middle of the 1950's that we lost a generation of salesmen because real sales effort did not seem to be required.

A more personal problem facing the student salesperson is that which arises from competition with his co-workers. Such competition from fellow salespeople or lack of it may be a considerable factor in the sales load. In some stores, salespeople compete vigorously for sales, while in others, the salesperson who dares to sell more than the group-formulated quota is labeled a "sales-grabber" and is chastised in one way or another by his fellow workers. In some firms, the more experienced salespeople develop a personal following made up of the more profitable customers; and they lay claim to them. This causes some additional problems for the novice salesperson. These and many other factors relating to competition make a considerable difference in the sales load.

Variable Group 4: The Salesperson

The salesperson himself is a sales variable, because he is not the same from day to day, or even from sales contact to sales contact. For example, there are days when it seems that nothing goes right—his co-workers say that he got up on the wrong side of the bed. On such occasions, the salesperson needs to overcome his own mood, a factor that makes selling more difficult. Time of day may be a factor. The fact that the previous sale was a very trying one may temporarily disturb the salesperson's emotional balance. Regardless of cause, the way the salesperson feels influences the weight of the sales load.

Even when his emotional condition is normal, the salesperson is a sales variable because his relationship to his customer is different in nearly every sale. For example, he may feel unkindly toward people from a certain section of town. He may be attracted more to some individuals than to others. Or he may feel inadequate when selling a product about which he is not well informed.

Another factor in the sales load, which may be attributed to the salesperson, is his background of experience and education. For example, a salesperson with

It takes an understanding saleswoman to make a shy customer feel at ease.

Courtesy National Cash Register Co.

little formal schooling might feel awkward when serving a customer who is a member of a college faculty. Or a city-born salesman may be handicapped for a while in dealing with farm trade.

Thus, in planning the sales load, the salesperson should consider himself— the way he feels, his attitudes toward particular customers, and his background of experience and education.

Variable Group 5: The Customer

The customer is one of the most important variables in determining the sales load. Some of the reasons for variation may be attributed to the situation in which the customer is placed, and others are brought about by individual differences among customers.

Differences Due to Sales Situations. Four of the more important differences in sales situations that are caused by customers are (1) the amount of time the customer has to spend, (2) the number of sales contacts made in shopping for an article, (3) the number of people making the purchase, and (4) whether or not the buyer is a professional purchaser.

Usually the customer with a limited amount of shopping time makes buying decisions quickly. Men seem to shop faster than women. Sales near closing time are frequently completed more quickly than those made in the mid-afternoon. Lunch-hour sales often take little time. When buying decisions are rapidly made, sales presentations should be correspondingly rapid and efficient.

Some customers make it a point to shop several stores before buying and consequently clarify (or clutter) their thinking before reaching the salesperson. When the merchandise being considered is a repeat sale or when the transaction involves a steady customer, the salesperson's load is usually lightened.

When a number of persons participate in a single buying transaction, this usually adds to the sales load, particularly for the novice salesperson. Lack of agreement concerning buying motives among group members may prolong decisions. On the other hand, two or more buyers may speed up the sale if the will of one clearly prevails.

In some instances, the sales load is greater when selling to the professional buyer. Certainly more sales information is needed, but also the purchaser is better informed and in a position to understand and appreciate good product information.

Differences in Individual Customers. Books have been written about individual differences in customers, and it is not possible to delve very deeply into this subject here. However, personal selling exists for the purpose of serving individuals; and some of the more important differences in customers should be discussed.

Whenever a customer and a salesperson meet, a relationship is created. The customer may feel (*a*) superior to the salesperson, (*b*) equal to the salesperson, or (*c*) inferior to the salesperson who, in turn, has developed also a feeling toward the customer. Whenever the customer feels inferior and the salesperson feels superior, the sale is usually easy. On the other hand, when the customer feels superior and the salesperson feels equal or inferior, the sales load is greatly increased.

Another factor affecting the sales load is the way customers think and reach decisions. The amount of time needed to help one customer may be double, triple, or even quadruple that required to help another. The customer's thinking pattern and the speed with which he makes decisions may differ from time to time and with the purchase of different products, depending on his experience with these products, his mental alertness, physical condition, and other factors.

The number of buying motives that influence a given customer and their intensity are sales variables that influence the sales load. A person may buy for very logical reasons one time and for emotional reasons at another time.

Individual differences among customers have caused salespeople to speak of them as belonging to a certain class—looker, silent, sophisticated, and talkative. While it is not sound practice to label customers as belonging consistently to a particular class, each customer has traits that influence his behavior at a given time. Customers may at different times be

This customer is inquiring about technical information and store service policies from the salesperson.

Undecided	Patient	Dignified
Impatient	Talkative	Doubtful
Well-informed	"Knows-it-all"	Silent
Fussy	"Just looking"	Curious
Grouchy	Argumentative	Happy
Timid	Cheerful	Preoccupied

As the customer-sensitive salesperson gains experience, he becomes familiar with his customer's drives, interests, and thought patterns and is able to adjust to his ways of thinking.

Trade Talk

business goods	sales variables
buyers market	sellers market
consumer goods	soft lines
hard sell	soft sell
sales load	hard lines

Can You Answer These?

1. What are the product variables? How do they influence the sales load?

2. How do the policies of the store influence the sales load?

3. How does competition affect the sales load?

4. In what ways is the salesperson a factor in determining the sales load?

5. From the standpoint of selling, what are the differences in customers that affect the sales load?

6. What are the differences in sales situations that affect the size of the sales task?

7. What are the benefits that may be derived from an understanding of the sales variables?

Problems and Projects

1. From your experience as a customer or salesperson, write a criticism of the poem on page 225.

2. Leaf through the yellow pages of a telephone directory. Classify the products listed on a number of the pages as to business or consumer goods; and hard lines, soft lines, or foods. Rank the products according to your concept of the effort required to sell them.

3. Make a chart or poster showing the groups of variables in the retail sales load. Include as many different kinds of variables in each group as you can.

4. Rank the sales situations arising from customer differences described on pages 229 to 230 according to their sales difficulty.

Learning Your Job

1. Make a list of your strengths and shortcomings as a salesperson. What kinds of merchandise do you seem best prepared to sell now? Do you think that in the future this list may change? Why?

2. Rank the five groups of variables in order of importance for the kind of products you sell. Explain the reasons for your ranking.

3. After reading the text material on management's concept of good salesmanship, describe on paper what you believe to be the beliefs of your store management with regard to salesmanship.

4. On the basis of the five groups of sales variables, compare on paper the sales load involved in three of your recent sales.

36 *Sales Resistance Is Natural*

Recall one of your own experiences in buying. Perhaps you anticipated the pleasure from your intended purchase. You may have given a great deal of thought to its selection, saving for it a long time. After finding what you wanted, you learned that it cost more than you planned to pay, so you hesitated, stalling for time to think through your problem; or you may have told the salesperson directly how you felt.

From your experience as a customer in situations like this, you will realize that resistance to buying usually is a natural situation in which many people find themselves. Good salespeople understand that customers often raise objections to justify in their own minds the purchase of an article. They are prepared to meet sales resistance with sympathetic understanding.

Kinds of Sales Resistance

Customers differ in the ways they reveal and conceal their buying resistance. Some are straightforward in expressing their feelings and come directly to the point that concerns them most. For example, a customer might say, "I can get it cheaper at Smith's" or "I don't like the color." This kind of resistance is called a *sincere objection.*

Many customers refuse to reveal their true objections—some because of pride; some because they are timid; and others because they want to elicit good reasons for making the purchase. A few even like to test the salesperson to see whether he knows his product and can be depended on to help them. Whatever the reason, evasion of the real objection is called an *excuse.*

There are a few customers who do not seem to reveal their thoughts at all. Usually, they are referred to by salespeople as "silent-type" customers. Generally, not "registering" their feelings is a part of their personalities.

Dealing with Sincere Objections

A good salesperson rarely side-steps a sincere objection. He is grateful to his customer for being sincere and for the opportunity to help him answer questions that lead to a wise purchase. Sincere objections reveal the customer's desire to have you show him a buying advantage, or to help fill in a missing buying decision. They are signals as to how to proceed with the sale.

A good salesperson never flatly contradicts a customer. There are definite ways of tactfully and effectively meeting objections. Through use of the following

Saleswomen must know how to handle a customer's objections.

Courtesy National Cash Register Co.

methods, you can meet customer objections without offending your customer and still keep the sale moving.

1. *Turning Objections into Selling Points.* This method consists of taking the customer's own statement and turning it back as a selling point, a reason for buying. An example of the application of this method is the following:

CUSTOMER: But this color is so bright.

SALESPERSON: That is the very reason why this article is to be desired at this time. The newest spring styles all show bright colors. When you wear this coat, it will be evident that your purchase has been made recently.

2. *Agreeing with the Customer and Presenting Another Angle.* This method is commonly referred to as the "Agree, but" or "Yes, but" method. It indicates that the salesperson apparently agrees with the customer's objection but interprets it in another way.

CUSTOMER: These shoes are so light that I do not believe they will wear well.

SALESPERSON: Yes, these shoes are made in a light weight, so that they will be comfortable on your feet. The leather that has been used in their manufacture is an especially strong, thin leather that wears better than most grades of heavy leather.

3. *Requesting the Customer to Explain the Objection.* When a customer has raised an objection, it is sometimes well to request him to explain his point still further. To a certain extent, this method places him on the defensive and often, in the attempt to explain, he answers his own objection or else shows that it is not a serious one. This method may be illustrated by the following example:

CUSTOMER: This washing machine will very likely injure our clothes.

SALESPERSON: We are always glad to obtain the opinions of our customers on the products we carry. I would appreciate your telling me why you think this machine will injure clothes.

4. *Admitting the Objection and Giving a Superior Point.* By this method, the salesperson concedes the correctness of the objection raised by the prospect, but at the same time points out advantages of the product that more than offset the disadvantages. An example of this method is the following:

CUSTOMER: This mattress seems rather bulky. I am afraid that it will be hard to handle.

SALESPERSON: Your point is well taken. The mattress is bulkier than others we carry in stock. You must consider, however, that the manufacturer has made it larger and heavier in order to improve its wearing qualities as well as its sleeping qualities. A full set of springs is built into each mattress. We have sold this type for several years, and our customers have been well satisfied.

5. *Asking a Question That When Answered Overcomes the Objection.* In this method, the customer answers his own objection when giving the answer to the salesperson's question. For example:

CUSTOMER: I do not believe that the action of the keys on the typewriter you are showing me is as smooth and easy as that of another make I have looked at.

SALESPERSON: Do you believe that the use of a ball bearing in a typewriter will insure better key action than the use of a plain bearing in which the friction is greater?

CUSTOMER: Yes, I believe so.

SALESPERSON: Do you know that our machine is the only one on the market that is equipped with ball bearings at the point where the action of the keys is greatest?

Dealing with Excuses

Most customers hesitate to buy because they have not completed all five buying decisions; others are the type who like to put things off. Some purchasers make rather trivial, obvious excuses that are immediately recognized as stalls; others are clever in covering up their real objections. Regardless of cause or method, after the resistance is revealed, the salesperson's job is to treat the customer courteously and probe for the real objection.

Experienced salespeople can detect excuses. They do not ignore them but deal with them tactfully, at the same time proceeding with their search for the real objection. For example,

When a customer says, "I'm only shopping for a friend," the salesperson may say, "If your friend trusts your judgment, why not try this model. Don't you think that it is a good value for the money?"

When a customer says, "I'm just shopping around," the salesperson may say, "Certainly, that's the best way to become familiar with our selection. Isn't this an excellent assortment from which to choose?"

When a customer says, "I want my wife to see it before I decide," the salesperson may say, "Certainly, that's reasonable. Does she prefer the table model to the cabinet style?"

You will note that, in side-stepping the excuses above, the salesperson also attempted to find the customer's real objection. He followed each acknowledgment of the excuse with a question concerning a buying decision—in these situations price, source, and item—in trying to uncover the true objection. Suppose that in the first illustration the customer had answered, "Yes, these are wonderful values, but I really had something a little less expensive in mind." It would be evident that the price decision had not been made, and the salesperson would have to work on that buying decision. Thus, the real objection usually reveals itself as a result of the salesperson's question or comes to light as the sale proceeds. The customer may state it directly, or the salesperson may detect it from his remarks and actions.

Dealing with Silent Resistance

"Silent-type" customers puzzle and sometimes vex the novice, but good, experienced salespeople take them in stride. They treat this kind of customer in a friendly way and present merchandise in much the same manner as in serving other customers. When it becomes apparent that there is unexpressed resistance to buying, seasoned salespeople probe for the underlying objection. They frequently use a *commitment question,* one that, when answered, commits the customer regarding his opinion. For example, "You agree that this is the right season of the year to buy a station wagon, don't you, Mr. Jones?" or "Would the tan or eggshell be the better color for your needs?" Thus without embarrassing or harassing the customer, they pleasantly pursue one buying decision after another until they find the troublesome one.

Ways of Controlling Sales Resistance

There are three basic ways of coping with sales resistance: (1) prevent it; (2) anticipate it; and (3) meet it when it is revealed.

Preventing Sales Resistance. Some salespeople do such a good job of selling that they answer most of the customer's questions concerning his buying decisions in a friendly manner as the purchase progresses. Thus, resistance to buying is at a minimum. This is the best way to deal with sales resistance, because too many objections tend to place the customer in a negative frame of mind. Once the customer states an objection, he feels that he must defend it; and unless it is properly handled, it grows in his mind. Many objections also focus attention on the less desirable merchandise features and often prolong the sale.

Anticipating Objections. Foreseeing and acting on an objection before the customer raises it—anticipating an objection—minimizes the importance

J. L. HUDSON, 1846–1912
Founder of the J. L. Hudson
Company, Detroit, Mich.

of unexpressed objections and builds the customer's confidence in the salesperson's ability to understand and cope with his problem. Anticipating objections is particularly important in educating customers, who are old users of a product, to accept a redesigned model or in selling high-priced merchandise to new users.

Alert salespeople soon discover the common objections to a product and dispose of them easily. For example, a stationery-department salesperson finds that most customers object to the way a particular brand of pen is filled. He knows that the pen is superior for many purposes, but that this feature interferes with its sales; he, therefore, disposes of the objection concerning the filling feature early. Thus, the way is cleared for the treatment of positive selling points.

The following example illustrates an effective way of anticipating the price objection.

> Very attractive, isn't it? This manufacturer's chairs sell for as high as $400. Our buyer was able to make a special purchase for this event enabling us to sell this chair for $198. It's something you'd treasure for many years. Please sit down in it and see how comfortable it is.

Thus the salesperson skillfully anticipated the customer's objection without being apologetic.

Naturally, the salesperson must use good judgment when anticipating objections, in order to avoid introducing negative ideas unnecessarily into the sale.

Meeting Expressed Resistance. It is virtually impossible for a store to stock a large enough assortment of items to meet all customers' needs within a given line of merchandise. Consequently, even the best salespeople encounter expressed sales resistance. The first step in dealing with it is to recognize it for what it is—identify it as an excuse or a sincere objection. Then it is treated as described above.

Skill in Meeting Sales Resistance

You are now familiar with the more common methods of meeting objections. Your success in using them will depend on (1) your judgment as to when to apply them, (2) your attitude toward your customer when you apply them, and (3) your skill in performing the procedure.

Always remember that the customer may be right in his objection. If this is the case, it is not wise to try to convince him against his will. Remember, too, that unless your attitude is one of understanding, friendliness, and sympathy for the customer's problem, your intentions will show through and you are not likely to succeed, regardless of how hard you try to persuade him.

What you say is important, but how you say it is even more so. Care must be taken to avoid the impression of being sharp with a customer. It is wise to point out that you understand your customer's point of view with such statements as:

"I'm glad you brought that point to my attention."
"Many customers have thought as you do."
"It's easy to understand why you feel as you do."
"It's perfectly natural to feel that way."

Thus, you appeal to the customer's sense of fairness, avoid an argument, and clear the way for the rest of the sale. If you know your product information well, you're bound to know a great deal more about your merchandise than your customer usually does.

After meeting an objection, it is important to point out further advantages or try to close the sale. Unless you do so, your previous good work is wasted. It is futile to wait expectantly for the customer to act, because his next action is likely to be another objection. It is surprising how easy it often is to close a sale immediately following the successful meeting of an objection.

Trade Talk

agree-but method   anticipate objections
commitment question   excuse
    sincere objection

Can You Answer These?

1. What advantages result from anticipating objections in a retail sale?
2. Why do people make excuses rather than tell the salesperson their true objections?
3. How does a good salesperson side-step an excuse?
4. What is the basic difference in procedure in handling an excuse and an objection?
5. What are the five methods of meeting objections discussed in the text? How are they performed?
6. In what ways does the retail salesperson meet sales resistance on the part of the customer?
7. What precautions must be exercised in meeting sales resistance?

8. What should the salesperson do immediately following the disposal of the excuse or objection?

Problems and Projects

1. Write a description of a recent purchasing experience in which you resisted buying. Criticize the salesperson's procedure.
2. Make a list of the excuses customers make when stalling the salesperson. Recommend procedures for handling five of them.
3. Choose an article you would like to sell. Then write a description of how you would anticipate an objection to (a) need, (b) item, (c) source, (d) price, and (e) time.
4. List the ways a salesperson distinguishes between excuses and objections. Interview experienced salespeople on the subject.
5. What is meant by "Winning a battle and losing a war," as it relates to meeting sales resistance?

Cite an example in your experience.

Learning Your Job

1. Make a list of common customer objections to three products sold in your department or store. Select one objection you think should frequently be anticipated for each product. Then describe on paper what you would do in handling it.
2. Select a product sold in your department or store. Then describe on paper the way you would deal with it under each of the five methods of handling objections.
3. Make mental notes of the objections or excuses made by customers during five sales contacts. Classify the objections according to the following: (a) need, (b) item, (c) source, (d) price, (e) time, and (f) excuse. Report to the class on the way you dealt with the various kinds of objections.

37 *What Makes the Difference Among Salespeople*

Two bright young men of the same age started retail sales work for the same company on the same day. Three years later one was head of stock, the other an assistant buyer. Five years from the time they were employed, the first was an assistant buyer, and the latter, a merchandise manager.

The interesting thing about these young men is that both had comparable abilities and similar backgrounds. Why, then, did one advance so much more rapidly than the other? Were "breaks" the reason? Very likely not. The difference was largely due to sales performance—first as a retail salesperson, and later as a department manager and buyer. Successful men usually make their own breaks.

Let us consider what makes sales personnel successful from four different angles: (1) sales attitudes and beliefs, (2) mastery of merchandising information, (3) choice of sales procedures, and (4) sales personality. Those who advance in sales and merchandising occupations almost always rank high in these sales characteristics.

The Salesperson's Attitudes and Beliefs

As you have studied the preceding text material or have observed successful salespeople, quite likely you have sensed many of the attitudes and beliefs of top-notch retail salespeople. Most of them (1) have a wholesome attitude toward customers and society, (2) have a positive attitude toward their occupation and position, and (3) are fair in their treatment of co-workers and competitors. They work under an unwritten code of ethics—a code to which successful people subscribe.

Attitudes Toward Customers and Society

Superior salespeople believe that they have a purpose in life—to serve society, as do doctors and lawyers, only in a different way. They do not impose their ideas and beliefs on customers. Rather, they figuratively prescribe merchandise for their needs when asked to do so.

Buying is not a charitable act; therefore, professional-minded salespeople do not appeal to the customer's generosity, hinting that they need the sale. They refrain from unduly praising the customer and do not ask for sympathy.

Usually, the customer is not aware of being sold something when dealing with a good salesperson. "You never hear the sales talk that sells you" is a well-known adage that characterizes his work. He is not overly aggressive, nor is he phlegmatic. He appeals to the customer's emotions, but judiciously so. This kind of behavior stems from respect for customers, regardless of class.

Professional-minded salespeople have a *customer following,* customers who ask for them by name or number. This following is built by giving superior in-

A well-informed salesperson becomes a consumer consultant—this one in a bridal shoppe.

Courtesy Fields Bridal Shoppe, Zion, Ill.

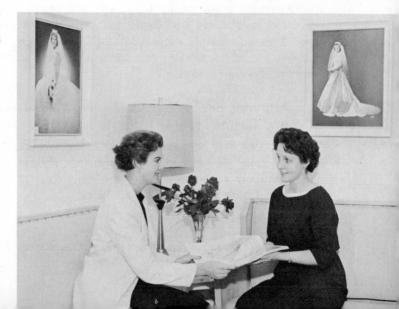

dividualized service, such as recording information about the customer's needs and notifying him when suitable merchandise is available.

A good business attitude toward customers is expressed by one firm as follows:

THE TEN COMMANDMENTS OF GOOD BUSINESS *

A CUSTOMER is the most important person
in any business.

A CUSTOMER is not dependent on us—
we are dependent on him.

A CUSTOMER is not an interruption of our work—
he is the purpose of it.

A CUSTOMER does us a favor when he calls—
we are not doing him a favor by serving him.

A CUSTOMER is part of our business—
not an outsider.

A CUSTOMER is not a cold statistic—
he is a flesh-and-blood human being
with feelings and emotions like our own.

A CUSTOMER is not someone to argue or match wits with.

A CUSTOMER is a person who brings us his wants—
it is our job to fill these wants.

A CUSTOMER is deserving of the most courteous
and attentive treatment we can give him.

Attitudes and Beliefs Concerning Occupation and Position

Good salespeople rarely consider switching occupational fields because they believe that selling is more than a means of earning a living—to them it is an opportunity to be creative and to express themselves. In spite of its short-comings, they prefer selling, enjoying the variety of work, the many contacts with people, and the congenial working conditions.

Also, successful salespeople have a warm feeling toward their company and believe strongly in the products they sell. They realize that idle gossip and the betrayal of confidences hurt those with whom they work and reflect on themselves. These salespeople are proud of their positions in the firm and concentrate on doing a good job, serving customers to the best of their ability, rather than dreaming about a promotion.

Attitudes and Beliefs Concerning Fellow Workers and Competition

Good attitudes and beliefs concerning fellow workers and competition complete the major elements in the salesperson's philosophy. Congenial relations with co-workers are important because they affect the salesperson's frame of mind. A bickering salesperson is not efficient.

* Kelly-Reed, Inc., Rochester, New York.

The superior sales worker respects the rules made for the sales staff. He sets a pattern of ethical practice, rather than retaliating for breaches of ethics. He believes in accepting his fair share of nonselling tasks; he serves customers in their turn and refrains from practices that hint of *sales grabbing*—picking only the most promising customers and beating fellow salespeople to them. He does not *steal sales*—take credit for sales to customers when another salesperson should be credited. On the other hand, he does not conspire with fellow salespeople in practices that restrict production.

Professional-minded salespeople respect the competition from other businesses. They refrain from making spiteful remarks concerning competing firms or products. Instead, they try to focus the customer's attention on helpful, factual information about their own products, services, and merchandising policies. They refer customers to specific competing firms when they are unable to meet the patron's needs within the required time.

Mastery of Merchandising Information

Sound attitudes and beliefs about selling help an individual to achieve the second characteristic of a professional salesperson—mastery of merchandising information. *Merchandising information* may be defined as all the knowledge needed to perform sales duties as a member of a merchandising team. The importance of balanced knowledge in order to succeed in any retail occupation was pointed out in previous units. We shall now discuss briefly the kinds of information for which sales personnel are particularly responsible.

Whether or not the salesperson intends it to be so, selling without adequate merchandising information may be deceitful to customers. As indicated earlier, the function of the salesperson is to represent management. He cannot truthfully do so without (1) having sufficient knowledge of the product he sells, (2) knowing a great deal about competing firms and their products, (3) having a good understanding of the customer services offered by his store, and (4) understanding the merchandising of the products and possessing basic merchandising facts concerning them.

The chart on page 242 lists 50 items of merchandising information commonly possessed by good retail sales personnel. Not all items in the chart may apply to a particular article. Additional items could be listed. Upon studying this chart, you will soon realize that merchandising information is almost inexhaustible. Recalling that many products sold by a store are changed frequently, you can appreciate why a professional-minded salesperson continually studies his merchandising information.

Proficiency in Sales Procedure

Sales procedure refers to the course of action the salesperson follows in carrying on the sale. Choice of procedure depends largely on the salesperson's attitudes concerning customers. Some follow procedures that tend toward dominating

50 ITEMS OF MERCHANDISING INFORMATION

I. Knowledge of Product

1. Who uses it
2. How they benefit from it
3. Advantages and disadvantages
4. When to buy it
5. Where it can be bought
6. How to use it
7. How to care for it
8. Who makes it
9. How it is made
10. Guaranty and warranty
11. Reorder possibilities
12. How to store it
13. How to recondition it
14. How to prepare it for sale
15. How to handle it
16. Precautions for users
17. Substitutes stocked by store
18. Rate of depreciation
19. Trade-in values
20. Stock locations
21. Customer buying problems

II. Knowledge of Competition

22. Competing brands
23. Competing substitutes
24. Qualities of competing items
25. Strength of competitors

26. Competitors' sources
27. Competitors' sales policies
28. Competitors' advertising
29. Competitors' services

III. Knowledge of Customer Services

30. Delivery services available
31. Delivery schedule
32. Policy on returned goods
33. Kinds of adjustments made
34. Credit arrangements
35. Lay-away policies
36. Servicing arrangements
37. How to wrap it
38. How to ship it

IV. Knowledge of Merchandising

39. Margin of profit
40. Fashion cycles
41. Markdown policies
42. Receiving date
43. Stock-control system
44. Quantity in stock
45. Seasonal demand
46. National advertising
47. Local advertising
48. Window displays of product
49. Business conditions
50. Business-condition forecast

their customers, while others choose methods that facilitate their "tuning in" with their customers' thoughts.

Basic Ways of Organizing Sales Procedures

There are three basic approaches to the organization of a sale: (1) the AIDA organization, (2) the salesperson's job organization, and (3) the buying-decision organization. Each serves a purpose.

The AIDA Organization. The letters A, I, D, and A stand for Attention, Interest, Desire, and Action—the mental stages a customer goes through during a purchase. This method of organizing sales is usually discussed in general salesmanship textbooks, because it applies to persuasion in all kinds of sales media. It is particularly suited to media, such as advertising, where customer contact is not on a person-to-person basis. It is difficult to follow in retail selling,

A salesmanship training class is reviewing the four basic approaches of a sale.

Courtesy E. I. du Pont de Nemours and Co., Inc.

because mental stages are abstract and unstable. Furthermore, this organization is not customer oriented.

The Sales-Job Organization. Organizing the sale according to the steps taken by salespeople in guiding customers to a buying decision is easily understood and is taught in many stores. The steps of the sale discussed in Unit 8 are (1) approach, (2) finding the customer's wants and needs, (3) presenting the merchandise, (4) meeting objections, (5) closing the sale, and (6) suggestion selling. Good results may be achieved when this method is skillfully applied. Its limitation, however, is that it stresses what the *salesperson* does during the sale rather than what the *customer* does. It tends to delegate the initiative to the salesperson, giving the impression that the customer follows along. This method of organization is usually applied to the sale of shopping goods.

The Buying-Decision Organization. The buying-decision organization of a sale—(1) need, (2) time, (3) place, (4) item, and (5) price, discussed in detail in Unit 9—is the newest of the three basic methods. It is customer centered and applies to all types of personal-contact selling. When this procedure is mastered, it is the fastest because it eliminates wasting time on buying decisions that are already made by the customer. It is effective because it avoids confusing the customer with unnecessary information.

Effective Sales Personality

Even with comparable attitudes and beliefs, equal command of merchandising information, and similar abilities in the use of sales procedures, one salesperson may produce much higher sales volume than another. The superior salesperson has a better *sales personality,* the ability to communicate favorably and effectively with customers. Communication in sales work is a three-way activity, involving listening, adapting, and conveying ideas.

**AARON MONTGOMERY WARD,
1844–1913**

A pioneer in the technique of selling goods from a catalogue by mail; founder of Montgomery Ward & Company of Chicago, Ill.

Listening

Customer-sensitive salespeople listen with their eyes as well as with their ears. Through their sense organs, they receive tips on what customers want and how they like to be treated. During the very act of listening and observing, they make friends because they do it in such a way that they flatter their customers through the attention given them. They are open-minded and find it easy to place themselves mentally in the customer's situation.

Adapting

Good salespeople are able to adapt their thinking to various kinds of individuals. They adjust to a customer's line of reasoning without losing track of good sales procedures. They sense when to reason with the customer, when to use testimonials or give opinions, and when to use various emotional appeals. They know how to react to humor and how to use it. They know when a customer wants assistance and direction and when he merely wishes support for his way of thinking.

Conveying Ideas

Customers are usually receptive to the information and suggestions of well-trained salespeople, because they readily understand them and enjoy their friendly manner. These salespeople use their voices to advantage and demonstrate or dramatize their ideas clearly. They are pleasingly persuasive because of their sincerity, self-confidence, and enthusiasm.

Trade Talk

Can You Answer These?

1. What kinds of attitudes do superior salespeople have toward customers and society? What practices do they avoid?

2. How do the better salespeople feel about (*a*) sales occupations, (*b*) their jobs, (*c*) the products they sell, (*d*) their superiors?

3. What are the attitudes and beliefs of good salespeople concerning fellow workers? concerning competition?

4. What does the better salesperson know about (*a*) the products he sells, (*b*) competing firms and products, (*c*) the customer services offered by his store, (*d*) merchandising the product he sells?

5. What kind of sales procedure do superior salespeople follow?

6. What are the three basic ways of organizing sales procedures? What are the purposes and advantages of each?

7. What characterizes the personality of superior salespeople?

Problems and Projects

1. Explain the ten commandments of good business given on page 240.

2. Write up a code of ethics for retail salespeople based on the text material on salespersons' attitudes and beliefs.

3. Plan a form for rating retail salespeople based on the four attributes of superior salespeople discussed in this part.

4. Make a list of the things a salesperson can do to develop a customer following.

5. Using a magazine advertisement, demonstrate the four mental stages of a sale (AIDA).

Learning Your Job

1. Drawing on your experience and the material on pages 239 to 241, describe your attitudes and beliefs relating to sales work.

2. List items of merchandising information needed to meet any situation that might arise in the sale of one of the products handled by your store or department.

3. On the basis of their sales personality, make a written comparison of two salespeople in your department or store. Do not reveal their identity.

Sale

99

poor w...
can co...
low pr...
Oh

Oher Shop

by silk, light...
...eiss new way !

DARK LUSTRE

GET IT AT

METAL MAGIC

RNITUR

al new blade devel-
...ssures you clean,
...with almost
and com

the costume

NEW D

HUG

4.50
4.00
4.00

o ...e new black-and-bea

shine at theatre, cockt...
at the edges with je...
..., in lines superbly new...
...izzle, a dark blaze of exc...

entle curv...

AVE

SALE

II. Visual Merchandising

eels

a rich girl. Go to

ing goil to deny herself high fashion, wher...
e to the rescue with smart clothes at
es. If you're loaded with taste, but not wit...
...and walk out looking like a m...

NEW

RONA

Unit 11

Part 38

The Importance of Good Display

How many times have you stopped on the street to admire a window display, then walked right in and purchased an article that drew your attention? And how many times have you, while wandering through a store "just looking around," been attracted to a counter or aisle display that made you want to buy? Chances are that these things have happened to you many times. Catching your eye and tempting you to buy is the job of *visual merchandising*—selling through display. And it is a powerful merchandising technique. It is used in grocery stores, drugstores, service stations, department stores, variety stores, and many other types of retail establishments. Manufacturers and distributors of nationally advertised goods are so convinced of the tremendous sales value of visual merchandising that they spend over a half billion dollars a year on display aids, literature, and "props," and in counseling retailers on effective display of their products.

An important new industry has grown up in recent years around visual merchandising. Included are manufacturers who deal exclusively in display equipment and supplies, display consulting firms that work with retailers, publishers of display magazines, professional display schools, free-lance display artists, designers, and so on.

Many stores regularly employ visual merchandising specialists, such as artists, prop men, and sign writers. In fact, the retailer's emphasis on display has made part-time displaymen out of many salespeople, both in small stores and in large ones. The modern salesperson is really not considered well trained unless he has a fair knowledge of display.

Types of Store Displays

Store displays range from a casual assortment of merchandise on a table top to the large department store's lavishly decorated corner window—the most expensive space in the building. All store displays serve either of two purposes. Most displays are called *promotional displays*, because their purpose is to achieve a sale as soon as possible. An example of this type of display is shown on page 251. A smaller number of displays are called *institutional displays*, because their purpose is to build customer good will—and, in turn, to increase sales in the future. An institutional display is shown on page 249.

Retailers also classify displays according to their location. *Window displays,* as the name implies, are those in the store's windows. *Interior displays* are inside the store on counters or ledges, in showcases, in open areas—such as in front of elevators—and in shadow boxes. Whether in the window or inside, the store displays are classified by displaymen into six general types: (1) open-type store front, (2) open, (3) closed, (4) built-up, (5) shadow box, and (6) ledge.

Open-Type Store-Front Display. Many stores now have an open-type store front. This is a front that is almost all glass and that has no backdrop, so that customers on the street can see the store interior. This type of window is classified as a window display although the interior of the store is also on display. The purpose of the glass front is to use the window and the attractive interior to attract customers and to encourage window-shopping after store hours.

Open Display. In open display, merchandise is not stored away in cases, boxes, and drawers, but put out where the customer can examine it. Open displays in the store enable the customer to study the merchandise by himself, if he cares to do so. Where open display has been tried, it has nearly always increased sales.

There are three general methods of exhibiting merchandise in open displays: (1) flat on the counter, (2) raised by a simple supporting prop, and (3) supported by decorative props or manikins.

Closed Display. While open displays are the order of the day, closed displays will always be necessary for some kinds of merchandise. For example, expensive glassware, which needs protection from dust and handling, is sold from showcases and back-of-the-counter fixtures. For obvious reasons, high-value merchandise, such as jewelry and silverware, is seldom sold from open display. Likewise, merchandise that is easily broken or soiled or is dangerous for children to handle is confined to closed display. Closed displays are sometimes used to please customers who object to purchasing articles that have received a great deal of handling.

Built-Up Displays. Built-up displays are those in which the merchandise is placed in a decorative setting and on platforms or built-up props to give added attractiveness to the articles displayed and to improve the general appearance of the store. They usually will be found in store windows, in front of the elevator, in full view of escalator passengers, and at important traffic points throughout the store. Model rooms in furniture departments are also classified as built-up displays.

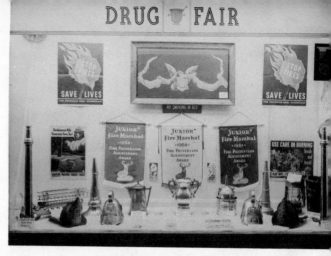

An institutional display window. An entire drugstore window is given over to a showing of Junior Fire Marshall achievement awards won by junior citizens.

Courtesy Drug Fair, Arlington, Va.

Shadow Boxes. Shadow boxes are relatively small display areas resembling a shallow box that is open on one side. They are usually found in the store's interior but may be used in display windows to isolate featured merchandise. Sometimes shadow boxes are built into interior walls or into store fixtures. Frequently they are erected for use above shelves or counters.

Ledge Displays. Displays on ledges, on store walls, or partitions are often used for the showing of merchandise. During certain times of the year, they are used for decoration only—spring flowers, Christmas trees, Easter rabbits, and so on. Some stores do not display merchandise on ledges continually because this may block the general view of the store.

The Job of Good Displays

The job of displays, whether on the sales floor or in a store window, is to stop traffic and influence those who look to buy. Good displays are "silent salesmen" for the store. They are effective salesmen because: (1) they show the product itself—not just a picture or a description; (2) they give the product a suitable setting—such as sports, holiday, fashion, or seasonal background or atmosphere; and (3) they help prepare the customer for the personal message of the salesperson by showing the customer in advance some things about the merchandise.

But good displays do more than sell merchandise. They contribute to the pleasing environment of the store. They stimulate favorably the emotions of those who see them—passers-by, customers, and employees—because people enjoy beauty. In addition, they influence employee morale favorably.

Store displays also lend a personal touch to a business enterprise—they symbolize the merchandising policies of the firm. Neat, well-designed displays indicate that the store is "on its toes." They say, in effect, to the customers, "We think you deserve our best and we will try to do our best for you."

How Visual Merchandising Increases Sales Volume

Effective window and interior displays help the store increase sales volume in five ways:

A very attractive interior open display of china and glassware.

Courtesy Grand Rapids Store Equipment Co., Grand Rapids, Mich.

1. *Displays Capitalize on Other Forms of Advertising.* Consumers often read advertisements in newspapers, magazines, and handbills, or listen to radio and television commercials. They make mental notes of the products that appeal to them. When they do their shopping, window and interior displays remind them of their intended purchases and the advantages featured in the advertisement.

2. *Displays Attract New Users.* The customer's attention may be drawn to a display that strikes a respondent chord. He stops to look. Further investigation convinces him that the product merits a trial, and he purchases it.

3. *Displays Remind Old Users to Buy.* Customers make mental notes of the products they plan to purchase. Yet it is only human to forget. When they go to the store to shop, "point-of-purchase" displays step in and remind them to buy.

4. *Displays Enable the Store to Meet Competition Almost Immediately.* Often, a merchant can have a window changed or modified within a few minutes. Thus, display is a flexible form of advertising.

5. *Displays Help Reduce Inventories by Increasing Sales.* Usually fast-selling merchandise is displayed prominently in a desirable sales location to increase stock turnover. Occasionally slow-selling goods are displayed for clearance purposes.

The Trend Toward Visual Merchandising

Visual merchandising is not new. In ancient times, sellers brought their wares to the market place and displayed them along the roadways and streets where people passed most often. But the full impact of visual merchandising has really been felt only in recent years. Only a generation ago, many retailers did not mind if their windows were cluttered with unattractive, unrelated merchandise; they paid little attention to interior display. What is the reason for the recent interest in good display? The answer is twofold. First, there is increasing competition for the customer's trade. Today's retailer knows he must bring customers into close contact with merchandise if he is to sell competitively. Secondly, expenses of doing business are rising; and the retailer must cut costs. To do this, many retailers have adopted self-service, a type of operation in which visual merchandising is essential. In self-service merchandising, open display gives the customer easy access to the goods and thus reduces selling expenses by reducing the amount of time a salesperson must spend with each customer.

And this is only the beginning. The importance of interior display was brought out in a national survey by the E. I. duPont de Nemours and Company, which revealed that two out of three purchases made in supermarkets are based on decisions made while the shopper is in the store! Window displays rank next to interior displays in sales power. A series of tests, sponsored by the Point-of-Purchase Advertising Institute, proved that window display substantially increased sales for certain nationally advertised drug and hardware products.

Store displays often repeat the same advertising message to shoppers who have been exposed to newspaper, magazine, and other kinds of advertising. To neglect point-of-purchase displays, as well as those in display windows and in the store's interior, is like dropping out of a race three feet short of the finish line. There is little point in spending money for advertising when there is nothing at the point of purchase to call the customer's attention to the advertised merchandise.

The reasons why customers buy more than they had planned upon entering a store are given in a survey by a national advertising agency, Batten, Barton, Durstine, and Osborn. Shoppers told interviewers that displays influenced them in three ways:

A promotional display of Everglaze cotton fabric; the design principle of dominance is also illustrated here.

Courtesy The Stewart Dry Goods Co., Louisville, Ky.

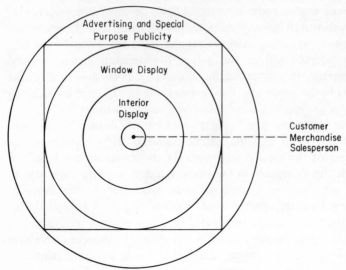

Importance of Sales—Promotion Media

Advertising and Special
Purpose Publicity

Window Display

Interior
Display

Customer
Merchandise
Salesperson

1. Displays sparked an impulse to buy small items, such as a candy bar, magazine, tooth paste, and shoe polish.
2. Displays reminded shoppers of something they needed or wanted, such as a new tie, a blouse, or a saucepan.
3. Displays sold customers on new uses or advantages of an article, causing them to buy.

Trade Talk

built-up display   open display
closed display   promotional
institutional   display
    display   shadow box
ledge display

Can You Answer These?

1. How has the growth of visual merchandising affected the salesperson's job?
2. In what ways does visual merchandising cause many customers to buy more goods than they expect to upon entering the store?
3. In what ways does the store benefit from visual merchandising?
4. What is meant by the statement, "Display is the final link in the advertising chain"?

5. In what ways are displays good salesmen?
6. Other than helping sell merchandise, how does visual merchandising contribute to a store's success?
7. What is the prevailing trend in visual merchandising?
8. What are the major kinds of displays? Describe each and explain its purpose.

Problems and Projects

1. Make an oral or a written report describing the recent development of visual merchandising and predicting its future. Procure your information from personal observations, interviews, and magazine articles located through *Readers Guide to Periodical Literature.*

2. Describe a recent experience in which visual merchandising influenced you. Analyze the thoughts that took place in your mind as you arrived at your decision.

3. Briefly describe an example in your business community of each of the following: (*a*) an open-type store front, (*b*) an open display, (*c*) a closed display, (*d*) a built-up display, and (*e*) a shadow box.

4. Without identifying the firms, compare point for point the visual merchandising done by two businesses of the same kind in your community—for example, department store, shoe store, service station, dry-cleaning establishment, food supermarket.

Learning Your Job

1. Classify the displays found in the store where you work according to the kinds described in the material you have just read.

2. Prepare a list of questions based on the material in this part to which you would like to have answers with regard to your store. Have your teacher approve the list; then ask your supervisor to answer the questions.

39 *Principles of Design*

Suppose that the displayman knows the advantages and the limitations of the space with which he is to work. After conferring with the department buyer, he decides on the merchandise to display and determines its sales features. From the fixture room, he brings the props that will be most appropriate. He gathers sufficient decorative material, show cards, and tools. His job is to visualize an idea for customers, for the purpose of display is to stop traffic and sell merchandise to those who stop to look. The good displayman uses the principles of design to create an attractive display, which will lead the customer mentally through the following steps of a sale:

1. Attract attention   2. Arouse interest   3. Stimulate desire   4. Cause action

Three underlying principles of design should be considered in constructing a display: (1) dominance, (2) balance, and (3) proportion.

Dominance

Dominance is the emphasizing of and directing attention to a particular item or idea. This is achieved by giving special prominence to the item by making one of the units of the display larger, stronger, or brighter. To put it another way, one kind of line, shape, color, or texture should predominate. For example, dominance might be achieved by a bright red background or a large, diamond-shaped prop on which the featured item is displayed.

Dominance is important because it provides a focal point to which the customer's attention is drawn. It is also the point to which all other parts of the display relate.

Balance

In a display, *balance* is the element that gives the impression that both sides of the display are equal in weight—that is, equal in importance. There are two types of balance—formal and informal. *Formal balance* is the placing on opposite sides of the axis (the center) one or more identical or similar elements. The concept of balance in design is illustrated below by weights on a beam that rests on a fulcrum (axis). Formal balance in a display is shown in the illustrations of shirts on page 258. Formal balance is the easiest and safest type of display for beginners.

Informal balance is the placing on one side of a display one or more elements and balancing them by one or more contrasting or dissimilar elements on the opposite side. Informal balance is much more interesting than formal balance, but it is more difficult to achieve. An example of informal balance in actual displays is shown in the illustrations on page 257. The principle of balance is very important in a design, for without it the design looks unattractive—literally out of balance!

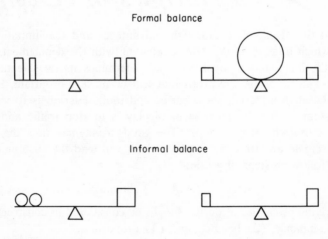

Formal balance

Informal balance

Proportion

The principle of proportion involves the relationships between two or more elements in a design. It means that one element is the right size when seen in relation to other elements. Because size is measurable, we say that proportion is a ratio. For example, two panels—one 4-by-2-feet and the other 8-by-4-feet—are in proportion because the ratio of height to width (2 to 1) is the same in each.

Many ratios are possible, but there is one that is commonly used in designing good displays. This is the Golden Mean:

$$\text{Golden Mean Ratio} = \frac{1}{1.618} \text{ or approximately } 1:1\tfrac{5}{8}$$

The rectangles shown below illustrate how the Golden Mean ratio looks.

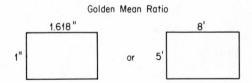

Golden Mean Ratio

Roughly speaking, the Golden Mean as used in display means that props, show cards, etc., should be about 1½ times as wide as they are high or vice versa. Thus, a show card that is 10″ high by 4″ wide would be out of proportion, because it would be 2½ times as high as it is wide.

Factors Used to Create Good Designs

In using the principles of good design, the displayman can employ several devices. They are (1) repetition and rhythm, (2) harmony, (3) contrast, (4) gradation, and (5) interference.

Repetition and Rhythm. In a display, repetition is the repeating of identical or similar shapes, lines, sizes, or colors. For example, an oval shape or the color blue might be repeated in the props, merchandise groups, and show card. *Exact repetition* is a regular, uniform repeating of one element; it is monotonous to look at—suppose everything were oval or blue! In contrast, *rhythm* is the more interesting form of repetition in which similar or identical shapes, lines, sizes, or colors are repeated at regular intervals. For example, the oval might be repeated in some props and in the show card, while the merchandise groups alternately are rectangular or triangular; or the color blue might be featured in one item of merchandise, a dress, and repeated in some of the accessories, such as shoes, gloves, and handbags. Repetition of line is shown in the display illustrated on page 271.

Harmony. Harmony is the combining in a pleasing arrangement of shapes, lines, or colors that are similar in one or more respects. When parts of a display are in agreement, there is harmony. For example, colors in a display may be harmonious hues of green and yellow, rather than the clashing of pinks and reds. Harmony of line is shown in the illustration on page 263.

Contrast. Contrast is the emphasizing of difference rather than likeness. It is achieved by placing near each other differing or opposing units. For example, contrast might be gained in a clothing display by using navy as the dominant

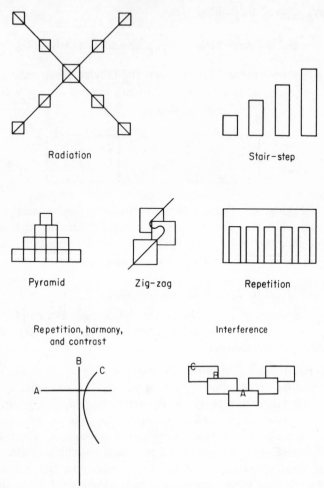

Arrangements

Radiation

Stair-step

Pyramid

Zig-zag

Repetition

Repetition, harmony, and contrast

Interference

color with accessories in white or straw hues. An example of contrast in lines is shown in the illustration above.

The figure at the left represents a very simple arrangement, using only the elements of line to illustrate repetition, harmony, and contrast. Lines A and B show repetition of line (both are straight), contrast of length (A is short and B is long), and contrast of direction (A is horizontal and B is vertical).

Lines B and C illustrate harmony of direction (both are vertical), contrast of line (C is curved and B is straight), and contrast in length (C is short and B is long).

Lines A and C show harmony in length (both are short), contrast of line (A is straight and C curved), and contrast of direction (A is horizontal and C is vertical).

Contrast is an important device in design because it stimulates interest and creates excitement. A display with too little contrast is monotonous and unattractive.

Gradation. The device called *gradation* is also known as *progression.* It refers to the gradual change in the units of a design—for example, units may range from small to large, dark to light, or bright to dull. Thus, gradation is a sequence in which the extremes are bridged by a series of in-between steps. An example of gradation is shown in the illustration below.

Interference. Placing merchandise or props in position, so that one overlaps or "interferes" with the next when seen by the customer, is called *interference.* This is a helpful device because it serves to unite the items of a group and links them with one another. See the diagram at the lower right on page 256.

A interferes with B which interferes with C. Also A interferes with the light and dark groups serving to unify them. Note in the illustration on page 271 how the shades of the lamps in the foreground interfere with those in the background.

Arrangements Used in Grouping Merchandise

The general shape of a display may take one of many different forms: (1) radiation, (2) stair-step, (3) pyramid, (4) zig-zag, and (5) repetition.

Radiation. In radiation, the elements of a design proceed outward from a common point. This type of design concentrates interest at the point of dominance from which the lines radiate. For example, a men's-furnishings window might have a male manikin as the focal point with various accessories displayed on platforms arranged in a circle around the manikin.

Stair-Step. In the stair-step arrangement, the fixtures holding the merchandise are arranged in a series of steps, mounting or descending from one level

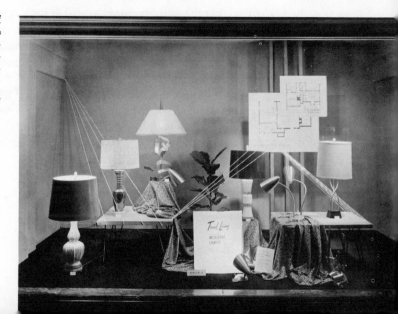

This window display of lamps illustrates three principles of design: informal balance, gradation, and stair-step arrangement.

Courtesy J. L. Hudson Co., Detroit

The window display of shirts is an illustration of formal balance and repetition.

Courtesy Younkers, Des Moines

to the next. For example, shoes might be arranged on ascending platforms, leading the customer's eye from one style to another.

Pyramid and Zig-Zag. The pyramid pattern is frequently used in food and drugstores, because it allows a mass display of one brand of merchandise to attract attention. On the other hand, department stores often use the *zig-zag* arrangement, especially in clothing displays. This pattern is good for light, open-type displays and is usually limited to three major items, such as a display of shoes, sweaters, and skirts.

Repetition. The repetition arrangement is also called the "continental" pattern. It uses items of the same general nature, aligning them in exactly the same manner such as height, spacing, or angle. The monotony can be broken by using panels or elevated platforms, displaying the items as a single unit or tilting the platform. For example, sweaters might be fastened in a line on a tilted board, so that the various colors available are contrasted for the customer.

Regardless of which type of arrangement is used, a well-designed display shows the careful application of the principles of dominance, balance, and proportion. In addition, the display will also have *unity* and *order*. A window that has unity has one principal theme or idea, a point of dominance, and the subordination of all units to the dominant one. A unified display does not distract the customer from the main point; rather it concentrates his attention on the main idea. Good displays also have order. This is the arrangement of the different parts into an easily understandable plan, so that the passer-by grasps easily and quickly the theme and sees the important things. A disorderly display distracts the customer and may even repel him because it is unattractive.

Trade Talk

balance	unity
contrast	continental
dominance	arrangement
gradation	pyramid
harmony	arrangement
interference	radiation
order	arrangement
progression	stair-step
proportion	arrangement
radiation	zig-zag
repetition	arrangement
rhythm	

Can You Answer These?

1. What are the three essentials of good design? Illustrate each.
2. What is the advantage of formal balance? informal balance?
3. What is the Golden Mean ratio? How does it apply to display?
4. What tools of design were discussed in your text? How do they serve as tools?
5. What is the difference between repetition and rhythm?
6. In what ways is harmony in design achieved?
7. Why is contrast needed in a merchandise display?
8. What purpose does gradation or progression serve in making a display? interference?
9. In what kinds of stores is one likely to find each of the display arrangements described in your text?
10. What purpose in display work does unity serve? order?

Problems and Projects

1. Using one of the illustrations of a display in your textbook as a visual aid, explain dominance, balance, and proportion.
2. Select a newspaper or magazine advertisement and from it illustrate repetition, harmony, contrast, gradation, and interference.
3. Make five rough sketches of displays, each illustrating one of the arrangements described in your textbook on pages 254–256.
4. Clip black-and-white pictures of merchandise from a mail-order catalogue, brochure, magazine, or newspaper and construct on paper a store display. List the principles of design used in completing the project.
5. Demonstrate with the use of books of the same size and color such as your textbooks or volumes of an encyclopedia the qualities of a display listed in "Trade Talk."

Learning Your Job

1. Classify the arrangements in three displays of competing retail businesses, including the store in which you work.
2. Sketch a display of merchandise in your store. Explain the principles of design that were followed or violated.
3. Sketch a display of merchandise in your store. Using the same articles, reconstruct the display using a different arrangement.

40 *Color in Visual Merchandising*

Color is more important than anything else in attracting the attention of a passer-by to a display. Pleasing color combinations favorably impress the customer's sense of sight and help put him in a receptive mood; and, of course, they make a display more lively, more interesting, and more dramatic. Color is an important factor in creating sales appeal and in making merchandise more attractive.

A large eastern department store uses a simple test in color selection as one means of selecting display personnel. The applicant is asked to build a display and is given free reign in selecting merchandise and props and in choosing colors. While many applicants are able to design good displays, the best ones always stand out for their ability to create harmonious, co-ordinated color schemes. Many who fail betray their shortcomings in the use of color. The importance of color in creating a display is well illustrated by the counsel of a master display-man who tells his pupils: it is much better to build a simple display in a becoming color than to create an elaborate display using poor color combinations.

Color Psychology

Colors have, for most people, definite mental associations or meanings. For example, many people traditionally think of purple as suggesting luxury, wealth, and splendor; red as associated with gaiety, anger, or fire; and white as meaning innocence and purity. These traditional meanings of color are, however, not very useful in merchandising today, because color is so widely used in our everyday living and people attach many different meanings to different colors. The important thing about color psychology today is its use in developing moods and illusions that help to sell the whole display to the customer.

Color can be used in displays to create mild illusions. Hues, or colors, with blue or green in them are *receding* colors; that is, they create the illusion of space by making objects look smaller or farther away than they actually are. For example, a pair of dark-blue (navy) shoes will appear to be smaller than the same size in white. On the other hand, colors containing red and yellow are called *advancing* colors because they create the illusion that objects are closer or larger than they actually are. For example, red velvet used as a chair fabric would make the chair stand out and appear closer than a similar chair in a subdued green upholstery. The lightness or darkness of a color also affects the illusion it gives. For example, a dark-blue object would look smaller and farther away than a similar object in light blue.

As used in merchandising, colors have other general meanings. For example, blues and greens generally give the impression of being cool and refreshing; however, one must remember in using colors meaningfully that blue is usually a calm color, while a bright green can be vivid and gay because it has lots of a warm color in it (yellow). The whole idea in using color psychology is to know what colors mean to the type of customer you are dealing with and to learn about shades, tints, hues, values, and other color qualities that can help create the illusions and the meanings desired in displays.

The Color Wheel

Sir Isaac Newton was the first to observe the colors of the solar spectrum. When he peered at sunlight reflected in a glass prism, he discovered seven colors—the same colors you see in the rainbow in which the drops of moisture in the air act as millions of tiny prisms. When he arranged the seven colors in a circular form, he created the first color wheel.

Later, the circle was made with six colors instead of seven. Indigo was omitted. These six colors are broken down into the three *primary colors:* red, yellow, and blue; and the *secondary colors*—which are made by combining primaries—red with yellow to make orange, yellow with blue to make green, and blue with red to create purple.

A third group—the *tertiary colors*—adds six more colors to the wheel by combining the primary and secondary colors and getting red-orange, yellow-green, blue-green, yellow-orange, red-violet, and blue-violet.

Color Qualities

In order to discuss color combinations, it is first necessary to define the qualities of color.

Hue is a technical term used to describe the color itself, as a red hue, an orange hue, etc. It is properly used as a synonym for the word color.

Value is a term used to distinguish light, pale colors from dark ones. For example, a navy blue is a dark value of blue; baby blue is a light value of the color. White or black is added to change the value of a true color. Light values are known as *tints;* dark values are called *shades*.

Intensity (*chroma*) is the degree of purity of a color. It represents the brightness or dullness of a color. For example, scarlet is an intense bright color, although some reds can be dark or of low intensity.

Color Schemes

Pleasing color schemes may be found by applying certain combinations of the color wheel. The simplest color scheme is the *monochromatic* arrangement, in which tints and shades of the same color are used, such as navy blue, pure blue, and baby blue. Another relatively simple color scheme is the *analogous* color combination, which is composed of colors that are next to each other on the

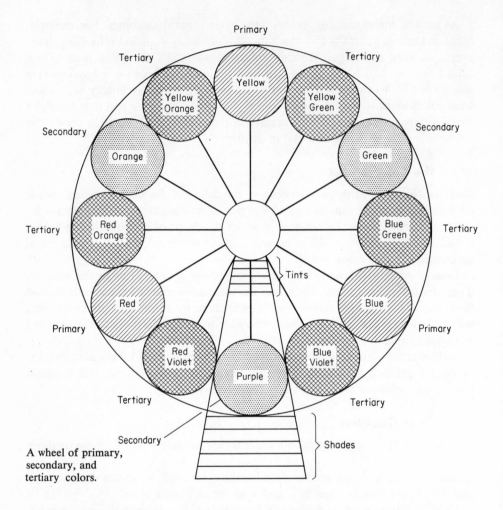

Primary

Tertiary

Tertiary

Secondary

Secondary

Tertiary

Tertiary

Primary

Primary

Tertiary

Tertiary

Secondary

A wheel of primary,
secondary, and
tertiary colors.

Yellow

Yellow
Orange

Yellow
Green

Orange

Green

Red
Orange

Blue
Green

Tints

Red

Blue

Red
Violet

Purple

Blue
Violet

Shades

color wheel, such as pure blue, blue green, and yellow green. One can use as many as five adjacent or neighboring colors, but it is more common to use three.

Complementary colors are two colors that differ most from each other. They are found directly opposite each other on the color wheel. You can be sure you will have color harmony if you use various tints and shades of two complementary colors. *Contrasting colors* are the same as complementary colors. Contrast may be applied to the three qualities of color—hue, value, and intensity.

The *split-complementary* color scheme is similar to the complementary pattern, but embraces three points of the color wheel. For example, yellow, whose complement is purple, has for its split complement blue-violet and red-violet. Any two colors equidistant from the complement blue-violet might be used.

The *double split-complementary* color scheme embraces four points of the color wheel. For example, the two neighboring colors to yellow (orange and yellow-green) may be combined with the two neighboring colors to purple (red-violet and blue-violet).

The *triadic* color scheme is composed of three colors forming an equilateral triangle on the color wheel, for example, red, yellow, and blue; but these colors should not be used in equal proportions.

Selection of Colors and Color Combinations

In order to create pleasing combinations of colors, the person building the display must have a clear understanding of tints, shades, intensity, proportion, and so on.

Balance of Colors. Most color combinations can be harmonious if the colors are used in correct proportions; for example, a small, bright area balances a large, dark one. Thus, many colors that are frequently considered as clashing may be used together in proper intensity and balance. A red and green combination may be very gaudy and disagreeable when two large pieces of furniture are placed side by side. On the other hand, a large area of a shade of green and a small area of bright red, like a red flower on an all-green dress, may be very appealing.

The various color schemes suggested here should not imply that a display must have a complicated color selection. The most pleasing displays are often those in which the simple analogous or complementary color schemes are used. In planning the colors of most displays, the variety of hues should be kept to a minimum; or the effect is likely to be one of confusion.

Limitations in the Selection of Colors. Of necessity, in planning a window or interior display, the color scheme is often controlled by the color of the merchandise. The goods to be displayed may be stocked in only one or a limited number of colors. Sometimes the purpose of a display window is to promote a particular color. Under these conditions, color manipulation is possible only through backgrounds, props, merchandise arrangements, and lighting. Through these media the display builder strives to achieve a color combination

An illustration of the use of color and harmony in a display.

SUGGESTED TABLE FOR BACKGROUND COLORS

Color of Merchandise	Black Background	White Background	Light-Gray Background	Dark-Gray Background
Yellow	Enhanced in richness	Slightly duller	Becomes warmer	Still brighter
Red	Far more brilliant	Darker, purer	Bright, but less intense	Brighter, but loses saturation
Blue	More luminous	Richer and darker	Little more luminous	Brighter
Green	Paler sharpens	Deepens in value	Takes on yellowish cast	Brightens, gray becomes reddish
Orange	Becomes more luminous	Darker and redder	Lighter and yellowish	Increases brilliancy
Purple	Loses in strength and brilliancy	Becomes darker	Brighter, gray becomes greenish	Gray becomes green

that (1) is appropriate for the purpose of the display, (2) possesses unity, and (3) is interesting.

Selection of Background Colors. The two most important areas, as observed by the customer, should be the merchandise and the background. The interaction of the colors of these two factors is of prime importance. The above table shows the probable effects of background color on the color of the merchandise.

Trade Talk

advancing color
analogous color
complementary colors
hue
double split-complementary colors
intensity
monochromatic
primary colors
receding colors
shade
split complementary
tertiary
tint

Can You Answer These?

1. How does color in a display

influence the customer's buying?

2. What mental associations are connected with blue? red? green? purple? white?

3. What are the advancing colors? the receding colors? How is this information used in display?

4. What is the purpose of the color wheel?

5. What are the qualities of a color? Why is an understanding of these qualities necessary in display work?

6. What use can be made of a knowledge of color schemes in display work?

7. What is meant by balance in colors?

8. How is color selection limited in display work?

9. What are the qualities of a good color combination?

10. Why is the color of the display background important?

Problems and Projects

1. Illustrate the use of color psychology with colored magazine advertisements.

2. Give at least five examples of how advancing and receding colors are used to advantage in business offices and the interiors of homes.

3. Using colored paper, make a poster illustrating each of the color schemes discussed in the text material.

4. Clip five color advertisements and identify the color schemes used. Criticize one of the ads from the standpoint of color usage.

5. Identify the color schemes used in three store windows. Criticize one of them thoroughly from the standpoint of color usage.

6. Make a poster illustrating what is meant by balance of colors.

Learning Your Job

1. Study a display in your store and criticize it from the standpoint of arrangement, color scheme, and background. Make suggestions for its improvement.

2. Construct an interior or window display in your store using a preplanned color scheme. Explain how you used your knowledge of color in planning and constructing it.

3. Window-shop two competing stores. Explain how they employ the psychology of color or fail to do so.

41 *Judging Store Displays*

Visual merchandising combines the principles of two fields—salesmanship and art. Without applied art, a display will not function to its fullest. On the other hand, a work of art that does not increase sales is a poor business investment. The retailer must know how to achieve a reasonable balance between these two complementary elements of visual merchandising. Learning to judge a store display helps you understand what makes visual merchandising "click"!

Elements of a Good Display

A display is evaluated on the basis of seven elements: (1) suitability, (2) power to attract attention, (3) selling power, (4) arrangement, (5) cleanliness, (6) lighting, and (7) technical excellence. The rating form on pages 268–270 shows how these elements are considered in determining the effectiveness of window or interior displays.

Suitability

A display that is suitable or appropriate for its purposes (1) fits the kind of store in which it appears, (2) appeals to the kind of audience that views it, and (3) achieves the particular objectives for which it was planned. Whether or not a display accomplishes these objectives depends on the answers to the following questions:

1. *Does the Display Reflect the Store Image and Merchandising Policies?* Some stores, such as Lord and Taylor in New York and Neiman Marcus in Dallas, achieve much of their sophisticated atmosphere by luxurious windows and artistic interior decorations. On the other hand, a supermarket or drugstore attempts to attract the bargain-conscious customer by using window streamers, mass displays, and point-of-sale aids.

2. *Does the Display Feature Fast-Selling Merchandise?* Many stores allot display space on the basis of sales volume produced by the display. This is done to realize maximum gross profits from expensive window and aisle table space. Store buyers, therefore, usually select the items to be displayed from among their best sellers, making sure there is sufficient stock on hand to fill all sales orders.

3. *Is the Motif Consistent with the Merchandise and Season of the Year?* The *motif* is the dominant idea that takes the form of decorative settings. It should harmonize with the season and the merchandise. *Dealer aids,* which are display materials usually furnished by the manufacturer, and show cards should also relate to the season of the year.

4. *Is the Theme of the Display Consistent with That of the Current Sales Promotion?* The *theme* of a display is the message, or buying appeal, of a *particular* display. When special sales events are featured, the theme of the display should be consistent with the motif of the sales event, e.g., jubilee sale, anniversary sale, or Halloween. Thus, the display can capitalize on the total sales publicity for this period.

5. *Is the Display Harmonious with Neighboring Displays and Other Surroundings?* Window-displaymen must keep in mind the store front as well as the next window: and those who create interior displays should consider the adjoining merchandise, fixtures, and decorations.

6. *Is the Display in Line with the Fashion Policies of the Store?*

Whether the policy is to handle high fashions or popular ones, the displays should be consistent with the store policy, lest the customer become confused.

Power to Attract Attention

The power of the display to attract attention is determined by:

1. The color scheme—the brightness of the color scheme and the contrast of the display as a whole with its surroundings attract attention.
2. The background—it should catch the eye of passers-by because of its pleasing color contrasts with surroundings and with the merchandise displayed.
3. The floor covering—it should harmonize with the merchandise and be in keeping with the rest of the display.
4. The props—they reinforce the theme and attract attention to the display.
5. The merchandise arrangement—the merchandise and props should be so arranged that the eye follows a path that leads to the center of interest.
6. The theme—it should be clever enough to attract attention and hold interest.

Selling Power

Visual merchandising is successful if it sells the merchandise that is displayed. Merchandise should be combined with proper accessories and shown in an appropriate setting. For example, fine china may be enhanced by the appropriate silver, linens, a centerpiece, and even furniture.

In a display that sells, the following characteristics are evident:

1. It is easy to find and concentrate on the most important item.
2. The features of the merchandise stand out clearly.
3. The theme emphasizes the strong features of the merchandise.
4. The props attract attention to the merchandise without overshadowing it.
5. Show cards bring out the important selling points.

Arrangement

Previous parts of this unit treat the subject of arrangement from the standpoint of color and design; therefore, only the merchandising aspects will be discussed at this point. Keeping in mind the type of store, the purpose of the display, and the nature of the audience, the following conditions should exist:

1. Neither too much nor too little merchandise is shown.
2. The units or groups of merchandise are well separated—they stand out clearly and orderly, avoiding the feeling of a cluttered display.
3. Related merchandise is displayed together, and each major item points to the next. Thus, the customer sees articles which are correctly used together; and his eye travels to the next item in the display.
4. Dealer aids from manufacturers—such as posters, banners, decorative cartons, mobiles, and cardboard props—are discreetly used.
5. Show cards are of the proper size and appearance and are in the correct locations and positions.

MERCHANDISE DISPLAY RATING FORM

Name of Firm_____ Merchandise Displayed_____

Location of Display_____ Name of Rater_____ Date_____

Check Type of Display:__ Window__ Table__ Counter__ Ledge__ Shadow

Box__ Show Case__ Open__ Closed__ Other:_____

Directions For Rating: Circle the most appropriate rating. If the item does not apply, check the column "Does Not Apply."

	Column 1	Column 2	Column 3	Does Not Apply
A. Suitability of the Display				
1. The display reflects the character and merchandise policy of the company	accurately	to some degree	very inaccurately	
2. Display features merchandise that has	large sales volume	average sales volume	low sales volume	
3. In relation to the season and merchandise, the motif is	very appropriate	fairly appropriate	inappropriate	
4. In relation to the current sales promotion, the motif is	consistent	fairly consistent	inconsistent	
5. In relation to the neighboring displays and other surroundings, the display is	very harmonious	reasonably well matched	out of tune	
6. In regard to the fashion merchandising policy of the store, the display is	in line	reasonably in line	out of line	
B. Power to Attract Attention				
1. Attention value of the color scheme is	strong	average	weak	
2. The background helps to highlight the merchandise	sharply	fairly well	very little	

268   *Unit 11* ■ *Visual Merchandising*

	Column 1	Column 2	Column 3	Does Not Apply
3. The floor covering is	very attractive	attractive	unattractive or missing	
4. The props are	very interesting	interesting	uninteresting	
5. The viewer's eyes move toward the merchandise	directly	haltingly	wander aimlessly	
6. Theme attracts and holds attention	easily recognized	slowly revealed	gap is not bridged	

C. Selling Power

	Column 1	Column 2	Column 3	Does Not Apply
1. The dominant item is identified	very easily	fairly easily	ineffectively	
2. Merchandise features are brought out	very effectively	fairly well	ineffectively	
3. The theme helps sell the items displayed	a great deal	some	very little	
4. The props attract attention to the merchandise	effectively	to some degree	little or none	

D. Arrangement

	Column 1	Column 2	Column 3	Does Not Apply
1. According to the display's purpose, the amount of merchandise displayed is	about right	too much or too little	very crowded or bare	
2. Units or groups of merchandise are	very well spaced	fairly well spaced	poorly spaced	
3. Related products are displayed together—each major item leads to the next	very well	to some degree	not at all	
4. Props and dealer aids	highlight the merchandise	do not affect merchandise	distract attention	
5. Show card is placed	properly	fairly well	improperly	

	Column 1	Column 2	Column 3	Does Not Apply
E. Cleanliness				
1. The merchandise is	fresh and immaculate	reasonably clean	soiled or damaged	
2. Background, floors, and glass are	spotlessly clean	reasonably clean	soiled or dusty	
3. Fixtures, props, manikins, and lights are	in good condition	in fair condition	soiled or damaged	
F. Lighting				
1. Lighting highlights the most important merchandise	very effectively	to some degree	absent or misdirected	
2. Lighting enhances colors in the window	very effectively	to some degree	spoils them	
3. Shadow treatment is	very effective	fairly effective	poor	
4. Lighting fixtures or glare does not distract from merchandise	no distraction	little distraction	obvious distraction	
G. Technical Excellence				
1. The use of color is	excellent	acceptable	annoying	
2. The theme of the display is	unique	conventional	trite	
3. The treatment of the merchandise and props is	unusual	conventional	overworked	
4. Attention to details-folding, draping, concealing pins, tags, etc., is	excellent	reasonably good	careless	

Instructions for Scoring:

1. Two times the number of items circled in Column 1........._____
2. Number of items circled in Column 2...................._____
3. Total of steps 1 and 2 immediately above..............._____
4. Number of items circled in Columns 1 and 2............._____
5. Divide amount in step 3 by amount in step 4 for rating of display ....

Deciding on How Much to Show. Perhaps no other problem in display is affected more by store policy than that of how much merchandise to display. Several policies are used. (*a*) In general, the more exclusive a store, the less merchandise will be shown in the window. Most retailers feel that one-item windows give the merchandise an exclusive appearance and the customer can easily observe the workmanship, design, or style of the item. (*b*) Stores featuring bargain merchandise usually show a large number of items. However, mass displays of unrelated merchandise do not always result in sales. (*c*) The best way to show large quantities of merchandise is to concentrate on one item—mass displays of handkerchiefs or shirts, for example. Progressive grocers use this method effectively. If peaches are in season, a mass display of peaches, boxed or in baskets, is used to bring desired results. (*d*) Specialty stores carrying only one line of merchandise will usually mass display their products. Shoe stores, for example, do so continuously. (*e*) There is also a tendency for stores in small communities to show more merchandise than similar stores in larger centers. A less hurried atmosphere in small communities gives the customer more time to observe the store window.

Cleanliness

To create a desire for ownership in passers-by, the merchandise must appear at its best; therefore, clothes are pressed, furniture is polished, carpets are cleaned. In like manner, backgrounds, floors, exposed walls or ceilings, and *valances*—short drape, banner, or other material extending across the front of the window at the top—all must be fresh and immaculate. Fixtures, props, manikins, and lights should be in excellent repair.

Lighting

Unless the merchandise on display can be seen readily and easily, the goal of

An illustration of the design principles of repetition and interference in a display of lamps.

Courtesy Sears, Roebuck and Co.

increased sales and profits will not be realized. The requisites for a well-lighted window display are as follows:

1. The brightest light is directed toward the most important merchandise.
2. The lighting enhances the colors used in the window.
3. No shadows are present except those designed for effect.
4. The lighting fixtures do not detract from the merchandise, and there are no reflections or glare that interfere with the vision of the passer-by.

Technical Excellence

The qualities of a display that give it a finished and professional look are referred to as *technical excellence*. This consists of:

1. The beauty of the display achieved through the skillful use of color and design principles
2. The uniqueness of the theme of the display and the way it is expressed as compared to most displays of similar merchandise
3. The unusual use of props and the use of unusual props
4. The care taken in folding, draping, concealing pins and tags, and careful attention to all other details of display

---

Trade Talk

dealer aids	valance
display theme	technical
motif	excellence

Can You Answer These?

1. How do the two main elements of a display contribute to its effectiveness?
2. What are the three qualities of a display that should be considered in judging its suitability or appropriateness?
3. What factors should be considered in judging the suitability or appropriateness of a display? How is each achieved?
4. What items are checked in determining the effectiveness of a display in attracting attention? How does each contribute to the power to attract attention?
5. What can the window-display-man do to make sure of the selling power of a display?

6. From a merchandising viewpoint, what points should be checked in rating the arrangement of a display?
7. What are the different policies concerning the amount of merchandise to be displayed in a window?
8. What should the window-display judge look for when rating a display on cleanliness?
9. What factors are considered in the appraisal of the lighting of a display?
10. What qualities of display are included in technical excellence?

Problems and Projects

1. Debate the proposition: "Display is more concerned with art principles than with merchandising principles."
2. Describe three examples of displays that you have seen that are appropriate from the standpoint of the merchandise displayed; three

examples from the standpoint of the audience; three examples from the standpoint of the particular purpose (e.g., sales promotion, institutional display, gift promotion, introduction of new merchandise).

3. Select three competing stores featuring window displays of the same kind of merchandise, e.g., shoes, hardware, stationery supplies. Copy the form on page 268 and rate one window for each store. Explain the superior points of the window rated highest.

4. Suppose that you were told to assign a specific number of points that total 100 for a perfect score on the rating form on page 268. How many points would you assign to each of the seven groups of qualities? Justify your recommendations. What are the advantages and disadvantages of this method of scoring as compared to the scoring suggested on the form in the textbook?

Learning Your Job

1. Copy the rating form on page 268 and rate two displays in your store. Make a written report explaining why you did not assign perfect scores to each of the items that did not receive one.

2. Construct an interior or window display in your place of business. Ask your training sponsor or supervisor to rate it on the basis of the form on page 268. Ask him to point out what changes he would recommend in your display.

3. Ask your training supervisor or someone in your store who is familiar with display work to criticize the merchandise-display rating form on pages 268–270. Report his suggestions to the class.

42 *Creating a Display*

Whether or not you intend to become a display specialist; to enter the field of merchandising hard lines, soft lines, foods, or petroleum products; to become a store manager; or to plan on a sales career—you will have many opportunities to use the ability to create a display. Fortunately, one need not be a gifted student to do excellent display work—nor need one have any special artistic talents. The only really essential qualities necessary in making displays are genuine interest and courage to proceed. Display work is not difficult if you are willing to start with building simple displays—and these are often most effective. To many people, creating a display is fun.

Steps in Creating a Display

1. Plan the display.
2. Select merchandise carefully.
3. Prepare the display space and materials.
4. Build the display in units.
5. Make needed adjustments.
6. Use good color combinations.
7. Keep the display well lighted.
8. Maintain cleanliness throughout.
9. Use show cards.

Plan the Display. Planning begins by determining the theme of the display, the kind of merchandise to be displayed, the size and nature of the space to be used, and the display properties available. Next, a sketch of the proposed display is made. It is important to know exactly what is to be done before going into a window or making an interior display, because valuable display selling time can be lost if merchandise and props are not ready. Changing a poorly designed display also wastes time.

Select Merchandise Carefully. The merchandise selected—both featured and accessory items—must be representative of the entire stock in the selling department. There should be sufficient stock on hand to meet increased demand resulting from the display. It is very important that the items selected emphasize the theme of the display. Related merchandise items must harmonize with the promoted items.

Prepare the Display Space and Materials. This includes (a) dismantling the previous display, (b) returning the merchandise and props to their proper places, (c) washing the glass and cleaning the floor, (d) checking the lighting equipment, (e) assembling and preparing the new props and necessary tools, and (f) assembling the merchandise to be displayed.

Build the Display in Units. In constructing the units within the display, several types of props are used: (a) *structural props,* major props supporting other props and merchandise; (b) *functional props,* those supporting merchandise only, including manikins; (c) *decorative props,* those used for decoration only. Props and merchandise are arranged into units, attention being

Distributive education students in their classroom demonstrating how to arrange an interior display.

Courtesy Patterson Vocational High School, Dayton, Ohio

Behind-the-scene display artists execute designs for windows and floor displays that dramatize and create desire for merchandise.

Courtesy L. S. Ayres & Co., Indianapolis

given to eye level, neatness, and selling features of the items. For example, in a women's shoe display when heel emphasis is important, the back of the shoe faces the window in line with the angle of sight. Finally, related items are included. The latter is called *accessorizing the unit*.

Make Needed Adjustments. Even though the general layout was determined before the construction of the display began, the actual execution may call for minor revisions, resulting in the improvement of position. Units may need to be shifted slightly, backgrounds altered or adjusted. Additional props may be needed to tie the units of the display together or to direct attention to some part of the display. In building and adjusting the units in the display, the displayman always keeps in mind the principles of design—balance, proportion, and a point of interest called dominance (see Part 39).

Use Good Color Combinations. Every element in a display has a color. Attention must, therefore, be given to the colors of the background, props, merchandise, show card, floor, and sometimes lights. The art of combining and arranging major colors, minor colors and using colors in harmony and with good taste was discussed on pages 263–264.

Keep the Display Well Lighted. The amount of light required will depend on the merchandise, the size and shape of the window, and the character of the adjoining windows or surroundings. In some cases, especially where colored lighting is used throughout the display, lens spotlights are used to direct a sharply defined spot of light on some article.

Maintain Cleanliness. Each piece of merchandise and equipment used should be cleaned before it is placed into position. Cleaning fluid and tissue paper are used to clean all glass fixtures, including the bases for manikins. The floor is vacuumed or washed, and tools are kept clean to avoid soiling props or merchandise. Manikins are handled with tissue paper and plastic bags are placed over their heads during the time the display is under construction in order to protect them.

A typesetter at work setting type for all kinds of show cards.

Courtesy L. S. Ayres & Co., Indianapolis

Use Show Cards. In displays, the show card is the "voice" of the merchandise. Customers often cannot see the hidden features or qualities in an article of merchandise, and these should be described briefly on the properly placed show card.

Show Cards Carry the Message

As a rule, no display is complete without a show card carrying the selling message. How is the merchandise used? What are its good features? Why should it be purchased now? Usually the price appears on the show card, or separate price cards are used for each item. Counter signs on which appear the price and several sales words are usually used with interior displays. Window cards in large stores should always indicate the location of the merchandise in the store and give the store name.

Copy That Clicks. In writing good show-card copy, the copy writer should keep in mind a few guiding principles:

1. Use everyday words—the copy must be easily understood.
2. Make use of trade names, trade-marks, and names of designers.
3. Be brief—concentrate on one thought or idea.
4. Use informative, educational copy—new ideas, new uses, new fashions.
5. Use persuasion—help the customer to make up his mind.
6. Be original—use humor in good taste.
7. Be truthful—do not exaggerate.
8. Aim at your largest interested group.

A good example of the value of good copy was revealed by a New York University study of show cards used with interior displays. In one store studied, women's belts were displayed on an open aisle table. Sign A read: "Bright Metal

5 units

SHIRT
SALE

TODAY

7 units

An outline of a show
card for a shirt sale,
showing the ideal pro-
portions for margins.

4 units   4 units

Belts—98¢ each." Sign B read: "Brighten Your Dress—Smart Metal Belts—
98¢ each." Sign B sold 24 per cent more merchandise than sign A.

Layout That Attracts Attention. Good layout with fair lettering results in a more attractive show card than good lettering with poor layout. Since
merchandising personnel are frequently responsible for determining show-card
copy and may be called upon to plan layouts, a few simple suggestions regarding
the latter may prove helpful:

1. Make thumbnail sketches—it takes the guesswork out of layout.
2. Use generously proportioned margins: bottom, 7 units; top, 5 units; sides,
   4 units.
3. Balance the layout: formal or informal balance.
4. Emphasize important copy; divide the copy according to importance and
   assign relative-size lettering.

FRED LAZARUS, JR.
Chairman of the Board of Federated Department Stores, Inc.

Lettering That Is Easy to Read. To make signs for window and counter use, only one style of lettering is needed—the "Speedball Gothic" shown below. Gothic letters are made with strokes of uniform width. Note how the various strokes forming each letter are numbered with the small arrows indicating the direction of the stroke. In hand lettering, most failures are caused by experimenting with too many different styles of lettering.

accessorizing   functional prop
  the unit   structural prop
decorative prop

Can You Answer These?

1. What are the steps in constructing a display?
2. What information is needed to plan a display?
3. What factors should be considered in selecting merchandise for a display?
4. What is included in preparing the display space and materials?
5. What is meant by preparing the units of a display?
6. In what ways does a person apply the principles of color and design while building a display?
7. What factors should be considered when determining the lighting of a display?
8. Why is cleanliness so important in the construction of a display?
9. What is the function of a show card in a display?
10. What suggestions should the composer of a show card keep in mind when writing copy?
11. What suggestions can you offer for show-card layout?

Problems and Projects

1. Make a sketch of a window or interior display indicating the colors used. Describe the factors you considered in arriving at the theme and tell how the proposed display carries out the theme.
2. Construct a simple classroom display with merchandise, books, or other available materials. List the main steps and minor activities you performed in making it.
3. Construct a display in your school outside the classroom, such as rearranging the trophy case. Use suitable props and accessory merchandise. Explain the procedure you followed to the class.
4. Using the suggestions given in your textbook, make a counter card or window card.
5. Procure from your counselor or other source literature describing occupations in the field of display or visual merchandising. Then prepare a report on career opportunities in this field.

Learning Your Job

1. Observe the construction of a display in your store. Make a list of the different activities the person engages in while building the display and report on them to your class.
2. Visit the display storeroom in your store. Make a list of the different kinds of props you see, noting the location of each.
3. Bring to class several discarded show cards from your store. Explain to your classmates the good and poor points of the cards. Reconstruct one of the cards as you think it should be.

12. Sales Promotion

METAL MAGIC

the costume

NEW D'

GET IT AT

FURNITURE

SALE

SAVE

HUG

METAL MAGIC
new blade devel-
sures you clean,
with almost
and com

4.00
4.00

e new black-and-bea

shine at theatre, cockt

at the edges with je

, in lines superbly new

zzle, a dark blaze of exc

entle curv

eels

s a rich girl. Go

ing goil to deny herself high fashion, when

e to the rescue with smart clothes at

es. If you're loaded with taste, but not wit

's and walk out looking like a m

NEW

RONA

Unit 12 Part 43

Everyone's Part in Sales Promotion

A gasoline service-station owner was asked how he accounted for his lucrative business. He replied, "Consistent sales promotion."

He explained that his sales of over $100,000 annually depended on the efforts of all his employees, who worked on a profit-sharing plan. He expected them to give quick and courteous service. Moreover, they were to suggest replacement of worn parts, such as windshield wipers and fan belts. If, upon inspection, the tires looked worn, the customer was to be reminded of special prices and trade-in allowances. Each time a car was lubricated, the oil changed, or other repair or tune-up work done, a file card was filled out. The card indicated the owner's name and address, the work done, the date, and the speedometer reading. The file was checked each month, and notices were sent to customers, reminding them of the need for a check-up.

The dealer also used other promotional devices. He displayed banners and signs supplied by the gasoline jobber. Letters of welcome, offering a free lubrication and oil change, were sent to new residents of the community. Charge accounts were available. Cars to be serviced were picked up and delivered to the customer's home or place of employment. Advertisements of "specials" on tires, batteries, and repair work were inserted in the local paper.

The service-station owner practiced what he preached. Sound sales promotion is consistent sales promotion, involving everyone in the firm.

Some people think that sales promotion is only advertising, but it is more than that. *Sales promotion* consists of all efforts of the store to sell merchandise and to persuade the customer that it is a good place in which to trade. Thus, sales promotion in a broad sense is the responsibility of the whole store and not the function of any one department exclusively. The advertising and display departments play a part. So do the salespeople. Still others are involved in promoting sales and customer good will, such as deliverymen—who must be careful and considerate; cashiers—who must be accurate; and credit personnel—who must be tactful and understanding.

Sales promotion that co-ordinates the efforts of all in the store pays big dividends. When all employees make an effort to give customers a good impression of the store—when they call attention to store services and merchandise—this teamwork results in greater customer satisfaction and increased sales.

To attract attention to his store opening, the florist is giving favors to his
customers.

Courtesy E. I du Pont de Nemours and Co., Inc.

Planning Promotional Events

A large store uses many sales-promotion activities. It advertises its merchandise
throughout the year and uses special sales promotions from time to time. The
subject of advertising will be discussed later in this unit.

Store sales promotions are of two types. One type, *sales events,* are promotions that feature merchandise at reductions in price—anniversary sales, white
sales, and end-of-the-month clearances, for example. Sales effort, carried on
regularly to increase the sale of merchandise at usual prices, is another form of
sales promotion.

Special promotions involve much planning. A *promotional calendar* must be
made in advance. This is a schedule showing the date of each event, the theme,
what merchandise is to be featured, and the departments involved. The promotional calendar serves many purposes. It tells the advertising and display
departments what preparation they must make. It informs buyers what merchandise must be ordered and when. It reminds stockkeepers and markers what
merchandise must be marked with special tickets and what must be brought to
the sales floor. And, it reminds the personnel department to give special sales
training to regular salespeople and to employ and train additional salespeople.

Retailers Use Other Promotional Methods to Increase Sales

Progressive retailers use many methods to increase sales volume. Among the
most used are credit and trading stamps.

Credit-Sales Promotion

Credit business is good business when it is properly controlled. Merchants view
credit as a major sales-promotion tool; therefore, the credit department must
be active in:

1. Securing new credit accounts
2. Persuading customers with inactive accounts to resume buying
3. Encouraging customers with active accounts to trade in more departments and increase their purchases

A well-planned credit-sales promotion program will seek out desirable credit customers from many sources. Among the best are:

1. Newcomers to the community, especially those employed in responsible positions as teachers, business executives, professional people, and skilled workers
2. Newlyweds, many of whom will be furnishing a home or apartment
3. Young people, especially those who are about to take their first job and begin leading adult lives
4. New homeowners, who will be in the market for everything from fertilizers to wallpaper

A program of soliciting new and old charge accounts may be carried out by personal visits, suggestions by salespeople, letters, telephone calls, newspaper advertisements, and radio announcements.

Trading-Stamp Plans

Many merchants find that trading-stamp plans are business stimulators. Such plans have been used since the turn of the century, but their great popularity has come since 1950. Stamp plans are now widely used, especially by food stores and gasoline service stations.

Trading-stamp firms may be independently owned or owned by a group of retailers. These firms sell stamps to the retailer for usually $10 to $15 for a book of 5,000. In turn, the retailer gives stamps to customers, commonly at the rate of one stamp for each 10 cents in purchases. When pasted in books, the stamps are redeemable for merchandise supplied by the trading-stamp firm. There is much argument over the value of stamps to the consumer. However,

This large drugstore is inviting customers to open charge accounts.

Courtesy Drug Fair, Arlington, Va.

The Thanksgiving Day parade—one of the most effective ways to promote a store.

Courtesy J. L. Hudson Co., Detroit

one study * shows that the merchandise obtained by one book of 1,200 stamps is worth about $3.20 at retail. The customer is, therefore, receiving, in effect, a discount of about 2 per cent on every dollar he spends in stores that give stamps.

Considering the percentage of gross sales he must pay for trading stamps, the merchant should obtain at least 15 per cent additional sales volume if the stamp plan is to be profitable to him. This raises a serious question as to whether trading stamps are good for the small retailer. Some argue that the money could be better spent for advertising. On the other hand, some merchants feel that stamps are necessary because so many other merchants use them. Experience seems to show that, like other promotional devices, their use should result in profit or they should not be used.

Other Promotional Devices

Retailers use many other promotional devices to supplement an advertising program. Fashion shows are favorites to introduce new lines. Novelties, imprinted with the store name, may be given away—pencils, ball-point pens, children's tee-shirts, and balloons. Stores also put on carnivals in parking lots, have concerts in the store, and plan "coke parties" for teen-agers. Any promotional device is valuable if it is in good taste, builds trade, and enhances the store's reputation.

The Role of Retail Advertising

Retail advertising is one method of influencing consumers to trade with the store—a method in which a variety of mass media are used to reach customers. Efforts within the store to create business—such as window displays, banners, fashion shows, and personal salesmanship—are not usually considered advertising. These are designated as promotional activities. Thus, advertising is only a part of the store's total sales-promotion effort.

* "Summary Information on Trading Stamps," *Business Service Bulletin 182,* U.S. Department of Commerce and Sperry & Hutchinson Co., Washington, D.C.

Purposes of Retail Advertising

The advertising done by a store is often termed "mass salesmanship" because it attempts to presell large groups of people on the store—its merchandise, services, and character. A particular advertisement, however, printed or spoken over the radio or television, attempts to achieve one or more of the following major purposes:

1. To sell goods. Advertisements create the interest and desire that will get the shopper either to come into the store and ask for the article or to telephone or mail in an order.
2. To bring the customer to the store. Merchants want customers to come to the store and look over the offerings. Often, "leader" advertising is used.
3. To create good will. Through advertising, the merchant can create a store personality and acquaint shoppers with store policies.
4. To level out sales. All stores have times during the week or month when sales volume is low. For example, many food markets advertise specials for Mondays and department stores often promote heavily for Wednesdays.
5. To attract new customers. In addition to holding old customers, advertising can develop new ones: young people as they enter adult life, new residents, and people whose rising incomes have made them customers for higher quality merchandise.
6. To introduce new ideas. Advertising can tell the customer about new fashions, new lines added to the inventory, new products on the market, or additional store services, such as parking and credit plans.

Advertising is a valuable sales-promotion tool, but the merchant must recognize that it cannot overcome bad store practices. Even an extensive campaign cannot offset poor merchandising. Advertising will not overcome a bad location, nor will it sell goods that people do not want. Above all, advertising cannot overcome careless service by salespeople, deliverymen, cashiers, and other employees.

Father's Day is one of the most effective promotional devices invented for selling all types of merchandise used by men.

Courtesy National Retail Merchants Assoc.

Two Basic Types of Advertising Used by Stores

Retail advertising may be classified according to two basic forms or types: institutional and promotional.

Institutional advertising attempts to sell the store rather than specific merchandise. It attempts to persuade customers that the store is a good place to trade. It emphasizes the reputation of the store and helps develop in the mind of the shopper an image or picture of the store's personality. Through institutional advertising, the store may boost civic projects to show its interest in worthwhile civic activities.

Through *promotional advertising,* the firm tries to sell specific merchandise. It emphasizes the selling points of the goods, whether promoted at the regular price or offered in a special sale. The rest of this unit will deal with the "how-to-do-it" of promotional advertising.

Forms of Promotional Advertising

Co-operative Advertising

Modern merchandisers are turning increasingly to co-operative advertising, which is a method rather than a type of advertising. In this method, the cost of newspaper advertising space or of radio or television time is shared by the local retailer and his supplier. The following example is common practice. A manufacturer of lawn mowers knows that more mowers can be produced and sold if customers know their good qualities. The manufacturer, therefore, employs an advertising agency to create an advertisement, or a series of advertisements. These appear in local newspapers with the local retailer's name and address inserted at the bottom of the advertisement.

Co-operative advertising has advantages for the retailer. The advertisements are usually well prepared with excellent art work. Since the manufacturer or distributor shares the expense of advertising, the cost to the retailer is substantially reduced. For this reason, the merchant may be able to use the more expensive methods of advertising, such as television. Retailers also derive a benefit when they tie in with a national promotional campaign that attracts much attention and presells the product. Some merchants feel, however, that co-operative advertisements do not really feature their store and emphasize its personality. Further, some feel that the advertising budget of a small store is too limited to have the store participate in an advertising campaign.

Circulars. Another method of advertising is also classified as co-operative. Sometimes merchants get together and share the cost of a special shopper's section of a newspaper or of a multiple-page circular delivered to homes in the merchant's trading area. The use of circulars is quite common in neighborhood shopping districts and in areas surrounding shopping centers. Merchants feel that the drawing power of this kind of advertising is greater and that the cost is reduced.

Charity Advertising. This may be considered a form of co-operative advertising to gain community good will. Retailers are often deluged by requests to purchase charity advertising. They are asked to contribute to civic projects by purchasing advertising space in programs for athletic contests or for plays by women's clubs, or in school newspapers and yearbooks, and in publications of fraternal associations.

The retailer faces a dilemma. The causes are usually worthy, and the good will of the community is an asset to the merchant; but, he recognizes that most charity advertising brings in little business. Accordingly, the intelligent merchant treats the cost as a donation—he does not charge it to his advertising budget.

Who Creates the Advertisement?

In the small store, the proprietor or his assistant usually prepares all the advertising. In the large store, this function is delegated to specialists in the sales-promotion or advertising department. Copy writers, artists, and layout men are employed in the advertising department of a large store and in the central headquarters of a retail chain. It is their responsibility to create ideas and to carry out these ideas in the form of finished advertisements ready to send to the local newspaper, shopping guide, or other media.

Retailers also rely on employees of newspapers and other media to help them prepare advertisements. Advertising agencies are seldom used by retailers, although smaller retailers sometimes employ the services of writers and artists on a part-time basis.

DOROTHY SHAVER, 1897–1959
Late president of Lord & Taylor, New York; outstanding particularly for her achievements in advertising and sales promotion.

Fair Trade Code

for ADVERTISING and SELLING
of the NATIONAL ASSOCIATION OF BETTER BUSINESS BUREAUS, INC.

I	Serve the public with honest values.
II	Tell the truth about what is offered.
III	Tell the truth in a forthright manner so its significance may be understood by the trusting as well as the analytical.
IV	Tell customers what they want to know—what they have a right to know and ought to know about what is offered so that they may buy wisely and obtain the maximum satisfaction from their purchases.
V	Be prepared and willing to make good as promised and without quibble on any guarantee offered.
VI	Be sure that the normal use of merchandise or services offered will not be hazardous to public health or life.
VII	Reveal material facts, the deceptive concealment of which might cause consumers to be misled.
VIII	Advertise and sell merchandise or service on *its* merits and refrain from attacking your competitors or reflecting unfairly upon their products, services, or methods of doing business.
IX	If testimonials are used, use only those of competent witnesses who are sincere and honest in what they say about what you sell.
X	Avoid all tricky devices and schemes such as deceitful trade-in allowances, fictitious list prices, false and exaggerated comparative prices, bait advertising, misleading free offers, fake sales and similar practices which prey upon human ignorance and gullibility.

Advertising Standards

In recent years, increasing effort has been made to improve advertising standards. This has been true of national as well as local advertising. National trade associations have promoted higher advertising standards by discouraging the use of ambiguous, misleading, or false statements by manufacturers or distributors;

by informing their members regarding proper and effective methods of advertising; and by keeping members informed regarding laws or regulations pertaining to advertising.

Local commercial organizations, such as the chamber of commerce and better business bureau, have contributed largely to improved local advertising practices. They have done this by drafting suitable codes of standards of advertising practice and by developing effective procedures for obtaining compliance with these codes. The codes, which have been adopted in various cities, attempt to clarify questions relating to advertising practices and to clearly define advertising terms. These codes usually prohibit the offering of "free" goods and the use of exaggerated statements regarding merchandise or prices; and they require that the advertiser accurately describe the merchandise he is trying to sell. In some communities, merchants who accept and follow the code of ethics prescribed by their local organizations are permitted to use a distinctive seal in their stores, in windows, and on advertising. A fair-trade code for advertising and selling prepared by the National Association of Better Business Bureaus is shown on page 288.

Trade Talk

sales promotion
promotional
   calendar
institutional
   advertising
charity
   advertising
leader advertising
promotional
   advertising
co-operative
   advertising

Can You Answer These?

1. What activities in a store are part of the sales-promotion program?

2. What is the difference between regular merchandise promotions and special sales events?

3. In what ways does a promotional calendar affect the work of departments in a store?

4. What practices are followed in credit-sales promotion?

5. What are the main purposes of retail advertising?

6. Who is responsible for advertising in a small store? in a large store?

7. How is a trading-stamp plan usually carried on?

8. What are the essential features of co-operative advertising between retailers and suppliers?

9. Why does the retailer usually find himself in a dilemma about charity advertising?

10. What poor practices in a store can advertising not overcome?

Problems and Projects

1. Make a list of the various kinds of workers in a store, such as stockkeepers, displaymen, etc. For each worker, explain how he does or does not play a part in the sales-promotion program.

2. Choose a kind of store that interests you. What types of people would you try to reach if you were responsible for credit-sales promotion in that store? Give reasons for your choices.

3. For each of the following types of retailers prepare arguments for or against offering a trading-stamp plan to customers: (a) chain food supermarket, (b) downtown fashion shoe store, (c) independent

gasoline service station, (d) neighborhood drugstore.

4. For a store with which you are familiar, describe possible promotional activities other than advertising, credit, or trading stamps.

5. In addition to the purposes of advertising given in the text, make a list of as many more as you can think of.

6. Study the advertisements in one issue of a local paper. Bring to class any that you feel are misleading or unethical. What proportion of the advertising did your study show to be up to ethical standards? Do you think a retailer can advertise dishonestly and "get away with it"? Why or why not?

Learning Your Job

1. Explain who is responsible in your store for sales-promotion activities, including advertising. What part do you play?

2. If possible, bring a promotional calendar to class, explain what it means, and how it is used. If you cannot bring one, make up one for a department in your store for the coming month.

3. Explain how your store engages in each of the following promotional activities: credit, trading stamps, co-operative advertising, and minor promotional devices such as give-aways. If your store does not participate, try to find out why.

44 *Retail Advertising— Mass Salesmanship*

Take a poll and "Mr. Retailer," large or small, will admit that he faces a truly bothersome question, "Which advertising medium is best for me?" By *medium* (the plural, *media*, is often used) is meant the means by which the advertising message is transmitted to the customer.

The merchant's first thought is likely to be "newspaper"—in fact, most large stores spend over 75 per cent of their advertising money in this medium. Radio and mailed circulars, however, are also widely used, often to supplement newspapers, sometimes exclusively. Less often used are such media as television, bus cards, and billboards.

Even when the basic means of advertising has been chosen, the retailer faces other questions. "Which newspaper will best reach my customers—newspaper X or newspaper Y? this radio station or that one? Which newspaper will give me the most help in preparing my advertisements? Which medium will give me the most sales for the least cost?" Only when the correct decisions have been made, will advertising prove to be profitable.

The Advertising Plan

All advertising must be carefully planned. If a store invests only a dollar in advertising, a plan should be made. An *advertising plan* is an outline of what is to be advertised, when time and space are to be purchased, and how much is to be spent. In larger stores, the advertising plan is made by the advertising manager, the sales-promotion director, the merchandise manager, and their staffs all working together. In smaller stores, the planning is usually the responsibility of the manager, who sometimes seeks the advice of experienced employees.

Advantages of Planning. An advertising plan is a part of the store's total budgeting procedure and has many advantages. It helps buyers to plan merchandise purchases far in advance, at a time when the right merchandise can be bought at the right price. Departments are more likely to receive a fair share of the advertising budget. Copy writers and artists have more time to be creative when deadlines are far distant. Writing advertisements is creative work, and the advertising manager and his staff artists and copy writers can do a better job if they know some time in advance what advertising is to be prepared. They can gather ideas by observing the advertisements of competitors and by studying the results obtained from the advertising of their own store. Most important, advertising can be spread over the entire selling season with enough money budgeted for important sales events.

What to Advertise

In deciding what merchandise is to be advertised, the merchant must remember one principle—while advertising results in many benefits, its main purpose is to sell goods at a profit. In application, this principle means advertising the "best sellers"; that is, merchandise that appeals to the public and that will produce a profit for the store. At times it may be desirable to advertise goods that have been marked down in price for clearance.

Best sellers are of several different kinds. Brands that are heavily advertised nationally may be partly sold already. Best sellers are often identified as a seasonal item—shoes for back-to-school, candy at Easter, garden tools in the spring. Since customers are price-conscious, best sellers are often popularly priced. Many wise merchants advertise heavily "fad" merchandise or fashion goods that are hitting the peak of their popularity. The important thing for the retailer to remember is that some items are best sellers everywhere, others only for a particular store and its clientele.

Finding Best-Selling Items. Several sources will help a merchant discover his best-selling items. His own stock-control records will show him what goods sold, when, and in what sizes, colors, and models. Alert salespeople and buyers can provide tips on what customers are asking for. Salesmen from reliable wholesalers and manufacturers bring news from other markets. In chain-store organizations, information is collected from all units of the chain; and reports are sent to managers telling about trends in different areas. Many times the small-town merchant can get ideas of trends by watching the advertisements in large city newspapers. Large and small retailers can find helpful information from figures obtained from the U.S. Department of Commerce reports and from trade associations and other business sources.

When to Advertise

In determining when to advertise, the retailer begins with his merchandising seasons. In most stores there are two six-month seasons: spring—February through July; and fall—August through January. Often an advertising plan is made for each season. In order to insure a continuous advertising campaign— even a minimum one—an advertising budget is made for a six-month period and then an allowance is made for each month and week. Extra money is allotted for heavy-volume weeks, for long promotion periods—such as Christmas and Easter—and for regular promotional events, such as anniversary sales and "Back-to-School Week."

Merchants are often perplexed about what day of the week is best for advertising. One indicator is the buying habits in the community. For example, in one community in which big payrolls come on Friday, Saturday is a big day on Main Street. In other towns, Friday is the big day. Merchants can obtain such information by checking their own records, by participating in chamber of commerce studies, or by reviewing shopping surveys made by local schools and colleges.

Experts advise most retailers to advertise as often as possible. This continuity keeps the store constantly in the customer's mind with one advertisement building on the next. Daily advertising, or weekly at a minimum, is advised. If necessary, because of a limited budget, special promotions may have to receive smaller allotments in order to keep up a regular campaign.

How Much to Invest in Advertising

How much money to budget for advertising is a question that perplexes many merchants. Experience is a guide, but only a partial one. A reliable method to start with is to look at the amounts other retailers spend. Trade associations often compile statistics on average advertising budgets. For example, the Bureau of Advertising of the American Newspaper Publishers Association cites the investments in advertising given in the table on the facing page.

Types of Advertising Budgets. Several ways of budgeting for advertising are in use:

1. Set the budget as a percentage of the previous year's sales. This method is very common but does not take into consideration factors causing a good or poor year. Nor does it take care of new situations, such as the addition of a new line of goods or a new competitor.

Types of Stores	Percentage of Net Sales Spent for Advertising
Department stores	
Sales	
Under $1,000,000	3.5
$1,000,000 to $2,000,000	3.9
$2,000,000 to $5,000,000	4.5
Drugstores	1.0
Furniture stores	7.3
General merchandise stores	2.0
Grocery stores	1.5
Hardware stores	2.5
Jewelry stores	3.9
Men's clothing stores	4.0
Shoe stores	2.9
Women's ready-to-wear stores	3.5
Restaurants	3.1

2. Allot money in terms of the sales forecast for the year. This method has merit because it means the merchant is thinking ahead; however, it also means that the retailer must be able to forecast accurately business conditions in the coming year—not an easy task.

3. Determine the budget by the objective-and-task method. In this method, the merchant determines his sales goals by department and merchandise line. As the year passes, sales are reviewed, usually monthly. If the sales goal is being met, the plan is followed. If not, advertising is increased.

Selection of a Medium

Once the advertising plan has been adopted and the budget determined upon, the retailer is ready to decide where to advertise—newspapers, circulars, radio, television, or in other media. The choice of a medium depends on several factors. The first criterion is whether the retailer wants his advertisement to have the effect of a shotgun or a rifle. In other words, does he want a medium like radio that conveys his message to thousands regardless of whether they are potential customers or not? Or, does he choose a method, like direct mail, that enables him to pinpoint his target—only those people who would be interested in the type of product he sells? Using a medium with a shotgun effect when a rifle is needed only results in waste circulation—a loss for the retailer.

The second criterion in choosing a medium is flexibility. This means the ability to change the advertising message quickly to take advantage of some event. For example, radio spot announcements have flexibility, since the spoken message can be changed immediately to advertise shovels when a snowstorm strikes.

Advertisement of a best-selling item.

A third criterion is the sales potential of the product being advertised. In other words, can enough of the item be sold to cover the cost of the advertisement? Here is a big difference between advertising by retailers and advertising done by manufacturers. The manufacturer can afford large sums for national television advertising, since the effort is concentrated on one product, or a line of products, that may have a sale of millions of dollars. On the other hand, the retailer must advertise many items, each of which may sell in limited quantities.

Other criteria involved are the size of the store and the amount it can spend for advertising and the amount of copy or the illustrations needed to fully describe the product.

Types of Media

Because each product advertised by a given retailer has certain advertising requirements, there is no "one best bet" among media. Studies by trade associations, such as the National Retail Merchants Association and the National Retail Hardware Association, however, come to one conclusion. The newspaper is used most extensively by retailers, especially those of large or medium size. Most experts, therefore, recommend a consistent, day-to-day newspaper advertising plan, supplemented by direct mail, radio, and other media to reach particular groups of customers at a given time for a given purpose.

In the following paragraphs, the

advantages and disadvantages of each of the media will be outlined briefly; however, the retailer should analyze each medium according to the criteria given in previous paragraphs.

Newspapers. The daily or weekly newspaper offers a number of advantages to the retailer. Newspapers reach a large number of people at a low cost per message. Also, their circulation area is often about the same as the trading area of the large retailer. Much of the circulation may, however, be wasted for the small neighborhood store with a limited trading area.

Newspapers are also read by many people because, in addition to news, special features are carried—such as sports, women's pages, church activities, financial topics, and society functions. In addition, special sections are devoted to activities in suburban areas and neighboring towns. Often an advertisement can be given a position in one of these special sections. In larger communities, the foreign-language paper offers a good chance to advertise to a special group of shoppers.

Timing is another advantage of newspapers. Copy can be changed, usually daily, to take advantage of special events or changes in the weather. Newspaper advertising offers also the opportunity to illustrate the product, often with low-cost art work. A major advantage of newspapers over other media is in the consumer's attitude. Many people consciously use it as a guide to shopping, looking forward to such features as Thursday's grocery advertisements, or the weekly shopper's guide section carried by many papers. A disadvantage, however, especially of small newspapers, is the low-quality reproduction of art work and the unskilled presswork.

Advertisement to launch the start of the Christmas sales-promotion season by a local chamber of commerce.

Direct Circularizing. The term, *direct circularizing,* is used to describe advertising distributed by mail or by house-to-house delivery. Included are sales letters, coupons, catalogues, handbills, and folders enclosed with monthly credit statements.

Direct circulars are very useful for the small retailer with a limited trading area and for specialty shops with a small clientele. For these merchants and others who wish to advertise to a special group, direct circulars can eliminate much waste circulation found in other media.

Direct circulars provide the opportunity to use longer sales messages, to illustrate the product better, and to attract attention by color. Handbills are economical if carefully distributed. They are excellent for small merchants who can often prepare and duplicate them themselves. The retailer should, however, use any direct circular with caution. Indiscriminate stuffing of envelopes with folders and literature only leads customers to throw it all in the wastebasket without reading it.

Direct circularization is a "rifle" method of advertising, but it depends on an accurate method of distribution. Mailing lists must be kept up to date. Names of customers who have moved, died, or become bad credit risks should be eliminated. New prospects should be added. Mailing lists can be compiled from store records—credit forms and sales slips—or from city directories. Lists of specialized groups of prospects—such as teachers, dentists, and country-club members—can be purchased from firms specializing in compiling direct-mail lists.

Radio. Since the advent of television, radio listening habits—and hence, radio programming—have changed dramatically. People no longer sit in the evenings in their living rooms listening to the radio. Instead they listen while they work in the home or at their job, or as they drive, fish, lie on the beach, or relax in the garden. Consequently, radio, with more listeners now than formerly, has turned to a new type of programming. Stations broadcast mainly news, weather, and music, usually relying on the popularity of the disk jockey. Commercial advertising consists primarily of short *spot announcements,* which are messages of 20, 30, or 60 seconds in length, spotted between programs or inserted in the middle of programs.

Advantages and Disadvantages. The new type of radio program has many advantages for the retailer. Spot announcements are low in cost and can be repeated frequently. The message can be changed quickly. The retailer also can tie in his store name with commercials prepared and paid for by national advertisers—his suppliers. Another advantage of radio advertising lies in the personal appeal of the human voice—friendly, exciting, and warm. The store and product also take advantage of the personal popularity that the disk jockey has with his listeners.

Radio, however, has disadvantages. Many products require illustrating which the spoken message cannot do. Also, radio can have much waste circulation if the listeners are outside the trading area; or, what is worse, if potential customers are not listening when the store's advertisement is being broadcast. However, radio is effective to supplement other media and to publicize special sales events.

Television. Today television reaches into almost every home and commands many hours of families' time. Yet, for most retailers, television is too technical and too high priced as an advertising medium. However, when it can be used, it has the advantages of large audiences, visual presentation, and the human voice.

Large retailers have used television successfully, usually by institutional advertising to gain prestige rather than to sell a specific product. Thus, they sponsor news programs, children's shows, and coverage of special events. The television advertising most widely used by retailers has been commercials between programs or between acts of the late evening movies. Retailers, even quite small ones, have obtained surprising sales results by messages tied in with commercials presented by national advertisers. Thus, television, like radio, is a supplementary medium for most retailers.

Other Media

Retailers also use other media to supplement their basic newspaper campaign. The yellow pages of the telephone directory bring surprising sales returns, especially for service businesses. Bus cards are low in cost and read repeatedly. Outdoor signs, or billboards, are useful especially for retailers in smaller towns. Advertising in a neighborhood theater presents a good opportunity for the small merchant to call attention to his store and to its merchandise.

Trade Talk

advertising plan media
advertising   flexibility of
  budget   media
direct   spot
  circularizing   announcement

Can You Answer These?

1. By what methods can merchants determine how much money to invest in advertising? Which method is best?
2. In what ways does a retailer benefit by making an advertising plan?
3. The text says that retailers should advertise best sellers. What characteristics mark such merchandise?
4. Where can the merchant find out which items are best sellers?

5. What advice could you offer a retailer who wants to know when it is best to advertise?
6. What criteria should be used in selecting a media?
7. Why have merchants used newspapers as their primary media?
8. How has radio programming changed in the last few years? In what ways has this affected its usefulness as an advertising medium for retailers?
9. Why is direct circularizing called a "rifle" method of advertising?

Problems and Projects

1. If television were to be less expensive as an advertising medium, would it be valuable for most retailers? Explain your opinion.
2. Find out what the advertising

rates are in your community for the following media: newspapers, radio, television, billboards, and mailed circulars. In order to compare rates, you may find it wise to set up a hypothetical case—that is, a type of store and an advertising plan for one sales event.

3. Organize committees to visit several stores of each of the following types: food stores, department stores, drugstores, and clothing stores. Find out approximately how much each store spends for advertising and which media are used.

4. Choose a type of store in which you are interested. Imagine that you are planning the advertising for this store. Make a chart of the advantages and disadvantages to the store of each of the advertising media listed in the text.

5. Using the amount of advertising carried in your local newspaper as a guide, rate the days of the week in order of their importance to retailers as shown by their advertisements. Explain why different types of stores advertise on different days of the week.

Learning Your Job

1. Retail advertisers must be able to determine which items are their best sellers. For your store or department make a list of at least ten best-selling articles. Explain why you chose each one and what sources of information you used.

2. Find out which advertising media are used by your store. Explain why each media is used and for what purpose. Your supervisor or the advertising manager can help you. Add this information to your store manual.

3. Try to obtain a copy of the advertising plan your store uses. Explain to the class what it provides and how it is used. If a copy is not available to bring to school, make notes on what the plan contains.

45 *The Results of Good Advertising Copy*

Time and time again experience has proved that the cash register will beat a merry tune if the advertising message strikes the customer's fancy. The following story is typical of the power of advertising copy that hits the right note: *

> A leading department store found that it had ordered four times the amount of men's jewelry it had originally intended to buy. To move the overstock, the store decided to use large ads in a local newspaper during the two weeks prior to Christmas, the only period in which the sale of the gift merchandise was practicable.

* *Printers' Ink,* February 15, 1946, p. 31.

Copy was developed, and a special position on the sports page was selected. The advertising representative from the newspaper, who knew how desperately the store executive wanted to move the merchandise, checked every two days to find out how well it was selling. Results were disappointing; only a few pieces had been sold.

Store executives finally asked the newspaper ad man if he could suggest any ideas that might step up sales. The representative asked them to switch the ads from the sports page to the women's page and change copy to read: "Give a man a gift a man would buy for himself." The changes were made, and within 48 hours the complete shipment of men's jewelry was sold out. New merchandise was ordered and the ads were continued.

Basic Newspaper Copy

We have learned that newspaper advertising is the principal form of retail advertising. The retailer, therefore, should learn first how to write the kind of newspaper copy that will bring customer response and result in sales action. What he learns about copy writing will help him with direct circularizing, show cards, and to some extent with radio and television advertising. With this in mind, the illustrations and examples in this part, and in the following one on layout, are based on newspaper advertising.

More small retailers could write their own copy if they would try. They are aiming at a local market that they know well. With this knowledge, they could try their hand at writing creative copy, the kind with a local, personalized appeal.

Even if merchants do not write copy, their understanding of the principles involved should serve two purposes. First, they can suggest ideas for copy because they know their merchandise and their customers well. Second, they are better able to judge the advertisements that are created for them.

Professional Advertising Services

The small retailer who wants to create his own advertisements has professional advice available. Space salesmen from local newspapers can suggest ideas for copy and layout. Radio and television stations employ writers to create messages that sell. In a large store, copy writers and layout artists are available; and the large store can consult an advertising agency.

A matrix, or mat, of an advertisement.

Courtesy National Cash Register Co.

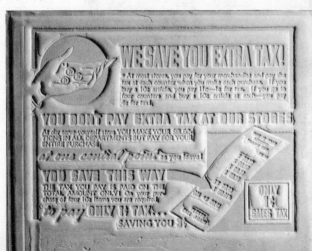

Mat Services. Excellent ideas are available from mat services. This advertising service is available through local newspapers. A *mat,* or *matrix,* is a sheet of papier-mâché on which is an impression of an advertisement that was set in type. Local printers use the mat to mold a stereotype plate that is used on the newspaper press. Mats of prepared advertisements are available also from distributors from whom the merchant buys. Mats are used also as sources of illustrations and headlines. The mat is valuable because the advertisement that it carries has usually been prepared by experts.

What to Say

The most important decision in creating an advertisement is deciding what to say. What description of the merchandise or service will appeal most to the reader's interest? What will create the desire to possess the merchandise? What will give the personal, human-interest touch that is so valuable? The preparation of an advertisement cannot begin until such questions have been answered.

Content of an Advertisement. An advertisement is composed usually of six parts: the headline, the copy or story, the illustration, the store signature or logotype, the white space, and the border. Occasionally, another part, such as a coupon, may be added.

An effective advertisement may be likened to a sales letter. In place of the salutation, "Dear Sir," the headline and the illustration go directly into action, attracting attention and building interest. The copy or story must create desire, build conviction, and move the shopper to action. But before the merchant's story can be told effectively, several preparatory steps must be taken.

The buyer and the copywriter study points of merchandise to be featured in the advertisement.

Courtesy L. S. Ayres & Co., Indianapolis

Steps in Preparing the Advertisement. In preparing an advertisement, the writer keeps in mind its resemblance to a sales letter. The importance
of the question, "Why should the customer wish to buy it?" cannot be over-
emphasized. To put the "you" angle into advertising, the retailer should:

1. Obtain all possible information about the product or service to be advertised. This can be obtained from salespeople, buyers, distributor's salesmen, and manufacturer's literature.
2. List the selling points—the ones that sizzle! From this list the copy writer
   can select the most important ones—and he will know that his information is
   accurate and not misleading. Selling points will be suggested by asking:
   What is the article? Who buys it, how is it used, and how does the customer
   benefit? Why does the retailer want to advertise it?
3. List other information necessary to provide correct information for the
   customer—is credit available, is the quantity limited, is the article guar-
   anteed, is the price correct as quoted, what colors, sizes, models, or styles
   are in stock?

Size of the Advertisement. Before copy can be written, the size of
the advertisement must be determined. The quality—not the size—of the advertisement generally determines the sales action that results; but, size also has
an effect. Large advertisements, splashed over a page or several pages, announce
the importance of a special merchandising event and create excitement among
shoppers and salespeople.

The size of an advertisement in relation to the size of the paper affects
visibility—the chance that a reader will see and read the message. For example,
a small advertisement has a better chance to attract readership in a small or
"thin" paper than it would in a many-page newspaper. Size also must be sufficient
for the illustration and the copy message.

Other considerations determining the amount of space that can be used are:
the advertising budget for the period, and the volume of sales possible on the
merchandise to be advertised.

How to Say It

After the size of the advertisement has been determined and the selling points
outlined, the copy writer must concentrate on the *headline* and the *body copy,*
the descriptive story and sales message.

Headlines with Attention-Getting Power

The headline has a definite purpose. It attracts the shopper's attention and
causes him to read the copy. Most advertising men feel that the headline is
worth at least half the value of the advertisement. All agree that if the advertisement is not "seen," it will not be read.

Headlines have several basic forms. They may ask a question, express a command, make a suggestion, or state a major selling point. No matter which form
is used, the headline must have three qualities:

. . . the "You" approach

. . . a newsy flavor

. . . a promise of gain or benefit

Use the "You" Approach. The headline is more likely to "stop" the reader if it involves him. To do this, it must have a "You" approach; and it must appeal to his self-interest. The headline should talk to the reader as a friend—in a person-to-person manner just like the salesperson does. For example:

GIVE YOURSELF FREE EVENINGS
WITH AN ABC DISHWASHER

Try a Newsy Flavor. A salesman who is excited about a product wants to tell his customer the big news. So should an advertisement! A newsy flavor stresses the new, the different, the unique, the latest thing. Thus, the headline should describe new products, new uses of an established product, or the latest styles, models, accessories, and colors. For example:

JUST ARRIVED—A PAINT THAT
COVERS RUST

or

IMAGINE, NO SCRAPING, NO CHIPPING
YOU PAINT OVER THE RUST

Promise the Reader a Benefit. Many customers pore over the advertisements; they hope to profit by making a "good buy." Therefore, the headline with "punch" and "sell" should promise the benefits of the product or service.

Retailers, advertising agencies, and media staffs have done much research in advertising. And the studies agree that the most effective headline contains a customer benefit. For example:

LOUNGE IN LUXURY
WITH A CHATHAM CHAIR

A famous salesman has said, "Sell 'em the sizzle, not the steak." This is good advice for headline writers. People buy the benefits of goods, not the goods themselves. Thus, the headline appearing like this:

TRY OUR TOP-QUALITY SIRLOIN

might be changed to:

TASTE THAT HICKORY FLAVOR!
TOP-QUALITY SIRLOIN FOR YOUR PARTY BARBECUE

The acid test of the headline lies in the answer to the question, "Will it stop the reader in his tracks?" An easy way to judge a headline's value is to place it next to several appearing in the current edition of your local newspaper. If it pales by comparison, throw it away and try again.

The "wash 'n' wear" feature as well as the name of a well-known brand in the headline will attract many buyers.

Body Copy That Convinces

The headline catches the reader's eye; the body copy must hold it. The copy story must also create desire and convince the reader sufficiently to arouse him to action.

The opening statement of the copy should follow up the headline, tying together the headline and the sales message. The opening is instrumental also in getting the customer to read the entire story. To do this, it refers to the reader's interests, for example, "Looking for ways to make your home comfortable?" The opening may be a striking claim for the quality or advantage of the article, an offer of an exceptional value, or refer to some unusual event.

Succeeding paragraphs usually go into detail, describing the product or service offered. Quality, price, service, use, and care, or combinations of these, may be emphasized.

The concluding paragraph is the "closer." It should induce the prospect to come into the store or telephone or mail in his order.

Copy With the Customer Point-of-View. In writing hard-hitting copy, the selection of the right appeal is important. If the customer viewpoint is kept in mind, the correct appeal should result. The many possible customer appeals were discussed in Unit 9. They apply to advertising just as they do to personal salesmanship.

A good copy writer talks directly to the persons he wishes to influence, using language they understand. The goal is to express thoughts vividly, in short words, and in short sentences. Simple words "pack the greatest punch." For example, *choose* is better than *select; go to bed,* better than *retire;* and *buy,* better than *purchase*. The advertising writer should avoid technical copy. Also, although he may have a great deal to say, he should stick to one idea in each paragraph. Remember, one idea is all a customer needs in order to take action.

A good practice is to read completed copy out loud. Test it for sounding clear, natural, friendly, and convincing. If it is not, try writing it again, for space is too expensive to waste words.

Trade Talk

mat (matrix)
visibility of an advertisement
mat service
body copy
headline
stereotype plate

Can You Answer These?

1. Should retailers write their own copy? What value is there in a retailer knowing how to write copy?
2. What services are available to help a merchant with planning an advertisement?
3. What are the usual parts of an advertisement?
4. Why is an advertisement likened to a sales letter?
5. In preparing an advertisement, what preparatory steps are necessary?
6. What factors affect the size of an advertisement?
7. Why is the headline so important? What three qualities must the headline have?
8. If you were assigned the task of

writing copy for a store advertisement, what rules would you follow?

9. What is the purpose of the body copy in an advertisement?

Problems and Projects

1. Bring to class at least three good and three poor examples of headlines and body copy. Explain your reasons for choosing your examples.

2. Select three effective advertisements of local stores. Explain to the class the purpose of the advertisement, the people the advertisement is trying to reach, and the buying appeal used.

3. Choose a product in which you are interested. For this product, write at least three headlines that have the qualities mentioned in the text. Then write convincing body copy for at least one headline.

4. For two products make a list of selling points that might be useful in an advertisement.

5. For your scrapbook select an effective advertisement and mark clearly each of its parts.

6. Collect several advertisements that are effective yet small in size. Explain why they are good even though they are small.

Learning Your Job

1. Write at least two examples of headlines and body copy that would be effective in an advertisement introducing a new item of merchandise in your store.

2. If possible, obtain some advertising mats supplied to your store. Show them to the class and explain how they are used. Explain also what other advertising services your store uses.

3. Find out in your store how the people who prepare advertisements get the information about the merchandise advertised. Are salespeople ever asked to supply such information?

46 *Layouts as Advertising Blueprints*

Publishing a newspaper is a complicated task, for almost all the material is new daily. Everything is done to meet an absolute deadline. Let us follow a newspaper sales representative as he leaves a retail store. He has picked up the copy for tomorrow's advertisement, a sketch of how it should look, some art work, and perhaps a photograph. The art work may be in the form of a mat or matrix.

At the newspaper plant, the copy goes to the composing room where directions are written on it showing the size and style of the type to be used. Body copy is set on a Linotype machine, which casts (molds in lead) an entire line in one piece. To change even one letter, the entire line must be recast. Large type for the headline is often set by hand.

The art work, if a mat, goes to the stereotyper who uses it as a pattern to mold a plate. Photographs are made into plates by an engraving process. All parts of the advertisement—type, plates, borders—are assembled according to the sketch made by the retailer. The parts are locked into a form, ink is applied, and a few sheets are printed by hand. These are called *proofs* and are checked by the retailer. The printer makes necessary corrections and readies the advertisement for the press. A creative idea becomes a printed sales message.

The Layout Invites Sales Action

When a person reads an advertisement, he is really being exposed to a sales talk in which the advertisement is the salesman. Thus, the advertisement must guide the shopper through the basic steps of a sale. Most advertisements aim to accomplish these four results:

1. Attract attention
2. Secure interest
3. Create desire
4. Obtain action

Layouts Are Blueprints. A printer, like other skilled craftsmen, needs a set of instructions in order to turn ideas into printed pages. The layout is a visual sketch—a blueprint. It shows the printer where the various parts of the advertisement go. It indicates to the compositor the type faces and their sizes. It tells the artist the number and kind of illustrations desired. In many cases, the rough layout shows the copy writer what copy is required.

Layouts, even in the most crudely sketched form, have another important value. They help the merchant judge whether or not the advertisement in final form will achieve the sales action he wants.

Who Does the Layout? If a retail store has an advertising department, specialized personnel will create layouts. If the services of an advertising agency are employed, its staff will design the layout. The smaller merchant often relies on the advertising staff of the local newspaper to design his advertisements.

Often the proprietor or a salesperson with a creative mind can provide ideas for effective layouts, even though the sketch may be very rough. Manufacturers sometimes supply him with mats and samples of layouts for their products. Mat services, discussed in the previous part, also supply hundreds of layout ideas.

Three Layout Forms Are Basic. In preparing an advertisement, the layout man generally uses one of three forms: one-item, group, or omnibus. In the *one-item* advertisement, it is possible to do a more thorough job with the copy and illustration.

In the *group* advertisement, several items are shown and described. For example, clothing may be shown with shoes and other accessories; or furniture, shown with linens, china, and draperies. In this way, suggestion selling may be done effectively; and more than one department in the store is given advertising space.

The *omnibus* advertisement contains a variety of items that are not related.

ANNIVERSARY PRESENT

Tiffany diamond flower clip-pin with

deeply curving petals, set with

round and baguette diamonds in a platinum setting.

Seventy one hundred dollars,

including federal tax.

TIFFANY & CO.

NEW YORK

Send for illustrated brochure "Tiffany Diamond Rings"

In this one-item adver-
tisement, the layout man
was able to show the fine
details and beauty of
workmanship of the dia-
mond flower clip-pin.

Courtesy Tiffany & Co.

This type of advertisement usually occupies a large space and pictures the diversity of the store's stock.

Most Layouts Have Similar Elements

A number of elements, or parts, are common to most layouts: (1) headlines, (2) copy blocks, (3) illustration or art work, (4) logotype—the store signature, (5) border, and (6) white space. In addition, layouts may include price and a coupon.

Illustrations. It has been said that a picture is worth a thousand words. The advertising message is thus made doubly effective when illustrations are used to attract attention and supplement the copy story.

Illustrative material consists of photographs, pen-and-ink drawings, wash drawings, and paintings. These are obtained from a number of sources. They may be done by the store's advertising department or by an advertising agency or commercial artist. Some illustrations are available from a mat service or from suppliers.

Logotypes. The *logotype* (also called a signature cut or "sig cut") is the name of the store or a design symbolic of the firm. This is set in type in

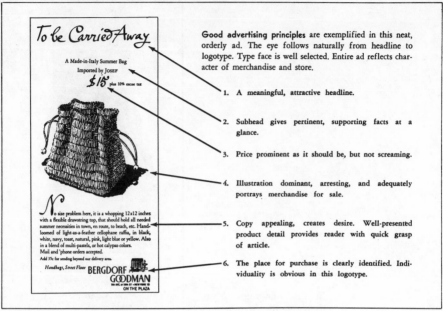

To be Carried Away

A Made-in-Italy Summer Bag
Imported by JOSEF
$15 plus 10% excise tax

No size problem here, it is a whopping 12x12 inches with a flexible drawstring top, that should hold all needed summer necessities in town, en route, to beach, etc. Hand-loomed of light-as-a-feather cellophane raffia, in black, white, navy, toast, natural, pink, light blue or yellow. Also in a blend of multi-pastels, or hot calypso colors.
Mail and 'phone orders accepted.
Add 35c for sending beyond our delivery area.

Handbags, Street Floor BERGDORF GOODMAN
ON THE PLAZA

Good advertising principles are exemplified in this neat, orderly ad. The eye follows naturally from headline to logotype. Type face is well selected. Entire ad reflects character of merchandise and store.

1. A meaningful, attractive headline.

2. Subhead gives pertinent, supporting facts at a glance.

3. Price prominent as it should be, but not screaming.

4. Illustration dominant, arresting, and adequately portrays merchandise for sale.

5. Copy appealing, creates desire. Well-presented product detail provides reader with quick grasp of article.

6. The place for purchase is clearly identified. Individuality is obvious in this logotype.

Courtesy National Cash Register Co.

different sizes and used in advertisements to identify the advertiser. A distinctive logotype is very valuable because it aids in achieving recognition and personality for the store.

Border. The border of an advertisement is like the frame of a picture. It unites the parts of the advertisement and attracts the attention of readers. Border designs, if properly used, can make the advertisement stand out from its neighbors. When poorly designed, borders may, however, tend to cheapen and clutter up the advertisement.

White Space. Modern advertisers use much white space in a layout in order to make the message stand out and command attention. There is a tendency, however, for the advertiser to want to crowd the space with type because he is paying for all the space. This tendency is unfortunate, for crowded copy is hard to read, unattractive, and cheapening.

Price. Merchants have debated long and loud over whether the price of an article should be quoted in an advertisement. The tendency now is to quote the price; however, there are exceptions. Some stores still maintain a long-standing company policy of not including price because they feel it tends to cheapen the advertisement. Others do not quote price for beginning-of-the-season merchandise—especially fashion clothing—which is being specially promoted. Many firms that attempt to maintain a reputation for exclusiveness never mention price in their advertisements.

Coupons. Sometimes coupons are included in the advertisement to invite requests for samples or for catalogues, more often to invite mail orders for the merchandise advertised.

What a Layout Should Have

The competitive strength of a layout should be tested by asking questions like the following: *

1. Does the design of the layout direct the eye movements of the reader from the top of the advertisement through the other elements? Is the most important element placed at the "optical center"—a spot just to the left of, and slightly above, the actual center of the space? Are the proportions about right, slightly deeper than wide?
2. Does the layout show a dominant element to stop the reader and direct his eye to the rest of the layout? This point-of-eye focus is sometimes the headline, but more often the illustration.
3. Is the price figure prominent? If price is counted on as a selling point, the figure should be near the article and should be given ample white space.
4. Is the advertisement competitive; that is, is the headline large enough to be seen against other advertisements? Does the logotype plainly identify the seller? Have special borders or distinctive typography been used on small advertisements to attract attention? Is the merchandise illustrated in sufficient detail so that shoppers know what it will look like? Have coupons been made noticeable by the use of solid or dotted lines surrounding them?
5. Is the design based on a standard format? Some stores follow a policy of using the same basic design for all advertisements except those for special sales. They feel that a standard format and place in the paper cause their advertisements to become familiar to the shopper. In this way, readers consciously look for the advertisements of their favorite store.

Layouts Become Printed Pages

Getting a layout into print is the job of the "back shop" of the newspaper, the place where engravings are made, type is set, and the actual printing is done. The methods used in the back shop need to be understood by the merchant even though he does not actually work with the printers. The advertiser must respect printer's deadlines and the work involved in making corrections in copy and layout. Lacking this appreciation and making frequent requests for last-minute changes cause resentment in the back shop. This in turn will cause the merchant to be turned down when he really needs help in changing his advertisement.

---

* Adapted from "Advertise . . . to Promote Your Business, to Sell Your Goods," National Cash Register Company, Dayton, Ohio, 1958, pp. 13–15.

Engraving Processes

The two most common processes for converting illustrative material into final form for printing are the line engraving and the halftone engraving. *Line engravings* (generally called line cuts or zincs) are made from line drawings; that is, drawings made with lines and dots and in which there are no shadings.

The Ben Day process uses screens to superimpose patterns upon line drawings, giving the appearance of textures and shadings to different parts of the drawing. The screened sections of the color wheel on page 262 are an illustration of this process. The finished product consists of a zinc plate nailed on a wooden block. Line drawings are especially useful when working with smaller newspapers whose equipment is not capable of turning out high-quality engravings of photographs.

Halftone plates are engravings made from photographs or other illustrative material consisting of shadings. Line cuts cannot be used for such material. In halftone engraving, the photograph is transferred to a copper plate through a "screen." In this way, the illustration is broken up into many little dots, each of which prints ink on the paper. The more dots, the closer together they will be, and the darker the part of the illustration will appear. The screen of the halftones can be detected by using a magnifying glass through which the dots can be seen.

A halftone plate is made with a varying number of dots depending on the quality of the paper to be used and the clarity desired in the finished advertisement. The most common screens are 55, 65, 85, 100, 120, 133, and 150, the numbers representing the number of dots to the square inch on the halftone plate. Newspaper stock usually requires a coarse 65-screen, while high-quality magazine paper needs a fine 120-screen.

Type Faces

There are many type faces. They are roughly classified as follows: text and display faces, roman and italic, lightface and boldface, old style and modern, serif and sans serif. (The text of this book is set in Times Roman, a serif face. The sideheads are in a sans serif boldface; the part titles in italic.) Some are simple and easy to read; others are more complex. There are a few cautions concerning the use of type in advertisements. It is good practice to use one type face, so that the store's advertisements become familiar to the readers. Faces should not be mixed as a rule, for mixed faces are displeasing. Mixed sizes are attractive if not overdone.

The type chosen for the headline and body copy can express the meaning or purpose of the advertisement.

Using the correct type can improve greatly the effectiveness of an advertisement; however, the subject of type and type faces is so large that the average merchant should consult a high-grade printer or his local newspaper. These firms employ experts in typography who are glad to advise on the preparation of an advertisement.

Trade Talk

logotype   linotype

border   line engraving

white space   halftone

"back shop"

Can You Answer These?

1. What purposes does an advertising layout serve?

2. Who designs a layout?

3. What are the differences between the three basic layout forms?

4. Why do many merchants value so highly their logotypes?

5. From what sources can a retailer obtain illustrations for his advertising layout?

6. What value does white space have in a layout?

7. Why do some merchants insist on a standard format for their advertisements as well as trying to place their advertisements on the same page of the newspaper?

8. What steps are necessary to turn ideas into printed advertisements?

Problems and Projects

1. One good way to study retail advertising is to examine carefully advertisements in newspapers and other media. Keep a scrapbook of newspaper ads, direct-mail circulars, and descriptions of radio announcements. Collect at least one example for each of the purposes of advertising outlined in Part 43 of this unit. In addition, collect several good examples of each part of an ad: border, logotype, etc.

2. Select three newspaper advertisements. On each, with a dark crayon, draw a line representing the eye movement of the reader. Typically, the eye moves from the headline or illustration toward the bottom of the page, sweeping through the copy to the logotype. Poor designs cause the eye to move off the page

without taking in the entire copy.

3. Whether to mention price in an advertisement is much debated in retailing. Make a list of the pros and cons. Show how the decision depends on the character of the merchandise and the store.

4. Using at least three advertisements, rate the competitive strength of each one according to the guide questions on page 309. In performing this project, try to select ads from different types of stores.

5. Printing and engraving processes can best be understood if they are seen. Ask your teacher to arrange a visit to the school print shop. Perhaps some industrial arts students could be your guides. If possible, visit the back shop of a newspaper.

6. Collect advertisements that use different type faces. Determine whether or not the type face has helped to express the meaning of the ad. Explain your opinion.

7. Using a headline and body copy you wrote as a project in the previous part, complete a layout showing the other necessary parts. Ask a local advertising man or layout artist to judge your class projects.

Learning Your Job

1. Find out and explain to the class your store policy concerning insertion of price in advertisements, the use of standard formats, and the use of the same position for its ad in your local newspaper.

2. If your store is part of a chain, explain how it differs from an independent store in its advertising policy. How much advertising preparation is done through the chain headquarters?

3. Design a sample layout for a coming promotional event for your store or department. Ask your supervisor to rate your layout.

13. Customer Services

the costume

GET IT AT

a rich girl. Go to deny herself high fashion, when to the rescue with smart clothes at If you're loaded with taste, but not with and walk out looking like a mil

Services Build Sales Volume

What attracts customers to a store? A large advertising agency, Batten, Barton, Durstine, and Osborn (B.B.D. & O.) conducted a survey to find out why customers trade at different stores and what they think of various customer services offered by these stores. Many customers said that they patronized the stores because of: (1) the merchandise carried, (2) the location and accessibility of the store, and (3) reasonable prices and special sales. However, as the chart on page 317 shows, many customers patronized the stores because of the services they offered. A large proportion of the customers placed great value on customer services such as charge accounts, free delivery, free gift wrapping, and time-payment plans. Also rated highly were parking lots, the accommodation desk, and check rooms. Customers also appreciated the convenience of such services as being able to pay utility bills, cash checks, have shoes and watches repaired, and have furs cleaned and stored.

Providing a large number of customer services is a comparatively recent development in retailing. In earlier years, merchants took the position that the interests of the store were best served by taking advantage of customers whenever possible. This practice was referred to as *caveat emptor,* or "Let the buyer beware!" The present theory, "The customer is always right," was, therefore, revolutionary and so was the idea of furnishing customers with extra services.

Types of Customer Services

Customer services can be classified according to two main categories: (1) shopping services and (2) convenience, or accommodation, services.

Shopping Services. Shopping services are the most widely offered group of services and are the most important in building sales volume. Some shopping services aid the customer in buying by giving him a place

Many stores have restaurants for the convenience of their customers.

Courtesy Corning Glass Works

to park, allowing him to pay later (credit and lay-away), enabling him to buy from home (mail order), and giving him personal shopping advice (the personal shopper). Other shopping services are said to encourage the customer to buy because they give him something extra—gift wrapping, delivery, alterations, and fashion-show information.

Convenience, or Accommodation, Services. *Convenience, or accommodation, services* are those that make shopping more pleasant and help to do some shopping tasks more conveniently; that is, they save the customer extra trips. Such services include check cashing, travel bureaus, rest rooms, strollers for children, utility payment desks, shoe and watch repairing, and restaurants.

Almost every retail store offers at least a few services. Those that offer the two essential ones—credit and delivery—plus other less-used ones are called *full-service stores* in the trade.

Factors Affecting the Store's Service Policy

One of the most perplexing problems for the modern merchant is that of deciding on how many and on what services to offer his customers. He knows that services are an important operating expense, and he watches them closely. He must constantly equate the cost of these services with the volume of business and the profit these services bring.

In the long run, of course, the customer must pay for store services in the price of merchandise. Would he rather pay less for his purchases and do without the extra services? This question puzzles all retailers today, especially since discount houses and supermarkets have thrived apparently by adopting self-service and eliminating major services such as credit and delivery. On the other hand, many full-service stores are thriving too. Thus, the retailer must carefully analyze many factors which will affect his policy of offering customer services.

Competition. An important factor in deciding on a service policy is that of the service practices of competing stores. For example, most department stores traditionally have offered a wide range of services; most of these stores would probably find it difficult to reduce these services. If services are reduced, a merchant must find another competitive weapon—location, lower prices, etc. An example of a successful minimum-service retailer is the Robert Hall chain of clothing stores. These stores offer few services, have plain interiors, but stress low prices as their competitive keynote.

Clientele. The clientele of a store is also important in deciding on what services to offer. Often the customer who wants exclusive, high-quality merchandise also wants many services for the higher price he is willing to pay. In contrast, there is the "do-it-yourself" type of customer, who will take his purchases home and make his own installation and repairs in return for a lower price. In general, as people do more shopping in suburban shopping centers, they seem willing to go without more services—credit and parking facilities being the exceptions.

Type of Merchandise Carried. The nature of the merchandise carried by the store also influences the services to be offered. Heavy, bulky items usually must be delivered. Most stores find that appliances and other mechanical items must be installed and serviced. High unit price items, such as furniture and jewelry generally must be sold on credit. Soft goods, such as clothing, require fitting and alteration service. Whatever kinds of merchandise the merchant sells, he must analyze his competition and his clientele to see whether or not the traditional offering of services in his line of business is justified. Following this analysis, he must be sure that his customer service policy is known by all store employees. Salespeople must be carefully trained to call store services to the attention of customers and to use store service policies as a selling tool.

Delivery Services

Retail stores deliver goods to customers by one or more of the following systems:

Individually owned and operated
    delivery equipment
Co-operative, or pooled, delivery

Consolidated delivery
Parcel post
Express

A fashion show is another customer service.

Courtesy E. I. du Pont de Nemours and Co., Inc.

Sewing instruction is a service offered to the customer by the yard-goods or curtain and drapery department of a store.

The choice of a delivery system is usually made by considering factors such as the volume of packages to be delivered, the distances customers live from the store, the cost per package delivered, the problems of owning and maintaining equipment, and the benefits the store desires to receive from delivery. As each type of delivery system is discussed in succeeding paragraphs, notice how each of these factors affects the final choice of a system.

Individually Operated Delivery Service. Individually operated delivery service is the kind most commonly used. In this system the store operates its own delivery service, using automobiles, trucks, or motorcycles. Some stores own the equipment used. Others lease vehicles from large trucking firms—a convenient practice, especially when extra vehicles are needed during rush periods, such as Christmas and Easter.

Advantages. An advantage for the small store of the individually operated delivery service is that the person making deliveries can perform other duties during his spare time. Another advantage—for both the large and small store—is that the sides of delivery vehicles may be used for advertising purposes. For many years, the delivery trucks of the Boston Store in Chicago carried the slogan, "Our truck before your neighbor's door means that the goods delivered are paid for"—an effective reminder of the store's cash policy.

A carefully selected delivery staff can serve as an additional effective contact with the store's customers. Courteous, helpful deliverymen reduce complaints and adjustments. Another advantage of individually operated delivery service is that the store can use its delivery equipment to pick up shipments of merchandise from railroad depots and from wholesaler warehouses.

Disadvantages. A big drawback of the individual delivery system is that of cost of operation. Because the volume of packages to be delivered varies from day to day, being large on some days and small on others, equipment may stand idle a part of the time. Too, the store must stand the expense of hiring, training, and supervising drivers or rely on part-time workers.

Co-operative, or Pooled, Delivery Service. Co-operative, or pooled,

SERVICES USED BY DEPARTMENT- AND SPECIALTY-STORE CUSTOMERS *

Shopping Services	Percentage of Customers Using	Convenience or Accommodation Services	Percentage of Customers Using
Regular charge account	64	Car parking lot	35
Free delivery service	54	Pay utility bills	26
Free gift wrapping	24	Shoe repair	17
Time payment	16	Accommodation desk (gather parcels)	12
Clothing alteration charge	11	Checkroom	11
Gift wrapping, minimum purchase	11	Check cashing (not for paying bills)	11
Fashion shows	9	Watch repair	5
C.O.D. orders	8	Fur storage	5
Local phone rate—suburban calls	6	Accessory repair (handbags, hosiery)	3
Free clothing alterations	6	Major-appliance repair	3
Delivery service, minimum purchase	6	Rug cleaning	3
Knitting instruction	5	Express, money orders, and traveler's checks sold	3
Needlework instruction	4		
Sewing instruction	4	Carpet laying	2
Brides' registry and advisor	2	Reupholstery service	2
Layette advisor (nurse)	2	Radio and TV repair	1
College fashion advisor	2		
Rug-making instruction	1		

* Table abstracted from Report by Batten, Burton, Durstine, and Osborn entitled *What Attracts Customers to Your Store . . . and What Services Your Customers Need.* Department Store Staff Presentation No. 3.

delivery service varies in practice; the essential feature of the plan is that stores work together to solve their delivery problems. Sometimes the equipment is owned and operated in common by the stores. In other cases, merchants divide the city geographically; and each merchant delivers in his zone the packages for all co-operating stores. This plan aids in eliminating duplicate routes or long routes where a store has only a few customers.

Consolidated Delivery Service. Consolidated delivery service is a method by which a group of local merchants contract for delivery service with a privately owned delivery firm. An example is United Parcel Service, a company that specializes in package delivery, charging merchants a fee for this service.

Packages from different stores are delivered together by the United Parcel Service delivery-man.

The main advantages of consolidated delivery service are the reduction of mileage by elimination of duplicate routes and usually lower costs per package delivered. The principal drawbacks of this type of service are: loss of the individual store's direct contact with customers, lack of control over delivery schedules, and loss of advertising value of the store's own trucks.

Parcel Post and Express Delivery Service. Parcel post and express delivery service are sometimes profitably used, especially when customers are a considerable distance from the store. Generally speaking, however, post-office and express systems are not adequately equipped to handle retail deliveries; moreover, this service would be too costly if used exclusively.

Is Delivery Service Worthwhile? In today's changing market, every retailer faces the question of whether or not to offer delivery service. Delivery service is costly—wages for those who pack orders, route shipments, and drive vehicles; gasoline, oil, and insurance; and vehicle maintenance—to name a few expenses. And costs go up as customers live farther from stores or insist that small, inexpensive items be delivered. The retailer must find answers to a number of questions. If delivery is not offered, will customers take their business elsewhere? Does the extra expense of delivery service pay off in additional sales volume and in profit?

The general trend in retailing is to reduce delivery service as much as possible or to charge a fee that covers the costs. Many small stores have decided to discontinue the service. Many supermarkets, drugstores, and variety stores have adopted a "cash-and-carry" policy, often advertising "lower prices" as a result of eliminating delivery service. Yet, some stores—especially department stores and other downtown merchants—still feel that delivery is an important service that they must maintain. In such stores, however, salespeople are usually told to encourage customers to take purchases with them.

Trade Talk

consolidated delivery
pooled delivery
leased vehicle

convenience service
caveat emptor
full-service store

Can You Answer These?

1. What reasons does the survey described in the beginning of this unit give for customers' patronizing stores?
2. What changes have taken place in the retailer's attitude toward customers and customer services?
3. What are the two main types of customer services? Give several examples of each type.
4. How has the customer's attitude toward customer service changed during the past fifty years?
5. What factors does a merchant consider before determining store service policies?
6. What types of retail stores offer the greatest number of customer services? what types the least?
7. What evidence is there to indicate that customers today will sacrifice services for lower prices?
8. What factors account for the decreasing need for certain stores to offer free delivery service?
9. Which factors would be most important in a merchant's decision to operate his own delivery service vs. contracting with a consolidated delivery service?

Problems and Projects

1. Read again the sections of this part that deal with methods of retail-store delivery. Prepare a class report in which you describe the various methods by which stores deliver goods to your home and to your neighbors. Discuss the advantages of these delivery methods as you see them.
2. Examine the B.B.D. & O. chart shown on page 317. Be prepared to defend the offering of so many services that so few customers actually use.
3. Make a list of the stores in your community that operate on a cash-and-carry basis. Explain how each can attract customers without offering full services.
4. Make a list of the types of services that each of the following kinds of customers would be most likely to want a store to provide: (*a*) a low-income family with children, (*b*) a retired couple living in a city, (*c*) newly married couples furnishing a home, (*d*) a teen-ager shopping for clothes, (*e*) a suburban, middle-income housewife who drives to a shopping center.
5. Make a survey of your family, relatives, and neighbors. Find out what store services they use often, occasionally, or never. Ask them also to rate these services as to their importance. Prepare a report.

Learning Your Job

1. Make a list of your store's delivery policies for various types of merchandise. List also your responsibilities, if any, for delivery services.
2. Prepare a brief statement of any responsibilities you have in connection with the customer services offered by your store.

48 *Credit as a Merchandising Service*

American salesmanship, searching for ways to make it possible for more people to buy the goods they want when they want them, found the answer in credit. When people had to pay cash for everything, many of them simply did without. Retail credit, once available only to the well-to-do, made it possible for nearly every wage earner to "buy now and pay later." Thus, by expanding business, credit helps to make mass production and mass distribution possible.

About one-third of the nation's retail sales volume is done on credit. Relatively few consumers today pay cash for a new car, a refrigerator, a kitchen range, or a television set. These purchases are more often paid for on the installment plan, a form of credit. Clothing, cameras, furniture, drugs, gasoline, and jewelry are examples of other purchases often made on credit.

Credit is used extensively at every level of business. The manufacturer buys on credit from the raw material suppliers; the wholesaler buys on credit from manufacturers; the retailer buys on credit from wholesalers; and the consumer buys on credit from retail stores. All borrow money from banks and other lending institutions, which is another form of credit.

Credit extended by retail stores to its customers is called *retail* or *consumer credit;* credit extended by one business firm to another is known as *mercantile* or *commercial credit.*

Why Consumers Use Credit

Of the various services offered by the retailer to his customers, credit is the one most demanded. There are two basic reasons why consumers use credit: (1) convenience, and (2) need. Some customers like the convenience of paying for an entire month's purchases at one time, thus avoiding the necessity to carry cash. For other customers, credit is a financial need as well as a convenience. They find it difficult to currently pay for the articles they want and thus need to charge their purchases and pay for these at a later date.

Advantages of Credit for the Retailer

Why do retail stores encourage the use of credit? There are six basic advantages of selling on credit:

1. *Credit Makes Regular Customers.* While cash customers are "everybody's customers," those who have charge accounts tend to be loyal to the stores where they have credit.

2. Credit Customers Are Less Price Conscious. A person with a charge account is less likely to hunt for bargains. He will buy an article because he wants it, not because it is a bargain. The average sale to the credit customer, therefore, is larger than that to a cash customer.

3. Credit Customers Buy More Freely. Credit customers like the convenience of saying, "Charge it," without having to worry about whether they have sufficient cash on hand to pay for their purchases. Several members of the same family often use the same charge account and do so freely because of this convenience.

4. Credit Builds Confidence. The fact that the store has sufficient confidence in the customer to grant him credit also builds the customer's confidence in the store. In other words, a mutual trust exists. Salespeople often know the charge customer by name, which is flattering to the customer and a big factor in building confidence and good will.

5. Credit Often Attracts a Better Trade. Stores that offer credit privileges often attract a better class of trade; that is, customers interested primarily in quality, service, and style, rather than in price alone.

6. Credit Smooths Out Business Peaks. Cash shoppers tend to buy heavily on certain days—Saturdays, paydays, and preholiday periods—and lightly on other days. Credit customers, on the other hand, buy whenever goods are needed. "Up-and-down" peaks in business are costly, and credit tends to smooth out these peaks.

Disadvantages of Credit for the Retailer

Selling on credit also offers a number of disadvantages to the retailer:

1. Credit Ties up Capital. When a customer buys on credit from a retail store, he is, in effect, using the retailer's capital. By offering credit, a merchant may be forced to borrow money from a lending institution and pay interest costs.

2. Losses Are Inevitable. Some people will not pay their bills, and the retailer suffers a loss from these bad debts. While the percentage of "no pay" customers is small, some losses are inevitable. Too, credit customers have a greater tendency to return and exchange goods than do cash customers.

3. Credit Costs Are High. The cost of doing business on credit is high for the retailer. Investigations of credit applications must be made, books kept, bills sent out, letters written, and collections made. These activities are costly.

4. Some Customers Are Lost. If the businessman is firm in collecting on past-due accounts (as he should be), he may turn the customer against him and lose his trade entirely. Unpleasant credit experience—regardless of whose fault it is—often loses a customer permanently.

Types of Retail Credit

Retail credit is found usually in two forms: (1) open-account (or open-book) credit and (2) installment credit.

Open-Account Credit. *Open-account credit* is so called because the customer's account remains open, permitting him to make purchases as he pleases during the month. In this type of credit, the purchaser is not asked to sign a contract or provide other security in order to use it. The articles bought on open-account credit belong to the purchaser as soon as the purchase is made; the store does not retain ownership in the goods as is the case in installment-credit sales. Obviously, in extending open-account credit, the retailer must have great faith in the customer's ability and willingness to pay.

In open-account credit, the customer is usually asked to pay his account in full at the end of the month. Even though the customer has no charges left against his account, the account remains open for future purchases. Some stores place a limit on the amount a customer can charge, basing the limit on their estimate of the customer's ability to pay. Usually no interest is charged on open-account purchases.

Variations. There are several variations of open-account credit.

1. One form commonly used by department stores and apparel stores is the *three-month charge account,* in which the customer is given regular open-account credit for the purchase of an article, such as a man's suit. The purchaser pays one-third of the amount each month for three months, after which the account is closed.

2. Another variation of open-account credit is the *coupon credit account.* In this type of credit, the customer is given a book of coupons (for example, a $50 book containing ten coupons worth $5 each) after credit is established. When the book is issued, his account is charged for the amount of the $50 coupon book. When a purchase is made, the salesperson removes coupons equal to the amount of the purchase and sends them to the credit department. After all the coupons are used, no more credit is available to the customer without special permission of the credit manager. This system is often used to limit the amount of credit a customer can obtain.

3. A third variation of open-account credit is the *revolving charge account.* It differs from the types just discussed in two ways: (1) there is an interest charge, usually 1 per cent a month on the outstanding balance, and (2) the customer must pay each month at least a stated minimum percentage of the amount assigned as a credit limit. Let us assume that Mrs. Brown has been granted credit privileges up to $150. Mrs. Brown may charge any number of purchases, so long as they do not exceed the $150 limit. At the end of the month Mrs. Brown must pay a portion—usually one-sixth or one-tenth—of the $150.

Revolving credit is used mostly in department stores, clothing stores, and other stores selling soft goods. The revolving charge account is gaining in popu-

Revolving charge accounts make buying easier.

larity. Of course, the interest charged makes revolving credit more expensive for the customer, but the objection is not serious.

The retailer likes revolving charge-account credit because less risk is involved. The interest received helps him to keep down his cost in servicing these accounts. Some large retailers, such as Sears, Roebuck and Company, who formerly gave no open-account credit have found revolving charge accounts very satisfactory and effective stimulants to sales.

Revolving credit is becoming especially popular in small stores. The expense of record keeping, billing, and collecting must be paid for and only by charging interest can the small retailer manage to offer this service to customers. Even larger stores encourage open-account customers to switch to the revolving charge accounts.

Installment Credit. Installment credit is offered principally by dealers in goods of high unit value, such as furniture, appliances, jewelry, boats, and automobiles. Installment credit is widely used by these retailers because many customers could not, or would not, buy high-unit-value merchandise if they had to pay cash.

Installment credit differs from open-account credit in several ways: (1) The buyer must usually sign a contract agreeing to pay for the purchase; (2) a down payment, a certain percentage of the total price, is required; (3) the ownership, title, of the goods remains with the store, although the customer has possession of the merchandise; (4) interest, carrying charge, is charged for the use of installment credit; and (5) periodic payments must be made until the goods are paid for.

Installment sales are usually made either on a *conditional sales contract* or a

To promote credit business, a medium often used is the newspaper. In this advertisment, three credit plans are offered and made available through the convenient application form.

Courtesy National Cash Register Co.

chattel mortgage. In a conditional sales contract, the seller retains title to the merchandise and may take the article back if the buyer fails to make a payment. A chattel mortgage differs from a conditional sales contract in that the title to the goods is transferred to the buyer upon taking possession. The seller, however, has the right to bring legal action to regain the title and repossess the goods if the buyer fails to fulfill the contract by not making his payments. In most cases, firms would rather be paid than to repossess the goods; they take back goods only as a last resort.

Nonretail Credit

Retail stores that do not offer credit often refer customers to banks, consumer finance companies, and other lending agencies. Some retailers have worked out co-operative arrangements with banks in which customers are referred to the banks for credit. In effect, these banks act as the credit department for the retailer. This arrangement makes it possible for small retailers with limited capital to build a sizable sales volume on the bank's credit facilities.

APPLICATION FOR CREDIT

ADOPTED BY AND FOR MEMBERS OF THE

NATIONAL RETAIL CREDIT ASSOCIATION

NUMBER __350217__   DATE __Feb. 8, 19--__

FULL NAME (SURNAME FIRST)	FULL GIVEN NAME	INITIAL	AGE	GIVEN NAME, HUSBAND — WIFE'S MAIDEN NAME	
Kincaid	Raymond	N	27	Irene Hays	

RESIDENCE	MAIL ADDRESS	TELEPHONE	HOW LONG
460 S. Maple Ave.		360	3 yrs.

FORMER ADDRESS		HOW LONG
Jarman Apts., Ash at Elm Street		1 yr.

BUSINESS OR OCCUPATION	BY WHOM EMPLOYED	BUS. ADDRESS	HOW LONG
Bookkeeper	Ajax Mfg. Co.	Danbury	3 yrs.

FORMER BUSINESS OR OCCUPATION	BY WHOM EMPLOYED	BUS. ADDRESS	HOW LONG
Payroll Clerk	same		6 mo.

WIFE OR HUSBAND EMPLOYED?	CAPACITY	BY WHOM
No		

OWN REAL ESTATE	(GIVE LOCATION)	MORTGAGED TO	AMOUNT
Yes	460 S. Maple Ave.	First Nat'l Bank	$ 9,500

		OWNER	MONTHLY RENTAL	CHILDREN	
				AT HOME	EMPLOYED
RENT { FURN. APARTMENT? / UNFURN. APARTMENT? / RESIDENCE?				2	

NAME OF NEAREST RELATIVE AND RELATIONSHIP (OTHER THAN HUSBAND OR WIFE)	ADDRESS
(father) Lee J. Kincaid	122 River Drive, Danbury

PERSONAL REFERENCE
R. O. Somerfield, Ajax Mfg. Co.

BANK { (NAME OF BANK)	(CHECKING) X	BRANCH
First Nat'l	(SAVING) X	

LIFE INSURANCE	NAME OF INSURANCE CO.	APPROX. INCOME	
$ 10,000	Mutual of N. Y.	$ 375 PER mo.	

TRADE REFERENCES

FIRM OR STORE	KIND OF MDSE. BOUGHT	ACCOUNT IS NOW	
		OPEN	DATE PAID
Sears Roebuck	Household	x	
Danbury Hardware	Hardware		Dec. 19--

LIST ON REVERSE SIDE OF THIS APPLICATION ANY UNPAID BALANCES ON INSTALLMENT ACCOUNTS AND MONTHLY PAYMENTS THEREON.

THE ABOVE INFORMATION IS FOR THE PURPOSE OF OBTAINING CREDIT, AND IS WARRANTED TO BE TRUE. I AGREE TO PAY ALL BILLS UPON RECEIPT OF STATEMENT OR AS OTHERWISE EXPRESSLY AGREED.

SPECIAL TERMS IF ANY.

SIGNATURE *Raymond N. Kincaid*

AMOUNT CREDIT	APPROVED
$	

PRINTED IN U.S.A.

In most stores, applicants for credit are required to fill out an application form.

Courtesy National Retail Credit Assoc.

Criteria for Granting Credit

In deciding whether to grant credit to a customer, the retailer takes into account the "three C's" of credit—character, capacity, and capital.

Character. Character is the most important of the three C's. It has to do with the individual's sense of fair play and his feeling of obligation in fulfilling a promise. A person may have plenty of money with which to pay his bills, but if he does not feel the obligation to pay, he is not a good risk.

Capacity. Capacity refers to a person's income—whether he has earnings sufficient to meet his obligations. Wage earners whose employment is subject to layoffs or who already have more obligations than their earnings will safely cover are examples of those who are checked on carefully for their capacity.

Capital. Capital, the least important of the three C's to most retailers, refers to the wealth of the applicant; that is, the physical assets he possesses. If persons own property that can be put up as security for an indebtedness, their credit potential is greater.

Retailers have learned through experience that the best credit risks are people who take their obligations seriously—who want to keep their credit reputation above reproach. Thus, when a person applies for credit, his credit history is studied carefully. It is almost certain that a credit applicant can be expected to pay his bills at one store according to the same pattern that he pays his bills at another store where he has been granted credit. In seeking credit information, the retailer saves a great deal of time and effort when he uses the facilities of a retail credit bureau.

Retail Credit Bureaus

Retail credit bureaus are found in most cities and towns throughout America. Often sponsored by the local chamber of commerce or retail-merchants association, credit bureaus are financed by membership fees paid by stores who use their services. A vast organization, closely related to the National Retail Credit Association, the Associated Credit Bureaus of America is made up of 3,000 credit bureaus and collection-service agencies. These bureaus and agencies form an interlocking network all over the nation—their files contain over 75 million credit records.

A retail credit bureau functions in collecting credit data as follows: All member stores supply the bureau with complete information on all customers with whom they have had credit experience. Let us assume that John Jones has applied for credit at the Blank Department Store. In investigating his credit application, the Blank Department Store asks for a report on Mr. Jones from the local credit bureau. The bureau's records show that Mr. Jones has a poor record of payment at other stores and still owes money to several. The Blank Department Store has the evidence necessary to refuse credit. The credit bureau saves the Blank Department Store the bother of checking all stores in the city where Mr. Jones has done business on credit. Even if Mr. Jones only recently moved into town, his credit record from his former address is available through the network of credit bureaus throughout the country. Thus, the saying "your credit reputation follows you wherever you go—you can't get away from it" is true. The job of keeping track of credit customers is the job of credit bureaus, and retailers depend on them heavily.

Trade Talk

chattel mortgage nonretail credit
conditional sales open-account
   contract   credit
coupon credit retail credit
   account revolving charge
credit bureau   account
mercantile credit title to goods

Can You Answer These?

1. What part does credit play in our distribution system?

2. Compare the advantages of cash and credit methods of store operation. What are the disadvantages of each?

3. What information about the personal characteristics of the prospective customer should a merchant consider before granting credit?

4. How does the adoption of a credit policy affect the retail prices of a store?

5. What are the kinds of merchandise that are sold mainly on credit? What are the characteristics of this merchandise?

6. What are the main differences between open-account credit and installment credit?

7. Why is revolving credit becoming so popular with customers? with retailers?

8. Why should retail management and salespeople know about nonretail credit agencies?

9. What advantages does a store gain by joining a retail credit bureau?

Problems and Projects

1. In a written report, discuss the advantages and disadvantages of installment-credit selling from the standpoint of the retailer as well as that of the customer.

2. Make a chart showing the various types of retail credit and the characteristics of each type.

3. Obtain credit application blanks from two or more stores. Explain why each item of information is needed by the store. Then compare the blanks for the kind and amount of information required.

4. Obtain copies of a conditional sales contract and a chattel mortgage. Explain the rights and obligations of both buyer and seller.

5. Assume that you are the owner of a women's or men's apparel store. What type of credit would you offer to obtain the benefits desired in each of the following cases: (*a*) to recover all or most of your expenses in granting credit; (*b*) to encourage customers to shop repeatedly for small items like hosiery or ties; (*c*) to limit your investment in merchandise the customer has not paid for in full; (*d*) to encourage parents to allow children to purchase by themselves; (*e*) to encourage customers to purchase at one time a complete wardrobe?

Learning Your Job

1. Describe to the class the procedure for opening a charge account in your store. Show the various forms used and then tell about the practices of the credit interviewer.

2. Find out from your supervisor what your store does to encourage credit sales and report your findings to the class.

3. Describe the procedure of your store in making and verifying credit sales.

4. Find out from your supervisor, or an executive responsible for credit policies, the extent to which credit contributes to your firm's business. What are the reasons for your store's credit policy?

49 *Other Customer Services*

In some countries shopping is a chore—a daily task to be avoided if possible. In the United States, on the other hand, almost everyone shops and enjoys it. Shopping is a pleasant experience when we have a wide selection of merchandise and meet with attentive salespeople. We have come to expect and receive a variety of store services that make shopping more convenient and pleasurable. In the United States generally, the customer is king and expects to be treated royally by the retailer and his staff.

In this unit, we have discussed the two most demanded customer services: credit and delivery. Now let us take a look at other services that customers appreciate—those that aid them in buying and in convenient shopping.

Good Parking Facilities Attract Trade

One of the most wanted customer services is good parking. If you have ever circled the block again and again in your car trying to park, you can appreciate why good parking facilities attract and hold trade. Parking service is so important in some cities that it is one of the basic reasons why stores move away from the downtown shopping district to the suburbs where space is available. The Southdale Center in Minneapolis has acres of parking space; the Northland Center in Detroit provides space for 9,500 automobiles!

Solutions to the Parking Problem. Most merchants know that their parking problems are going to get worse—the population is growing rapidly, and more families drive two and even three cars. Retailers located in congested areas therefore have tried several solutions to the parking problem: (1) building and operating their own parking garages, (2) co-operating with other merchants in providing off-street parking lots, (3) working with local government to encourage the development of privately or publicly owned parking lots and garages. Most stores, however, prefer not to engage directly in the parking business. In some cities, retail-merchants associations have formed organizations to build and operate garages and parking lots. A more recent and successful solution is the "Park and Shop Plan," used in Tucson (Arizona), Lansing (Michigan), and in other cities. Under this plan, the stores encourage the city government and private operators to establish lots and garages. Stores participating in the plan give parking stamps with each purchase. Such stamps (for example, 20 cents worth on a $5 purchase) can be used by the customer to pay all or part of the cost of parking.

Parking areas like this one are a "must" in suburban shopping centers.

Courtesy Circle Plaza Shopping Center, Manasquan, N.J.

Parking services, like other services offered the customer, are of little help in building trade if customers do not know about them. Thus, every salesperson should aid customers with their parking problems by: (1) encouraging the use of store-sponsored parking, (2) reminding them of city parking regulations, (3) validating customers' parking checks or attaching the necessary stamps, and (4) parking their own cars in spaces that customers will not use.

Shopping Services

In Part 47 of this unit, customer services were classified as being either a shopping service or an accommodation (convenience) service. The two groups are somewhat alike, but there is a difference. *Shopping services* are those that are defined as aiding or helping customers with their buying problems rather than merely making their shopping pleasant or convenient. Thus, credit and delivery are shopping services because they help the customer directly to purchase; while dining rooms, check-cashing services, and parking make shopping more convenient, easier, or more pleasant.

Personal Shopping Services

A number of shopping services can be conveniently described as personal shopping services, because they allow the customer to shop from his home; or if he comes to the store, they provide help for his unique shopping problems. Among the personal shopping services are the telephone order board, the mail-order department, the personal shopper, and the special customer consultant.

The personal shopper is a specially trained sales consultant who provides special help to customers with unique shopping problems. The personal shopper may learn of the customer's needs by mail (a letter from an invalid, for example), by telephone, or by talking with the customer in the store. Personal shoppers may be asked to help an overseas visitor who does not speak our language, help an invalid buy a gift, or give advice on a gift for a special occasion. The personal shopper is not a substitute for the regular salespeople who can meet most needs, but a specialist who has a wide knowledge of the store's merchandise selections, and who is skillful in working with people. Personal-shopping staffs are often featured in television, radio, and newspaper advertising and generally are known by fictitious names such as "Kate Hemingway" (Wanamaker's, Philadelphia) or "Betty Lane" (The Hecht Company, Washington, D.C.).

Telephone Shopping Services. Telephone shopping services are of two types: the telephone selling practiced by departmental salespeople and the telephone order departments operated by larger stores. The latter are usually telephone order boards, manned by a specially trained group of telephone saleswomen who take orders for merchandise that has been advertised. These operators also answer inquiries from customers and suggest goods that will meet the customer's needs.

Telephone shopping saves time and energy for both customer and retailer. It also eliminates the parking problem for the customers who use it. Retailers use several methods of encouraging customers to shop by phone. Newspapers, television, and radio advertisements announce telephone "specials." Some stores publish merchandise catalogues especially for telephone shoppers during special promotions, such as "Back-to-School Week," "Spring Fix-up Time," and the Christmas gift season. The small store, especially when it offers fast, free delivery service, can use the telephone order service to compete with larger firms.

Mail-Order Service. Mail-order service is an important form of personal shopping service for customers. Nearly everyone is familiar with the large mail-order houses—Sears, Roebuck and Company, Montgomery Ward and Company, Spiegels, and Aldens. Thousands of small and large stores sell by mail, too, reaching customers through catalogues, newspaper advertisements, handbills, and direct-mail circulars.

Customers respond well to store efforts to sell by mail, buying because they have confidence in the quality of the merchandise. They also are encouraged to purchase because of the attractive illustrations and descriptions of merchandise and because of the convenience of ordering by mail.

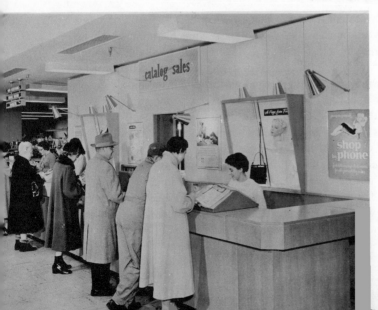

An important service in every Sears, Roebuck and Co. retail store is a catalogue sales desk, such as the one shown here.

Courtesy Sears, Roebuck and Co.

Every sale is important to the retailer, but mail orders are especially valuable. In fact, some retailers consider mail-order business as "gravy," because they feel it results in extra sales volume that they might not otherwise get. And, mail orders are usually more profitable because the retailer does not have to use expensive display or stock space, nor does he have to pay for a salesperson's time. For these reasons, large numbers of specialty stores, department stores, and discount houses in recent years have added or enlarged their mail-order departments. One large store, Younkers of Des Moines, personalizes its mail-order service by calling it the "Jane Wilder Mail Order Shopping Service." Services like this are advertised in Sunday newspaper editions that have large circulations, covering a wide geographical area. These ads pull heavily in rural areas and small towns. Many stores also circulate special mail-order catalogues at Christmas and get heavy sales volume. A good example, well-known in the Midwest, is the Christmas *Daytonian,* of the Dayton Company in Minneapolis.

Because the mail-order service is so profitable to the store and so important to customers, getting mail orders ready for shipment is considered an important job. Salespeople are often asked to fill orders from their departmental stock, and they must be sure items selected are exactly as ordered. In large firms, a special staff is often trained to handle mail orders exclusively. These people must make special effort to avoid errors, must learn how to pack shipments to prevent damage, and must sometimes select items that can be substituted for articles not in stock.

Shopping Consultants. Shopping consultants for special sales problems are sometimes employed by department and specialty stores. These are specially trained salespeople who provide a customer service by helping the customer in planning and buying for a special event. For example, bridal consultants assist with choice of gowns and accessories, invitations, wedding-reception planning, and the selection and co-ordination (harmonizing) of patterns in crystal, silver, and china. Interior-decorating and home-building consultants counsel customers about materials, color schemes, and room planning. These consultants differ from the personal shopper discussed on page 329, since they advise on only one type of problem and are really salespeople attached to one department or to a group of related selling departments. In smaller stores, the regular salespeople are expected to provide such professional shopping counsel. Some smaller stores also contract with a firm of consultants for their services. For example, a furniture store in Tucson, Arizona, offers new homeowners who purchase their furniture a special certificate worth $100 in a private decorator's services.

"For Men Only" Shopping Services

Some stores operate departments for men only, where special consultants assist male shoppers with their gift selections. Marshall Field and Company (Chicago) features a "Stagline" shop; at Bonwit Teller (New York), the special men's shop is called the "721 Club." Other stores set aside certain evenings as a service for men only.

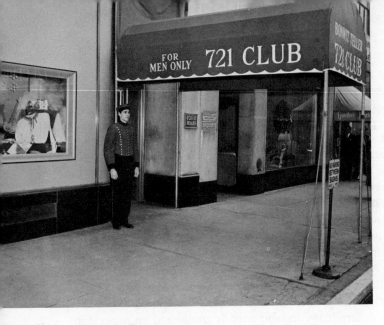

The entrance to Bonwit's well-known 721 Club where men receive special help in shopping.

Courtesy Bonwit Teller

Store Facilities

One group of customer services that are especially important in building sales volume are store facilities. One of the most important of these, delivery, was discussed in Part 47 of this unit.

Gift Wrapping. In many stores, large and small, gift-wrapping services are among the important services that attract trade. This is especially true in stores featuring high-quality merchandise in exclusive lines. There are several variations in the gift-wrapping services offered: (1) some stores provide gift boxes without charge during the Christmas season; (2) some stores provide throughout the year gift wrapping and gift boxes at no extra charge on purchases over a given amount—usually $5; (3) throughout the year some stores will, for a small charge, box gifts and wrap them in decorative paper and ribbon that suit occasions such as birthdays, weddings, and anniversaries; and (4) a few stores provide free gift wrapping the year around.

If there is a good deal of gift wrapping to be done, the store will hire specialists for this purpose. These people work in gift-wrapping centers especially constructed for this purpose. In many stores, however, every salesperson is expected to gift wrap when the occasion demands it. Because customers value the gift-wrapping service so highly, salespeople should use it as a selling point, reminding customers of its availability.

Other Trade Builders

In addition to the major services discussed so far, stores offer almost an infinite variety of services in the hope of drawing trade. Sometimes classes are conducted in such hobbies as knitting, needlework, sewing, and weaving. For example, classes in clothing construction have long been a major promotional activity in stores operated by the Singer Sewing Machine Company.

Another trade builder for many stores is the fashion show. Stores may hold shows in their own buildings or in community buildings and often sponsor them in connection with women's clubs and high school groups.

In apparel stores, a valued customer service is free clothing alterations. In addition, some stores offer to make custom-made draperies and slip covers, and to do upholstering.

Accommodation Services

Accommodation (convenience) services were defined earlier as those that make shopping easier and more pleasant—services that accommodate the customer's personal needs. These services are designed to build trade and increase profits in an indirect manner. A list of some of these services is given below. Many are offered by large stores, some can be used effectively in smaller stores.

1. *Check Cashing.* Customers appreciate the convenience of being able to cash personal and payroll checks in the store.

2. *Utility Payments.* Another valued convenience is that of paying utility bills—telephone, gas, water, etc.—in the store. A plus advantage for the store is that customers see other merchandise as they pass through the store to pay their utility bills.

3. *Repair Services.* Repairing of shoes, furs, watches, jewelry, appliances, and furniture is a service offered by some stores. The repairs may be done by workers employed by the store, by firms that lease space in the store, or by firms that contract with the store.

C. R. WALGREEN, JR.
President of Walgreen Drug Stores.

Free art classes for children are a regular customer service at this department store.

Courtesy John Wanamaker, Philadelphia

4. Checkroom and Nurseries. Customers like the convenience of checking their wraps and parcels, so that they do not have to carry them while shopping. Mothers with small children especially appreciate nurseries where they can leave their children while shopping. They also value strollers provided by the store.

5. Dining Accommodations. Many large stores offer a complete range of dining facilities: snack bars, soda fountains, cafeterias, tearooms, and elegant dining rooms. In some cases, private dining rooms are available for private luncheons, dinners, and parties.

6. Miscellaneous Services. Clean and comfortable rest rooms, lounges, exhibit halls, and beauty salons are but a few of the variety of extra services that may be offered.

Trade Talk

accommodation shopping
services consultant
personal shopper shopping services

Can You Answer These?

1. Of what value is each of the following services to customers? How does the store benefit from these services? (*a*) wrapping purchases, (*b*) delivery service, (*c*) returned goods and adjustments, (*d*) personal shopping service, (*e*) mail-order service, (*f*) telephone-order and sales services, (*g*) nurseries and playrooms, (*h*) dining accommodations and club-room facilities, (*i*) parking facilities, (*j*) will-call, lay-away, and C.O.D. services.

2. To what kinds of people do the personal shopping services prove most helpful?

3. In what ways do merchants solve the problem of providing parking facilities?

4. In what ways do retailers adver-

tise the merchandise that can be ordered by telephone? by mail?

5. What are the common gift-wrapping practices in stores?

6. What are the more common store accommodation services? How do they build trade?

Problems and Projects

1. What are the methods used in your community for providing parking facilities for store customers? Describe the various arrangements.

2. Prepare to debate the proposal, "Retail stores should reduce the number of customer services so that prices might be lowered."

3. Make a list of the customer services offered by the larger stores in your city. Repeat the activity for small stores. In what types of stores within each group do you find the greatest number of services offered?

4. Basing your questions on the text material, interview a merchant on the advantages and disadvantages of the customer services he offers. Report your findings to the class.

5. List the ways in which a salesperson can use store services to increase his sales.

Learning Your Job

1. For your store manual, make a list of the customer services offered by your store. Describe your own responsibility for each service on your list.

2. List the customer services offered by your company's competitors. Give reasons for the differences in the offerings of your store and those of your competitors.

3. Interview one of your store executives or supervisors asking him to review his experiences with competition in the field of customer services. Describe these experiences to your class.

14. Fashion Merchandising

Unit 14 Part 50

Becoming Fashionwise

We live in a world where styles and fashions are the keynotes for everyday living. Phrases like "in step," "the thing to do," and "very smart" tell us that it is important to be fashionwise. A quick look around us reveals that good design and pleasing color combinations are found increasingly in the things we wear and use—in automobiles, apparel, furniture, kitchen utensils, appliances, and sporting goods. Styling even affects the packages in which goods are sold. Containers for foods, cosmetics, toilet articles, and patent medicines are styled by distinctive use of color, shape, and materials.

When fashion is mentioned, many people are apt to think first of words like: "apparel," "Paris," or "Fath." And it is true that fashion is the hallmark of apparel merchandising. Yet, fashion affects many lines of merchandise that the retailer stocks and sells. Together with price and quality, it is a ruling factor in the sale of merchandise. Since World War II, consumers have become educated to demand better design; they are becoming very style-conscious. Like it or not, few retailers, or their employees, can ignore the psychological force of fashion. More and more, they must understand fashion and learn how to use it as a merchandising tool.

Fashion Terminology

The field of fashion has a language of its own. Some terms are specific to a phase of fashion—an example is the term *high fashion,* which denotes one part of the fashion cycle. Specific terms such as these will have to be recognized and studied by each student according to his fashion interests, for this text could not begin to cover every field. There are, however, several important, general terms the student of fashion must know.

Style. The style of an article lies in the characteristics that make it different from others of its kind. For example, a narrow crown, a wide brim, and saddle stitching around the brim are three characteristics of a hat that make up its style. Color, material, and workmanship are also elements of an article's style.

In the furniture field, the style is often described by the term *period,* which denotes the span of time during

337

which the style was introduced. For example, furniture may be of the "Early American" period. In furniture, as in many other lines of merchandise, modern design is said to be functional or "clean lined," meaning that nothing is included in the design solely for the sake of ornamentation. A good example is Danish Modern furniture. This illustration shows that style can be described as the design of an article.

Vogue means a style that is extremely popular at a given moment, or it may be defined as that which is in fashion at a particular time. For example, one vogue in furniture was the style Chinese Modern; in apparel, a vogue was the chemise dress.

A *fad* is a style that is popular for a brief time but which quickly loses its popularity. It has been described as a "craze followed with exaggerated zeal." Usually it is adopted by a particular group of people. Fads often have their beginnings in a novelty; for example, yo-yo's and hula hoops. Smaller articles of clothing sometimes become fads, for example feathered hats and painted neckties.

Fashion. The terms *style* and *fashion* are sometimes used interchangeably. There is, however, a difference in their meanings. A *fashion* is a style that is adopted by a large number of people over a period of time. Fashion represents that which is "right" or "the thing to do." When a fashion loses its popularity, it is still a style; but it is no longer a fashion. For example, one can still buy furniture with the design characteristics that identify it as Chinese Modern in style, but it is no longer in fashion. In men's clothing the detachable celluloid collar on shirts has not been in fashion for a number of years.

The Fashion Cycle. Fashions usually follow a cycle of acceptance, popularity, and decline. First a new style is favored by a designer or manufacturer. Then it is usually adopted by a limited number of people, often those in prominent positions, those who desire exclusiveness, or those who are not afraid to try a new design. At this point in the cycle, a style is called "high-fashion." As the cycle continues, more people adopt the style; and quickly a large segment of the public begins to buy the article. By the time the item has been accepted by the masses, the original adopters have turned to something new. The more exclusive shops cease to carry the item, the style declines in popularity and is usually abandoned. In some lines, however, such as furniture, many styles are not abandoned but remain favored by a limited number of people. Furthermore, some styles, once abandoned, come back; and the cycle begins again. This tendency is more often seen in men's and women's apparel styles.

The Psychology of Fashion

Fashion merchandising has been described as a "tricky business" because fortunes can be made or lost depending on the whims and fancies of customers. Thus, the person who wishes to merchandise fashions must understand why people accept or reject a style.

High fashion is exemplified by
this model and emphasized by
the modern display fixture.

Courtesy Bonwit Teller, New York

Fashion Motives. Fashions stem from a desire for social approval and, to a lesser degree, from the desire for newness and variety.

The wish for distinction and for approval is almost universal. Hardly anyone desires to be mediocre. It is a human tendency to call attention to oneself— one's appearance and one's intelligence. We aspire to leadership. We have a strong underlying desire to be recognized. This is one of the psychological factors that enters into fashion and fashion merchandising.

Fashion seems to be a paradox—it satisfies not only the desire for distinction, but also the desire to be a member of a group and to have its approval. Most people want to conform to accepted standards of dress. For example, a man who is fashion-conscious will refuse to wear a necktie or a suit that is "out of style" even though it is not worn out. Similarly, businessmen feel they cannot afford to wear outdated clothes because of the poor impression they might make on customers. Women often discard garments and shoes because they are last year's fashion.

The desire for newness and variety is present in most people. It is particularly important to women who like changing styles. They like a new hair style, new clothes, new drapes, or new household accessories. Women show a decided adaptability to change and seek variety in their daily lives. They have more time than men to read fashion articles and advertisements in magazines and to shop in stores. They see things that make them dissatisfied with the old. For these reasons, merchandise purchased by women is subject to more rapid change in fashion than that purchased largely by men.

Some fashions have their origin in the common sense and good taste of fashion leaders. They gain acceptance because the advantages attached to their use are easily recognized. For example, as early as 1940 only a few men were brave enough to appear on the streets of American cities wearing shorts. During World War II, however, many G.I.'s serving in warm countries experienced the comfort of men's shorts in hot weather; and following the war, the style was gradually accepted.

Changes in Fashion. The fact that we have the desire to follow the leadership of people whom we admire is a determining factor in rapid fashion changes. We are willing to imitate the clothing worn by social leaders who have the means and the desire to be distinctive.

In former days, kings, queens, and nobility started fashions. Many styles used in clothing and furniture are directly traceable to, and named for, royal personages; for example, furniture—Queen Anne and Louis XIV. The instincts of imitation or emulation still create the desire in people to own, use, or wear clothing or articles of merchandise similar to those adopted by the wealthy, the socially elite, or the professionally popular.

Fashion in Apparel

London and Paris before World War II were the centers of fashion influence for the whole world. Men's styles were primarily the work of London designers and clothiers. Although American designers are still influenced by their counterparts in London and Rome, they have had remarkable success, especially in casual clothing and sportswear. New York, Chicago, Los Angeles, and Dallas are centers for the manufacture of men's clothing. The clothing manufacturers located in these cities produce men's clothing that is superior to much that is produced in Europe.

Paris has been, and still is, a primary source of fashions for women for the entire world. Among women, the names of famous designers are well known—Patou, Lanvin, Schiaparelli, Mainbocher, Molyneux, Fath, and Balenciaga. Italian designers, especially in Rome, have influenced markedly women's apparel styles. However, New York and the Pacific Coast cities are now prominent fashion centers of the world.

The American Contribution to Fashion

The grooming of American women has been described admiringly by visitors from other countries. Typically, they are amazed that such fashionable clothing can be acquired so inexpensively. But, it has not always been so. Before 1940, American women of means chose mainly Parisian clothes. Garments designed by Americans were considered less desirable. A Paris label in a gown insured its salability. In spite of this discouragement, American dress designers maintained their original ideas and individuality. Now the United States fashion industry is given credit for maintaining a generally high level of fashion. Its major contribution has been the democratization of fashion through mass production, mass advertising, and mass distribution.

Fashion in Other Merchandise Lines

Manufacturers and retailers have taken advantage of changing fashions as an opportunity to appeal to the customer who owns outmoded articles. As we have seen, this is particularly true of women's apparel. This tendency on the part of manufacturers and distributors to capitalize on obsolete design is increasingly evident in other lines; for example, automobiles, appliances, sporting goods, home furnishings—and even housing!

Not many years ago—in the twenties—all automobiles were painted black. Now a car may have two or three colors, and pastels account for a majority of the units sold. This change is illustrative of how fashion has come of age in the nonapparel fields. How did this change come about?

Before the Industrial Revolution, most articles were made by craftsmen, or artisans. They tried to combine utility and beauty in the designs which they produced for their customers—the wealthy and the noble. With the adoption of power machinery and principles of mass production, the artisan gradually disappeared. In his place, came the engineer and the production experts who designed goods primarily with use, not style, in mind. Products were useful and they were cheap to make, but they were anything but beautiful.

Since World War II, a fundamental change has taken place in industry. The task of correlating design with customer tastes has been turned over to the stylist, or industrial designer, as he is often called. The industrial designer is fundamentally an artist, interested in the appearance of things—line, shape, and color combinations that have emotional appeal. Yet, the stylist remains alert to scientific developments. He works closely with engineering, production, and marketing-research departments to incorporate their ideas into his design. One result has been the application of fashion merchandising to nonapparel lines.

A sitting room furnished in authentic Victorian style from carpet to lighting fixture.

Courtesy W. & J. Sloane Inc., New York

Trade Talk

style   fad
vogue   fashion
period   fashion cycle
fashion motive

Can You Answer These?

1. Is fashion more important in merchandising apparel or in merchandising nonapparel lines? Why do you think so?
2. What factors have made styling and design so important in merchandising?
3. What is the difference between the terms, "style" and "fashion"? Show the difference by using one type of merchandise as an example.
4. What causes styles to come into fashion and then decline?
5. What are the motives that govern fashion?
6. Why do present-day fashion tastes change more frequently and rapidly than those of the past?
7. What has been the American contribution to fashion?
8. How has the change in industrial production affected design and styling in nonapparel lines?

Problems and Projects

1. List the items in your classroom that are subject to the forces of fashion. Place them in order of the rate at which they show a change in fashion, starting with the most rapid.
2. In making your most recent purchase of (a) apparel and (b) a nonapparel item, to what extent were you influenced by its style features? Was the item in fashion? Explain how this affected your decision.
3. Select two articles—one apparel and one nonapparel. For each, point out the fashion motives to which the article appeals.
4. Name two articles that are examples of basic styles that are no longer in fashion, two articles that are examples of fads or vogues.
5. For two articles of merchandise point out all the characteristics that go to make up their styles.

Learning Your Job

1. For your department or store, make a list of merchandise that is important from the standpoint of fashion. For at least four items, list the fashion motive governing their sale and write some selling phrases or sentences incorporating these motives.
2. Select two articles sold in your store. For each draw a diagram of the fashion cycle for this article, showing the approximate dates of each stage, both those that have occurred and those that you think will occur.

51 *Buying Fashion Merchandise*

Buying fashion merchandise in New York or some other fashion market can be an exciting event, like that described in the following experience: *

> You have an appointment. And you go. You're prompt. Seats are at a premium. Let's say it's at Dior, on upper Fifth Avenue—away from hectic Seventh Avenue. His showroom is exquisite and simple—as all expensive things are. It's like a theatrical production for an opening. There's a hush! . . . hush! . . . atmosphere. You are handed a program, a pencil. Then, out come the models. We know them . . . applaud quietly as they pass our chair and give us a smile of recognition. You concentrate on the beauty of the clothes you see; the facts can come later.
>
> A representative of the establishment stands in the corner and describes the gown, very genteely and very softly, as the model promenades. No prices are quoted, just numbers. As the model passes your chair, she repeats the number. If you like it, you jot it down. That's where a buyer's memory comes in. She has to know if this black crepe at $125 is better or worse than Rosenstein or Carnegie. What are its important new fashion points? It can't be like one from last season.
>
> Occasionally you let your gaze wander to the other buyers or advertising managers . . . they all look smart. They try to wear one of the designer's outfits when they go to see her collection. But they look tired. Two major collections a day . . . of about 135 pieces . . . almost 3 hours each. And perhaps a half dozen other minor ones during lunch hours . . . looking at garments on hangers at 5:00 o'clock, or later. When the last model comes out, there is usually a tremendous burst of applause.
>
> During the "looking" time, buyers are cheerful, happy people. They go to the theater . . . are normal. At "order-writing" time they are unapproachable . . . nervous. You know how you feel when you start to buy your own outfit. Well, imagine spending tens of thousands of someone else's money. Hoping, praying you'll be right. This is the procedure that all store buyers follow.

Buying for the Fashion Cycle

In Part 50 of this unit, you learned how the fashion cycle operates from the consumer point of view. It must also be considered by the buyer as a guide to purchasing a stock of fashion goods. He should consider the following factors:

___

* From a talk, "Fashion—We Love It," given by Mrs. Thelma Kennedy, Director of Advertising, Harzfelds, Kansas City, Missouri, to a woman's club in that city.

A fashion show for buyers of high fashion staged in the salon of a leading couturier.

Fashion Desires of the Store's Clientele. A successful retail store gears its fashion policy to the desires of its clientele. If its customers are willing to pay for merchandise that is an original design, or is exceptionally distinctive, then the store operates near the beginning of the fashion cycle. Such stores are known as "high-fashion" shops. These firms and other stores known for their exclusiveness introduce the fashion to the community.

Inasmuch as copies of the original article are produced with less detail and from less expensive materials, the style is handled by stores with a reputation for quality at a reasonable price. At this point in the cycle, the popularity of the item is growing rapidly; and the item is stocked by popular-price department stores, chain stores, and mail-order houses. As the style declines in popularity, the item is sold by cut-rate establishments, especially surplus outlet stores.

Fashion merchandise is handled in different departments of a department store also according to the fashion cycle. As a distinctive original, the item is usually offered in a very exclusive shop within the store or at a branch catering to the elite trade. As the style—a dress, for example—begins to catch on, the item is transferred to the "Better Dresses" department. At the height of the cycle, the dress is sold in "Budget Dresses." As the style declines, the item is transferred to the downstairs store (basement) or sometimes is sold to another store to be closed out.

Variations in the Cycle. So far, it appears that all a buyer needs to know about the fashion cycle is the age of the fashion. This is far from true, because the cycle varies in several ways:

1. Some fashions are short-lived: they are almost fads.
2. Some fashions are more universally accepted than others.
3. Most styles tend to come into fashion slowly and decline rapidly; however, some styles remain popular longer than others.

4. The more basic a style is, the longer it will be in fashion.
5. Styles in nonapparel lines tend to stay in fashion longer than do apparel styles.

Styles will also be in fashion with different groups of consumers at different times and in different sections of the country. For example, Oxford-cloth shirts with button-down collars at one time enjoyed general popularity with men. Later, they came into fashion with smaller groups—college men in the East and young business executives. Another example of consumer acceptance of style is the type of men's shoes with what is known as a "French toe." This style has not been popular with city residents for many years, but it is still in fashion in many rural areas. The wise store buyer also remembers that living habits differ in various parts of the country—what is in fashion in New England may never be in vogue in the Southwest where living is more informal.

Analyzing Customer Fashion Preferences

In the final analysis, it is the customers who accept or reject the merchandise of the store. Thus, before merchandise is purchased, the buyer must determine the style preferences of his clientele. One of the best sources of information is close at hand—the salespeople. Many buyers discuss styles with their salespeople and obtain recommendations from them. In addition, valuable information can be procured from want slips and stock-control records. Many buyers also put in some time on the selling floor. Through personal contact with customers they keep abreast of current preferences.

A buyer uses many other ways to obtain answers to fashion questions. He knows that his decisions must be based on facts, not on guesswork or his own personal preferences.

Manufacturers. The buyer learns from the manufacturers what styles they have decided to make and which ones they will "push" (promote heavily). At the beginning of the season, manufacturers have private showings of their new lines or exhibit them at trade shows. The buyer gets the feeling of the fashion

A "Little Shop" within a woman's apparel department of a large department store, where original Paris models as well as other high-fashion merchandise are sold.

Courtesy Macy's New York

trends in the market by "shopping" these shows. He also utilizes other aids and forecasts offered by manufacturers—for example, the color charts brought out in advance of each season by textile, shoe, handbag, or hosiery manufacturers. He studies advance information about fabrics, materials, and accessories, for he must know which are going out and which are coming into use.

Fashion Counts. Manufacturers, publishers of fashion magazines, fashion marketing services, and some large retailers predict fashion trends by making *fashion counts.* These are tallies of the frequency with which a certain style is observed. For example, fashion observers visit fashionable restaurants and resorts where smartly dressed women are. They observe and record the number of women wearing a particular style of dress or shoes. They may even concentrate on a style feature, such as a certain type of heel or collar. The fashion count is repeated from week to week or month to month to determine how the style is progressing on the cycle.

Resident Buying Offices. Large department stores and specialty stores, as well as groups of stores that form voluntary buying groups, maintain resident buying offices in large market centers such as New York and Chicago. These offices gather information about fashion trends and about merchandise resources. This information is available to buyers who visit the market and is often summarized in news letters that are sent to member stores.

Fashion Marketing Services. Some firms specialize in providing retailers and others with fashion marketing information. For example, Tobé in New York, a merchandising, fashion, and market service, issues a weekly report. The Tobé staff, specialists in their own field, keep constantly in touch with market conditions and fashion developments. They "scout out" new resources for merchandise and report on them. They make studies of trends in different lines of merchandise, and clients may consult them on fashion problems.

Other fashion marketing services conduct semiannual fashion clinics in New York that are attended by representatives of the merchandising, personnel, advertising, and store-management divisions of stores. The purpose of these clinics is to summarize fashion developments for store personnel and to enable them to take home this story of fashion and apply it to their local situations.

Trade Literature. The alert buyer reads the trade papers and magazines in his field. In the apparel field, two trade papers are very valuable—*Women's Wear Daily* and *Men's Wear Daily* (Fairchild Publications, New York). Both papers have on their staffs a number of fashion editors, each assigned to a special market or field. In addition, the trade magazines in nonapparel fields now devote considerable space to design and color in merchandise.

Consumer Magazines. In addition to reading trade publications, those who merchandise fashion should keep up with consumer magazines. Many women now read avidly magazines that supply fashion information—*Vogue, Harper's Bazaar, Glamour, Town and Country,* and others. And, they read eagerly the

DRESS NEWS

Tobé
• 11 West 42nd Street • New York

cone skirts add deep center fold-pleat

Updating dresses and ensembles
for fall are new-looking skirts,
so the cone, as we said, stands
pre-eminent in its several
variations. With a deep in-
verted center front fold or
pleat, the gently flared cone
is part and parcel of many
smart dresses and ensembles.

To illustrate - our sketch
combines three important
points. First, the inverted-
pleat cone skirt, barely
covering the knee. Second,
the pared-down blouson,
often in contrast. Third,
the longer cutaway open
jacket, with a tiny collar.
All three are Bohan-Dior
signatures that are
carrying into fall.
Here in navy blue wide
vale twill with a
red jersey pared-
down blouson.

This easy, young look
is now seen in many
topflight collections,
in a wide gamut of
fabrics from silk-and-
worsted to satins and
brocades for after-five.

Sketch Portfolio 2

A page from the fashion report of Tobé giving advance information on fashion trends.

Courtesy Tobé

fashion sections in magazines, such as *McCall's* and the *Ladies' Home Journal.* In addition, they find fashion advice in syndicated columns in newspapers. College, career-girl, and teen-age groups find appealing fashions in magazines such as *Mademoiselle* and *Seventeen.* Many men shoppers read *Esquire,* a publication that features men's fashions in apparel and other goods, such as sporting equipment. In the home-furnishings field, many magazines feature fashion information on furniture, household equipment, and decorating. Among the most widely read and influential publications are *Better Homes and Gardens, House Beautiful,* and *Living for Young Homemakers.* Almost all of these consumer magazines have developed extensive national advertising campaigns for manufacturers and distributors. The fashion merchandiser should know how to tie in his local promotions with them.

Planning Fashion Assortments

In planning the amount and kinds of fashion merchandise to stock, the buyer often uses a *model stock plan.* This is an assortment that is balanced according to anticipated customer demand on such characteristics as size, color, style or model, and price line. This method allows a buyer to plan for an anticipated dollar volume of sales and then estimate how many of each kind of goods should be stocked to attain the sales quota. The model stock differs from the basic stock (discussed on pages 119 and 138) that is essentially a list of the lowest quantities that should be on hand and is based on the number of units of each item sold in the previous year.

To illustrate how a model stock aids a buyer, a men's shoe department can be used as an example. The first step is to determine the broad classification of shoes carried. Assume that these are sport shoes, dress shoes, and work shoes. Sales records will indicate the proportions of the previous year's sales accounted for by each classification. Knowing this, the buyer next determines the proportion of the stock sold last year in each size for each classification. Next, data must be procured showing the price lines that have proved most popular. Usually sales will "cluster" at three points—a majority at a medium price and small numbers at a higher price and a lower price.

When the buyer knows what proportion of the stock should be in each size, each price line, and each classification, he is ready to apply his judgment of fashion trends. He will apportion part of his stock to the colors that have been popular, adjusting these according to fashion forecasts. He will also buy some stock in shoe styles that have proved to be in demand almost constantly, but he will buy more stock in styles that he thinks will be in vogue. This illustration shows that a model stock is based on (1) the previous year's sales records showing how many of each style were sold, and (2) the fashion forecasts for the coming season.

Trade Talk		*Can You Answer These?*
high-fashion store	fashion marketing	1. Why is there more risk in merchandising fashion items than staples?
fashion count	service	
elite trade	model stock plan	2. What information does a buyer need to make successful purchases of fashion goods?

3. From what sources does a buyer obtain information about fashion in the lines he is buying?

4. How does a store determine at which point in the fashion cycle it will operate?

5. What information does a model stock plan provide for a buyer?

6. Explain how consumer magazines and television aid the buyer in doing his job better.

Problems and Projects

1. Make a list of items that are in fashion and show the different groups of consumers who favor them. Explain which ones seem to be appealing only to limited groups of people.

2. After consulting with the managers of two or three local stores, prepare a report on the manner in which these stores deal with fashion problems in men's and women's clothing. From what sources do these store managers obtain fashion information?

3. Knowing the names and special abilities of the principal fashion designers in Europe and in the United States is worthwhile information to possess. From your reading of fashion magazines and from conversations with fashion buyers in your city, prepare a list of such persons. Below each name, write the fashion accomplishment for which the person is known.

4. Read two articles in a trade magazine that deal with new fashions or buying fashion goods. Prepare a report to the class on them.

5. Select a certain style in some line of apparel. Make a fashion count in school (such as in the cafeteria) or at some out-of-school location to determine the extent to which this style has been adopted. If you wish, make the count only on a specific style feature of an item, such as a certain type of heel on a shoe.

Learning Your Job

1. Find out what your store's fashion policy is. Make a list of competing stores and classify them as to where you believe that they operate in relation to the fashion cycle.

2. Describe the ways in which your store keeps up to date on fashion or style trends.

3. Report on the fashion trends in the merchandise you handle.

4. If your store uses a model stock plan, find out how it works and report to the class. If possible, bring a copy of the plan to class.

52 *Promoting Fashion Merchandise*

Designers, manufacturers, and fashion magazines all play an important part in promoting fashion goods. But, in fashion merchandising as in other lines of retailing, it is the local store promotion that sells the goods. Advertising, fashion shows, window displays, and the store's reputation as a fashion center attract the fashionwise customer. Then the salesperson takes the spotlight, for it is her ability, interest, and fashion knowledge that convince the customer. Customers read and enjoy fashion magazines and are excited by the glamour of Paris showings and designers' reputations. But, when the final choice is made, it is made on the basis of what the salesperson shows and says. The customer will be happy when she is sure that she is "fashion-right." The customer will be both if the salesperson has made a careful study of fashion and applies this knowledge.

Building a Career in Fashion

Merchandising fashion goods in retail stores offers many attractive careers for those who have talent and are willing to study. In almost every case, an individual begins a career in fashion by becoming a top-flight salesperson. The individual must know selling techniques; but what is more important, intensive study must be made of color, line, design, and materials in the field in which the individual is interested. A high school education is sufficient, but further study in adult evening schools, community colleges, or college is desirable.

The Fashion Co-ordinator. Large department stores and specialty stores often employ a fashion co-ordinator, and perhaps, several assistant co-ordinators. A fashion co-ordinator has many duties. She collects fashion information to assist buyers in deciding what to purchase and what to promote. She is responsible for planning and carrying out fashion shows for customers and employees. Another duty is to keep salespeople informed about fashions and show them how to use fashion information in selling. Her most important responsibility, however, is co-ordinating fashion for the store. In doing this, she helps buyers in different departments to be consistent in the colors and styles they buy, advertise, and display. She also develops fashion themes for advertisements and displays.

The Fashion Consultant. All salespeople who sell fashion goods should be fashion consultants. Some stores, however, employ people with special training and experience in the fashion field to serve as fashion consultants in

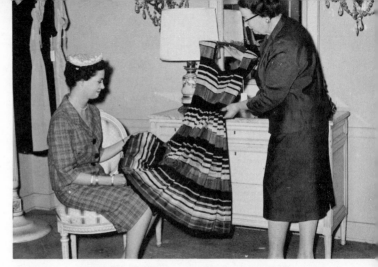

The salesperson in one of the special shops of a large department store becomes a fashion consultant for the customer wanting advice on suitability, accessories, etc.

Courtesy L. S. Ayres & Co., Indianapolis

departments where fashion is primary. For example, a bridal shop or department may have a bridal consultant whose job is to advise customers on bridal gowns, trousseaus, invitations, and receptions. Home-furnishings departments employ interior-decorating consultants and color stylists. In some cases, these consultants do not sell merchandise; they only advise customers. In other cases, the consultants are, in essence, highly trained salespeople.

The Fashion Buyer. Although many stores employ fashion co-ordinators and consultants, most opportunities in fashion merchandising are in the positions of buyer and assistant buyer. In some departments, fashion knowledge and discriminating judgment are the most important qualifications for a position as buyer. In most stores, assistant buyers are selected from the ranks of experienced and trained salespeople.

Planning Fashion Promotions for Special Groups

Stores that enjoy a reputation for fashion promote it in many different ways. They feature style and color in displays and advertisements. They make sure that salespeople are trained to act as fashion counselors. They also carry on major promotional efforts directed at different customer groups.

Teen-Age Promotions. Manufacturers and retailers are aware of the sizable (and very profitable) teen-age fashion market. In fact, distributors have taken steps to foster the growing fashion interests of teen-agers. Manufacturers have special designers to create apparel based on teen-age ideas and activities. Publishers make special appeals by creating teen-age columns or sections in their magazines, or, as in the case of *Seventeen,* establishing a new magazine for this important group.

Many stores have established teen-age fashion departments. They have also organized fashion boards composed of high school girls. An example of a teen-age fashion board is that conducted by the William H. Block Company, a large Indianapolis department store. Block's wanted to keep in touch with the high schools in its trading area, in order to find out the current fashions that girls

THE J. L. HUDSON COMPANY
1962 COLLEGE FASHION SURVEY

Name *Helen S. Appleton* Age *19*

School *Wayne University* School Address *Detroit*
Year of Graduation *1966* Number of Students Enrolled *18,000*
Your Activities in School *Glee Club, Dramatics*
DATE CLOTHES *5 dresses, 2 skirts & blouses*
Please list the clothes and the **number of each** you think would make an ideal wardrobe for school.
CAMPUS CLOTHES *6 sweaters, 3 skirts, 2 tailored dresses*
FORMAL ATTIRE *3 formals*

Is an all-white dress required at your school? Yes___No ✓ If yes, type needed _____ Purpose _____

Do you have a Rush Week? Yes___No ✓ If yes, is it at the beginning of school or is it deferred? _____ If deferred, when? _____

Please list the different parties that make up Rush Week and the clothing required for each party _____

If you are near a metropolitan center or a men's college and go there week-ends, please name the city or college and what you consider appropriate and essential for such trips _____

A fashion survey taken by a department store of clothes worn by college girls.

Courtesy J. L. Hudson Co., Detroit

prefer. Girls, representing high schools within a radius of 75 miles, are now on the board.

The board members attend meetings held on Wednesday of each week. At these meetings, the girls report on observations about their local communities and then select the fashion clothing "item-of-the-week" from merchandise carried in the "High School Hangout," the teen-age department. Different girls on the board write the advertisements describing the fashion item of the week. The board also publishes a monthly paper, called "The Clothesline," which gives a summary of the news and gossip from the various high schools that co-operate with Block's.

College Promotions. Many stores have recognized the importance of the college-age group in the fashion market. Stores have college-fashion departments and also appoint fashion boards whose members represent different colleges and universities. For example, the J. L. Hudson Company, a large department store in Detroit, has a college-fashion advisory board made up of young women from some twenty-five colleges and universities located in different parts of the United States. Under the direction of this board, periodic surveys are made among young women in colleges to find out the clothes they consider essential in an ideal wardrobe for school. The variety of information called for is shown in the questionnaire given above.

Career-Girl Promotions. Another important group of fashion-minded women are the "career-girls." For this group, clothes are important to their job success, and many spend considerable portions of their income on apparel. For this reason, stores plan special promotions for them.

Men's Fashion Promotions. Stores that emphasize fashion in men's clothing usually use different promotional efforts than those used for women customers. The man is not so likely to want to "let the world know" of his interest in style. Thus, the store usually attempts to promote men's fashions through a personal relationship between salesperson and customer. In addition, the store usually tries to make men more fashion-conscious by advertising and display. Knowing that women buy much of the clothing worn by men, stores also advertise heavily in a way that will attract the woman's eye.

Building Fashion Appeals on Color

It is said that we live in a technicolor world. The wise merchandiser knows this to be true, and in almost every line of goods he builds fashion appeals on color. For example, since World War II, there has been a marked shift in customer preferences to brighter colors and to pastel hues.

Besides being more conscious of color, the American customer readily adopts a color that is in vogue. For example, a few years ago it was fashionable to have a dark-color wall in the living room; hence in many homes, rich and poor, a dark wall was the center of the decorating scheme. Similarly, each year or season finds a "new" color in apparel in fashion; perhaps it is "tangerine," "avocado green," or "charcoal." When promoting merchandise, the retailer recognizes these vogues in color, whether in apparel, toys, kitchen utensils, or appliances.

Color in fashion also has another important effect on merchandising. The customer not only wants the color that is in vogue, but he also wants co-ordinated colors. That is, he is conscious of the color harmony necessary in articles that are used together—in clothing and accessories and in furniture and home furnishings. In promoting merchandise, colors must be co-ordinated; and these harmonies are pointed out to the customer in displays, advertising, and personal selling.

Color, therefore, enters into sales promotion; and the retailer must understand this when buying his merchandise. In addition, his salespeople, to serve

The college girl has her own special shop in many stores.

Courtesy F. & R. Lazarus & Co., Columbus, Ohio

Color used to advantage in a fashion promotion.

Courtesy Sears, Roebuck and Co.

customers intelligently, must be able to recognize, match, and harmonize colors and know how to apply this knowledge to their own goods. This is equally important whether the store sells clothing, paints and varnishes, household goods, or the wide variety of accessories in any field of merchandise.

The fashion-minded merchandiser recognizes that color can give special appeal to merchandise that is basically similar to that offered by other stores. For example, a promotional appeal in appliances is that the color of the appliance can be co-ordinated with the decorating scheme of the kitchen. In fact, one manufacturer offers refrigerators with colored door panels that can be changed when the kitchen color scheme is changed. The promotion-minded salesperson knows that the color of the carpet, draperies, floor tile, or walls can make a room seem longer, wider, or shorter. He knows also that certain colors in dishes make food seem more appetizing. In this way, he uses color fashions to sell merchandise. The buyer and salesperson also know that some colors stay in fashion almost indefinitely. For example, for years the most popular color for the handles of kitchen utensils has been red, with yellow a distant second—items with green handles are almost impossible to sell!

Trade Talk

fashion co-ordinator

fashion consultant

fashion buyer

fashion promotion

Can You Answer These?

1. What part does the salesperson play in fashion merchandising and selling?

2. Why is it good business for merchants to try to develop fashion interest among teen-agers?

3. In what ways do stores cultivate teen-age interest in fashion?

4. How do retail stores keep their finger on the pulse of college fashions?

5. Of what value is a knowledge of color to a salesperson? In what lines of merchandising do you con-

sider color information especially important?

6. Where does a person usually begin a career in fashion? What study is necessary to prepare for such a career?

Problems and Projects

1. From your examination of various fashion magazines be prepared to answer the following questions: (*a*) What use can consumers make of these magazines in preparing to buy clothing or household furnishings? (*b*) How can salespeople best obtain selling points that will help them in the sale of fashion merchandise?

2. Procure from your school or city librarian one or more career monographs on occupations in fashion industries. Report on two or three of the careers described.

3. Cut two advertisements from your local newspapers, one of which emphasizes style in clothing and the other style in furniture. How effective in bringing out the style feature do you consider these advertisements?

4. Obtain a color chart for insertion in your notebook. Using this chart as a basis, prepare a list of color combinations that would be harmonious and pleasing in (*a*) a fall suit with appropriate clothing accessories, (*b*) a living room you have been asked to decorate and furnish, (*c*) an automobile for which you are buying seat covers.

5. Observe carefully the teen-age fashion promotions carried on by your local stores through newspapers and other advertising media and through window and store display. Can you suggest ways in which these promotions may be made more effective?

Learning Your Job

1. Ask your supervisor whether or not he can recall items that have sold slowly because of a buyer's error in judgment of fashion. How did the store dispose of the merchandise?

2. Examine at least five advertisements of your company or for products sold by your company. List the ways in which they appeal to fashion motives through their copy and illustrations.

3. Write ten selling sentences for a product of your choice that appeal to fashion motives. Check them with your teacher before trying them out on the job.

4. Make a list of ways in which your firm, in promoting business, could appeal to teen-agers, to young adults, and to young parents.

Sale 99

GET IT AT

RNITURE

METAL MAGIC

the costume

NEW D

HUG

4.00
00

new black-and-bea

ne at theatre, cockt

the edges with je

in lines superbly new

le, a dark blaze of ex

ntle curv

eels

15. The Changing American Market

s a rich girl. Go t

ng goil to deny herself high fashion, whe

to the rescue with smart clothes at

s. If you're loaded with taste, but not wit

and walk out looking like a mi

NEW

BONA

Unit 15 Part 53

Keeping Pace with the Times

Your future in distribution depends on your ability to understand customers and the changing American market.

If we had a crystal ball, perhaps we could foresee the merchandising techniques of the future. But even without one, we can do some predicting, for we do have a crystal ball of a kind—today's customers.

Customers—millions of them—are the great American mass market that consumes the goods and services pouring from a gigantic system of mass production. As a retailer, you will become customer oriented. You will watch and study your market—a market composed of people. How many? What are they like? Where do they live? How much do they spend—and for what?

The Consumer Market Is a Giant Sponge

The July, 1961, issue of *Survey of Current Business,* published by the U.S. Department of Commerce, describes

The first half of the twentieth century is known as the "Age of Production." The second half merits the title, the "Age of Distribution." Now for the first time in our history, more people are engaged in distributing goods and services than in producing or manufacturing them. Now, more than half of the people gainfully employed are in the fields of wholesaling, retailing, financing, real estate, insurance, business transportation, communications, public utilities, and personal and government services.

We must examine this age of distribution because it is the setting in which successful retailers make their management decisions. In the remaining units, we shall turn our attention to studying the function of retail management. But, first, let us find out about the "Changing American Market."

graphically the huge American consumer market. In this issue, it is stated that in 1959 the American consumer spent 78 billion dollars for food, 33 billion for clothing and accessories, 84 billion for housing and household operations, 19 billion for medical care, 39 billion for transportation, 18 billion for recreation, and 44 billion for other products and services.

Some retailers feel that this national market does not concern them. They believe that their local market is the one that really counts. They fail to realize that every local market is a part of the national market and reflects to some degree the changes that take place in the national market. For this reason, understanding the national market helps retailers know what to look for in their local shopping areas. For example, surveys of national trends show that older people are buying more goods. The local retailer should find out the percentage of older persons in his town.

The Mass Market Has Money

Today's consumer has more money to spend than ever before. In order to understand how much more, we must first define two terms—*disposable income* and *real income*. People usually think of their income as all the dollars they earn. Yet, their actual spendable income is the amount of money they have left after taxes and other fixed deductions. This amount is called a person's *disposable income*—the amount he actually has to spend. The merchandise and services that a person can buy with the money he has to spend vary with the purchasing power of the dollar. During inflationary periods (when prices are rising), a dollar buys less than it formerly did. The term *real income* then reflects the value of the dollar. It means how much a person's given income will actually buy at a given time.

Changing Income Groups. Customers today have much more purchasing power than in former years, for changes have taken place in the number of people in different income brackets. In the first place, the United States is tending to become more of a one-class market composed of prosperous, middle-income families. For example, in 1958, over 50 per cent of American families had personal incomes between $4,000 and $10,000. This same 50 per cent of the family units had a total personal income in this year amounting to over one-half of the total national personal income of 342 billion dollars.*

Secondly, people today have more *discretionary buying power*. This is the money the consumer has left after he pays for his essential living expenses—taxes, food, housing, and clothing. It is income available either for saving or for buying luxuries. Today it is usually considered necessary that a family have an income of at least $4,000 before it has any noticeable discretionary buying power. Retailers should plan their operations knowing that about 50 per cent of American families are above this income level.

* *Survey of Current Business*, April, 1961, Office of Business Economics, U.S. Department of Commerce.

Several other factors also should be noted. Regional differences in income are diminishing; that is, people in different sections of the country have incomes more nearly the same size. More wives are working and more teen-agers are employed part-time.

Meaning for the Retailer. These changing income levels add up to one conclusion for the retailer—more consumer buying power, especially in the growing middle class. For these families, a new standard of living is developing. They buy recreational and leisure-time goods, luxury clothing, more appliances and gadgets, better furniture and housing, and more prepared, packaged, and frozen foods. Retailing is, therefore, changing to capture this middle-class market!

The Population Is Zooming

Every minute of every day in the United States, eight people are born and three people die. Going beyond the experts' past predictions, the population is growing now at a pace that will see it reach at least 217 million by 1975. This growth is equivalent to adding a new place at the table of every family in America!

More Younger and More Older People. Americans are living longer, and there are more teen-agers and children. The U.S. Census of Population shows that in 1950 there were 47 million persons under 18 years of age. In 1960, this number had grown to 64 million, an increase of 37 per cent. In 1950, there were 12.2 million persons 65 years of age or over; in 1960, this number had increased to 16.6 million persons, a 34.7 per cent increase.

New Households. The number of new households has risen rapidly. As young married couples go through the family-life cycle, their needs change. After furnishing a house, they will concentrate on buying articles for children. Later, when the children are grown, the parents' income will be spent for entirely different items.

A Mobile Population

The American consumer moves often. Every year, a substantial proportion of the population changes residence. People move from one state to another, from one city to another. Migration from rural areas to the cities or their suburbs continues. Many of these changes are for economic reasons; some for health and other reasons. When consumers move, they take their buying habits with them, and they look for "old friends"—the types of stores and branded products they are accustomed to.

Meaning for the Retailer. Local markets may vary, but general population trends are important everywhere. New markets are opening for the aggressive retailer. The "baby boom" has meant a greater demand for baby foods, children's clothing, furniture, and appliances. When the babies become teen-

Young couples are buy-
ing homes in the suburbs.

agers, what will the market be for clothing, recreation equipment, soft drinks, hamburgers, or . . . ?

On the other hand, the increased number of older people purchases less furniture and appliances. Instead, they often enter the luxury-goods market, buying items such as cameras, phonographs, special foods, and leisure-time goods.

There Is a Rush to Suburbia

The barbecue on the patio, the three-bedroom house, commuting miles to work, and do-it-yourself projects are well-known aspects of the rush to live in the suburbs. The suburbs comprise a large portion of the 168 metropolitan areas that account for about two-thirds of the nation's total retail trade. In fact, suburban residents plus the residents of smaller towns make up about 60 per cent of the nation's population. Although not all customers live in suburbia, many innovations in retailing, such as the shopping center and night openings, stem from this important group.

Suburban Shopping Habits. Suburban living tends to be informal and seems to revolve around the home and children. It is fostering a new set of shopping habits, such as the family shopping tour in the "super," the shopping center, or the branch store. The suburbanite, besides having middle-income purchasing power, is a relatively sophisticated consumer. He is well educated, but he also is responsive to advertising and ideas from today's mass communications —TV, radio, newspapers, and home magazines.

Because suburbanites are remarkably homogeneous (alike) in their habits as consumers, they are becoming today's most important market. In fact, suburban dwellers are characterized as mass purchasers of fashion and specialty goods. They want—and they buy—station wagons, modern furniture, barbecue and outdoor equipment, power tools, picture windows, children's toys, and fashionable clothing.

Luxury Markets Are Growing

We know that the American consumer today has more discretionary buying power than ever before. We also know that he tends to spend this extra income on items formerly considered luxuries. For example, consumers are turning increasingly to processed foods that cost more but are more convenient to prepare. More sportswear and fashion clothing fill closets and drawers. Substantial sums are being spent for recreation and leisure—on hi-fi, boats, motors, water skis, hunting and fishing equipment, and camping outfits.

This extra purchasing power is being spent also for the second car and for extra laborsaving devices like clothes dryers, air conditioners, home freezers, and floor waxers. In addition, these new consumers in huge numbers enthusiastically tackle do-it-yourself projects in homes and gardens, spending increasingly for hand and power tools, garden supplies, lumber and paint, floor tile, and plywood.

More Services Are Purchased. Increasingly, the consumer with discretionary purchasing power buys more services. He has his clothes dry-cleaned more frequently, purchases more insurance, keeps his car and appliances serviced, and seeks better dental and medical care.

Not every American is a purchaser in the luxury market, but the large number who are compose an important segment of the market for the progressive retailer. The new mass market is wide open to competitive selling because of the large amount of discretionary buying power in the hands of consumers.

This new shopping center features indoor courtyards designed to make shopping pleasant and convenient.

Courtesy Southdale Shopping Center, Minneapolis

What Does It Add Up To?

At this point in our study of retailing we cannot do more than skim the surface in our look at the changing American market. However, we have briefly viewed:

. . . the people: more youngsters, more oldsters, more families
. . . the shift in income levels: more middle-class families with greater purchasing power, greater common demand for luxury goods
. . . suburbia: a new mass market

What does this mean for the future retailer? First, it says "Watch the people because they are your market—your customers." Secondly, it means that the "old way" is not good enough. The modern merchandiser must always be alert to market trends and adapt his business techniques constantly. Thirdly, the young person will see in these market trends new and promising opportunities for careers in retailing and other areas of distribution. Finally, the changing American market demands that retail personnel know thoroughly the basic principles of retailing if they are to keep up with a changing world.

Trade Talk

disposable income
discretionary buying power
real income
suburbia
mass market
luxury market

Can You Answer These?

1. In what ways will a local retail-store manager or salesperson benefit from understanding what is happening in the national market?

2. What changes have taken place in recent years in the distribution of incomes? How do these changes affect retailing?

3. What three population trends does the text describe? Explain what these trends mean to the retailer.

4. Why are suburban residents described as "today's single most important market"? Explain why you agree or disagree.

5. In your opinion, would it be fair to say that only consumers with high incomes are in the luxury-goods market? Defend your opinion.

6. In what ways is it important for a future retailer to study the changing consumer market?

7. What do you consider to be the single most important feature of the changing consumer market? Why do you hold this opinion?

Problems and Projects

1. Prepare a list of ten or more articles of merchandise that your family owns that you feel would have been considered luxuries a few years ago. On your list underscore any items that you think many families would still consider as unnecessary.

2. If two families both have incomes of $5,600 per year, would both have (a) the same disposable income, (b) the same discretionary buying power? Explain how you arrived at your answer.

3. Real income takes into account the purchasing power of the dollar. With your teacher's aid, try to find out how much a dollar will buy today as against 5, 10, and 20 years ago. If no facts are available to

you, ask some older people to estimate the value of the dollar today.

4. Using the resources of the library or the local chamber of commerce, find out what the distribution of incomes is in your community. Prepare a report comparing your community with others in your state.

5. The annual incomes of three families are respectively (*a*) $4,-200, (*b*) $6,200, and (*c*) $7,800. Make a list of factors that would determine how much discretionary buying power each family could have. By using some imaginary figures, show how the three families could possibly have the same discretionary buying power. What does this mean to the retailer?

6. Prepare a report showing the population of your community in different age groups. Show also the changes between 1940 and 1950 and 1950 and 1960. The Census data in the library is a good reference for this project.

Learning Your Job

1. Make a list of the major features of the consumer market that are listed in this part of the text. For each feature, indicate what meaning it has, if any, for the operation of your store. For this project, ask your employer for his opinions.

2. Using as an example a line of merchandise sold in your store, explain why some consumers would class it as a luxury while others consider it a necessity.

3. Explain how changes in the national market affect your store's local market.

54 *The Value of Distribution*

On a back street in the Chinese quarter
of Hong Kong, there is a craftsman who makes
camphorwood boxes with dragons and lotus
blossoms carved on them. He loves his work and
turns out many beautiful and unusual products,
but very few tourists ever wander down his
alley and business isn't so good.

The box-maker is working on the sidewalk now
because his workshop-home is jammed to the
ceiling with beautiful, unusual, unsold

camphorwood boxes. He can carve dragons and
lotus blossoms with the best of them, but unfortunately he doesn't know about the other
half of the business picture—distribution.*

Like the Chinese craftsman in the story above, many Americans know little
about distribution. They are familiar with their local retailers from whom they
buy food, clothing, gasoline, and hardware. They are, however, largely unaware
of the wholesalers, brokers, and other distributive businesses who make available
the products of farm and industry. In this part of the unit, we shall learn of
the value of distribution to all of us.

The Process of Distribution

The economic activities of any country fall into three categories: (1) production,
(2) distribution, and (3) consumption. A wagon wheel illustrates very well how
goods and services are produced, distributed, and consumed in our economy.

1. The *hub* represents the producers—the factories turning out goods by processing raw materials and assembling parts; the farmers, miners, foresters,
   and fishermen who wrest raw materials from the earth and sea.
2. The *rim* of the wheel represents consumers—you and me, the people who
   buy goods and services for their own use; the businesses that use goods and
   services to produce other goods.
3. The *spokes* of the wheel, necessary to keep the hub (producers) and rim
   (consumers) turning together smoothly, are the distributors. As fast as
   distribution can create demand for goods, producers make them. Distribution is indispensable, because it builds demand for goods and services
   through such techniques as packaging, display, advertising, and personal
   selling.

From this wheel illustration, we can see that *distribution* is defined as the
steps necessary to get goods from where they are grown or produced to where
they are purchased by the ultimate consumer. This process is also called *marketing*. In fact, many people use *distribution* and *marketing* as synonymous terms.

Functions of Distribution. In a country as large as the United States,
the process of distribution is very complex, but for our purpose it can be simplified. Basically, the process of distribution is composed of a series of functions
carried on by many types of distributive businesses—retailers, wholesalers,
brokers, railroads, banks, trucking companies, advertising agencies, manufacturers' sales offices, and many others.

The main functions of distribution, simply defined, are: buying, selling (including sales promotion), transporting, financing, and storing. In addition, the
function of risk bearing is involved, since goods may be damaged and destroyed

* White, L. T., "Wanted! More Spokes and Spokesmen for Distributive Education," *Business
Education Forum*, X: 7, April, 1956.

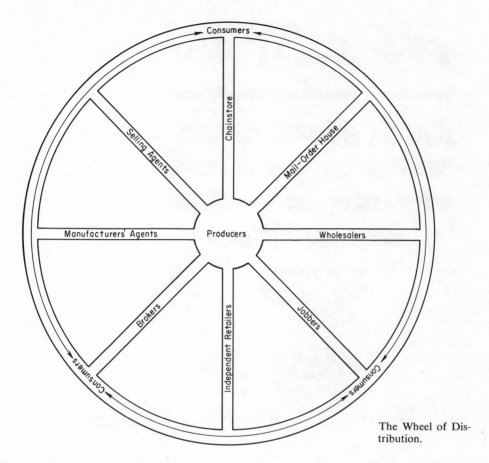

The Wheel of Distribution.

or may drop in price. Depending on the kind of goods involved—such as appliances—customers have made related services such as installing and servicing an additional function of distribution.

Channels of Distribution. A principal reason why we are able to purchase the merchandise we want, when and where we want it, is that networks of distributive firms provide routes through which we can obtain such goods. These routes, over which goods travel from manufacturer to consumer, are called the *channels of distribution*. For example, the orange grower sells carloads of oranges packed in crates to fruit wholesalers in several states. They resell the crates of oranges to grocery retailers, who, in turn, sell them in smaller quantities to consumers.

Several channels are used in distributing goods, depending primarily on the character of the goods and on customer buying habits. The most used channels are:

1. Producer or manufacturer, to retailer, to consumer
   Examples: shoes, garments, meat products

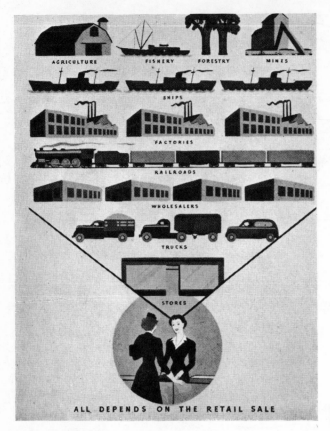

ALL DEPENDS ON THE RETAIL SALE

Courtesy Committee for
Economic Development

2. Producer or manufacturer, to wholesaler, to retailer, to consumer
   Examples: Hardware, drugs, groceries
3. Producer or manufacturer, to consumer (house-to-house selling)
   Examples: cosmetics, household products

Sometimes several channels are used by the same producer because he wishes to cover several different markets.

Mass Production and Mass Distribution. Large-scale, or mass, production in factories is made possible by a production line on which each worker and machine performs a specialized job. In this way, each worker produces more goods per man-hour of work than he could if products were handmade. On the distribution line, which stretches from the factory to the final consumer, each specialized worker—whether wholesaler, broker, jobber, retailer, salesman, or advertising man—performs a specialized job. Unless the goods are sold to consumers, mass production breaks down. Thus, the often repeated slogan that continued progress means "production and more production" is a half-truth.

Values Added by Distribution. A well-known manufacturer in Battle

The production line is speeded up by the consumption line.

Courtesy Committee for Economic Development

Creek, Michigan, buys wheat and processes it into cereal. He expects to be paid for this service and also to receive a reasonable profit for the wheat and for his manufacturing expenses. Most people are willing to pay his price, because he has added value to the raw material (wheat) by changing it into a more useful form for consumers (breakfast food). But, if the cereal is stored in cartons in the warehouse in Battle Creek, it has only limited value. It has full value only when wholesalers, retailers, and other distributors make it available to the consumer when and where he wants it. Thus, distribution, as well as manufacturing adds value to products. Distributors also add value when they change the form of the product to make it more desirable to the customer. Dividing a crate of oranges into bags of a dozen each is one example of creating form that customers want. Cutting a side of beef into steaks and roasts is another example. It may be truly said that distribution adds form, place, and time utility to products.

Freedom in Our Economy

Our competitive, capitalistic economy has nurtured the development of a system of production and distribution unequaled anywhere in the world. As a result, one of the great and enduring values of our American system of free enterprise is the truly enormous selection of goods and services available to consumers. In our country, one is not forced to buy what a few manufacturers (or the government) think one should have. The consumer can exercise his own taste in determining what product, what brand, and from what store he will purchase.

Competition for the consumer's dollar is the principal reason why we are privileged to select the merchandise we desire at the time and place we want it. By and large, producers and distributors survive and prosper if they make available the kinds of products consumers want. Those who are unable to do this are eliminated.

The American Standard of Living. How has America attained the most envied standard of living on earth? Many people would answer, "production"! But, the often unrecognized ingredient is distribution. Unlike his counterpart in other countries, the American distributor is no mere order taker—he is a promoter. He is a merchandiser, not a storekeeper. He arouses in us a need, then stimulates a desire for the good things that are available to fill the need. The American system of distribution has helped make past luxuries into today's necessities. Without an active and aggressive system of distribution, we would still be an agrarian country, living at a horse-and-buggy pace.

Allied Forms of Distribution

Distribution a century ago was a relatively simple process. Consumers obtained the goods that manufacturers produced through rather simple methods of distribution and without requiring many services. However, the demands of the changing American market have increased the importance of distributive businesses other than retail stores.

Service Businesses. Many types of nonmanufacturing businesses that provide services to consumers are now considered a part of distribution. Among them are: (1) *personal services*—such as dry cleaning, laundering, shoe repairing, banking services, television and radio servicing, (2) *business services*—such as record-keeping services and advertising-agency services, (3) *the selling of intangibles*—such as insurance, stocks, and credit, or (4) *acting as a broker* as in the sale of real estate.

The selling of service today is a big business. Our changing way of life has resulted in consumers' doing less for themselves. Their desire for a higher standard of living, plus their higher incomes, leads to a demand for many kinds of services. In addition, the increased technical complexity of many products makes necessary their repair and service by skilled technicians.

This demand for services will not only continue but in all likelihood will increase greatly. For this reason, the young person seeking a career in distribution should consider carefully the service businesses. Retail knowledge and training can be valuable when transferred to the service part of distribution.

Modern Wholesaling. The wholesaler, or jobber, traditionally assembled goods, stored them, and then made deliveries to retailers; but the modern wholesaler goes much farther. He is no longer a passive order taker;

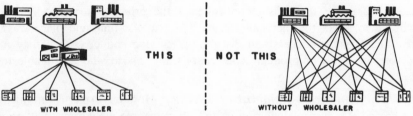

WHOLESALERS SIMPLIFY THE WORK OF RETAILERS

THIS | NOT THIS

WITH WHOLESALER | WITHOUT WHOLESALER

Courtesy National Association of Retail Grocers

The warehouse of a large grocery wholesaler contains a wide variety of merchandise drawn from many parts of the country. The wholesaler serves both the manufacturer and the retailer by providing storage and distribution facilities.

Courtesy Red Owl Agencies, Minneapolis

instead he is developing into a dynamic force in business progress, providing considerable information and many services to his retail customers.

Today's wholesalers provide display services and co-operative advertising assistance to retailers. In addition, progressive wholesalers help with the analysis of store location and with problems of store modernization and layout. Another important service is that of providing sales-training programs and merchandising assistance.

The trend toward large-scale retail outlets affects wholesale distribution because the supermarket, chain store, and shopping center are changing the traditional patterns of distribution. The wholesaler helps independent, smaller retailers to adapt themselves to the changing patterns of distribution and to meet the competition of chain stores and supermarkets.

Manufacturer's Distributive Functions. The modern manufacturer has many distributive functions. The most important is selling and sales promotion. In large businesses, the sales force may be extensive with sales offices in different parts of the country. The sales division also may conduct extensive advertising efforts, train the sales personnel of the retail dealer, and conduct consumer studies.

Other distributive functions of manufacturers involve packaging, providing parts and service, and financing sales to dealers or consumers. In addition, large manufacturers often maintain their own warehouses from which they carry on the wholesaling process to retailers. These large-scale distributive efforts by manufacturers employ many people and often provide excellent career opportunities for young people who have retail-store experience.

Facilitating Agencies. Manufacturers, wholesalers, and retailers all add value to products by performing their distributive functions. Yet, they often utilize the services of allied distributive businesses. Advertising agencies help by planning sales campaigns, preparing sales literature and advertising copy, and conducting consumer-research studies. Credit agencies, including banks, provide financial aid for expansion of inventories and sales, offer financial advice, and set up credit plans for the distributor's customers. These and other facilitating agencies, such as warehouses, not only help provide the goods consumers want, but also offer excellent career opportunities for the young person with a retail background.

Trade Talk

distribution   channel of
marketing   distribution
service business

Can You Answer These?

1. What could a knowledge of marketing do for the Hong Kong craftsman described in the story on page 363?

2. What are the common functions of distribution?

3. Why is mass distribution so necessary to keep mass production going?

4. In what way does distribution add value to a product?

5. In what way is distribution related to a country's standard of living?

6. Why are service businesses considered a form of distribution?

7. What services do modern wholesalers provide for retailers?

8. What distributive functions do manufacturers often perform?

Problems and Projects

1. Draw the economic wheel. Label as many spokes as you can with the names of different types of distributive businesses.

2. Select some type of merchandise in which you are interested. Describe how each of the distributive functions is necessary to make this merchandise available to consumers.

3. List the three most used channels of distribution. For each channel, list several types of goods (and their brand names, if possible) distributed through this channel. Local stores can help provide this information.

4. On a sheet of paper, list the three types of utility that distribution adds to products (time, place, and form utility). Give several examples of merchandise to which at least one type of value has been added by distribution.

5. In addition to the examples given in the text, name as many of each type of service business as you can.

6. List as many reasons as possible for consumers being willing to buy services rather than to perform them themselves.

Learning Your Job

1. For several types of merchandise sold in your store describe the channels of distribution through which they are obtained.

2. List the distributive functions performed by your store. Explain why they are necessary and how each benefits the customer.

3. Find out if your store deals with a wholesaler, either an independent one or one owned by the stores he serves. Explain what this wholesaler does for your store.

55 The Origins of Modern Merchandising

The earliest written records, together with relics of commerce discovered in ancient ruins, show that even the earliest civilizations carried on trading enterprises. Factories, however, did not exist, so that distribution in early times was largely concerned with importing and exporting raw materials and foodstuffs. Hence, the great cities of Carthage, Rome, Athens, and Alexandria were trading centers serving the whole Mediterranean—almost the limits of the known world at that time.

Trading declined when the Roman Empire collapsed. Europe became a medieval land, containing many kingdoms or domains, in which the people lived under the protection and rule of a king or lord. For over five hundred years, ending in the tenth century, distribution in Europe was maintained by itinerant traders. Carrying their wares on their backs or on animals, these peddlers traveled from castle to castle, offering their goods for sale.

We can see the origins of modern merchandising by looking at Europe in the fourteenth century. In England particularly, the establishment of shops heralded the beginning of the system of retailing that the colonists later brought to the New World.

The Establishment of Shops in Europe

In England, as in much of Europe, up until the eighteenth century, distribution of goods was conducted largely by traveling peddlers. However, when people began to settle in towns, many peddlers also settled there and opened small shops to display their wares. In addition, many artisans—shoemakers, bakers, silversmiths, and weavers, for example—began the sale of their products through their own shops.

Early shops were small and carried a special line of goods. In this respect, they were the forerunner of our modern specialty stores. An interesting example of the ancestors of the grocery stores were the spice dealers. They were usually Italians—called Lombards then—and were known as "pepperers." Gradually they added more lines of goods and became grocers.

By 1376, no less than 48 different classes of retailers had shops in London. As was then common practice in Europe, the English retailers grouped themselves in certain localities—a practice present in American cities today. In London, the corn merchants gathered near Corn Hill; the fish dealers, in Fish Street; the ironmongers, in Lothbury; and the goldsmiths, in Cheapside.

The Early Department Store. In 1570, the forerunner of modern department stores was established in London. A large building, known as the Royal Exchange, was divided into numerous booths, or stalls. In turn, these stalls were leased to merchants who displayed a wide variety of merchandise—foods, fabrics, shoes, furniture, jewelry—all under one roof. This type of retailing was copied in other English cities. As a consequence, nearly every sizable city had a "department store" by the end of the seventeenth century. Out of these early European practices and improvements came the retailing policies and practices that the colonists brought to the New World.

Pioneer Retailing in the United States

The early colonial times in our country saw the familiar pattern of the import-export trade that Europe had experienced centuries before. The progress of retail distribution in the United States, however, can be seen best by beginning with a study of the frontier trading post.

The Frontier Trading Post. The earliest type of retailing in the United States was the trading post, established as an outgrowth of the activities of the fur traders. These adventurous men made their way by land and water through the Indian territories. They established trading posts on navigable streams, at portages, and at intersections of Indian trails. The Indians bartered (exchanged) furs for wares such as knives, fabrics, hatchets, firearms, jewelry, and similar items.

Both French and English companies established chains of trading posts throughout the middle and western parts of what is now Canada and the United States. Many present-day commercial centers, including Detroit, Chicago, St. Louis, New Orleans, and Des Moines, were originally settled as trading posts.

After the American Revolution, American businessmen took over the trading posts formerly operated by the French and the English. Settlers from the coastal states migrated westward in search of farm lands and changed the character of the trading posts. In addition to the goods necessary to continue the Indian trade, the posts began to carry general stocks of merchandise suitable for farm families. In this way, they became the forerunner of the general store that was to play so potent a role in the development of American retailing.

The Yankee Peddler. During colonial times, most of the common household goods needed by the colonists were imported. Such items, however, were expensive, and soon a number of small industries sprang up in New England, manufacturing items such as cloth, pins, needles, scissors, buttons, oil lamps, and kitchen tinware. These items were in great demand by the settlers in the frontier communities. Quickly seizing upon this opportunity, Yankee peddlers spread throughout the western territories, carrying their stocks of merchandise on the backs of horses or on wagons. Many of these itinerant peddlers later settled down as merchants in frontier communities. In fact, some

The Yankee peddler was a welcome sight in the early days of the West, bringing there the goods manufactured in the East.

Courtesy Sears, Roebuck and Co.

of today's prominent stores in the West had their origin in these humble beginnings.

The General Store. As we have seen, the early English shops usually specialized in one line of goods. In the United States, however, the general-merchandise store grew out of the needs of the frontier life and made a unique and significant contribution to American retailing.

The general store, which still survives in some smaller communities, was the direct opposite of the modern retail store in its layout and equipment. A general stock of goods—including notions, dry goods, groceries, hardware, and liquors—was sold or exchanged for furs, hides, dairy products, grain, lumber, and other products offered by the store's customers. The merchandise was often scattered about in bins, barrels, and boxes without regard for display or systematic arrangement. Long-term credit was the rule, with accounts often settled when the crops were harvested and sold. Often the general store housed the village post office and sometimes was operated in connection with an inn or a tavern.

The contribution of the general store was twofold. First, it was the center of commercial activity for a new community, attracting trade that brought other businesses, and eventually, a bank and small industries. Secondly, it not only provided the necessities for the frontier settlers, but also became the social center for the men of the community and a meeting place for the discussion of political questions.

Main Street with its shops in an American small town at the turn of the century. Compare this with the principal business street in your city.

Courtesy Sears, Roebuck and Co.

The variety of merchandise carried by the general store made it impossible to offer a wide selection in each merchandise line. As a result, stores specializing in a single or related line came into existence in the United States, as they had in Europe earlier.

The Development of Modern Retailing

During the middle of the nineteenth century, the population of the United States increased rapidly; towns grew into large cities, and industries developed. These changes brought about numerous changes in retailing, greatly altering the comparatively simple methods of distribution that had served frontier communities.

New Types of Stores. Within a few years of one another, several new types of stores were developed: department stores, mail-order houses, variety stores, and chain stores. Each type was destined to play a major role in our modern system of mass distribution.

The 1860's saw the introduction of department stores in a number of cities. Jordan Marsh and Co. in Boston and A. T. Stewart in New York were among the best known. The Great Atlantic and Pacific Tea Co. began the modern chain-store idea in 1859, followed by the well-known Kroger Co. in 1882. The mail-order concept of distribution is traced to the late nineteenth century, also with the establishment of two mail-order houses—Sears, Roebuck and Company and Montgomery Ward & Company. F. W. Woolworth's idea of variety-store merchandising also began in this period.

Changing Policies to Attract Customers. The late nineteenth century also saw the advent of new retailing policies designed to attract customers. Retailers, following the leadership of men such as Marshall Field, John Wanamaker, and A. T. Stewart, discontinued bargaining with customers. Instead, they generally adopted the one-price policy, which today is characteristic of American retailing. Many stores shortened the credit periods or began operating strictly on a cash basis. Retailers also developed more ethical standards in salesmanship

Wide aisles, good lighting, escalators, and open display characterize the modern store.

RETAIL TRADE—1958—UNITED STATES *

Kind of Business	Stores (number)	Sales Entire Year (thousand dollars)	Total Paid Employees (number)	Active Proprietors of Unincorporated Businesses (number)
Lumber, building materials, hardware, farm-equipment dealers	108,248	14,309,206	445,403	99,274
General-merchandise group stores	86,644	21,879,106	1,326,671	79,421
Food stores	355,508	49,022,333	1,183,633	380,058
Automotive dealers	93,656	31,807,877	720,877	82,995
Gasoline service stations	206,302	14,178,203	465,550	233,922
Apparel-accessory stores	118,759	12,525,451	648,703	100,911
Furniture, home-furnishings stores	103,417	10,074,227	392,743	96,911
Eating, drinking places	344,740	15,201,481	1,575,667	382,856
Drugstores, proprietory stores	56,232	6,778,926	347,627	53,127
Other retail stores	240,140	18,468,340	580,509	233,458
Nonstore retailers	74,679	5,401,313	223,698	75,733
United States Totals	1,788,325	199,646,463	7,911,081	1,818,666

* From 1958 Census of Business Retail Trade

WILLIAM T. GRANT

Chairman of the Board and founder of W. T. Grant Co.

and sales promotion, which resulted in increased confidence on the part of the public.

One change, especially, had a major influence on the growth of retail stores. Many stores, and especially department stores, began extensive advertising and sales-promotion efforts. In place of the very modest advertisements they had placed in newspapers, stores turned to continuous and large-scale advertising, and some even dared to advertise on Sundays!

Retail Stores Today

As the twentieth century unfolded, retail distribution grew rapidly. New types of merchandising practices evolved from the pressure of many influences. Among these were the great expansion of the population, the development of large urban centers, the rising incomes of families, the outpouring of goods from a gigantic system of mass production, and the market and product research that developed articles that customers wanted. It was from these forces that the twentieth-century "Age of Distribution" began.

Trade Talk

general store   Yankee peddler
trading post   barter

Can You Answer These?

1. Of what value is it to study the history of retailing?
2. Describe trade in England around the fourteenth century. How did practices current at that time affect the development of retailing in the United States?
3. What part did the trading post play in the progress of retailing?
4. What was the contribution of the general store to distribution on the frontier?
5. What new types of stores were developed in the United States during the last half of the eighteenth century?
6. Of what service was the Yankee peddler to small manufacturers in New England and to people on the frontiers?
7. In what ways did merchants change their store-operating policies in the late nineteenth century? Which of these policies are in effect today?

Problems and Projects

1. On a map of the United States, indicate the trading posts in existence before 1850. Which of these have developed into present-day trading centers?
2. Collect magazine pictures and drawings or other suitable illustrations describing the following: trading posts, Yankee peddler, general-merchandise store, specialty store, and changes in American retailing.
3. The instructor will appoint several students to interview some of the leading merchants in your city and obtain from them brief histories of their stores. The information thus obtained should be prepared as a class report.
4. From your grandparents and

other older people obtain information about methods used in store-keeping in the locality or country in which they grew up. Present this information to the class as an informal report.

5. Use the latest U.S. Census of Business, Retail Trade, to secure for your state, county, or city the same type of figures that appear in the table on page 375. Using your figures, construct a new table and analyze the retail trade in your area.

Learning Your Job

1. From your employer or from any literature available, obtain information that will help you compile a brief history of your store. Try to determine the factors that influenced its development. Add this information to your store manual.

2. List the ways in which policies and practices in your store have changed due to new conditions or customer demands. Use your employer as a source of information.

16. Store Location, Layout, and Organization

Unit 16 Part 56

Store Location

For our grandmothers, shopping was an adventure. It was, first of all, a chance to get away from a week of heavy household chores—Monday was washday; Tuesday, ironing; Wednesday, mending; Thursday, shopping; Friday, baking; and Saturday, cleaning. But it was also an opportunity to meet with friends from scattered parts of the countryside and catch up on the local news. The day was considered an outing—unhurried and sociable.

Today's homemaker shops far more often (she depends on retail stores for practically all her family needs, whereas her grandmother provided a great many of the family needs herself). In most cases, the modern homemaker is in a hurry. While her household duties are lightened by such conveniences as frozen foods, prepared mixes, an automatic washing machine, dryer, dishwasher, and garbage disposal, she has a far more active life outside the home —the church, the school, youth groups, and clubs. She may even have a job in an office, a store, or a factory. Thus, she wants her shopping to be efficient.

Recognizing the needs of today's homemakers for more efficient shopping, progressive retailers are giving more attention to location, layout, and organization of their stores.

For many years, Frank Cochran operated a successful hardware store in a neighborhood shopping area in a large city. In the same area was a grocery store, a drugstore, and similar small stores that catered to the surrounding neighborhood. But in recent years, Mr. Cochran felt the "squeeze" of changing times and living habits. His store prospered when the surrounding area was made up of large, one-family houses. But gradually these homes were replaced by apartment houses. The people who moved into the apartment houses seemed to have little need for hardware items or preferred to buy these in large department stores. Consequently, Mr. Cochran decided to follow his former customers to the suburbs, where again there would be individual private houses whose needs he could supply. By doing this, Mr. Cochran illustrated a principle of retailing—the success of a retail business depends heavily on its environment.

379

Importance of the Trading Area

In locating a retail store, the merchant must consider the *trading area* the store will serve—that is, the geographic boundaries within which his customers live or are likely to shop. Knowing this, he can estimate how many people live within this area, their standard of living, their tastes, and their needs for his products or services. For some stores—for example, a large department store or an exclusive furniture shop—the trading area may be an entire city or town, including surrounding suburban and rural communities. For other stores—such as a small drugstore, florist shop, or bakery—the trading area may be restricted to a surrounding few blocks.

A merchant should also know who and where his competitors are in his trading area and estimate their effect on his sales potential. The merchant can obtain this information about his trading area from many sources: the local chamber of commerce, retail merchants bureau, trade associations, wholesalers, census data, studies made by colleges and business publications, and from various community leaders.

Selecting a Trading Area

In looking at possible locations for a store, the retailer must decide which area in a community is most suitable for his type of retailing. Often, he may choose from several types of shopping districts.

Central Shopping District. The central shopping district is the downtown area in a city or town—the "main drag," so to speak. Here are located the big department stores and a wide variety of specialty shops. This area is characterized by heavy customer traffic. The customers come from all over the city and from the outlying suburbs and communities to shop where wide assortments of goods and services are available.

Secondary Shopping Districts. In most cities, there are several secondary shopping districts, which are smaller replicas of the central shopping district. These secondary shopping districts primarily serve a specific section of the city; but since they are usually located on main traffic routes, they often attract shoppers who live outside the area. Many people like to shop at these secondary shopping districts because it is more convenient to do so, and parking space is generally available.

Neighborhood Shopping Districts. In nearly all cities and towns,

A map is helpful in locating the **probable limits** of the trading area of a store.

Courtesy National Cash Register Co.

there are neighborhood shopping districts. Located in residential districts, often at intersections, these districts include smaller businesses, such as shoe-repair shops, meat markets, florists, bakeries, and small grocery stores. Neighborhood shopping districts are ordinarily patronized only by those living nearby.

String Streets. Cities usually have a "string" of retail stores often extending for miles on an important highway leading into the city. These are called *string streets.* This type of shopping district depends on passing traffic for its support. Typical of establishments located in this district are diners, fruit and vegetable stands, gas stations, garden centers, and the like.

Planned Shopping Centers. As you know, planned shopping centers are usually located in suburban areas where there is plenty of parking space. In some instances, they are located in older sections of the city, often on property where factories, schools, or streetcar and bus "barns" have been razed. Many large downtown stores have branch stores in these shopping centers. The larger planned shopping centers provide the shopper with "one-stop" facilities—just about everything he needs can usually be found in this one general area.

General Factors in Store Location

The Community. The prospective retailer will be wise to take a good over-all look at the community before deciding on locating there. He should find out all he can about the growth trends of the community—whether it is "going places," merely standing still, or losing ground. Once he has satisfied himself on this point, he will want to get detailed information on the following:

Competition. Is there room in this area for an additional establishment such as he is planning, or is the community already saturated with satisfactory outlets?

Rentals and Property Values. If he plans to rent, is the rent reasonable for

Good locations develop into retail centers. Typical of this is the famous Petticoat Lane in Kansas City.

A choice location for a store is here where shoppers can walk unimpeded by traffic from one store to another.

the type and location of the store? Are property values such that he can afford to buy a building?

Labor Conditions and Wages. Can the retailer find a sufficient number of qualified workers to "man" the store and at wages he can afford to pay?

Local Taxes. How do local taxes compare with tax rates in other cities?

Advertising Media. What is the situation regarding newspapers, radio, TV, and other media useful for advertising his store?

Business Services. Does the community have available accounting services, banking and credit facilities?

The Site. Chain stores have developed highly successful methods for determining store locations. Before choosing a site they do a great deal of research, tapping every available source of information—real estate dealers, chambers of commerce, civic groups, "scouts," and various specialists in their own employ. Often they make traffic counts; that is, a person stands at the proposed site and actually counts for several days the number of people who pass by. All retailers, chain or independent, would do well to practice the chain-store methods of locating store sites.

Following are some general factors to be considered in choosing a site:

Buying Habits. Buying habits vary in different trading areas. Goods that are considered necessities in one area may be luxuries in another. A store must therefore locate in a suitable price area. For example, a ladies' dress shop specializing in high-fashion garments at high prices would probably not find it profitable to locate in a section where incomes are low.

Transportation. Proximity to buses, streetcars, and other kinds of transportation should be carefully considered when an accessible location is sought.

Parking Space. The availability of parking space is a big factor today in store location and its importance continues to grow.

Specific Factors in Store Location

Although the merchant may be fairly certain about the community and the trading area in which he wants to locate his store, several specific factors must be considered before buying, constructing, or renting a building.

The "100 Per Cent" Location. Many retailers base their choice of an exact site on what is known as the *100 per cent location*. This is defined as the ideal location from every point of view for that particular type of store. A merchant judges all store sites in terms of the ideal: for example, a site in a good general area, but located on a side street with less sidewalk traffic might be rated as an "80 per cent location." Of course, what is a 100 per cent location for one store may be only a 60 per cent location for another. For example, an auto-parts store would be very poorly located in the same block with high-grade clothing stores, millinery, etc., even though on the best side of the street with plenty of traffic passing by. For many years, foot traffic past the store was considered the most important indicator of a good location; however, the general use of the automobile makes foot traffic less reliable today in judging the sales potential of a site.

Following are some basic principles to be considered in judging an available site:

Proximity to Similar Stores. There are several advantages in locating near stores selling similar or complementary articles. For example, a furniture store may locate next to a successful carpet and rug store; a ladies' shoe store may locate next to a dress shop; and so on.

Corner Locations. Corner locations are often 30 to 70 per cent more valuable, since there is more window-display space, double traffic, better light inside the store, and usually two entrances.

Shady or Sunny Side. Rentals on the side of the street that is shady in the afternoon may be as much as 20 per cent higher than those on the sunny side. Many shoppers prefer not to walk on the sunny side, particularly in warm climates. Furthermore, on shady streets, displays in the windows are protected from destructive heat and light.

Street-Level Locations. Upstairs and basement locations are considerably lower in rent than ground-level locations. Window display cannot be very effective in such locations, and often heavy advertising must be done to attract trade.

"Fringe" Benefits. If the merchant plans to rent, he should consider carefully such details as the terms of the lease, equipment provided by the owner, amount and shape of the floor space, storage space available, condition of the building, adequacy of plumbing and heating, and so on.

Trade Talk

trading area	secondary	neighborhood	string street
central	shopping	shopping	100 per cent
shopping	district	district	location
district			

Can You Answer These?

1. In what ways have changes in buying habits and the use of the automobile affected the choice of store location?

2. What should a merchant know about his trading area?

3. Where can a retailer obtain information about his prospective trading area?

4. What are some of the things about a community that the retailer should investigate before locating there?

5. Why is it important for a retailer to know about the different types of shopping districts?

6. Why is customer foot traffic less reliable nowadays as an indicator of sales potential than it formerly was?

7. Why are corner locations usually more valuable?

8. Why are basements and upper floors usually less desirable as store locations?

9. Why is it an advantage for a store to locate near stores selling similar or complementary merchandise?

Problems and Projects

1. Choose a type of store, such as apparel, food, drug, or hardware store. Explain briefly how changing customer buying habits might affect the location of such a store.

2. Make a list of at least five factors basic to choosing a store location. Rate each factor on its importance in choosing a site for each of the following retail businesses (be ready to explain your ratings): (a) low-priced, chain shoe store, (b) suburban branch department store, (c) gasoline service station, (d) drive-in restaurant,

(e) apparel shop, (f) florist shop.

3. Name two store buildings that have been vacant for some time. What reasons can you give for their remaining unoccupied?

4. Interview the owner of a recently opened store. Try to find out his reasons for choosing the location. Report your findings to the class.

5. Attach to the chalkboard or bulletin board a large map of your community and surrounding areas. On this map indicate with crayon the principal shopping districts and streets. Using different colored thumbtacks, locate department stores and their branches, food supermarkets, variety stores, drugstores, and principal apparel stores. Using your map as a guide, (a) point out the different types of shopping districts as described in the text; (b) determine to what extent shopping areas are located in the suburbs; (c) make a list of other things that the map tells you about store location.

6. A committee of students can make a check on pedestrian traffic at some corner, or outside a selected store in the middle of a block or in a shopping center. Select several such points for comparison purposes. Count the pedestrians who pass these points over a 30-minute period. Tabulate the information and report on the value of these points as store sites.

Learning Your Job

1. Find out from your supervisor or store manager what advantages your store has in its present location. Determine, if possible, what disadvantages the location has and what methods the store uses to offset them.

2. Make a map showing the location of your store and that of your principal competitors. Outline on the map your estimated trading area. This information can probably be obtained from your supervisors, the credit or delivery departments, or by checking the customer addresses from sales checks.

57 Modern Store Buildings and Equipment

Modern consumer buying habits have brought about many changes in the appearance not only of the outside of stores but also in the interior arrangement of fixtures and display of merchandise. The store front, the display windows, and the entrance are the first things the customer will see. If these are well designed and attractive, they will draw the customer to the store; and if he is sufficiently interested in the merchandise on display, he will enter the store. There the salespeople and interior displays take over.

Adequacy of the Building

As discussed in Part 56, the choice of a store location involves many decisions. In addition to the location of the store, the building itself is of very great importance. Here are four fundamental factors to be considered:

1. The building must contain ample space for the display of the merchandise and also adequate space for the nonselling activities of the store.
2. The building should be large enough to allow for future expansion.
3. The plumbing and heating systems must be adequate.
4. The rent or purchase price of the building should be low enough to permit the retailer to alter the building to suit his purposes. This may involve the installation of modern lighting, modernizing the store front, lowering the ceiling, installing air conditioning, and a general redecorating. If the alterations require a heavy investment, the retailer must have a long-term lease in order to spread the expense of such improvements over a period of years.

The Store Front and Entrance

First impressions are important. If a customer has a favorable impression of a store, he is more likely to want to shop there. The store front and entrance are powerful factors in the customer's decision as to whether or not he will go inside.

Store-front design has made great progress in recent years. Fronts with consumer appeal—inviting entrances, open display, soft lighting, interesting construction materials—have replaced the "gingerbread" architecture of past years. In one interesting experiment, doors have been eliminated. Instead, air is forced downward, forming an "air curtain" between sidewalk and store interior, screening out dirt and dust. At night, movable panels slide into place to safeguard the property.

A widely adopted design is the *open-type store front*—a front of large areas of glass through which the sales floor is seen on display. The purpose is to make the store interior really a part of the window display, attracting shoppers when the store is open and drawing attention after store hours.

Another development in store-front modernization has been the improvement of store signs. The sign should be an integral part of the front and contribute to the distinctive character of the store. The sign is an effective sales reminder if it can be seen at some distance—reminding shoppers of the merchant's location. Many retailers consider that spending a few cents to illuminate the sign and store front at night is excellent and economical sales promotion.

The rules for modernizing store fronts and entrances have been well summarized by the Kawneer Co., Niles, Michigan, a well-known manufacturer of store equipment:

1. Locate the entrance doors in accordance with interior layout and traffic circulation needs—not to satisfy a decorative urge.
2. Identify the entrance so the customer can quickly and easily find it. (For example, the door can be identified by a special kind of handle or by signs on the glass, such as "In" or "Out."
3. Design a store front as two basic elements:
    a. The sign area, or "billboard," for identification and advertising.
    b. The entry area for display and invitation.

An attractive store front on a modern drugstore. Note the authentic Old English exterior that suggests a page out of Dickens' Old Curiosity Shop.

Courtesy The Chemist Shop, Fort Lauderdale, Fla.

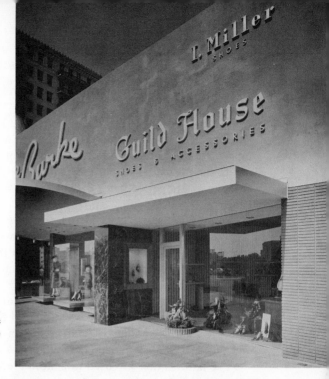

A modern open-front store front, permitting shoppers to see the displays inside.

Courtesy The Kawneer Co., Niles, Mich.

4. On busy streets, set the front back a few feet to allow the customer to concentrate on displays without feeling conspicuous or without being subjected to elbowing by the passing crowds. Building codes need to be observed in connection with store-front planning.
5. Make use of contrast between light and dark colors and textures of materials. Remember that the eye will always be attracted to the source of strongest light, contrast, and color.
6. Use color boldly, but not carelessly. Avoid the use of too many colors. A few, well-placed colors are superior to many competing with each other.

Windows. The display windows of a store are of very great importance; they serve as a constant advertisement of the merchandise on sale. Consequently, stores plan to have their windows as large as possible, so that the merchandise can be displayed attractively. Two basic kinds of construction are used: (1) Windows that are closed off in the rear, so that a passer-by will concentrate on the merchandise displayed in the window. This type of display window is used in furniture stores, where an entire room may be shown in a window, or in a display of clothing. (2) The window without a background permits the passer-by to look into the interior of the store. This is done in food supermarkets, in flower shops, and in motorboat showrooms.

One advantage of the open background is that merchandise can be removed and sold easily, which is more difficult in the closed-background type of window; however, merchandise is more protected in the closed-background window.

Store Fixtures

Modern stores are equipped with shelves, display cases, wall racks, and other merchandise fixtures. Some of these fixtures may also have built-in display aids, such as pegboard or corkboard.

Fixtures are needed in stores for several reasons: To display the merchandise, to help sell the merchandise, to guard the merchandise, and to provide a storage space for the merchandise. Although counters, racks, display cases, and storage units should be attractive, they should never detract from the merchandise but should always aim to focus the customer's attention and interest on the merchandise.

Self-service stores will, therefore, have certain types of display cases and shelves that serve a dual purpose: display as well as easy accessibility of the goods for selection. In a jewelry store, on the other hand, the display cases will be different, for here the merchandise must be displayed as well as guarded against theft.

Fixtures, such as shelves or drawers, are used for storage. This makes the goods more easily accessible when needed than if left in original packing boxes. Storage fixtures should be built in such a way that they will assist in keeping the stock in the best possible condition.

The fixtures that are used in a store are determined by the type of merchandise sold by the store, as well as by the class of customers patronizing the store. A dress shop selling expensive, high-fashion clothes will have more expensive display fixtures than one handling moderate-priced merchandise. The high-priced store may show only a few dresses on manikins and keep most of its stock "behind the scenes." The moderate-priced shop may be partly self-service, so that most of its stock will be on the floor, easily accessible to the customers. Its fixtures will, therefore, be quite simple and serviceable.

Effective Lighting

No matter how attractively the store is decorated and the stock arranged, much of the effectiveness of the displays is lost if the lighting is inadequate. It is, therefore, important that careful consideration be given to effective lighting. Sometimes a merchant wants to save a few pennies by turning off the lights, failing to realize that customers are discouraged by the gloomy atmosphere.

The job of spreading an even curtain of light over all merchandise on display may be done by general illumination throughout the store, which in many small stores may be of sufficient intensity. Most stores, however, need some additional, localized lighting to highlight special displays and showcases, help bring out colors, and generally relieve the monotony of an even, over-all light. Contrast is essential in large stores, where vast quantities of merchandise are on display and one group must be visually separated from another. It also has a useful place in small stores to draw attention to specific articles or departments.

Types of Lighting. Lighting may be either direct or indirect with variations of these two. On the whole, more stores use indirect or semi-indirect lighting because of the diffused and soft light produced. This type of lighting

A very effective use of indirect lighting.

Courtesy Stix, Baer and Fuller, St. Louis, Mo.

is more expensive, however, than the direct lighting because of the greater cost of the fixtures. Another relatively new development is the use of fluorescent lamps. These are cheaper to operate than filament bulbs, because they give more illumination for each watt. The fluorescent lighting is, however, more expensive to install.

The type of store as well as the type of merchandise for sale will determine the kind of lighting to be used. In a food store, direct lighting is more appropriate; while a high-class specialty shop will use some indirect lighting to throw a soft, diffused light that is more flattering to the customers as well as to the merchandise on display.

Advantages of Good Lighting

In Windows

1. Bright, cheerful lighting of window displays draws customers to the store.
2. In the case of the store with an open front, a brightly lighted interior makes the entire store a display window and attracts passers-by into the store.
3. Controlled lighting of display windows makes it easier for passers-by to see merchandise even though daylight reflections appear in the glass.

Interiors

1. Good lighting reveals the true color, texture, luster, and other qualities of merchandise and brings quicker, more accurate buying decisions. The result is a reduction in the time required per sale and fewer merchandise returns.
2. When used skillfully to provide varying degrees of brightness, strong contrasts, silhouettes, and color, lighting draws attention to featured items and increases their appeal.
3. Good lighting increases the alertness and efficiency of salespeople, improves their morale and reduces mental fatigue.
4. Good lighting promotes store cleanliness and neatness.

5. Proper blending of light and color in a store's decorative scheme helps to give the store a distinctive character and atmosphere.

Other Store Equipment

In addition to sales, display, and storage fixtures as well as lighting, many retailers have installed air-conditioning units or combinations of heating and air-cooling systems. Although expensive, the comfort provided by these attracts shoppers to the store and keeps them there longer. Furthermore, the merchandise is kept fresh, dirt and dust are eliminated, and employee fatigue is kept down to a minimum. In most parts of the country, air conditioning is a "must" during the summer months.

These are the fixtures and equipment the customer is aware of. In addition, many electrical devices and machines help the employees to expedite sales and routine work connected with them. Among the devices are bookkeeping machines, calculators, files, safes, machines for price-marking goods, addressing machines, duplicating machines, to mention but a few. The use of these time-saving machines will provide faster and better service to the customer and will eventually increase the profits of the store.

It is, therefore, to the advantage of every store manager to read the trade magazines in his line, which will discuss and feature the latest developments of machines and fixtures that can be used in his store.

Trade Talk

open-type front   direct
indirect   lighting
  lighting   store fixtures

Can You Answer These?

1. Name four fundamental factors to be considered in choosing a store building.
2. What matters should be considered in building a store front?
3. What are the advantages of good lighting in the windows and interior of a retail store?
4. What is meant by the statement, "The store sign is an effective sales reminder"?
5. What purposes should the store fixtures serve?
6. What advantages are claimed for stores having air conditioning?
7. What is an advantage of fluorescent over filament electric lighting?

Problems and Projects

1. Visit several different types of retail stores. Prepare a report on the kinds of store equipment used. To what extent do you find open or visual display? closed glass counters? What kind of merchandise do you find displayed in each type? What advantage does open display have over the closed counter?

2. In the business section of your city, locate one good store front and one poor one. Describe both to the class. Why is the good store front more inviting to persons passing the store? For this project, use the rules for modern store fronts that are listed in the text.

3. Consult your local electric company on the subject of correct lighting of stores and store windows. Obtain as much helpful information

on the subject as you can, and prepare a special class report.

4. With your teacher's permission, invite a store-front or store-equipment salesman or a local architect to talk to your class on effective store fronts and equipment.

5. From real estate men, attempt to find out the rental or purchase price of some unoccupied store buildings. Report your findings to the class.

6. Prepare to take part in a discussion on the topic, "It's not the appearance of a store, but the merchandise and service that really count."

Learning Your Job

1. Analyze the front of your store and prepare a brief report on its good features. Point out also improvements that might be made. Be sure to explain how each feature attracts or deters customers.

2. Rate your store on the effectiveness of its lighting and store equipment. To do this, explain the purpose of each item, and determine whether the purpose is being served.

3. If possible, find out how much rent your store pays or would pay if it were not owned. Then figure the monthly rent per square foot of floor space and per front foot.

58 Effective Store Layout

There are tricks in all trades including retailing. One is to direct customer traffic to all parts of the store, including the upper floors. Here's how one large department store did it. A washing machine, filled with water and clothes, with a salesman demonstrating it, was placed directly in front of the elevators on the first floor. In addition, there were radios playing pleasant music and a refrigerator stocked with food nearby. Customers who were attracted by this display and who became interested were then directed to the departments that carried the items on display.

This story will illustrate the point that good interior display, well located, can be a valuable aid to increase the sales volume of a store.

Principles of Store Layout

The term, *store layout,* refers to the interior arrangement of a store for its selling and nonselling activities: the location of counters, display areas, aisles, elevators and stairways, for its selling activities; storage areas, the bookkeeping department, the receiving department, etc., for its nonselling activities.

In the past, many stores overlooked the importance of store layout. All too often, new lines of merchandise were added without a plan, resulting in a haphazard arrangement in which merchandise was sometimes hidden or located so poorly that both customers and salespeople were unaware of it. In recent years, however, store layout has been approached scientifically, especially by department stores and chain stores. Wholesalers, retail trade associations, and store-equipment manufacturers have also studied this problem and are prepared to help retailers with layout planning.

Store layout is important for several reasons: rising costs of store operation and increasing competition among stores have forced the retailer to achieve as fast a stock turnover as possible. He has learned that his turnover is greatly increased by effective store layout. Furthermore, floor space in the modern store building is too expensive to allow any of it to go to waste through poor planning. Following are some of the principles of store layout that must be applied by today's merchants.

1. Remove excess barriers, such as walls and counters, that prevent maximum store circulation by customers.
2. Use aisle arrangements to "lead" customers past many departments and display areas.
3. Maintain sufficient aisle space, so that customers are able to examine merchandise without being jostled or feeling that they are in the way.
4. Concentrate stock in the smallest space possible without giving a look of crowdedness.
5. Use arrangements that encourage as much self-service as the type of merchandise and store policy will permit.
6. Display openly as much merchandise as possible. Goods should be given display space in relation to the profit returned and seasonal importance.
7. Design the interior to permit the shopper to handle and inspect the merchandise (except perishable or fragile items).
8. Place related merchandise lines near each other to obtain suggestion sales.

Factors Affecting Store Layout

The factors that affect the layout are: (1) the type of merchandise carried; (2) the need for directing customer traffic, and (3) the merchandising policies of the firm. Each of these factors is discussed in the following paragraphs.

Type of Merchandise Carried. The kind of merchandise carried strongly influences store layout. There are things people buy on impulse because they admire them and want them. These goods must be displayed to catch the eye of the customer. Items such as jewelry, gloves, drugs, candy, handbags, notions, and toilet goods fall into this category. Such items are therefore placed on the main floor of a store, near the main aisles, elevators, or entrances. In smaller stores, impulse items sell well when placed near cash registers or self-service check-out lanes.

Convenience goods are goods that a customer buys frequently, usually in

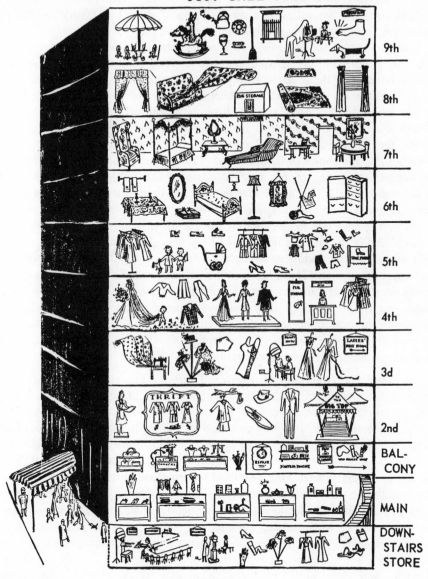

JUST CALL YOUR FLOORS!

9th

8th

7th

6th

5th

4th

3d

2nd

BAL-CONY

MAIN

DOWN-STAIRS STORE

Customer guide to a department-store layout.

small quantities. Hosiery and handkerchiefs fall into this group. These need not be placed so conspicuously as impulse goods, but they should be close enough to the main stream of traffic, so that they can be featured when the need arises.

Shopping goods may be placed at some distance from the main entrance, because customers usually plan such purchases and are willing to spend some time in locating these items. This is especially true of more common articles such as sweaters, domestics, and sporting goods, as well as luxury articles such as antique furniture, Oriental rugs, fine silver, and furs.

If the layout of the store is well planned, the customer on the way to the shopping goods will pass many displays of impulse goods as well as displays of special features or items reduced in price for quick clearance. This principle of arrangement holds true in the department store as well as in a small food store. In the latter, for example, special displays of canned goods on sale may be placed along the aisle leading to the meat department.

The type of merchandise influences not only the choice of location in the store but also the choice of fixtures needed for proper display. Thus in the clothing department, fitting rooms must be provided that will give complete privacy to the customer. The layout of that department therefore requires careful planning, so that valuable aisle space can be kept for display purposes. Seasonal goods and special sale items, such as potted gift plants, are often displayed on tables placed in the aisles or near them. They may also be sold on closed counters with a space in the middle in which the salesperson stands providing service to customers on all sides. These tables and counters are called *merchandise islands*. Stores must be careful, however, not to fill the aisles with too many special tables and counters, which may hinder customer traffic and give a cluttered, untidy appearance. If possible, the merchandise near the entrance should lend itself to an attractive display. This selection should also be determined partly by principle number 6 given on page 392.

Need for Directing Customer Traffic. The circulation of customer traffic is not a problem in the small specialty shop dealing in articles such as furs or jewelry. In most stores, however, the use of modern merchandising methods stresses ways of routing customers to different parts of the store. Large stores have observed that customers will automatically walk to the right when entering a store. Stores have tried various ways to divert customer traffic to the left or straight ahead. One way used was to place particularly attractive displays to the left of the entrance to catch the customer's eye. Elevators and escalators are placed in sections less frequented by customers, in that way bringing the customer to those departments on their way to the elevators. Large stores often place customer services—particularly restaurants, lounges, shoe-repair shops and cashiers—in basements or on upper floors to direct the flow of traffic past merchandise counters. In smaller stores, placing cash registers or items in high demand near the rear will help draw shoppers through the store.

Merchandising Policies. Store layout is influenced strongly by the firm's merchandising policies. In a store featuring personalized salesperson service, fewer goods need to be displayed because the salespeople will show the customers the right items. In prestige stores, the layout should give a spacious, un-cluttered, and dignified look. In fact, small "shops" may be created by partitions or low walls to provide a feeling of exclusiveness. On the other hand, stores competing on a low-price basis need to put on display as much merchandise as possible.

A recent trend in store arrangement is to place quick-selling, low-profit items in the rear of the store. Consequently, the more valuable space just inside the entrance and along the main aisles can be devoted to slower-moving, high-profit items.

When stores sell many different types of merchandise, related items should be grouped. For example, accessories and shoes should be located close to clothing; gifts, near wrapping supplies; and paint, near wallpaper. Placing related items together reminds the customer of something he will need later. Also it saves the salesperson's time and helps him perform suggestion selling.

Stores following a policy of simplified selling (self-service or semiself-service) must have wider aisles in order that aisle tables, merchandise islands, and display racks can be placed in the traffic flow without causing congestion. Like full-service selling, simplified selling also requires layouts that give an unobstructed view of selling departments. In addition, cashiering-wrapping stations should be provided near high-demand merchandise displays.

The principles of store layout are better understood when some typical store layouts are studied in detail.

Department-Store Layout

Typically, department stores are located in multistory buildings and are highly departmentalized. Consequently, departments must be assigned to floors according to their sales volume and the value of the space to be occupied. The main floor is usually reserved for:

     . . . Seasonal goods
     . . . Impulse items
     . . . Convenience goods
     . . . Low-priced and popular shopping goods, such as apparel accessories, stationery, and rainwear

Men, as a rule, are in the minority as shoppers in a department store. They

The layout on the ground floor of a modern department-store suburban branch.

Courtesy John Wanamaker, Philadelphia

The layout in a food supermarket.

Courtesy McGaughan and Johnson, Washington, D.C.

are usually in a hurry and go into a store to buy specific items. They want to get in and out as fast as possible. For that reason, men's clothing and accessories are usually located on the main floor, away from feminine detractions. Some stores may have this section on an upper floor and run a special elevator to it. Some stores cater to men in another way at Christmas time, having a special gift shop for them to which no women customers are admitted. In this shop, appropriate goods from all other departments have been assembled, so that the male shopper can look at them undisturbed.

Floors just above the main floor have considerable customer circulation. Here are featured popular lines of shopping goods—budget dresses, millinery, and children's clothing. The upper floors have less traffic, and the space is less valuable. Located on these floors are:

  . . . Bulky items—carpets, furniture, and appliances
  . . . Specialty items—fashion clothing, toys, china
  . . . Customer services such as restaurants and decorator's studios
  . . . Store offices and nonselling departments

Food-Store Layout

Most food stores are now arranged for self-service. Hence, layouts feature open display and the use of island shelving to form lanes for customer circulation. Shoppers are guided through departments carrying high-profit, impulse items—cosmetics, bakery goods, frozen foods, and "fancy" groceries such as preserves, pickles, party snacks, and soft drinks. Meat departments are located in the rear close to processing rooms and refrigerated storage areas. Fresh fruits and vegetables are usually displayed near a wall toward the rear of the store, in order that bulky items like potatoes do not fill up the shopping cart at the beginning of the shopping tour.

The layout of a variety and drug store.

Courtesy Drug Fair, Arlington, Va.

Variety-Store Layout

Variety stores feature open-display layouts regardless of whether the store offers self-service or salesperson service. Characteristically, merchandise lines are alloted space according to their rate of turnover:

> . . . Fast-selling items such as candy, notions, greeting cards, costume jewelry, and cosmetics are given the more valuable space—near entrances, on main aisles, and on the right-hand side.
> . . . Hardware, housewares, pet supplies, and other goods and items that make less attractive displays are located at the rear or in the basement.
> . . . Fountains or snack bars are often in the rear or along the sides, partly for ease in servicing but also because they draw traffic past other departments.

Nonselling Activities

We have discussed so far only the layout for the selling activities of stores. But even the smallest store needs space for the nonselling activities, such as receiving goods, storage, delivery, bookkeeping etc. In very large stores, some of these activities may be carried on in separate buildings. As a rule, however, space is provided in the same building in those areas less suited for selling, such as lower basements and upper floors. The layout for these activities must be planned carefully in connection with the layout for the selling activities. Some of the nonselling activities, such as the credit department, for example, can be placed in such a way that customer traffic will pass many selling departments in order to reach it. This holds true for such customer services as restaurants, beauty shops, fur storage, gift wrapping and many others found in a large department store.

Trade Talk

store layout   aisle table
customer   merchandise
   circulation   island

Can You Answer These?

1. Why must merchants study and plan store layouts so carefully?
2. Where is the most valuable space in a store located? Why is this true?
3. What advantages are gained from store arrangement that emphasizes display?
4. Why do progressive merchandisers pay so much attention to the problem of customer circulation?
5. In what ways does the classification of merchandise affect the planning of a store layout?
6. For what purposes are aisle tables and merchandise islands useful?
7. What lines of merchandise are commonly displayed on the various floors of a department store?
8. What are the keys to effective food-store arrangement?

Problems and Projects

1. Do you agree with the principle that "Store layout should put on display as much merchandise as possible"? List reasons to support your point of view.
2. Using stores you know as examples, describe the methods used to route customers through or past departments.
3. Select two types of merchandise —one hard line and one soft line— and for each one, list the principles of store layout that best apply.
4. Choose a type of store in which you are interested. Explain to the class how its merchandising policies would (or should) affect the layout.
5. Using trade-association journals such as *Stores* or *Chain Store Age,* prepare a short paper describing some innovations in interior layout.
6. Visit a supermarket and make a sketch of its layout. Show the changes you would make to improve it.
7. With your teacher's permission, invite a representative from a chain store, wholesaler, or store-equipment manufacturer to speak to your class on trends in store layout.

Learning Your Job

1. Rate the layout of your store according to the principles in the text on page 391–392. Give reasons for each rating.
2. Make a scale drawing of the present layout of your store, or your department if you work in a large store. Then make a second drawing showing the changes you would make. Explain how these would improve the situation. Perhaps your supervisor has ideas he will share with you. Add these drawings to your store manual.

59 *Types of Store Organization*

Shortly after Phil Ashler, a young veteran, was released from military service, he used his veteran's benefits to obtain a business loan. Phil had worked part time in a grocery store during his high school years and remembered this experience with pleasure. He and his wife, therefore, decided to make use of this experience and training and buy a small grocery store in a large city. They thought that, if things worked out well, they would have a better chance to expand in a large city than in a small town; and—they dreamed on—maybe someday they could own a supermarket.

At first, Phil and his wife did all the work—buying, stocking shelves, serving customers, cashiering, keeping records, and cleaning. Because of Phil's previous experience and the couple's pleasant personality, the store was a success, so that after two years Phil thought the time had come to expand by adding a meat market. A butcher with chain-store experience became his partner, contributing to the partnership not only his skill in meat merchandising but also the capital needed for remodeling the store and adding new equipment.

The store did very well, gradually adding more departments and consequently adding many more employees. Phil's dream had come true—he had his supermarket. But in reaching this goal he and his wife and his partner were no longer able to watch all the details of the store. They had to let some of the employees take over some of the work they themselves had done on a small scale in the original grocery store. In order to keep their supermarket running smoothly, they realized they had to plan, or organize, the work of all employees. The supermarket required more working capital. Consequently, Phil and his partner had to find ways of procuring this capital.

Forms of Ownership

Phil had come a long way from the simple grocery store, an individual proprietorship. When he took on his partner, a partnership was formed; and finally when the store had grown to a supermarket and needed more operating capital, Phil and his partner formed a corporation in order to obtain money from shareholders.

The table on page 400 reveals that the choice of type or form of ownership depends primarily on three factors: (1) the degree to which the owners wish to be active in the management of the store; (2) the size of the business and the amount of capital needed to start and operate it; (3) the amount of capital needed to develop a well-established business.

Advantages of a Sole Proprietorship

1. Easy to organize   No "red tape" or complicated legal problems; little cost.
2. Freedom of action   Not necessary to consult others in order to reach a decision.
3. Profits not shared   Owner keeps all profits for himself.
4. Low taxes   Taxes are not levied against the form of ownership itself.
5. Personal pride of ownership   Owner has more incentive to work and gets more satisfaction from his work.

Advantages of a Partnership

1. More capital available   Additional owners increase possibility of obtaining more money for expansion.
2. Better management   Combination of skills and ideas lead to better operating procedures. "Two heads are better than one."
3. More interest in the business   Ea h partner will have much keener interest in the success of the business than if he were only an employee.
4. Simple organization   Compared with the corporation, the partnership is relatively easy and inexpensive to organize—few state regulations.
5. Low taxes   Just as in the sole proprietorship, a partnership has tax advantages over a corporation. The form of ownership itself is not taxed as is a corporation.

Advantages of a Corporation

1. Limited liability   Each stockholder is liable only to the extent of his original purchase of stock.
2. Only designated officers can bind in contracts   No one owner can make a contract that will bind the company, as a partner can do.
3. Continued existence   The corporation life is not affected by death, disability, or disagreement of a stockholder.
4. Tremendous growth possibilities   The public corporation can grow large by selling securities to the general public.
5. Opportunity for expert management and large-scale economies   The large public corporation can afford to hire the most skilled personnel and save money by large-scale purchases and integrated operation.

The individual proprietorship form and the partnership form of ownership are used in small retail stores, such as groceries, hardware stores, drugstores, radio and TV repair and supply shops. As soon as a business plans to expand

and needs more capital, organizing a corporation is the next step. Thus, almost all department stores, women's and men's apparel shops, and supermarkets are corporations. A few chain-store organizations are owned by individuals, often families, or by partners; but most chains are incorporated.

Principles of Store Organization

Why must there be organization in a retail store? Phil and his partner found the answer to that question soon after they had expanded. Employees seemed to be getting into one another's way—some duplicating one another's work and leaving other jobs undone; some assuming responsibility that was not theirs; others shirking all responsibility. Phil and his partner realized that very definite organization was needed in order to fit the activities of all into one unified whole which would operate smoothly as a unit.

This smooth functioning could be obtained by

1. Planning an organization to fit the type of merchandise being handled and not following some plan intended for a different type of business. For example, a furniture store would be organized differently than a large department store.
2. Assigning definite jobs to each employee and holding him responsible for the carrying out of his job.
3. Giving adequate training to individual employees for the performance of their duties, in that way making specialists of these employees in their particular phase of the work.
4. Supervising the operation to ensure the proper performance of the work.
5. Grouping related activities and establishing the interrelationship of departments, showing definite lines of authority.
6. Freeing top executives from detail work, so that they can plan the operation of the entire organization.

These are the general principles that have been accepted by most retail stores as fundamental to sound organization. Management and supervisors should give the organization enough supervision, so that each worker can function efficiently while developing a feeling of job importance.

Departmentized Organization

With the exception of the very small retail store, most stores will find it to their advantage to departmentize; that is, to combine the various items sold by the store into well-defined groups. The Merchants Service Bureau of the National Cash Register Company advises the merchant to divide his store into departments wherever possible. In the small store, this can be done simply by grouping related merchandise together; for example, paint and wallpaper. Departmentalization results in several advantages: (1) Profitable lines or individual items of merchandise are revealed more quickly, thus speeding up the turnover of the stock. (2) Inventory is more easily kept and checked, so that a better merchandise control is obtained. (3) Store layout can be simplified by grouping related items near each other. (4) In large stores, as a result of departmentalization, the buyers and salespeople will become specialists in their particular line.

Types of Store Organization

The organization of stores is determined to a great extent by their size.

Small-Store Operation

In the very small store the proprietor or partners often do all the work, possibly assisted by members of their families. As the store becomes larger, employing several people, organization becomes necessary. The six basic principles of organization, given on page 401, should then be followed. The chart given below shows one type of organization that may be used.

To be effective, even the best organization plan must be supplemented by continuous training of personnel—orientation of new employees, explanation of new policies and products, and retraining where performance shows the need. In the small store, the manager will do this training, assisted by experienced employees, salesmen from his suppliers, and instructors in adult distributive education courses offered by local schools.

SMALL-STORE ORGANIZATION

Merchant	Head Salesperson	Second Salesperson	Third Salesperson	Deliveryman
Supervise buying displays advertising selling credits deliveries office	Sell goods Supervise and train salespeople	Sell goods Arrange stock Report slow-moving stock	Sell goods Keep store, stock, and shelves clean	Responsible for correct delivery
Watch departments finances and collections for leaks	Assist in buying Watch credits Check price changes Plan advertising window and interior displays	stock shortages Check invoices received outgoing merchandise	Clean and arrange price tickets Put up "send" orders Maintain stock	Report all complaints Watch for new customers en route Keep delivery equipment in good shape
Analyze records of salespeople Control expenses Plan business Win trade Sell goods				Collect slow accounts Sell goods during rush hours

Large-Store Operation

As the store grows larger, the need for organization increases. While the details of large-store organization cannot be listed here, the student should take advantage of his work experience, even part time, and study the organizational patterns of large firms. The five operating divisions of large department and specialty stores were discussed briefly in Unit 2 in order to show the career opportunities in retailing. We must now study these divisions again to see how large stores are organized and to introduce the functions that will be studied in later units.

Merchandising Division. All activities in a store that have to do with the purchase and sale of goods and the adjusting of merchandise offerings to customer demand, such as planning of stock and planning of special sales, are known as *merchandising*. At the head of this division is the general merchandise manager. Directly responsible to this executive are the department managers and the merchandise buyers of the various departments. Under their charges are the assistant buyers. The work of buyers is discussed in Unit 17.

In addition to buying, the buyer is in charge of sales in his department, fixing the prices of the items and estimating the total sales and profit for his department; consequently, he must provide adequate stock control.

To the merchandise division also belong heads of stock, salespeople, and stock clerks. Although in most stores the buyer is not responsible for the general training of salespeople, he must instruct them on the merchandise of his department and train them in the best ways of selling it. Salespeople and heads of stock who have done outstanding work in their departments are frequently promoted to positions as assistant buyers.

Sales-Promotion, or Publicity, Division. The main functions of the sales-promotion division are to gain the good will of the public, to attract people into the store, and to overcome their sales resistance. At the head of this division is the sales-promotion manager. It is his duty to supervise the store's advertising, in all forms—in newspapers, radio, circulars, etc.—to promote various sales events, and to arrange for effective window and interior display. He usually is assisted by a staff that includes copy writers, artists, sign writers, decorators, and displaymen. The sales-promotion division emphasizes not only merchandise but also the various services that the store offers, skillfully combining these efforts to impress on the public the character of the store.

Store-Operation, or Maintenance, Division. The store superintendent, in charge of the operation and maintenance division, supervises many store functions.

1. *Maintenance of Building.* He is responsible for the condition and appearance of the building and its equipment. The staff of engineers, custodians, deliverymen and stockmen, and store detectives look to him and his assistants for instructions.

2. *Customer Service.* A large department store offers its customers many services that are not related to the merchandise it carries. Such services as restaurants, rest rooms, playrooms for children, branch post offices, delivery service, and similar conveniences for customers are under the general supervision of the superintendent of the store. Likewise, within his jurisdiction fall the making of adjustments and handling of complaints.

3. *Supplies and Equipment.* He and his assistants are in charge of purchasing the supplies and equipment needed by the various departments of the store, receiving, checking, and in some cases giving them identifying marks. He is in charge of distributing the supplies to the departments and maintaining a supply room.

Finance and Control Division. The fourth major division, finance and control, is of more recent origin than the other three and has been made necessary because of the growing complexity of business management and government taxation. In large retail stores, this division is under the direction of a trained financial and accounting executive known as the *controller*. His staff consists of bookkeepers, cashiers, billing clerks, file clerks, credit interviewers, office-machine operators, accountants, and auditors.

1. *Credit and Collection.* In this division is placed the credit and collection department, responsible for the granting of credit to customers and the billing and collection of accounts.

2. *Bookkeeping and Accounting.* Another department in this division is the accounting department. Statistics of past performance are obtained from its records. Buyers are assisted by these statistics in their preparation of budgets for future purchases. This department also has a complete record of the firm's liabilities; that is, the amounts owed to the firm's creditors.

3. *Control.* This division also supervises the taking of merchandise inventories. It also receives and disburses all cash, checking to see that all departments are operating at a profit.

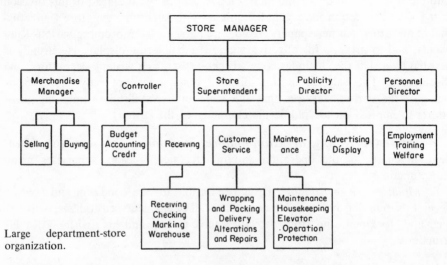

Large department-store organization.

Personnel Division. The task of employing, training, and supervising store workers and of attending to their welfare is considered of such importance that, in many large stores, the personnel function has been made the responsibility of a major store division—the personnel division. The personnel director usually has the assistance of a trained employment manager who interviews and engages employees. A special training director supervises the training of new employees and organizes training programs for experienced workers. Many stores carry on a program of employee services, such as medical and nursing service, financial aid and advice, and recreation.

Leased Departments

Many stores, especially department stores, have adopted the practice of leasing (renting) departments to individuals or firms outside the store. Leased departments are separate operations, but to the customer they appear to be part of the store's regular operations.

Leasing of a department is commonly used by a store to provide a specialized customer service or merchandise that the store is unable to furnish profitably or for which it does not possess the necessary capital. Examples are: photographic studios, shoe-repair shops, optical-goods departments, restaurants, camera shops, and millinery departments. Leasing offers several advantages to the store. It reduces the inventory and makes it possible to operate on a smaller investment. Customers benefit from better service of specially trained personnel. The store also can offer a wider range of services to shoppers than it could do by itself. The operators of leased departments sometimes pay the store a fixed rental for the space they occupy, but more often they pay a percentage of their total sales or of their net profit.

Chain-Store Operation

The central office of a chain store is responsible for purchasing merchandise and

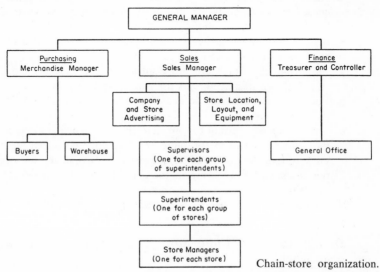

Chain-store organization.

supplies, for the sale of merchandise, and for finance and control of all the stores in the chain. In the purchasing division are the merchandise managers and buyers who are in charge of the large-scale buying that is necessary to take care of the combined orders of the many stores in the chain. Merchandise is often stored in central, regional, and district warehouses for delivery to individual chain-store units.

The sales division is charged with supervision of the individual stores. Usually the direction of store units is decentralized through the use of regional and district offices. Supervisors in these offices are in direct contact with managers of store units.

The chain organization offers excellent opportunities for advancement to merchandising and sales supervisory positions. The gateway to such supervisory and executive positions in the district offices and central headquarters is a managership of a chain store.

The chain-store type of organization has grown steadily ever since Woolworth started operating several stores in several communities by selling the same type of merchandise. Since then various types of chain stores have developed. (1) A chain store selling similar merchandise, controlled by centralized management and buying goods through a centralized office, such as a food chain or drug chain. (2) A chain selling only the goods manufactured by one manufacturer, such as men's clothing, hats, sewing machines, etc. This type of chain is called a *manufacturer's chain*.

Advantages of Chain-Store Organization. The principal advantages of chain stores are as follows:

1. Operating costs are lower. This is due to division of labor, employment of specialists, higher rate of turnover, reduction of wholesale expenses, no loss from bad debts in the cash-carry stores, and no delivery expenses.
2. Almost always, goods are purchased by the chains at lower prices. Purchases are made in larger quantities. Some merchandise is manufactured by the chain organization. Expert buyers are employed.
3. Better stockkeeping systems are maintained. Fresher stocks are kept, and markdowns are decreased.
4. As a rule, the stores are more attractive and cleaner. Goods are better arranged and displayed, and the stores are better lighted.
5. Locations are carefully selected on the basis of volume of traffic and potential sales.
6. There is an advertising advantage, especially when a number of stores of the same chain are in the same city; the cost of advertising per dollar of sales is reduced. In addition, advertising advantages are gained by national chains by preparing in the central office advertisements to be used by all the stores.
7. Merchandise that does not sell readily in one store can be shipped to another store in the chain.

Disadvantages of Chain-Store Organization. Some of the disadvantages are as follows:

1. Some consumers consider that chain-store operation is too impersonal. They prefer to receive the personal attention that a small independent merchant can give them, who also can order for them articles that they especially want. They also prefer to buy on credit and to have goods delivered to them.
2. Managers of chain stores sometimes find it difficult to adjust their company policies and merchandising practices to special local requirements. They also are unable in many cases to gain the same kind of community friendships and acceptance that the local merchant enjoys.

Trade Talk

partnership   corporation
leased   store
  department   superintendent
individual   store controller
  proprietorship merchandising

Can You Answer These?

1. Why is some form of organization essential to good storekeeping?
2. What are the differences in the organization problems of a small retailer and of a large retailer?
3. Name three advantages of departmentized organization.
4. What are the functions of the sales-promotion division?
5. What do you understand by the term controller? What activities take place in the division controlled by this official?
6. What part does the personnel division play in the operation of a large store? What are its relationships to the other store divisions?
7. How can the small-store owner go about organizing his store?
8. Why does a large store find it desirable to have leased departments?
9. Mention five advantages of chain-store organization.

Problems and Projects

1. Three forms of legal ownership are discussed in this part. Each has advantages and disadvantages. Which form of ownership is best suited to the owner of a small store? the owners of a large store? Use this subject for a panel discussion.
2. Compare the store-organization problems of the small store with those of the large store. Do their problems differ because of the difference in size of the stores?
3. Prepare to debate the statement, "Organization is a good thing, but too often it creates 'red tape' and stifles initiative and creativity."
4. A personnel-management specialist has said, "The best organized system is one that operates in a way so that no one can see it at work." What did he mean? Can you give examples from your club or church groups showing how good organization works?

Learning Your Job

1. Using the list of principles of organization on page 401, describe how each operates in your store. Explain how each principle applies to you or affects your job.
2. Draw a chart of your store organization showing the various departments or divisions and their relationship to each other. If you are employed in a small store, draw the chart so that it shows the major responsibilities of each person and how their jobs relate to the others. (The charts on pages 402, 404, and 405 can be used as models.)

17. Buying to Meet Customer Demand

the costume

METAL MAGIC

NEW D'

Sale

GET IT AT

99

poor w
can co
low pr
Oh

a rich girl. Go to
ing goil to deny herself high fashion, wher
to the rescue with smart clothes at
If you're loaded with taste, but not wit
and walk out looking like a mi

NEW
RONA

Unit 17   Part 60

The Buyer and His Job

"You Can't Do Business from an Empty Wagon!"

The Yankee peddler, once a mainstay of distribution in the United States, knew that "you can't do business from an empty wagon." His wagon creaked under the weight of housewares as he started out on Monday, and it rattled home empty on Saturday.

Knowing what and how much to buy was the peddler's specialty. If he didn't do this well, he knew he could not stay in business. Knowing what and how much to buy is still a fundamental factor in retailing. Profits are made on goods sold. Repeated buying of a dozen items when a gross is needed is wasteful and expensive to manufacturer, distributor, and consumer alike. Empty shelves create customer suspicion or fear. Full stocks of fresh merchandise stimulate confidence. A variety of merchandise invites attention and action.

At the same time, inventories are dangerous when they are the result of wrong selection or poor timing. Good buying means sufficient stock to meet daily or seasonal needs.

Buy confidently, but buy wisely. Act as if you knew you were going to be in business this year, next year, and the year after. Don't let dust gather on empty shelves; but, at the same time, don't let dust gather on merchandise that won't sell. You can't make a profit without a sale.

Adapted from Dun and Bradstreet, Inc.

As you know, in order for a merchant to succeed in his business he must have on hand the *right goods* in the *right quantities* at the *right time* and at the *right prices*. This is the basic function of the buyer in the retail store. "Goods well bought are half sold," is a famous axiom that guides every successful retailer, regardless of the type of merchandise he handles. The person who buys merchandise for resale is really a purchasing agent for the store's customers. He cannot buy merely to satisfy a personal whim; he buys merchandise only for the purpose of selling it to the customer—and at a profit to the store. It is easy to see that buyers have an enormous responsibility, both to the store and to the customer.

What Is a Buyer?

A buyer is one who purchases merchandise for resale. The job of buyer is not assigned to just anyone. Only those who are thoroughly experienced in all aspects of merchandising are

409

promoted to the position of buyer. It is one of the best paid jobs in retailing and calls for an enormous amount of know-how and experience.

Qualifications of a Buyer

Among the desirable qualifications for this job, the following six are essential.

1. *The Buyer Must Be a Merchandise Specialist.* He must be able to judge quality, workmanship, and style and be able to buy the type of goods that fits in with the merchandising policies and standards of his firm. When new merchandise arrives, the buyer must know enough about it to explain to the sales staff the advantages, selling points, style, construction, and quality of the goods.

2. *The Buyer Must Be Profit-Minded.* Goods are purchased to be sold at a profit. The buyer must have the ability to calculate what each article will cost, how much it will sell for, and how much profit can be expected. Without this knowledge he can lose money, rather than earn profits for his company.

3. *The Buyer Must Be Sales-Minded.* He has an enormous responsibility to the store or department for which he buys. This responsibility does not really end until the merchandise is sold. He observes the salespeople to be sure they are getting across the sales story to the customers. Occasionally, for the purpose of gaining firsthand information, he waits on customers himself. He must also see to it that his department or store is attractive in appearance and that merchandise is displayed in such a manner as to bring out its best features.

4. *The Buyer Must Know Merchandise Sources.* The buyer must be thoroughly acquainted with the best sources of merchandise—sources that he can depend on to provide the right goods at the right prices. And he must be able to count on these suppliers to provide goods exactly when they are needed and in the quantity needed.

Here the toy buyer and his assistants are selecting merchandise for the Christmas season.

5. *The Buyer Must Be a "Trader."* He can save many thousands of dollars for his store if he knows how to get the best possible terms from his suppliers, how to effect savings on discounts, and how to speed up delivery schedules when necessary. In addition, he obtains as many special privileges for his store from suppliers as he can manage, such as the privilege of returning defective or unsalable merchandise.

6. *The Buyer Should Have a "Sixth Sense" about Consumer Tastes.* He should be able to recognize merchandise with special appeal—fashion and fad items, for example—and capitalize on whims and fancies of his customers. The smart buyer can often predict a "hot" item, and stock just the right quantity for quick turnover and quick profits.

Duties of Buyers Differ

In small retail establishments, the manager does most, if not all, of the buying. In larger stores, each major department has its buyer, such as Women's Shoes, Furniture, Men's Clothing, and so on. Sometimes a buyer in a large store is responsible for two or three departments that carry related merchandise. For example, he may be responsible for the department that carries handkerchiefs, gloves, and handbags, as well as the department that carries umbrellas and rainwear.

In chain operations, there is usually a buyer for each important line of merchandise—toys, paint, radios and TV sets, and so on. These buyers are located in the regional or central headquarters of the chain. From this vantage point they purchase in huge quantities for all branch stores. The individual units of the chain buy a very limited number of items for resale. Sometimes they will take advantage of local markets when there is a need; for example, a supermarket may purchase fresh fruit, vegetables, and eggs from local producers. As a general rule, however, the chain-store manager is required to order merchandise from the stock list of the chain's regional or main offices.

In many independent stores, and especially in variety, drug, grocery, and hardware chain stores, experienced salespeople are often asked for advice on what and how much to buy. In this way, they have a big influence on buying decisions.

Planning the Merchandise Assortment

A merchant must often buy his merchandise assortment months before the beginning of a selling season. For example, he must buy in the fall and winter the goods he will need for the coming summer; in the spring, the goods he will need for fall; and so on. To buy effectively this far in advance, the buyer must consider various factors carefully and scientifically.

1. He must consider what he thinks his customers will want—anticipating their basic needs and, insofar as possible, their anticipated wants.

2. He must forecast economic conditions, answering as accurately as possible such questions as: Will consumers have more money or less money to spend? Will the store's financial resources be adequate for the goods that are to be ordered?

3. He must make decisions concerning

    a. the number of manufacturers' lines he will carry
    b. retail price ranges he will maintain
    c. sizes of inventories in relation to desired turnover

4. In order to compete more effectively, he must be alert to the efforts of his competitors in their merchandising plans.

Estimating Customers' Wants

A successful restaurant operator, famous for his fine food, says that the best way to find out what people like to eat is to find out what they do not eat. To do this, he checks periodically each tray of dishes as it is returned to the kitchen and notes what food was not eaten. Similarly, the retail-store buyer can obtain accurate information about what customers want by the goods they pass up. A good source of information is the stock record. Items that are not selling will, of course, show up time and time again on the stock cards.

Estimating the Store's Purchases

Estimating what the store will buy may be done in a number of ways:

1. *Sales Records.* The store's sales records—if kept in sufficient detail—are excellent indicators of what customers want. These records and various other records in the store will show how many of each item have been sold and will reveal the most popular models, colors, sizes, and price ranges.

2. *Contact with Customers.* Personal contact with customers on the sales floor is very helpful to a buyer. Watching for customer reaction to articles shown—what he says, facial expression, hesitation about style or price—will communicate a great deal to the buyer.

3. *The Want Slip.* The *want slip,* a form for use of the sales staff in reporting requests from customers for items not carried in stock, is a valuable source of information. If a large number of customers want a certain style or size of article, then the buyer knows that the article should be stocked. The buyer must make sure that salespeople take the want slips seriously. The use of want slips as a part of good stockkeeping was described in Unit 6.

4. *Comparison Shopping.* Comparison shopping is another method of determining customer demand. The buyer watches the advertisements of his competitors; window-shops at various stores; and assigns salespeople, or others hired especially for the purpose, to visit stores as though they were customers. In this way, the buyer finds out how his store's prices compare with those of

competitors, as well as how various goods are moving. Of course, a great deal of other information may also be obtained from display techniques, merchandise assortment, services offered, and so on.

5. *Trade Publications.* The buyer reads the major trade papers in his field. For example, if he is buyer for a women's wear department, he will probably read *Women's Wear Daily;* for hardware, *Hardware Age;* and so on. For just about every specialty in retailing there are newspapers and magazines containing information helpful to the buyer. Also, literature issued by manufacturers contains important information for the buyer.

6. *Reporting Services.* The buyer may make use of reporting services. These are periodic bulletins, issued daily or weekly, that provide complete information about certain items of merchandise, customer response to them in various cities, and sources from which they may be obtained.

7. *Sales Representatives.* Sales representatives of reputable suppliers are often sources of valuable information to the buyer. These salesmen are in a good position to know what items are selling well for other stores on whom he calls, market trends, and comparative prices.

The Merchandise Plan

In successful merchandising it has become a standard practice for the buyer to make up what is called a "buying plan" or "merchandise plan." The purpose of this plan is (1) to encourage the store management, including buyers, to consider carefully in advance the purchases that will be made, based on expected sales, and (2) to decide on the supporting activities that will be necessary to

Buyers are selecting gowns at a wholesaler's showroom.

Courtesy E. I. du Pont de Nemours and Co., Inc.

make a success of the business period for which these purchases are to be made. The value of even a simple merchandise plan is illustrated in the following story:

> Some years ago when I was a merchandise manager, the floor-coverings buyer suddenly decided to leave us. We were sorry to see him go, for he had made a consistently good showing, in spite of the fact that he was no believer in scientific merchandising and had never made out a buying plan in his life.
>
> The outlook for the immediate future of the department was not bright. We had to beat a very good record made the previous year. The assistant buyer and myself went over the stock, checked up on what had been selling insofar as possible, talked with the salespeople, and finally arrived at a list of the merchandise we thought we needed to buy.
>
> Then we went to New York to look over the various lines of floor coverings available. That night we decided what we wanted, and we placed our orders the following day. When the results were all in, we found that the department had gone far ahead of the previous year's record, and through the use of the same methods, it continued to make all the old records look sick.
>
> Buyers can make money with rule-of-thumb methods. But if they knew how much better they could do with a little systematic study and careful planning, there's not one of them who wouldn't change his habits.
>
> *Foresight in Buying, Bigelow-Sanford Carpet Company*

In a merchandise plan, the buyer bases the amount he will buy on the amount he expects to sell. He arrives at this estimate by a careful consideration of a number of factors already described and prepares a budget based on all available information—past sales, inventory turnover, discussions with salespeople, and so on. His merchandise plan is for a definite period, usually from three to six months; and he divides this period into months, weeks, and even days. A plan is usually made up by each department in a large department store, and it is ordinarily broken down by size, color, and price. The small-store owner's plan may be fairly simple—perhaps just a rough general plan. In the larger store, it is likely to be much more elaborate and will include budgets for sales promotion, advertising, and the cost of training personnel.

The following factors will influence the merchandise plan:

Past sales figures	Competition from other stores
Performance in recent months	Market, price, and labor conditions
Business conditions	in particular commodities
Style trends	Relation of inventory to sales
Time needed for delivery	Individual department requirements
Transportation conditions	

The tendency in recent years in buying has been to keep on hand a relatively moderate stock of each type of goods—to buy only a small amount at a time, but to buy often. In this manner, all stock is "working" all the time; and the owner does not have the heavy investment in inventory. At the same time, he does not run the risk of stocking up on merchandise that will not move and will have to be marked down later. Except in peak seasons, it is not generally necessary to have large reserve stocks, which use storage space and tie up capital.

In the merchandise plan, it is best to show all figures in terms of retail prices, rather than cost prices. In this way, all other figures may be expressed as percentages or ratios of these prices. As a result, comparisons of figures both within the store and with other stores may be more easily made.

The Basic Stock List

Among the aids to a good merchandise plan is a *basic* stock list. This list includes from 70 to 80 per cent of the items normally carried by the store. This list is most useful when it is prepared by the store; however, basic stock lists for various types of stores are available from wholesalers and from other sources, such as trade publications. The basic stock list is, of course, a list of the items that are in steady and predictable demand. The founder of the largest variety retailing chain in the United States built his business on the principle of the uniformity of customer demand—the principle that underlies the use of a basic stock list. Through a careful analysis of the sales of every item and of all customer requests, it was possible for him to develop a list of the merchandise that customers wanted to buy in a variety store. By doing so, he eliminated slow-selling, unwanted, and unprofitable articles. Once the basic stock list has been made up, it should be used as a basis for future buying and sales promotion. The illustration given below shows a partial basic stock list.

Controlling the Merchandise Plan

The merchandising work of the buyer is not finished with the completion of the plan, however. As this plan is put into operation, it is necessary for him to see to it that the various estimates dealing with sales and purchases have been met. He must watch the stock in each department to be sure that it is low enough

Dept. K								SUBLINE Electrical Supplies (Contd.)											
Merchandise Description & Stock No.		PACKING	COST	RETAIL PRICE	WORKING STOCK	STORE CLASS.	ON HAND ORDER	1	2	3	4	5	6	7	8	9	10	11	12
STOCK NUMBER	FCTY. NUMBER																		
Sockets							O.H												
							ORD.												
K-B345	KXA-1531-4						O.H												
Monowatt Brass Shell Push Through Sockets ¼-in. nozzle cap. Medium base. Rating 250 watts, 250 volts. UL Approved.		10 in 1½ lb	Ea .27	40c		C	ORD.												
K-B346	KXA-1520-2						O.H												
Monowatt Stay-Lock Sockets Ivory plastic. Pull chain. All-purpose cap locks securely and cannot pull out when in use. 250 watts, 250 ... UL Approved.		10 in 1½ lb	Ea				ORD.												

A basic stock or checking list prepared by a progressive wholesaler for use by his retailer customers.

Courtesy Butler Bros., Chicago

to ensure quick turnover but still high enough to offer a satisfactory variety of merchandise to customers.

From the planned budget and the present condition of stocks, an open-to-buy allowance can be arrived at for each department and for the store. A department is said to be *open to buy* when additional stock must be purchased to take care of estimated future sales. The amount that the buyer is open to buy is usually indicated on the department budget sheet prepared by the merchandise or general office. At times, the buyer must guard against overoptimism in purchasing goods beyond the budget requirements. A definite proportion of the monthly budget, or open-to-buy, allowance should be set aside for staple, reorder items.

Trade Talk

buyer
open-to-buy
merchandise
  plan
budget

basic stock
  list
comparison
  shopping

Can You Answer These?

1. What is the basic function of a buyer?
2. What is meant by "goods well bought are half sold"?
3. Discuss the abilities needed by a buyer.
4. How do the duties of a department-store buyer differ from those of a small-store owner?
5. What is a merchandise plan? What factors influence the preparation of it?
6. What factors must the merchant consider in planning his merchandise assortment?
7. What methods can a retailer use to estimate customer demand? Discuss each.
8. What types of information may be obtained by comparison shopping?
9. Why should a buyer keep in close touch with salespeople? with customers?

Problems and Projects

1. A knowledge of the place of brand lines and price lines in retail merchandising is valuable to a person who desires to succeed in retailing. Based on recent experiences you have had in buying clothing or other articles for yourself or for members of your family, be prepared to discuss the following questions: (*a*) To what extent do stores in your city feature manufacturers' brands? their own private brands? (*b*) What price lines seem to be most popular in: (1) men's suits, shoes, and hats? (2) women's dresses and shoes?

2. Visit a store buyer of your acquaintance. Request him to explain to you the basic stock list used in his department or store. How was this list prepared? In what ways is it used as a basis for buying? Try to obtain a copy of this list.

3. Estimating customer demand is quite difficult. Give illustrations, from your experience or by guessing from advertising, of merchandise for which local stores have either under- or overestimated demand.

4. By interviewing retail managers or buyers, find out what career opportunities are open in merchandising management. Prepare a report of your findings, showing the routes of advancement and positions open to beginners.

Learning Your Job

1. Talk with a buyer or the person in your store who is responsible for buying merchandise. Find out what abilities he thinks are necessary to performing the job well. Summarize your findings in a brief report, comparing them with the abilities described in the text.

2. Procure, if you can, a sample of a merchandise plan, or planning work sheet. Find out how it is developed and how it is used. Prepare a brief report to the class.

3. Find out in your store the methods that the buyer uses to estimate customer demand. Rate the methods on their usefulness to the buyer.

61 *Selecting Merchandise That Sells*

In selecting merchandise for today's market, the store buyer faces an increasingly complex problem. The range of products available is great; and there are hundreds of variations in styles, models, colors, and construction that must be judged. In addition, the buyer is bombarded with sales literature and various promotional devices from manufacturers, each hoping to convince the buyer that his is the best buy.

As you learned, the buyer's problem of selection is partially solved by carefully analyzing his customer's demands and by adopting a thoughtful merchandise plan. Armed with such a plan, the buyer begins his search for items that will (1) achieve a rapid turnover, (2) attract a large volume, (3) decrease the number of markdowns, and (4) return a reasonable profit on the investment. Selecting such items calls for real know-how about where to buy, when to buy, and what to buy.

The Buying Process

When choosing merchandise, the buyer bases his decisions on several important considerations. He must determine whether a given article is of the type and description his customers want. He must decide whether to stick with his present lines only, add new lines, or switch entirely to new lines. He must calculate from cost prices the probable retail prices the merchandise will bring; if the cost price is too high, he must bargain for reductions or seek similar items of lower quality. Finally, he must determine which supplier will in the long run provide the best services for delivery, credit, reorders, and returned-goods allowances.

What to Buy

The task of the buyer is very interesting, but it is also serious business. The buyer consults with sales representatives from many suppliers. When he goes to the market, he visits showroom after showroom looking for the articles that fit into his buying plan. He rarely buys at first sight, but jots down notations and descriptions of the articles that appeal to him, checking the offerings of many different manufacturers. He then analyzes his notations, makes his comparisons, and decides on his purchases. Sometimes he may find it necessary to go back for a second or a third look before coming to a decision. One manufacturer may have a lower price, but the other may have better workmanship or style. The buyer must decide which will sell better in his store, always asking himself the question, "Will my customers want to purchase the article I am thinking of buying?" The following "five-point-star test" is an effective guide in selecting merchandise: *

1. The article must be right as to type, style, or kind. Depending on the nature of the item, it must be judged as to style, weight, size, color, shape, height, width, mechanism, strength, and material.
2. An item must have popular appeal; that is, it must be wanted by people.
3. The article must have real value. It must be fully worth what the merchant intends to ask for it.
4. It must be priced at a popular price, a price people like to pay.
5. An item, if it is packaged, bottled, or wrapped, must be so put up as to influence sales profitably, not adversely.

Where to Buy

Knowing what to buy is a key to successful selection of goods. On the other hand, the buyer must know where to find the goods he wants—seeking out a number of merchandise resources.

Traveling Salesmen. Thousands of salesmen, representing many manufacturers, call on retailers throughout the nation. Many buyers place orders for merchandise directly with these salesmen.

Wholesalers. The wholesaler performs a real service for the retailer. He buys from manufacturers in large quantities—often in carload lots—stores this merchandise in large warehouses, and then sells it to the retailers in the quantities they desire.

Buying from the wholesaler saves much time for the retailer. He can, with little effort, purchase at one time a large number of different items from the wholesaler's representative. As a rule, wholesalers can give quicker deliveries and better service than can manufacturers. Wholesale firms will take a greater interest in a merchant's problem and offer him more liberal credit terms if he concentrates his purchases with them. They are also an important source of market information for the retailer. The wholesaler knows price trends; he

* Bedell, *Seven Keys to Retail Profits*, pp. 15–35.

knows the demands for, and supply of, goods; new merchandise; and resources.

In recent years, significant changes have taken place in wholesale distribution. Large national wholesalers have decreased in number, giving way to wholesalers who service a limited geographic area. There are hundreds of grocery wholesalers, for example, whose territory covers only one or two states—in many instances, only a large city and its immediate suburbs. Some wholesalers, such as Hibbard, Spencer, Bartlett and Company (hardware), service dealers in a number of states. Butler Brothers, through their branch houses, provide merchandise and specialized store service to their affiliated distributor outlets (Ben Franklin Stores) and, in addition, sell such merchandise as floor coverings to a large number of retail stores on a regular wholesale basis.

Chain organizations, as you have learned, maintain their own district and regional warehouses. Managers of local chain stores count on their regional warehouses for speedy delivery of orders and for help with various merchandising problems.

Central Markets. Due to economic conditions and to the location of natural resources, certain industries and markets are centralized in various sections of the country. For example, the major furniture markets are Grand Rapids, Michigan; Jamestown, New York; High Point, North Carolina; and Chicago, Illinois. Apparel markets are located in New York City, Los Angeles, San Francisco, Dallas, St. Louis, Kansas City, Cleveland, and Minneapolis. Central markets are a great help to a buyer, for here, in one place, he can inspect the goods produced by hundreds of manufacturers.

Some manufacturers and wholesalers own buildings in convenient locations and display their merchandise in them for buyers. Others exhibit their goods in special buildings devoted to the display of sample merchandise from a great many manufacturers. The Chicago Merchandise Mart is an excellent example of the opportunities open to a buyer visiting a central market. This building contains

A wholesaler's salesman is calling on a retailer.

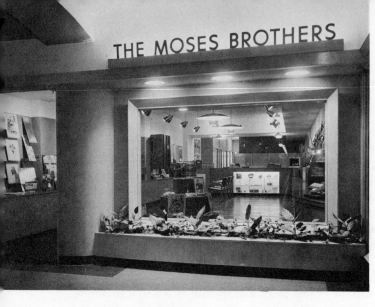

THE MOSES BROTHERS

Even the showrooms in the Merchandise Mart, like this one, have large picture-front windows that permit the buyer to see the exhibits inside.

Courtesy The Merchandise Mart News Bureau

the largest home-furnishings market under one roof in the world, as well as exhibits of men's, women's and children's apparel, toys and gift wares. More than 2,500 manufacturers' lines of home furnishings are displayed in showrooms that are open all year. These include furniture, floor coverings, housewares, home appliances, lamps, curtains, draperies, glassware, and china.

This enormous building has 93 acres of floor space. Adjacent to the downtown Chicago business district, it attracts thousands of buyers—more than 500,000 buying visits are made to the Merchandise Mart annually. Housefurnishings markets are conducted twice a year, and men's and boys' wear markets are conducted at various times during the year. Style shows and merchandising clinics are conducted in connection with some of these apparel markets. A merchandise service bureau is operated by the Merchandise Mart for the benefit of store buyers. From its exhaustive files and library, this bureau offers buyers information on the location of sources, on prices, brands, and trade-marks, and on the quality of consumer products.

Another very large commercial building, the American Furniture Mart, devoted to the exhibits of the furniture industry, is also located in Chicago. Hundreds of manufacturers of furniture, home appliances, and floor coverings exhibit their products in this building. Seasonal markets are held at least twice a year—the January market being the more important.

Buying Offices. Many large department and specialty stores purchase merchandise through buying offices located in principal key cities. To meet chain-store competition, smaller stores also have been forced to associate themselves with such offices in order to buy on some basis of equality with the chain store and large department store. Buying offices are of three kinds:

1. Those owned and financed by a group of associated stores
2. Those owned by large individual retailers
3. Independent buying offices operated by individual buyers who work on a commission basis

Most buying offices are located in New York City. In certain merchandise lines, such as clothing, it is the world's chief wholesale market. However, because of the constant expansion of trade, buying offices have been opened in such important cities as Los Angeles, Chicago, St. Louis, and Dallas.

Rapid changes in styles, fluctuations in prices, and the necessity for keeping in constant touch with new offerings have made it necessary for thousands of stores to do at least part of their buying through buying offices. The men in charge of these offices spend their entire time studying merchandise, styles, and prices. The information they gather is sent regularly to each member store, and the buyers of these various stores place their orders as the result of the information received. The following statement well describes the services of buying offices and also illustrates additional aspects of the buyer's job: *

> By working closely with her resident buying office, the buyer can greatly cut down her time spent in the market. The service of resident buyers and buying offices usually includes both buying and research assistance. Buying information is given both when the buyer is in the market and when he is at home. Not all offices perform the same services, but in general the following help is given when the buyer is in the market or is planning a trip to market:
>
> 1. Preparing for the buyer's visit: (a) locating merchandise in advance if a copy of the buying plan is forwarded; (b) surveying specified lines of merchandise in advance; (c) making appointments with resources for the buyer.
> 2. Providing desk space, sample-room space for examining merchandise, and stenographic, typing, mailing, telephone, and telegraphic service.
> 3. Accompanying the buyer to market on request.
> 4. Providing personal service to the buyer, such as hotel accommodations.
>
> Resident buying-office services to the buyer when he is in his home store or department include:
>
> 1. Answering requests for information on such matters as (a) prices and styles available in the market; (b) the supply condition in the market; (c) trends of purchasing; and (d) location of new resources.
> 2. Placing orders for the buyer.
> 3. Following up and checking on deliveries. This is a vital service and a time-consuming one. Without the knowledge that overdue orders will bring a protest from the resident office, manufacturers would be less careful about living up to their delivery promises. Most resident offices anticipate by calling up each manufacturer on the day a delivery is supposed to be made, and checking to make sure that the shipment is going forward complete.

The resident buying office also mails weekly or monthly reports to all the buyers it serves on prices, fashions, what other stores are doing, good buys, and other general market and retail information.

* *Departmental Operating Manual, Sports and Casual Wear,* National Retail Merchants Association, 1950, pp. 56–57.

Trade Talk

merchandise   buying offices
   resources   resident buyer
central market

Can You Answer These?

1. Describe the task of the buyer when he goes to the market.
2. What are the provisions of Bedell's "five-point-star test"?
3. From what sources may a merchant buy goods for his store?
4. What are the advantages of a central market to a retail merchant? to a manufacturer? Describe the activities of the Chicago Merchandise Mart.
5. What helpful information may a merchant obtain when he buys from traveling salesmen?
6. What buying advantages has a wholesaler to offer to retailers?
7. In what ways do buying offices located in key cities serve the interests of the stores affiliated with them?
8. What are the three types of buying offices? In what ways do they differ?
9. What is meant by the term "market" when used in expressions such as "the buyer has gone to the market" or "he is visiting the annual apparel market"?

Problems and Projects

1. Choose two or more items or brands of some type of merchandise in which you are interested. Apply Bedell's five-point-star test to these items and determine whether you would buy them for resale in a store that you managed.
2. Look over carefully several retail-trade papers or journals that your instructor or you have been able to obtain. In your opinion,

what help in buying can a merchant receive from reading the trade papers published for his own field of retailing?
3. Some lines of merchandise—such as groceries, candies, and tobacco products—are distributed through wholesalers to retail stores. Visit a wholesaler in your city and for the purpose of preparing a class report obtain information about the following: (*a*) What is the size of the trading area covered by the wholesaler? (*b*) How many salesmen does the wholesaler employ? (*c*) What products does his firm sell? (*d*) What special services does the wholesaler offer to his retail customers?
4. Visit one of the larger department stores in your city and obtain information about the buying office in New York or elsewhere with which it is affiliated. How does this buying office assist in the store's buying?
5. With your teacher's permission and aid, invite a store buyer to talk to your class. Ask him to describe a trip to the central market and the methods he uses to select goods.
6. If a trade show or regional market is close to your town, visit it and report to the class on how it helps a buyer do his job.
7. Grocery stores usually buy most items from wholesalers. Fashion-goods stores usually buy from manufacturers or distributors in central markets. List other goods bought in these two ways. Explain why each item is purchased in the way that it is.
8. Assume the role of a store buyer. When you go to a central

market, what features or characteristics will you look for in selecting items of the following types? (*a*) men's or women's suits, (*b*) children's sweaters, (*c*) coffee tables, (*d*) everyday china.

Learning Your Job

1. Prepare a brief report about your store, commenting on (*a*) the store's sources of merchandise, (*b*) buying policies with regard to quality and prices.

2. If possible, obtain your employer's permission to observe him when he talks with a salesman about a possible purchase. What kinds of questions are asked about the merchandise? Did you feel the salesman was helpful to your store?

62 *Obtaining the Best Terms*

It was mentioned earlier that "goods well bought are half sold." It may also be said that goods bought on favorable financial terms return a profit before they are delivered, in that the cost of the goods to the store is actually reduced.

The Trading Process

When a buyer has located the merchandise best suited to his needs, he must arrange for its purchase on financial terms most advantageous to his store. The buyer's shrewdness in bargaining can pay big dividends. Saving a few pennies on a ten-dollar item may not seem important, but those pennies multiplied by hundreds of items may mean the difference between profit or loss for his department. There are many ways in which a buyer can save money for the store. Selecting the best method of shipping can save hundreds of dollars. Desirable credit terms and discount privileges can result in considerable savings to the store. Buying some items on consignment can reduce the investment in the inventory and make the money available for other purposes.

The trading, or bargaining, process usually takes place before the buyer definitely gives an oral or a written purchase order. Of first importance to the store is, of course, the desirability of the merchandise to customers. Other important considerations are: the right quantity, correct packaging, prompt delivery, discounts, credit arrangements, and the general reliability of the concerns with which the buyer proposes to do business.

Important Purchasing Details

The following matters should always be considered by the buyer and, when decided upon, entered on the orders he places with different supply houses.

Date and Method of Shipment

The manufacturer or wholesaler must understand clearly the date on which goods are to be forwarded; the method of shipment—parcel post, express, rail, truck, air, or freight—and name of carrier; and the route the goods will travel. If more than one carrier is available, the buyer may specify the one he prefers.

F. O. B. (Free on Board) Point

This term has two meanings: (1) the point to which the shipper pays the transportation charges; and, (2) the determination, from a legal standpoint, when title (legal ownership) passes to the buyer. It is a general rule that the buyer assumes the responsibility for the goods as soon as they have been delivered to the common carrier by the vendor.

There are several methods of paying the transportation charges. The following are the most commonly used:

1. *F. O. B. Shipping Point.* The shipper assumes the responsibility for the goods until they reach the carrier's shipping point. At this point the title passes to the buyer, and he pays the rest of the charges.

2. *F. O. B. City of Destination.* The shipper pays all transportation charges to the city in which the buyer is located. The buyer pays the cartage from the carrier's freight station to his own store. The title passes to the buyer when the goods arrive at the city of destination.

3. *F. O. B. Store.* The shipper pays all transportation charges. The title passes when the shipment arrives at the buyer's place of business.

Discount

The term *cash discount* means the amount that the seller allows the buyer to deduct if the invoice is paid within a specified period of time. It is expressed as a percentage of the price. For example, a discount of 2 per cent may be allowed if payment is made within 10 days of the date of the invoice.

Manufacturers and wholesalers offer cash discounts to stores to encourage prompt payment. They feel that they are justified in lowering the purchase price to this extent to cash buyers because they receive the earlier use of the money and because this practice reduces their credit risks. It is to the advantage of the retail merchant to use the cash-discount privilege wherever possible. Not only does he improve his credit standing by doing so, but he also saves money. If he does not at times have the necessary cash to take advantage of a discount, it will often pay him to borrow from his bank.

DISCOUNT VALUES	
½% in 10 days, net 30 days	9% a year
1% in 10 days, net 30 days	18% a year
1½% in 10 days, net 30 days	27% a year
2% in 10 days, net 30 days	36% a year
2% in 10 days, net 60 days	14% a year
2% in 30 days, net 60 days	24% a year
2% in 30 days, net 120 days	8% a year
3% in 10 days, net 120 days	10% a year
3% in 10 days, net 60 days	21% a year
3% in 30 days, net 60 days	36% a year

Note: Values figured on period between discount time and net

Another form of discount is the quantity discount. Some suppliers make a practice of giving retailers a discount if they buy in larger quantities. For example, items normally purchased by the dozen may earn a discount of 5 per cent per dozen if purchased in six-dozen lots.

Dating

There is considerable variation in the length of time that sellers extend credit to buyers. This period of time is known as *dating.* Ordinarily, a buyer is allowed 30 days within which to pay, with the inducement of a cash discount if the invoice is paid within 10 days.

Dating is determined by three things: (1) the length of the marketing period; that is, the time that elapses between the purchase of goods by a store and the payment for these goods by the store's customers; (2) length of the selling seasons; and (3) competitive conditions. Following are the more common types of dating:

Regular Dating. Current dating of an invoice, such as 1/10/30 or 2/10/30, constitutes *regular dating.* An invoice marked "1/10/30" allows the buyer to take a cash discount of 1 per cent if payment is made within 10 days, or he may pay the net amount within 30 days.

Extra Dating. An invoice marked "2/10/90 extra" would give the buyer an opportunity to deduct 2 per cent for cash within 10 days plus 90 days, or within 100 days. This is known as *extra dating.* The extra days are added to the normal number of days within which the buyer is expected to make payment in order to obtain the cash discount. Terms of 30 extra, 60 extra, and 90 extra are common.

Advance Dating. By arrangement, an invoice may be made payable at some future date instead of on the date of the invoice. This method of billing is known as *advance dating.* For example, goods invoiced January 1 may have a March 1 dating; and terms of payment, therefore, would be figured from March 1 instead of from the date of the invoice.

Manufacturers give advance dating to merchants in order to encourage them to buy ahead of the selling season. This practice helps the manufacturer to plan his production schedule to better advantage and is an aid to the merchant whose buying funds are low.

A common form of advance dating is season dating. In *season dating* the time for payment is determined by the date of opening of the sales season for the merchandise. For example, on an invoice for toys that are shipped in July to be sold during the coming Christmas season, the terms may be 2/10/30 December 1. These terms will enable the buyer to obtain a cash discount 10 days after December 1. If he decides not to take advantage of the cash discount, he need not pay the invoice until December 31.

E.O.M. Dating.   Dating an invoice "1/10 E.O.M." gives the buyer an opportunity to take a cash discount of 1 per cent within 10 days of the end of the month in which goods are shipped and invoice is dated.

Consignment Sales

As mentioned earlier, the title to goods bought on consignment remains with the manufacturer. The merchant does not assume the financial risk involved in an ordinary purchase; rather, he assumes only the responsibility for safeguarding the property. He may return all or any part of the merchandise if he is unable to sell it. This is often a desirable arrangement if the retailer is uncertain as to the sales possibilities of the goods and does not wish to tie up his money. On the other hand, the manufacturer is willing to ship on consignment in order to induce retailers to stock his line.

Buying Merchandise on Credit

A merchant has funds, called *working capital,* that are used to pay for salaries

A retailer discussing a loan with his banker.

MARY WILLIAMSON
Personnel Director, Younkers, Des Moines, Iowa; formerly local teacher co-ordinator and state supervisor of distributive education.

and other current store expenses. He uses this capital also to pay for merchandise. Yet, few retailers have working capital sufficient to maintain a complete inventory. This is especially true in fields where the sales volume is highly seasonal. For this reason the merchant must seek sources of credit for his purchases.

Trade Credit

Trade credit is extended to a merchant by the manufacturers or wholesalers from whom he buys. As you have just found out, the terms on the invoices may allow discounts within 10 days, and the net is due if the invoice is paid within 30, or 60, or 90 days. Sometimes it is to the merchant's advantage to use the full credit period. For example, it may be possible within that period for him to receive the goods, sell them, and receive payment from his customers before he has to pay for the goods. However, the merchant should be sure he is not paying too much for this privilege. It may be better for him to borrow money and take advantage of his discount and the lower prices offered to cash buyers.

Bank Loans

Many commercial banks derive a good share of their business from short-term loans to retailers. Short-term loans are commonly used (1) to obtain cash discounts, (2) to take advantage of sudden, favorable offerings in the market, (3) to expand the inventory for a peak period such as Christmas, and (4) to buy additional stock of some sudden fad merchandise or "hot seller." A progressive merchant who maintains a sound relationship with his banker will also find that his advice concerning current economic trends is most helpful.

Trade Talk

F. O. B. point   consignment
cash discount   sale
trade credit   working
quantity discount   capital
dating

Can You Answer These?

1. What are the two major sources of credit available to a retailer for buying goods? How do these sources differ?
2. What does the F. O. B. point tell the retailer about his obligations for the goods?
3. What are the commonly used F. O. B. points?
4. What are the different types of dating commonly used in retailing? For each type, describe: (a) the characteristics of each type, (b) why a vendor might choose each type.
5. In what ways are goods sold on consignment advantageous to both retailers and vendors?
6. In what ways is it useful for a merchant to know the point at which title to goods passes?

Problems and Projects

1. The *Tot Shop* receives a shipment of children's shoes. The invoice for $100 is dated February 14 and shows the terms as 2/10/30. Explain: (a) when the shipment must be paid for in order to be eligible for the discount; (b) the amount due if the discount is taken; (c) the last date for payment in full.
2. How would your answers to Problem 1 be different if the terms were 3/10/30 extra?
3. If a $500 invoice for some dresses is dated September 5 and the terms are "3/10 E.O.M.," (a) how much is the discount worth? (b) what is the last date the store is eligible for the discount?
4. An invoice for $450 arrives with a shipment of golf clubs received on May 5. The invoice is dated July 1 and carries terms of 2/10/30. (a) How much must be paid if the discount is taken? (b) When is the last day for the discount? (c) When is the entire bill due?
5. Obtain schedules of air, rail, and truck freight rates by calling or visiting the offices of the carriers. Find out how much it would cost to ship a 100 lb. shipment to your city from a major market. Compare the differences in costs and in the services offered by each type of carrier.
6. Using the procedure in Problem 5, compare the cost of five shipments of 20 lbs. each against the cost when they are combined into one shipment.
7. Working as a member of a committee directed by your teacher, choose several types of goods that vary in size and weight. Find out what percentage of retail price the usual transportation charges are. Do you think the average customer knows how much of the retail price consists of transportation costs?

Learning Your Job

1. Find out from the buyer in your store what his usual datings, discounts, and shipping terms are on different types of goods. Also, ask about his opportunities to bargain on the terms of an order. Record your findings in your notebook.

2. Using your employer or a local banker as a source of information, find out under what conditions and terms the bank will lend a store money to pay for goods.

18. Pricing for Profit

Unit 18 Part 63

Pricing Merchandise in Today's Market

In many countries, it is customary for the storekeeper and the shopper to haggle over the price of an article until each is satisfied with the deal. In the United States, retail stores generally adhere to the *one-price policy*—the practice of setting a fixed price for an article and refusing to deviate from it. Although discounting is common in some types of stores, notably appliance stores, direct bargaining with customers is seldom done.

This has not always been the case. About the time of the Civil War, John Wanamaker of Philadelphia and A. T. Stewart of New York are said to have led the movement to establish a one-price policy. Other merchants also found that this practice built customer confidence in their stores, because each shopper believed he was given the same advantages as every other shopper. The practice of uniform prices saves valuable selling time for both the store and the customer. It helps the merchant to calculate in advance the amount of money he can count on to finance his operations.

A survey made by Dun & Bradstreet, Inc., the national financial rating agency, showed that haphazard pricing was one of the main reasons for failures in retail-store operation. Other reasons were lack of sufficient capital, lack of management training, and inadequate accounting records.

Fixing the selling prices of merchandise is not difficult when the merchant knows the cost of his goods. The first rule in establishing a selling price is to make sure the seller will realize an adequate profit on the article. At the same time, retailers are no longer able to charge "what the traffic will bear" —the highest price that customers will pay. The price must be competitive, and it must result in the inventory turnover desired by the merchant.

Methods of Determining Prices

Ideal prices are those that will move the largest quantity of goods in the

431

shortest time at a reasonable profit to the store. In most stores, the sale of a large number of items at a modest profit is more to be desired than large profits on few items.

Traditionally, merchants have determined retail prices by adding to their cost price an amount that will cover the store's expenses and leave a fair profit. Although many other factors—such as competition and customer services—were considered, the merchant used his delivered cost as the basis of his calculations. This method is still used in most stores and for most merchandise.

Pricing in Reverse. Some large stores and chains use a different approach when determining retail prices. In certain lines these stores are known for giving a certain quality at a traditional price. For example, the J. C. Penney Co. for years has maintained a $3.25 line of men's dress shirts. Thus, when the company buyer desires to keep to this usual price at retail, he must calculate how much he can pay for the dress shirts (cost price), still cover expenses, and leave a profit at the desired retail price. Under such pricing policies, the store buyer seeks a manufacturer who will produce merchandise to order at the desired cost price.

Factors in Retail Pricing

In addition to considering the expenses of doing business and the desired profit, the merchant must take into account other factors when setting prices.

Desirability of Goods. The desirability of the article to the customer is an important factor in retail pricing. Although two articles may cost the same, their value in the eyes of the customers may be different. By carefully considering the customer point of view, the store buyer may be able to mark up one of two similar items to a higher retail price than the other and still have it sell well. For example, in a shipment of men's suits to the retailer, all suits may cost the same. Because of a difference in appearance and materials, the retailer may set a higher retail price on some of the suits than he does on others. This same practice is followed sometimes in the case of women's clothing, house-furnishings, art goods, and other merchandise that is not too highly standardized.

If a merchant has the exclusive right to the sale of an article, he has the advantage of monopoly. Having this, he is free to charge whatever he wishes for the article. However, the merchant is usually more interested in treating his customers fairly and in selling the largest possible quantity of goods. He, therefore, sets his prices as low as is feasible.

Competition. Competition among stores handling similar merchandise is a great leveler of prices. The pricing policies of other merchants must be considered before the storekeeper can make a final decision on the amount of profit margin he should try to obtain. The extent to which a merchant must consider competition depends, however, somewhat on the character of his store and the good will it enjoys. His customers may be willing to pay a higher price in return for better services and a more attractive store environment.

Both large and small stores follow the custom of comparing their merchandise and prices with those of competing stores. To meet competition, a store may find it necessary to sell at prices lower than those required to yield a normal profit. Some stores announce as a matter of policy that they will not be undersold by competitors. For example, Gimbels Department Store in New York publicizes the slogan, "Nobody, but nobody undersells Gimbels."

Pricing Customs. Habits and customs of both consumers and store buyers are of considerable importance in price setting. If customers have been used to paying a certain price for an article over a period of time, they naturally expect to continue to pay this price. They will be suspicious of a selling price that is much lower; at the same time, they will resent a substantial increase. For example, if a woman has been accustomed to paying $10 for a certain type of leather handbag, she may not want to pay more than that; but she may question the quality if the price is much lower.

Service Policies. The service policies of a store are factors in pricing. For example, credit, delivery, service by salespeople, and other customer services add to a store's expenses. These additional expenses must be added to the prices asked for the merchandise. Customers of stores that offer such services are usually willing to pay somewhat higher prices.

Kind of Merchandise. The kind of merchandise carried has a direct bearing on the retail price. Merchandise that may depreciate in value must be sold quickly at a high enough price to cover possible loss. For example, high-fashion merchandise should be priced high enough to provide for losses. Merchandise of a staple nature, such as sugar, canned goods, or hardware, does not depreciate in value as do fashion goods. Such merchandise can therefore be priced at a lower profit margin.

Managing Price Lines

Prices for some goods, women's dresses for example, are established at certain price levels. Dresses that are somewhat the same in quality and appearance are priced at this level rather than having each article marked up separately in price. Price lines or levels were established because customers prefer to buy within certain price ranges. For example, some women may be willing to pay from $14.95 to $16.95 for dresses while others will pay from $22.50 to $24.50. If a large number of dresses are priced at $14.95 and at $22.50, customers can make comparisons more easily within the store and in other stores. Stores establish price lines especially in shopping goods; that is, in clothing and housefurnishings that can be sold within popular price ranges. When an article is received in the store, the buyer or his assistant decides into which price line the article should fall.

Just as it is important for the store buyer not to carry too many different brands or lines of merchandise, it is also important that price lines be kept at the level at which the greatest sales occur. This is a large factor in increasing stock turnover and in reducing retail inventories. By limiting the number of prices, the storekeeper likewise may reduce the number of items that must eventually be marked down and still maintain his sales. Another advantage from a sales standpoint lies in the fact that customers can make up their minds more readily when there are only a few prices than when there is a wide range. The establishing of price lines also simplifies the work of the buyer. Knowing his store expenses and his consequent markup, the buyer can readily ascertain the amount he can afford to pay for any given article or class of merchandise.

Many stores require their buyers to keep price-line control forms. A report of this kind shows at a glance what price lines are popular and those that are not. An example of such a form is shown below.

Establishing Other Pricing Policies

The increasing competition for the consumer's dollar leads many retailers to adopt price policies that are frankly promotional in nature. Various price appeals are used to attract customers and to increase sales.

Pricing in Odd Numbers. Some stores follow the practice of pricing goods, especially those of low or medium values, in odd numbers. The odd num-

DEPT. 27

PRICE LINE REPORT for Week of May 15 (Mark-down Price Lines not included)

Classification	Sold		Price Line	On Hand	
	Units	Net Amount		Units	Amount
Blouses	30	88.50	2.95	126	361.70
	8	28.00	3.50	46	161.00
	40	198.00	4.95	102	504.90
	35	243.25	6.95	112	779.40
	6	65.70	10.95	51	558.45
	17	220.15	12.95	56	725.20
Bathing Suit	6	33.00	5.50	26	143.00
	8	55.60	6.95	30	208.50
	10	89.50	8.95	41	366.95
	12	155.40	12.95	48	620.60
	16	223.20	13.95	60	837.00
	4	76.00	18.00	25	450.00

A typical price-line report.

ber draws attention to the lesser round sum. For example, if an article which would normally sell at $3 is priced at $2.97, the customer will think of $2 rather than $3. The odd prices are said to have a psychological effect—customers who might hesitate to pay $3 for an article may be persuaded to make the purchase if the price is $2.97.

The practice of pricing in odd numbers is, in general, used by stores that feature price appeal in their advertising. This is one of the devices used to impress upon customers the fact that the store's prices are established at the

This advertisement shows the manufacturer's list prices and the store's considerably lower retail prices, which also are in odd numbers to further attract the buyer.

Courtesy Alexander's Department Stores, Inc., New York

Quality + Economy at your MORNINGSIDE CO-OP SUPER MARKET

Open late Thurs. and Fri. Nights till 9 P.M.

SPECIALS-Thu, Fri, Sat, June. 8, 9, 10

Meat Dept.

CHOICE
Round Roast
    Top & Bottom   75¢ lb

CHOICE Eye Round
        Top Sirloin   85¢ lb

WEBSTER Bacon   53¢ lb

SELECTED Beef Liver   49¢ lb

Produce Dept.

FANCY
Blueberries
    PT box   29¢

FANCY Peaches   2 lb For 35¢

LARGE Canteloupes   29¢

HARD RIPE Tomatoes carton   15¢

For Better Buys Shop Co-op

CO-OP Green Label Pears 2-1/2   33¢

O.C. Potato Sticks   10¢

CO-OP Cider Vinegar PT   10¢

SUNSWEET Prune Juice   49¢

DUCHESS Strawberry Jam 12oz 25¢

BUMBLE BEE
    Chunk White Tuna 1/2   29¢

CO-OP Red Label Catsup 20oz 25¢

DROMEDARY
    Corn Muffin Mix pkg of 3   29¢

SNOWKIST Pea & Carrots 10oz   2/29¢

BREAKSTONE Sour Cream PT   37¢

PILLSBURY'S
    Golden Dinner Rolls   21¢

This co-operative super-market is advertising its weekend leaders in the various departments.

Courtesy Morningside Co-Op Supermarket, New York

lowest possible level. Stores catering to people who are more interested in quality than in price generally price their goods in round numbers. They depend on other appeals to convey the thought that they are giving good values.

Leader Pricing. To attract people into the store, some retailers often price certain items just above their delivered cost price. These items are known as *leaders.* Usually the price covers part, but not all, of the expense of handling the item. Sometimes these articles are called *loss leaders;* however, a *true* loss leader not only is priced too low to cover expenses, but is actually sold for less than its cost to the store.

Merchants use leaders on the theory that once customers are in the store they will purchase other items. Some stores believe leaders create the impression that all their prices are lower. Food stores often use items such as butter or coffee as leaders. In some states, cigarettes and gasoline are sold as loss leaders during "price wars."

The practice of using loss leaders, as followed by a number of stores, has been criticized by customers and by manufacturers. Customers object particularly when stores carry only a very limited stock of the articles advertised at the low price, and then, when this is exhausted, attempt to sell substitute merchandise at a higher price. The ethics of such practices are certainly open to question. Manufacturers whose national brands are used as leaders, because their quality and retail prices are well known, object to the use of their products as "bait" to attract customers. Price cutting on such national brands is often injurious to future sales.

Minimum Price Laws. In some states the law prohibits leader pricing and requires that merchandise be sold at a price that covers both the cost of the goods and the store operating expenses. In some states, the law also permits a manufacturer to establish a minimum retail price for his branded products. Such laws, however, seem to have little real effect since a discounting from the manufacturer's suggested retail price is a very common practice in many parts of the country.

Advertised List Prices. In recent years, there has been a trend by stores to advertise substantial reductions off the "manufacturers' list price." This practice is common in the appliance field and has spread rapidly to other lines. An honest reduction in the retail price is legitimate to clear inventories or to spur sales. The practice of advertising, however, or marking price tickets, with "phoney list prices" cannot be condoned. Furthermore, quoting "original" prices that never were that high can only lead consumers to question all prices and invite price "haggling." Pricing policies designed to trick customers into thinking they are obtaining "wholesale" terms are unethical and are shunned by retailers who take the long-run point of view.

Trade Talk

price line   leader pricing
promotional   loss leader
  pricing   list prices

Can You Answer These?

1. What factors should the retail merchant consider before adopting a price policy for his store? Explain.

2. What advantage do you see in the merchant's maintaining a minimum number of price lines?

3. How do customers benefit from the practice of stores of grouping merchandise into price lines?

4. Should retail stores, in your opinion, use "loss leaders" to attract customers? What is the effect of this practice on (*a*) customers, (*b*) retail stores, (*c*) manufacturers?

5. Give two reasons for pricing merchandise in odd numbers.

6. What are the two basic methods of pricing retail merchandise? Why do some stores use the less traditional method?

7. Describe the practice of promotional pricing using "list prices." In what ways are "phoney list prices" disadvantageous to stores and customers?

Problems and Projects

1. List the reasons why, in your opinion, it is important for a retail store to establish a pricing policy. From your observations of store advertising in your local newspapers and from your own experiences in buying goods, what stores in your community do you consider have definite pricing policies?

How do they make these clear to the public?

2. Bring to class illustrations of store advertising in which prices have been given in odd numbers. Does this method of pricing add to the effectiveness and pulling power of the advertisement?

3. Bring to class newspaper advertising or evidence from other promotional devices such as handbills or TV of (*a*) leader merchandising, and (*b*) use of manufacturers' list prices. Do these methods of promotion appear effective? Give examples of customer reactions to such promotions.

4. Prepare to debate both sides of the idea that the use of "phoney list pricing" tends to cause customers to haggle over prices.

5. Make a list of examples of merchandise for which you believe stores in your town set the price according to habit or custom. Use magazines to find national brands that attempt to maintain a customary price.

Learning Your Job

1. Talk with your supervisor, buyer, or manager. Find out your store's policies, and the reasons for them, concerning (*a*) odd-number pricing, (*b*) leader pricing, and (*c*) list pricing.

2. Make a list of the price lines maintained on at least two types of goods sold in your store or department. Find out the reasons why these price lines are carried. Judge for yourself whether the number of lines carried is good for the store.

64 Planning for Desired Margins

Recently the following conversation was overheard on a downtown bus. A woman passenger said to her companion, "You know, the other day we bought Suzy a new tennis racket. It was a good one, we paid $12 for it. But, I think the price that store charged is outrageous! Why, my husband told me that the store probably only paid $6 for it, and that's a 100 per cent profit!"

Like the woman on the bus, some customers think of profit as all the money a merchant receives above what he paid for the goods. They fail to recognize that from the customer's dollar the retailer must pay for the cost of goods and the operating expenses of the store, before he can start to figure on a profit for himself or his stockholders.

Consider the sale of a dress or man's suit. Typically, the cost of such items to the retailer is about two-thirds of the retail sales price. The other third must pay for salaries, rent, taxes, advertising, and other expenses of the store. Anything left is net profit. Setting a retail price is not a simple affair. Determining necessary markup is the heart of a store's pricing policies.

Understanding the Basis of Markup

Before a retail merchant determines a price policy—that is, the prices at which he will sell his merchandise—he must consider carefully the financial side of his store's operations.

Classifying Operating Expenses. The merchant must have an accurate picture of the items of operating expense, or overhead, that are included in his cost of doing business. The following list illustrates the expense classifications often used by department and specialty stores.*

1. Payroll
2. Rent
3. Advertising
4. Taxes
5. Interest
6. Supplies
7. Services purchased (such as light, heat, power, and delivery service from outside agencies)
8. Unclassified (such as cash shortages, supper money for employees, bad debts and fraudulent purchases, pensions and retirement allowances)
9. Travel (buyers, for example)
10. Communications (telephone, telegrams, cables, and correspondence)
11. Repairs
12. Insurance
13. Depreciation
14. Professional services (legal and accounting services furnished by outside firms, services of buying associations, credit bureaus, and store-planning organizations)

Determining the Margin

Every businessman prepares periodically a profit and loss statement, which gives him a picture of the way his business looks financially. This statement gives the merchant the information he needs to determine retail prices—the cost plus the markup. To arrive at the selling price that will yield a profit, the merchant begins with his sales. Suppose that estimated sales for the coming year are $100,000, that the cost of the merchandise to be purchased is $70,000, that total estimated operating, or overhead, expenses are $25,000, and that the merchant desires to obtain a net profit on sales of 5 per cent. He considers that this profit on sales is fair and in keeping with that earned by retailers in the same line of business. A simple profit and loss statement, summarizing these estimated figures appears as follows:

* A Manual of Expense Accounting for Retail Stores, National Retail Merchants Association.

PROFIT AND LOSS STATEMENT

Income from net sales	$100,000
Less cost of merchandise sold	70,000
Gross margin	$ 30,000
Less operating expenses	25,000
Net profit (5% of sales)	$ 5,000

At this point the merchant will determine the margin on which he must operate in order to obtain the desired profit; thus:

Operating expenses	$25,000
Net profit (5% of $100,000)	5,000
Margin	$30,000

Margin here has the meaning of *gross margin,* a bookkeeping term that expresses the difference between net sales and total merchandise costs. All operating expenses plus net profit are included in margin or gross profit. The term *gross profit* also is used to mean margin.

From the illustration we can see how the merchant determines what percentage of his estimated total sales this margin represents:

$$\text{Margin} \div \text{Sales} = \text{Markup}$$
$$\$30,000 \div \$100,000 = .30, \text{ or } 30\%$$

The merchant now knows that, in order to cover his operating expenses and earn a profit of 5 per cent, he must work on a 30 per cent margin on sales. In other words, he must price his goods—that is, mark them up over the cost price—at a figure sufficient to give him the margin he needs.

Determining Markup

The merchandise that the retailer purchases from the wholesaler or the manufacturer is invoiced to him at the cost price. He must find a method for changing this into the selling price. To do this, he must find out the markup; that is, the amount he must add to the cost in order to arrive at the selling price. For example, if a shirt costs a store $3 and is retailed (sold) at $4.50, the markup is $1.50. This markup is called *dollar markup* because it is expressed in dollars and cents. The relationships between cost, retail, and markup are illustrated as follows:

$$\text{Cost } + \text{ Markup} = \text{Retail}$$
$$\$3.00 + \$1.50 \quad = \$4.50$$

$$\text{Retail} - \text{Cost} \quad = \text{Markup}$$
$$\$4.50 - \$3.00 \quad = \$1.50$$

$$\text{Retail} - \text{Markup} = \text{Cost}$$
$$\$4.50 - \$1.50 \quad = \$3.00$$

Markup Calculated as a Percentage. In the preceding illustration, markup is shown in dollars. However, it is often expressed as a percentage either of the cost price or of the retail price. Using a percentage makes possible comparisons of markup even though the price is different.

Again we can use the illustration of the shirt. We already know the cost, retail, and markup in terms of dollars. To translate dollars into percentages the following methods are used:

(1) Markup (on cost) $= \dfrac{\text{Markup in dollars}}{\text{Cost in dollars}} \times 100$

$$\text{Markup} = \frac{\$1.50}{\$3.00} \times 100 = 50\%$$

(2) Markup (on retail) $= \dfrac{\text{Markup in dollars}}{\text{Retail in dollars}} \times 100$

$$\text{Markup} = \frac{\$1.50}{\$4.50} \times 100 = 33\tfrac{1}{3}\%$$

Using a Markup Table. Being able to compute markup helps in understanding and solving basic pricing problems. Many stores, however, have markup tables to provide information quickly and easily. Reference to the table on page 442 indicates the retail equivalents of retail markup and vice versa. It also aids in determining the retail price when cost and markup percentages are known.

Markup Is Usually Based on Retail. Most stores calculate markup as a percentage of retail rather than of cost. There are two main reasons for this. First, expenses and other items such as profits are commonly expressed as a percentage of net sales. Thus, it seems logical to express markup the same way in order to compare markup with other available figures.

A second reason for basing markup on the retail price is consideration for the customer who thinks in terms of retail prices. A markup of 50 per cent of retail is (see table on page 442) equal to a markup of 100 per cent of cost. Customers who do not understand markup would consider a markup of 100 per cent unreasonable, if not downright dishonest!

Calculating Initial and Maintained Markup

Two kinds of markups are commonly used in pricing—the *initial* or *purchase markup* (also called markon) and the *maintained markup*. The initial markup is the difference between the cost of the goods and the original retail price. The original retail price and actual sales price are, however, often different, as goods frequently are reduced in price in order to sell them or they may even be sold at a higher figure than the original retail price. The maintained markup is the difference between the cost of the goods and the actual sales price.

Our previous example of shirts showed they cost $3 and were priced at $4.50 initially. Thus, the initial markup (or markon) was $1.50 or 33⅓ per cent of retail. If these shirts were reduced in price and sold at $4, the markup

MARKUP TABLE

Margin Percentage on Selling Price	Markup Percentage on Cost	Margin Percentage on Selling Price	Markup Percentage on Cost
4.8	5.0	25.0	33.3
5.0	5.3	26.0	35.0
6.0	6.4	27.0	37.0
7.0	7.5	27.3	37.5
8.0	8.7	28.0	39.0
9.0	10.0	28.5	40.0
10.0	11.1	29.0	40.9
10.7	12.0	30.0	42.9
11.0	12.4	31.0	45.0
11.1	12.5	32.0	47.1
12.0	13.6	33.3	50.0
12.5	14.3	34.0	51.5
13.0	15.0	35.0	53.9
14.0	16.3	35.5	55.0
15.0	17.7	36.0	56.3
16.0	19.1	37.0	58.8
16.7	20.0	37.5	60.0
17.0	20.5	38.0	61.3
17.5	21.2	39.0	64.0
18.0	22.0	39.5	65.5
18.5	22.7	40.0	66.7
19.0	23.5	41.0	70.0
20.0	25.0	42.0	72.4
21.0	26.6	42.8	75.0
22.0	28.2	44.4	80.0
22.5	29.0	46.1	85.0
23.0	29.9	47.5	90.0
23.1	30.0	48.7	95.0
24.0	31.6	50.0	100.0

Find your margin or gross profit percentage in the left-hand column. Multiply the cost of the article by the corresponding percentage in the right-hand, or markup column. The result added to the cost gives the correct selling price.

that would be realized would fall to $1 and the maintained markup would be 25 per cent ($1 is 25 per cent of $4).

Markup on Individual Articles

In pricing individual articles, the merchant does not apply uniformly the markup percentage that he has found necessary to meet his expenses and realize a profit. On some articles, such as fashion goods or slow-moving items, a higher markup than average is generally desirable. On staple, fast-selling merchandise, such as groceries, a lower markup is possible. Even in food stores, however, retail prices vary widely above and below that price which is based on the average markup for the entire store. For example, on one wholesale grocer's price list, the lowest suggested markup was for 10-pound bags of sugar; the highest, for whole cloves. In view of the wide variations in the markup on individual items, the only method of maintaining a reasonably uniform margin is to keep a balance between the sales of both low and high markup items.

Using Markup in Buying

The store buyer computes his possible markups when he is determining which goods to buy. His supplier quotes him the wholesale (cost) price, which the buyer must translate into a retail price. Referring to our example of shirts once more, the buyer might be quoted a cost of $3 each. Knowing that he needs a markup of 33⅓ per cent of retail price, he uses the following method to find the retail price at which he should sell the shirt:

$$\text{Retail} = \frac{\text{Cost in dollars}}{100\% - \text{Markup percentage}} \times 100$$

$$\text{Retail} = \frac{\$3}{100\% - 33\frac{1}{3}\%} \times 100$$

$$\text{Retail} = \frac{\$3}{66\frac{2}{3}\% \ (66.66)} \times 100$$

$$\text{Retail} = \$4.50$$

Knowing the retail price he must charge, the merchant can decide whether or not his customers will consider the shirts to be a good value at that price.

Sometimes a buyer goes to market knowing the retail price at which he customarily sells goods. For example, the store may have a reputation for offering fine quality shirts at $4.50. In this case, the buyer can figure out how much he can afford to pay by using his known retail price ($4.50) and his desired markup percentage (33⅓ per cent) like this:

$$\text{Cost} = \text{Retail} \times (100\% - \text{Markup percentage})$$
$$\text{Cost} = \$4.50 \times (100\% - 33\frac{1}{3}\%)$$
$$\text{Cost} = \$4.50 \times 66\frac{2}{3}\%$$
$$\text{Cost} = \$3$$

Reducing the Retail Price

There are various reasons why the original retail prices are reduced. Articles may be marked down in price for a number of reasons—to attract trade, to move slow-selling items, or to clear odds and ends and shop worn goods. Reductions in the sales price also occur from discounts given to customers and employees. Any factor accounting for a reduction in the retail value of goods is classed as a *retail reduction*.

Probably competition has caused the retailer to advertise his new low prices.

Courtesy National Cash Register Co.

Causes of Markdowns

The need to mark down goods is one of the persistent and vexing problems of the retailer because it cuts into his margin. Some of the following reasons may be held to be responsible for markdowns.

Errors in Buying. Even expert buyers make mistakes in purchasing merchandise. When they do, it becomes necessary for the store to assume some loss in order to move the goods.

Rapid Style Changes. Rapid style changes date merchandise quickly. It must therefore be reduced in price and sold promptly before it becomes out of date.

Shopworn Goods. Goods sometimes become shopworn or deteriorate. As an inducement to customers to buy them, they are reduced in price.

Competition. Competition often makes it necessary for the merchant to lower prices on merchandise that is in good condition. He does not wish to create the impression that his prices are higher than those of his competitors, so he marks down the competitive articles.

Loss Leaders. Reference has already been made to the use of articles of merchandise as loss leaders. When merchandise is used for this purpose the selling price is marked down from the original retail price.

Miscellaneous Reasons. Unfavorable weather conditions, seasonal changes, and unwise original pricing of goods are other causes for markdowns.

Amount of Markdown

Experience and close observation will help the merchant in determining the percentage of markdown he must take.

One rule of thumb is that the markdown must be large enough to move the goods. Sometimes the slash in price must be drastic. At any rate, one large markdown is usually more effective than several smaller ones. If the merchant finds his markdowns becoming large, he should make a closer study of what his customers want; give greater care to pricing, advertising, and displaying goods; and instruct his salespeople in better methods of retail salesmanship. The merchant can obtain markdown information that will be of help to him from the trade associations in his own field and from other sources, such as the Harvard University Bureau of Business Research.

Timing the Markdown

Determining when goods should be reduced in price is difficult. The merchant often hopes that volume will increase if he waits a "few days more." However, even a few days may find fashion or fad merchandise completely unwanted except at a price below cost. In other cases, the "few more days" stretches into weeks while goods deteriorate, become shopworn, and take up space and money that could be invested more wisely in new stock. Again the wise retailer through experience learns to mark down goods quickly when there is evidence that they are not going to move. Desired turnover and adequate sales volume depend on taking substantial markdowns, timed to move slow sellers.

Some stores use a system known as *automatic markdown*. Briefly, this system sets a time period in which an item stays at its original price. If unsold at the end of that time, it must be marked down by a given percentage.

JOSEPH B. HALL
President, The Kroger Company.

Trade Talk

initial markup   overhead
maintained   expenses
   markup   operating
markdown   expenses
margin   retail reductions

Cost of Article	Margin Percentage of Selling Price	Selling Price
$1.00	18	
1.50	20	
1.80	25	
3.00	25	
6.00	40	

Can You Answer These?

1. Why is it important for the merchant to know the difference between margin and markup?

2. What is the difference between initial and maintained markup?

3. What are some common reasons for a merchant's marking down merchandise?

4. How can one explain the differences in the percentage of markups necessary for different kinds of articles?

5. On what kinds of items do retailers usually obtain minimum markups?

6. In what ways does tight control of a store's operating expenses affect pricing and markup determination?

7. Why is timing important in marking down the original price of merchandise?

Problems and Projects

1. Study three or four newspaper advertisements in which markdowns are featured. What reasons do the stores featuring these advertisements give for the markdowns?

2. Copy the following table in your notebook, heading a third column "Selling Price." Then, using the markup table on page 442, compute the selling prices on the following articles:

3. Ask a store owner of your acquaintance what items of expenses he includes in his margin or overhead. How does this store's list of expenses compare with that given on page 439.

4. Using a bookkeeping text, find several samples of profit and loss statements for retail stores. For each one: (a) calculate the margin on which the merchant must operate, and (b) explain what each of the items in the statement is and what it tells the merchant about his business.

5. Make a list of items for which you believe the initial markup is (a) low, and (b) high. Explain the reasons for each choice. Compare your list with those of other students.

6. Make a list of stores in your town which you believe operate at low or high markups. Give reasons why each store operates at such markups.

Learning Your Job

1. Select several lines of merchandise sold in your store, choosing those that differ considerably in value and nature. Find out what the initial markup is on each line. Indicate why the markup is of the size it is.

2. Find out what your store does to attempt to control and reduce markdowns. What responsibilities do you have in this effort?

3. Determine what over-all average markup your store management attempts to achieve. On individual items how large is the range of markup above and below this figure?

19. Accounting and Control

Part 65

Managing Capital Wisely

People have said that "anyone with a little common sense can run a store." Unfortunately this is not true. A good example of this can be given by telling the true story of a middle-aged man who lived in a midwestern town of 14,000 population. He was employed as a factory supervisor but had some part-time retailing experience. His wife had been employed most of her married life, and they had a modest savings account. Desiring a higher living standard and more independence, they decided to open a store.

They reasoned that the population was growing—more families with children. At women's club meetings, the wife gained the impression that good children's clothing stores were scarce. The couple found a well-equipped store building just off the main street, a lease was signed, and capital was invested in a stock of merchandise. At first, the Tot Shop, as the store was called, did a reasonable sales volume. But then, the volume dropped noticeably.

What was wrong? The inexperienced retailers had invested too much capital in high-fashion children's dresses and suits and not enough in play clothes and everyday shoes. The best-selling items were out-of-stock. But even worse, the owners had used up their savings and their borrowed funds on their initial inventory. The Tot Shop struggled on for a while, but eventually had to close, because customers couldn't find what they wanted and stopped coming.

The free-enterprise system in America offers many opportunities to the person who can obtain enough money to finance a business venture and who understands how to use financial facts in managing his business wisely.

In the United States, there are about 4 million individual, separate business establishments outside of agriculture, and 6 million more in agriculture, producing some 8 million different items. This provides 10 million centers of initiative and enterprise, 10 million places where experiments may be tried, usually without any outside authorization or control. Under 10 million separate business budgets, the managers are constantly striving to minimize costs and maximize net gains. Out of this vast, divergent, and multitudinous effort, the more aggressive and enterprising are constantly stumbling upon, designing or inventing the new. Successes are imitated, and under competition they must get imitated.*

* *How Competitive Is the American Economy?* Chamber of Commerce of the United States, p. 6.

Management's Need for Capital

A business analyst employed by Dun & Bradstreet, Inc., has said that, in order to start a retail store, capital should be sufficient to acquire enough inventory of merchandise, to obtain enough volume of sales, to provide enough profit, and to carry on the business successfully and maintain a satisfactory financial position.

Capital is required for two principal purposes: (1) to acquire the fixed assets, such as the building, equipment, and the fixtures; (2) to conduct the business. The funds used to buy a business or purchase the equipment and opening stock are called *initial capital*. The funds used to run the business are known as *current,* or *working, capital* and are used to purchase merchandise, pay salaries, and take care of the many other expenses necessary to the operation of a retail store.

After the store is in operation, the merchant may find that he needs additional capital. He may want to enlarge the store and add a few fixtures, or he may find that so much money has been tied up in merchandise and in customers' accounts that additional funds are needed for inventory replacements. The retailer should analyze many sources of capital before choosing the one that best suits his needs.

Sources of Capital

Small businessmen obtain capital to finance a business in a number of ways. They use personal savings, loans, the proceeds of a mortgage on real estate, and trade credit. Larger businesses tap some of the same sources of capital, but more often incorporate to obtain funds from investors.

Additional funds to meet operating expenses or to expand come from the sources listed in the previous paragraph plus the use of profits from the business. The advantages and disadvantages of each source of capital will be discussed in the following paragraphs.

Personal Savings

There is an old saying that "it takes money to make money." Thus, the future retail-store owner will find his personal savings very helpful in starting his business. Almost no one will lend money to an individual who has none of his own in the business. The amount of savings necessary will be determined by the size of the store, whether it is to be rented or purchased, the amount and value of the inventory and fixtures, and the kind and size of the operating expenses for the first few months. The owner, however, should not put all his savings into the business. Enough cash should be withheld to meet his family living expenses for the first few months.

Loans

Capital to start or operate a business may be borrowed from relatives, friends, or financial institutions, such as banks. The U.S. Small Business Administration, an agency of the Federal government, aids small retailers in obtaining capital to operate their businesses. Frequently, these loans are made through the co-operation of local financial institutions.

Loans may be long-term or short-term in length. Long-term loans usually run for a year or more. They are usually secured by mortgages on store real estate or on the fixtures and equipment (such as refrigeration cases or units) to be bought with the borrowed funds.

Short-term loans usually run for only 30, 60, or 90 days. They are used typically to meet current obligations (such as payrolls) or to take advantage of favorable prices on goods needed in the inventory. Funds for permanent improvements are not usually obtained on a short-term basis.

The bank or financial institution making the loan ordinarily judges the store owner's loan application according to:

> . . . the purpose for which the funds are to be used
>
> . . . the credit reputation of the merchant—the manner in which the applicant has met his past obligations, particularly in his relationship with the bank
>
> . . . the probable ability of the borrower to repay—as shown by examination of the financial statements submitted, particularly the balance sheet and the profit and loss statement.

In addition to the history disclosed by the financial statements, the banker will be interested in the current affairs of the business: (1) the trend of sales, (2) the trend of balances in customers' accounts, (3) the trend of cash accumulations and merchandise inventories, and (4) the trend of operating costs and of net profit.

Trade Credit

The terms of the credit extended by manufacturers and wholesalers to retail merchants were discussed earlier in Unit 17. Some additional ideas are useful, however, in illustrating how trade credit is used in financing a business.

The opening inventory is often obtained from wholesalers on a credit basis. Thereafter, additional merchandise is bought usually on 30-, 60-, or 90-day terms. Some manufacturers and distributors also install retail equipment on credit terms—for example, a frozen-foods case or specialized display rack to encourage the retailer to stock a given line of merchandise.

Trade credit is almost a necessity in retailing; however, the wise merchant is cautious about the interest he pays and is careful not to use credit to over-expand.

Profits

If the merchant has enough money of his own to start his business and can pay for improvements and expansion out of profits, he is undoubtedly using the safest and best method of financing his business. Even though the business may seem to grow slowly, the storekeeper owns the property he is using; and he does not face the problems of the merchant who rushes from one loan maturity date to the next.

Financing out of profits is practicable when the sales of a store show little seasonal fluctuation and the amount of stock that is required remains fairly constant. For example, grocery stores, meat markets, and drugstores should be able to take care of their financial requirements out of earnings, unless they desire to build or to make other substantial improvements. Stores whose business is seasonal in character—ladies' and men's apparel stores, department stores, and various specialty shops, for example—may find it necessary to arrange for short-term loans at certain periods during the year to build their inventories and cover their payrolls.

Partnerships

A store proprietor can increase his capital by entering into partnership with others. The additional partners not only provide new funds but also may bring specialized knowledges or skills needed by the business. For example, an appliance-store owner who is an excellent salesman and buyer may seek a partner who knows the service end of the business and who can keep accurate financial records.

Incorporation

Forming a corporation has financial advantages, especially for larger firms. The company is able to procure considerable funds by selling stock to a number of investors. Additional stock may be authorized and sold to finance a building-expansion program or the purchase of additional stores in order to form a chain. Incorporation and selling stock is, however, not a good method of procuring short-term funds.

Management's Need for Financial Facts

At the beginning of this unit it was pointed out that men and women can enter or leave the field of retailing with ease, and that their good or bad fortune is shared with manufacturers, wholesalers, and other suppliers. This freedom of enterprise, which benefits so many thousands of small retailers, carries with it a responsibility for good management that many retailers do not assume. Young people who wish to advance to store management or ownership need to learn the principles of good management and, particularly, the importance of complete and accurate record keeping.

Causes of Business Failures

Whenever a retail business fails, people are curious as to the reasons. Some

Why does a business close after 30 years? One of the reasons given below is probably the answer.

Courtesy E. I. du Pont de Nemours and Co., Inc.

blame bad luck; others cite poor location or a bad business year. Yet, the cause of retail-store failure is more basic—poor management.

Dun & Bradstreet, Inc., reports that in 1956 over 70 per cent of the failures could be traced to lack of ability by the management—40 per cent were judged incompetent and 33 per cent lacked management experience or previous experience in the retail line they were managing. This management weakness showed in their inability to deal with these reportedly apparent causes of business failure:

50 per cent—inadequate sales volume
21 per cent—competitive weakness
12 per cent—inventory difficulties

The table on page 454 shows the number of retail business failures since 1946; however, the number of failures is a small percentage of all businesses. In fact, in 1951 the 4,088 failures represented only 2.7 per cent of all retail businesses. The study indicates also that a large proportion of failures occurs in the second or third year of operation. Businessmen that survive the first few years apparently have acquired the "know-how" to operate successfully.

The Value of Good Records

Much of the incompetent management, reported as the major cause of business failure, is due to lack of financial facts. Without financial facts, retail management acts on "hunches" when trying to devise ways of meeting competition. Studies of bankrupt businesses show that sometimes no bookkeeping records were kept; in other cases, the records were inadequate for business requirements. One successful retailer says that his records are "worth their weight in gold" when they show him where sales are dropping and what expenses are climbing.

FAILURE TRENDS IN RETAILING		
Year	Number	Liabilities
1946	304	$ 6,273,000
1947	1,222	21,459,000
1948	2,185	39,819,000
1949	4,246	71,273,000
1950	4,429	72,691,000
1951	4,088	72,936,000
1952	3,833	75,547,000
1953	4,381	117,299,000
1954	5,491	145,473,000
1955	5,339	121,619,000
1956	6,341	156,048,000
1957	6,895	186,847,000
1958	7,514	225,277,000
1959	6,873	226,832,000
1960	7,386	241,094,000

Adapted from Dun & Bradstreet, Inc., reports, 1945–1960.

Records Needed in Retailing

The kind and number of records required vary with the size of the store. In the small store, the owner is usually active in the business and personally supervises many of its functions. From direct contact he has a more intimate knowledge of what is happening and may need only simple records. In the larger store, no one person, no matter how active, can follow and supervise all functions. The large store, therefore, requires more records and reports.

Since each store presents a different record-keeping problem, no specific systems are presented here; however, the retailer has many sources of help. For example, retailers' associations, such as the National Retail Merchants Association and the National Association of Retail Grocers, promote the cause of good accounting records among their members. Some private companies, such as the National Cash Register Co. and the Burroughs Adding Machine Co. have developed simplified systems of bookkeeping that can be adapted to different types of stores. Progressive wholesalers, especially those sponsoring a voluntary chain organization, offer standardized accounting systems to member stores. In addition, retailers can attend special bookkeeping courses for adults that are sponsored by the distributive education program in the public schools.

Store Operating Ratios

A retailer will find it helpful to compare periodically his costs of operation

OPERATING RATIOS FOR FURNITURE STORES

Items	Annual Sales Volume $250,000 to $500,000	Annual Sales Volume $500,000 to $1,000,000	Annual Sales Volume Over $1,000,000
Gross Sales	106.89%	107.37%	107.49%
Less Returns and Allowances	6.89	7.37	7.49
Net Sales	100.00	100.00	100.00
Cost of Merchandise Sold	61.61	61.24	61.23
GROSS MARGIN ON SALES	38.39	38.76	38.77
Operating Expenses:			
Administrative (Including Buying)	12.38	11.50	12.15
Occupancy (Store and Warehouse)	5.69	6.35	6.65
Advertising and Publicity	5.12	4.97	6.44
Selling	6.54	6.88	6.58
Handling	3.71	3.70	3.96
Delivery	3.48	3.40	3.03
TOTAL OPERATING EXPENSES	36.92	36.80	38.81
NET OPERATING PROFIT	1.47	1.96	−.04
Other Income:			
Cash Discounts Earned	1.11	1.13	1.18
Income from Credit Service Charges	4.94	4.51	5.07
Interest Earned (on Notes and Investments)	.20	.18	.26
Recoveries on Bad Accounts	.20	.21	.20
Miscellaneous	.30	.39	.46
Total Other Income	6.75	6.42	7.17
TOTAL INCOME	8.22	8.38	7.13
Other Charges:			
Discounts Allowed	.47	.25	.38
Interest Paid (Other than Mtge. Indebtedness)	.88	.70	.83
Provision for Bad Accounts	.67	.55	.63
Loss on Repossessions	1.60	.38	.30
Loss on Trade-Ins	.23	.50	.72
Miscellaneous	.94	.43	.46
Total Other Charges	4.79	2.81	3.32
NET PROFIT (Before Income Tax Deductions)	3.43	5.57	3.81
NET PROFIT (After Income Tax Deductions)	1.49%	2.62%	2.50%
Stock Turnover (times per year)	2.68	2.80	2.78
Amount of Average Sale	$69.81	$99.10	$77.00
Dollar Sales per Sq. Ft. of Selling Space	$21.36	$38.32	$35.30
Cash Sales—Per Cent of Total Net Sales	11.14%	13.68%	11.21%

Courtesy National Retail Furniture Association

A section of the record-keeping department of a large department store.

with those of retailers in similar lines of business. To do this, he must express his costs as percentages of sales. Such figures are referred to as *operating ratios*.

Comparison of operating ratios has several purposes. It enables a retailer to make revealing studies of his costs, item by item. The ratios serve as yardsticks for measuring his efficiency. Using intelligent guides such as these, many retailers have turned losses into profits, and small profits into larger ones. A sample showing the ratios for furniture stores having an annual sales volume from $250,000 to $1,000,000 and over is shown on page 455; another one may be seen on the profit and loss statement of the J. Maxwell Hardware Company on page 464.

Store operating ratios are compiled by the U.S. Department of Commerce, by such organizations as Dun & Bradstreet and the National Cash Register Co. and by such retail associations as the National Retail Merchants Association.

Trade Talk

working capital
short-term loan
source of
 capital

operating ratio
initial capital
long-term loan

Can You Answer These?

1. For what two major purposes does a retailer require capital?
2. For what reasons might a retailer need capital after his business was started?

3. In what three ways may a merchant obtain capital for running his business? Under what circumstances should he use each method?
4. What factors does a banker consider when approached by a retailer for a loan?
5. What do studies reveal as the major causes of business failures?
6. What is the major value of good financial records?
7. What can the study of store

operating ratios show the merchant?

Problems and Projects

1. The banker in your community is called upon to make loans to store owners. If possible, ask him what bookkeeping statements he examines before loans are granted and to explain the basis on which he is willing to make loans.

2. Make a chart listing a retailer's sources of capital. For each source indicate the purposes for which that type of capital is used.

3. Prepare a brief paper suggesting what a retailer could do to reduce the risk of business failure. Base your ideas on the causes of failure reported in the text.

4. Find out, if possible, approximately how much capital is required to open different types of retail stores. This information can be obtained from retailers who are family friends, the local chamber of commerce, bank officials, and representatives of firms, such as oil companies and drug chains that lease stores. Be careful not to appear too inquisitive but ask for information only in general terms.

Learning Your Job

1. If your employer will give you such information, ask him approximately how much money is currently invested in the stock, equipment, and fixtures of the store. If your employer prefers to keep such information confidential, then estimate as best you can the capital required to open your store, or a department in it.

2. Ask your manager or employer what he thinks are the best sources of capital for a business such as the one in which you are employed.

3. From information supplied by your employer, write a brief report on the types of trade credit available in your type of retailing.

66 *Preparing Financial Statements*

A few years ago during a sales clinic, a retail lumber dealer was asked how his business was going. He replied that he was making "a little money." He then went on to explain that all he had to do was compare his checkbook balances at the beginning and end of the year!

It was true that the lumber dealer knew whether he had more dollars in the bank, but he did not know about his actual profits. He did not realize that some profit might have been invested in equipment, thus increasing the value of his business. He had no idea how much was tied up in the inventory. He did not know whether his expenses had gone up or down. In other words he did not possess enough financial information about his business to start improving it. Carefully prepared financial statements were his greatest need.

Accuracy in Customer Accounts

Among the most important store records are those showing what customers owe the store. When goods are bought on credit, the information from the sales check must be summarized and transferred to several records. Charge-sales information is entered finally in what is known as the *accounts receivable,* or *customers, ledger*. This ledger is a record of all charge sales and payments made by customers. See the illustration of a charge sales check on page 97.

Methods of Recording Credit Sales

There are many different ways of recording charge sales. Some small stores merely clip the sales checks of each customer together and file them alphabetically. Most small stores enter customer charges and payments directly in the customers ledger, one ledger sheet or card being kept for each customer. These sheets or cards are arranged in alphabetical order.

In large stores, charge sales checks usually are sent first to the sales audit department. Here, the extensions and totals are checked and verified. Sales are compiled and recorded separately for each salesperson and department. Sales checks are listed on tallies, to be sure that each check has been accounted for. Any missing ones are traced and located; and if necessary, the third, or tissue, copy is used to replace the missing copy.

Charge sales checks are routed from the sales audit department to the billing, or accounts receivable, department. Here they are stuffed in the customers ledgers behind the proper account name. This work is often done by clerical workers called *stuffers*. After the charge sales checks of one or more days have been stuffed into the ledgers, machine operators post them to the proper account, recording the date, department, description of the merchandise, and the charges.

Some large stores enter all charges from sales checks directly on an invoice or statement form that contains the customer's name and is kept in a binder or

CUSTOMERS LEDGER

Name _M. K. Custom_

Address _516 Fifth Avenue, City_

DATE	EXPLANATION	POST. REF.	DEBIT	CREDIT	BALANCE
Apr. 1	n/30	S1	25 —		25 —
26	n/30	S1	50 —		75 —
28	Returned merchandise	J1		3 —	72 —
May 9	Cash	CR5		72 —	— —

folder for an entire month. Any charge sales made to this customer and any payments made by the customer are entered on this invoice form. By means of carbon paper, a duplicate record is made of all charges and payments. This duplicate is then placed with the records for other customers, and together, these records constitute the customers ledger illustrated on page 458.

Ways of Billing Customers

Regardless of how credit sales are recorded, each customer usually is billed by a monthly statement, or invoice, showing the sales, interest charges, if any, and payments. The form shown below is typical. Installment credit, granted on the basis of a sales contract, is handled similarly, except that customers often are given a book, like a bankbook, in which payments and interest are recorded.

Cycle Billing. The *cycle method of billing* customer accounts is being adopted increasingly. In this method, the usual customers ledger is discontinued

The monthly statement form.

Courtesy Recordak

and replaced by the credit-history record, a month-by-month record of totals of purchases, returned merchandise, payments, and balances due. Each customer's account is assigned alphabetically to one of some twenty sections. Instead of waiting until the end of the month to send out statements at one time to all accounts, each alphabetic section is assigned a certain day of the month. On that day, statements are mailed to the customers whose names appear in the section. Copies of all sales checks issued during the preceding thirty days are attached to the statement. Before these are mailed, they are photographed together with the statement. The film is kept so that it can be projected whenever a question arises. A customer's record is easy to find since the statements and tickets are shown in alphabetical order on the film.

Advantages of Cycle Billing. The cycle method of billing has a number of advantages, the chief ones being those of (1) spreading of the work of sending out statements over the entire month, (2) supplying copies of sales tickets to customers to check with the statements, (3) better use of office equipment and personnel, and (4) more efficient handling of customer questions and complaints.

Elements of Good Bookkeeping Systems

Although the customers ledger is really an integral part of a good store bookkeeping system, it was discussed separately because of its importance in maintaining good customer relations.

Requirements of Good Bookkeeping Systems

A great deal of expense need not be incurred in maintaining bookkeeping and accounting records. Many successful stores spend no more than 2 per cent of net sales on accounting and other records. Lack of necessary information costs more than this, because of the waste and other losses it causes.

The requirements of a good bookkeeping system for a retail store may be listed as follows:

It Should Be Simple. In the small store, the entries may have to be made by a person who is not trained in bookkeeping. Nevertheless, that person must understand what he is doing. In the larger store, a greater number of, and more complex, records will be required. These should be compiled and tabulated in such a way that the store executives can readily tell the condition of the store at any time.

The System Should Be Complete. It should satisfy the requirements of good bookkeeping, of the government's annual call for tax information, and of the banker's demand for credit information. Today the retailer's books are used as a basis for determining the sales taxes, Federal social security taxes, Federal excise taxes, and Federal and state income taxes. The banker to whom the retailer applies for a loan will want to study financial statements, the information for which has been obtained from the retailer's books.

A Good Bookkeeping System Should Show the Store Owner How to Stop Losses and How to Increase Profits by Cutting Expenses and Increasing Turnover. Competition governs, to a large extent, the costs of the merchandise the storekeeper buys and also the retail prices at which he can sell it to his customers. It is quite obvious, then, that within this margin between cost and retail, which is largely determined for him, he must so plan his expenses that he will be able to make a profit. An effective bookkeeping system will help him obtain this result.

Types of Accounts

In addition to a customers ledger, most stores keep two major records: the creditors ledger and the general ledger.

Creditors Ledger. The *creditors,* or *accounts payable, ledger,* is similar in operation to the customers ledger. Charges against the merchant (credits) are posted from invoices received and are added to the balance owed. Payments on account (debits) are posted from the merchant's own check stubs and are subtracted from the balance due. As in the customers ledger, a separate sheet or card is kept for the account with each wholesaler or manufacturer; and a daily balance is extended on each account.

The General Ledger. The general ledger gives a summarized history of all activities of the business—a bird's-eye view of the business in action. There are five main divisions of accounts in the general ledger:

1. Asset accounts
2. Liability accounts
3. Proprietorship accounts
4. Income accounts
5. Expense accounts

The Recordak machine expedites obtaining information about a customer's account.

Courtesy L. S. Ayres Co., Indianapolis

Asset Accounts. The asset accounts show the value of everything owned by or owed to the business. The Cash account, the Accounts Receivable account, the Merchandise Inventory account, the Notes Receivable account, the Furniture and Fixtures account, and the Delivery Equipment account are illustrations of asset accounts.

Liability Accounts. The liability accounts show everything owed by the business. Examples are the Accounts Payable and the Notes Payable accounts. When subtracted from the assets, they show the *net worth* of the business.

Proprietorship Accounts. Proprietorship accounts indicate the actual amount the proprietor has invested in the business. These accounts are credited with profits and charged with losses and withdrawals. The principal accounts shown under this classification are the Proprietor's Investment account and the Proprietor's Drawing account.

Income Accounts. Income accounts include the Sales account, the Discounts Earned account, the Interest Earned account, and Miscellaneous Income account.

Expense Accounts. The general ledger expense accounts show the merchant's expenditures for rent, light, heat, postage, telephone, telegraph, salaries, taxes, insurance, delivery, and other expenses.

Informative Statements

At the close of the month, or such fiscal period as the merchant considers best, financial statements should be prepared. These statements usually consist of a profit and loss statement and balance sheet.

Profit and Loss Statement. The profit and loss statement (see page 464) contains income and expense accounts taken from the general ledger. It presents a summary of the operation of the business over a particular period of time.

Balance Sheet. The balance sheet (see page 465) contains asset and liability accounts also taken from the general ledger. It is a picture of the condition of the business at one particular time.

The balance sheet and profit and loss statement, containing figures for the entire year, are used to prepare the tax statements required by local, state and Federal governments.

Aids to Better Record Keeping

As the American business system has grown more complex and competitive, the retailer has sought help in his efforts to gather financial facts. Among his most important aids are cash-register systems and bookkeeping service organizations.

Cash-Register Systems

At one time, many merchants used simple cash drawers or small cash registers that served only to ring up the total sales and to provide a change drawer. Modern registers, however, record much more financial information. The sales register lists and totals the individual prices for each item the customer buys. Some registers also calculate change. Many provide a record of cash or charge sales by departments and salespeople and of taxes paid. These totals can then be transferred to the accounting records at the end of the day. Because the cash register is a versatile piece of store record-keeping equipment, the retailer can select one that will give the necessary information needed in his business.

Bookkeeping Service Organizations

Of great value to smaller stores has been the development of bookkeeping service organizations. For a fee, such a company does the record keeping for a small store, also preparing its financial statements and tax reports.

Typically, the merchant mails in weekly to the bookkeeping service his

Cash Register Audit-Strip

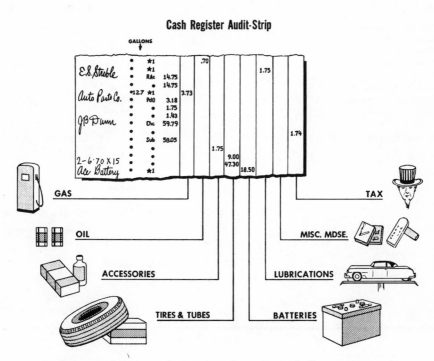

This audit-strip from a modern cash register automatically segregates sales and other transactions into eight columns. When a gas sale is made, the quantity sold is registered at the same time the sale is recorded.

J. MAXWELL HARDWARE COMPANY
Profit and Loss Statement
For Year Ended December 31, 19—

			Per Cent of Sales
Income from Sales		$25,264.82	
Less Sales Returns and Allowances		410.03	
Net Sales		$24,854.79	100
Cost of Goods Sold			
Merchandise Inventory, January 1, 19—		$ 5,000.00	
Gross Purchases	$16,210.50		
Less Purchases Returns and Allowances	215.00		
Net Purchases	$15,995.50		
Add Freight In	50.00		
Cost of Purchases		16,045.50	
Total Cost of Goods Available for Sale		$21,045.50	
Less Merchandise Inventory, December 31, 19—		8,000.00	
Cost of Goods Sold		13,045.50	52.2
Gross Profit on Sales		$11,809.29	47.8
Operating Expenses			
Rent Expense		$ 1,700.00	6.8
Miscellaneous Expenses		525.15	2.1
Salary Expense		3,877.82	15.5
Freight Out		150.10	.6
Bad Debts Expense		125.00	.5
Depreciation Expense		400.00	1.6
Supplies Expense		225.00	.9
Insurance Expense		70.00	.3
Total Operating Expenses		7,073.07	28.3
Net Operating Profit		$ 4,736.22	19.5
Other Income			
Purchases Discount		$ 114.16	
Interest Income		122.83	
Total		236.99	.95
Total Operating Profit and Other Income		$ 4,973.21	20.45
Other Expenses			
Sales Discount		$ 206.40	
Interest Expense		130.24	
Total		336.64	1.35
Net Profit		$ 4,636.57	19.10

financial figures, such as sales totals and expenses. A good example of how such systems work is the "Mail-Me-Monday Bookkeeping and Tax Method," provided by the Accounting Corporation of America. It describes its services as follows:

J. MAXWELL HARDWARE COMPANY
Balance Sheet, December 31, 19—

Assets

Current Assets			
Cash		$1,255.12	
Notes Receivable		1,420.00	
Accounts Receivable	$3,264.90		
Less Reserve for Bad Debts	325.00	2,939.90	
Merchandise Inventory		8,000.00	
Accrued Interest Receivable		60.00	
Supplies on Hand		75.00	
Prepaid Insurance		50.00	
Total Current Assets			$13,800.02
Fixed Assets			
Equipment		$4,550.00	
Less Reserve for Depreciation		900.00	3,650.00
Total Assets			$17,450.02

Liabilities

Current Liabilities			
Notes Payable		$2,675.00	
Accounts Payable		1,123.24	
Accrued Interest Payable		50.00	
Total Current Liabilities		$3,848.24	
Total Liabilities			$3,848.24

Proprietorship

J. Maxwell, Capital, January 1, 19—		$9,550.00	
Net Profit	$4,636.57		
Less Drawings	584.79		
Net Increase in Capital		4,051.78	
J. Maxwell, Capital, December 31, 19—			13,601.78
Total Liabilities and Proprietorship			$17,450.02

This service provides complete income and disbursement control and is designed especially for the smaller business venture. The client is not required to maintain any form of bookkeeping journals, ledgers, or summaries. Mail-Me-Monday relieves him of all record-keeping detail and permits him to devote all his time to the management and conduct of the business. The service includes preparation of all tax returns.

The detailed general ledger accumulates all data pertaining to income and expenses of the business. Summary profit and loss statements, furnished monthly, provide a clear and concise picture of the client's operating position. Complete identification of source documents and simplicity of tabulated form meet the requirements of all tax authorities.

accounts
   receivable
   ledger
cycle billing
asset accounts
proprietorship
   account
balance sheet

accounts
   payable
   ledger
general ledger
liability accounts
profit and loss
   statement

Can You Answer These?

1. What are the requirements of a good retail bookkeeping system?
2. What are the basic differences in the ways that credit sales are handled in small and large stores?
3. For what reasons is cycle billing being increasingly adopted? Do you think customers like this method?
4. What is the basic difference between an asset account and a liability account?
5. Into what main divisions is a general ledger usually divided?
6. What types of financial information can a merchant obtain from a modern cash-register system?
7. For what reasons do you believe small merchants have patronized bookkeeping service organizations?

Problems and Projects

1. Using the equation, Assets − Liabilities = Net Worth, prepare a balance sheet showing your net worth. Use the balance sheet given below as a guide.
2. The profit and loss statements and the balance sheets of many manufacturing concerns and retailing firms are published in pamphlet form or in newspapers. Obtain several copies of these statements and analyze them. Try to answer this question: "If I were a banker who was asked to make a loan, or an investor with surplus funds, would I invest in the firms whose statements I have analyzed?"
3. As you make purchases in stores for yourself or your family, observe carefully the cash-register operation in these stores. What common purposes do all serve? How do they differ from each other in terms of record-keeping purposes served?

ALFRED HART
Balance Sheet, May 31, 19—

Assets (things owned)		Liabilities (things owed)	
Cash	$ 3.40	Unpaid balance	
Loan to sister	1.00	on school annual	$ 3.00
Clothing	110.00	Owed to father	2.00
Radio	25.00	Total liabilities	$5.00
Activity ticket	5.00	Net worth	139.40
Total assets	$144.40		
		Total liabilities	
		and net worth	$144.40
	Total assets	$144.40	
	Total liabilities	5.00	
	Net worth	$139.40	

The cashier or store manager may be able to explain the features of his cash register to you. Prepare a report of your findings.

4. If possible, visit the office of a local bookkeeping service. Report back to the class what you find out about their services and charges. Perhaps a representative of the firm will talk to your class about good store records.

5. Prepare a chart showing the five divisions of a general ledger. Under each division list the names of as many accounts as possible that fall in that category.

1. Using information supplied by your supervisor, prepare a list of the types of financial information provided by the registers used in your store. If possible, describe briefly how each type of information is used to control store operation.

2. Make an analysis of the way your store handles the billing of credit sales. Write a brief report of your findings and include (*a*) a diagram of the billing process and (*b*) samples of the forms used in this process.

67 *Maintaining Budgetary Controls*

In retailing, as in most businesses, timely and accurate information is precious. With it, limits can be set on inventories and operating expenses. Without it, the retailer can only guess when preparing budgets. The owner of a small business usually can secure budget information from his own simple records. On the other hand, large retailers, especially chains, use more complex accounting systems, such as electronic computing equipment, to provide up-to-the-minute data.

Montgomery Ward & Company, Inc., in 1957, became one of the first retailers to install electronic accounting and statistical control equipment. Their electronic unit provides rapid tabulation and analysis of inventory and financial data obtained from a network of stores. It provides efficient control over buying, pricing, stockkeeping, and expenses. If present plans bear fruit, the next few years will see the introduction of smaller, less expensive computers into medium-sized stores.

Preparation of Retail Budgets

Intelligent consumers plan their personal and family spending in advance, basing their plans on their estimated incomes and on their needs for food, clothing, recreation, and the like. It is even more logical for a retail-store manager or executive to estimate future sales and to set up a budget for operating expenses that will leave him a profit. Retail budgetary control calls management's attention to business facts that enable him to:

Reduce expenses

Increase stock turnover

Expose and reduce mistakes
in buying and pricing

Spot merchandise
that does not pay

Build better credit

A retail budget has been called "a plan for the future, based on past experience and the present economic situation, together with any changes that may be anticipated." Essentially, preparation of a retail budget involves a careful estimate of future sales, purchases, and expenses.

The Sales Budget

The sales budget is made for a definite period of time, such as a month, three months, or a year. Estimates of sales volume are made for the entire store, for various divisions or departments, and for various lines of merchandise. These anticipated sales possibilities are based in part on past sales; however, con-

FINANCIAL BUDGET

B-Budget / A-Actual		Jan.	Feb.	Mar.	Apr.	May	June	July	Aug.	Sept.	Oct.	Nov.	Dec.	Total
① Bank Account 1st of Month	B	500	644	610	73	106	183							
	A													
② Sales	B	2750	2625	3350	3850	3950								
	A													
③ Total Funds Available	B	3250	3269	3960	3923	4056								
	A													
④ Merchandise Payments	B	1651	1750	3400	2813	2365								
	A													
⑤ Fixture Payments	B	164	164	164	164	164								
	A													
⑥ Expense	B	791	745	823	840	844								
	A													
⑦ Total Disbursement	B	2606	2659	4387	3817	3373								
	A													
⑧ Balance End of Month	B	644	610	(427)	106	683								
	A													
⑨ Additional Requirements	B			500		(500)								
	A													
⑩ Bank Balance End of Month	B			73		183								
	A													

03-4189

Courtesy Butler Bros.

sideration is given to other factors, such as local and general economic conditions, competition, fashion changes, availability of credit, weather, and trends in consumer shopping habits and preferences.

Sales quotas provide a basis for merchandise budgets and for planning such operations as sales promotions, displays, advertising, and maintaining the proper staff of selling and nonselling employees. In short, the sales budget tells the manager what he needs and how much money he has to spend for it.

The Expense Budget

As discussed earlier, the net profit of any store, or department within the store, is determined by the amount by which the gross margin exceeds the expenses. This margin depends partly on skillful buying; however, operating expenses can "eat up" even a sizable margin. On the other hand, expenses may be increased —say, for advertising—in order to obtain greater sales and a higher margin.

In any event, the retailer must plan his expenses, using his sales budget as a guide. He also considers other factors, such as wage trends, and the expected future costs of items such as wrapping materials, utilities, rent, insurance, and the like. The sales budget helps the manager allot expense budgets to departments. In this way, the department head knows how much he can spend for advertising, personnel, and other things that will be necessary to achieve his sales quotas.

Good expense control involves setting up classifications of expenses, establishing budgets for each expense classification, and continual analysis of expenditures in relation to the established budgets. (A suggested classification of operating expenses was discussed on page 439.)

Simply cutting down on expenses is not good business, for money must be spent to obtain the desired sales volume. Budgetary controls, however, show which expenses are resulting in profitable sales and satisfied customers.

Prevention of Inventory Difficulties

Good store managers adopt a control system that will prevent inventory difficulties—carrying too much stock, losing sales because of inadequate stock, or buying items that the public no longer desires. In this way inventory control systems serve as a merchandising tool.

As a buying tool, inventory control:

1. Points out what merchandise classifications are selling well; what should be ordered, and what should not
2. Indicates when to buy, so that stock will be on hand at the proper time
3. Shows the quantity of stock on hand at any time without the need for a physical inventory
4. Reveals inventory shortages

As a selling tool, inventory control:

1. Points out aging stock where markdowns are desirable
2. Reveals merchandise that is popular and worthy of extra sales promotion
3. Serves as a guide in planning special promotional events by showing how much stock is on hand
4. Indicates whether stock is on hand in the stock room or warehouse

To provide the inventory-control advantages listed above, two techniques are used: (1) stock-control record systems and (2) stock-turnover calculations.

Stock-Control Systems

In Unit 6, the elements of unit-control systems were viewed from the salesperson's point of view. At this advanced stage of retail study, stock control must be considered from the point of view of merchandising management.

As described earlier, there are three general sources of information on sales—stubs, sales slips, and physical inventories. The kind of information needed varies, of course, with the type and the size of store. Certain basic information is likely to be needed, however, on nearly all stock-control cards:

1. The amount and kinds of purchases. Information concerning goods on order and goods received can be obtained from the records of the order department and the receiving department.
2. The names of manufacturers from whom merchandise is ordered
3. Accurate information on styles, colors, sizes, patterns, and price lines
4. A record of all markdowns. This record enables the buyer to observe the effect of markdowns on sales.
5. A record of returns. Returns include both goods returned by the store to manufacturers and goods returned to the store by customers.
6. Sales record

If the buyer understands the principles of stock control, he can create a suitable system for his department or store; or he can obtain a system from his trade association or wholesaler and modify it to suit his needs.

Stock-Turnover Calculations

Turnover was defined in Unit 6. Its importance, however, in the intense competition of modern merchandising cannot be stressed too strongly. The calculation of turnover rates is a basic part of effective inventory control, leading a merchant to an awareness of the causes of low turnover and methods of increasing turnover.

Causes of Slow Turnover. A number of causes tend to contribute to slow turnover of goods. If a merchant carries too many price lines, too great a variety of stock, and too many sizes of stock, some of this merchandise will tend to stay on his shelves. Style changes, unusual weather conditions, lack of proper stock-control records, poor sales promotion, lack of interest and skill on the part of salespeople, and buying too much at one time in order to obtain large trade discounts—all tend to slow up sales and to decrease stock turnover.

Ways to Increase Turnover. Turnover can be increased by a number of methods. One way is to install a simple stock-control system. In addition, the merchant watches his purchases carefully—avoiding overbuying—devises special means to move "sleepers" from his shelves, and trains his salespeople in better methods of retail salesmanship.

Local conditions will influence the rate of turnover. It is well for the merchant to check his own results with those of other merchants in his field; however, the retailer should remember that averages are not necessarily standards. The merchant can obtain information on rate of turnover from trade journals and trade associations in his field and from other sources interested in the improvement of retailing, such as the National Cash Register Company and Dun & Bradstreet, Inc.

INVENTORY TURNOVER PER YEAR FOR VARIOUS BUSINESSES *

Kind of Business	Stock Turns Each Year
Appliance, radio, and television dealers	4.2
Automotive accessory and parts stores	3.9
Department stores	2.7
Drugstores	4.0
Dry-goods and general-merchandise stores	2.5
Floor-covering stores	3.7
Gasoline service stations	21.3
Grocery and meat stores	17.2
Grocery stores (stores handling groceries exclusively)	13.6
Hardware stores	2.1
Jewelry stores	1.3
Lumber and building-material dealers	4.3
Men's furnishings stores	2.1
Paint and wallpaper stores	3.2
Shoe stores	1.9
Sporting-goods dealers	2.5
Variety chain stores	3.4
Women's ready-to-wear shops	4.1

* *Standard Ratios for Retailing*, Research and Statistical Division, Dun & Bradstreet, Inc.

Ways of Figuring Turnover. Three methods are commonly used in calculating turnover rates:

1. *By using physical units.* In this method, the total number of units sold is divided by the average number of units in stock. *Example:* if the home-appliance department sells 60 electric refrigerators during a given period, and

the average number of refrigerators carried in stock is 15, the stock turn is 4. It is difficult, however, to use this method of figuring stock turn, because many store departments do not keep a record of units sold and on hand.

2. *By using retail figures.* Stores using the retail method of inventory usually find stock turnover by dividing net sales by the average stock at retail during the period. *Example:* if the net sales of a store for a year amount to $100,000, and an average of inventories for all months is $10,000, the stock turn would be $100,000 divided by $10,000, or 10 times.

3. *By using cost figures.* In this method, the sales at cost are divided by the average net inventory at cost. *Example:* first find the cost of goods sold; assume that the beginning inventory at cost for six months is $12,000. Goods costing $68,000 have been purchased during the period; and the closing inventory, also at cost, is $10,000. Cost of goods sold will, therefore, be $70,000. Thus:

Beginning inventory	$12,000
Add purchases	68,000
	$80,000
Deduct closing inventory	10,000
Cost of goods sold	$70,000

Next find the average stock, obtained by adding each monthly inventory and dividing by the number of months. Thus, monthly inventories:

January	$12,000
February	8,000
March	9,000
April	11,000
May	7,000
June	13,000
Total for 6 months	$60,000
Average monthly inventory	$10,000 ($60,000 ÷ 6)

The number of stock turns, therefore, will be 7, obtained by dividing $70,000 sales at cost by $10,000, the amount of the average inventory at cost.

It is advisable for the merchant not only to find the total rate of turnover on all stock lines but also to find the turnover by lines and even by separate items. A suitable stock-control system will help him obtain this information at any time. It is not wise to wait until the end of a six-month or a yearly period to ascertain the rate of turnover. An attempt should instead be made as soon as possible to learn the approximate rate of turnover on all merchandise carried.

Control of Credit Service

Consumer credit, increasing rapidly in use since the end of World War II, has become a major sales-promotional device. In fact, many retailers doubt that they could exist but for their credit sales.

Types of consumer credit were discussed in Unit 13 from the point of view of providing services to customers. At this point, credit must be studied as a merchandising technique—powerful in drawing sales but expensive if not carefully controlled. The retailer must learn to manage his customer credit program. He must marshal information and facts that (1) aid in the analysis and decisions necessary in credit granting and (2) reduce the probability of risk from bad debts or from tight policies that rob him of potential customers.

In setting up a controlled credit policy, the merchant can apply six fundamental credit principles that are applicable to any kind of retail business:

1. Investigate thoroughly and select new charge customers carefully.
2. Explain clearly to each new charge customer just what your terms are and get his definite agreement to pay on those terms. Also, establish his credit limit.
3. Follow up promptly, sending out the first reminder on the next day if possible (or within five days at the latest) after bills have become past due.
4. Suspend slow-pays, those who have not paid by the end of your credit period, from further credit until they have paid up.
5. Help delinquents, by showing them how they can pay immediately, instead of merely dunning and threatening them.
6. Act decisively with those who are able but apparently unwilling to pay, by promptly using collection pressures, collection agencies, or legal services.

Select Risks Carefully.   The first step in controlling credit is to select credit customers carefully. Every new customer who desires the credit privilege must be investigated thoroughly. When appraising a credit applicant, the credit manager must grade the risk to the store on the nine basic qualities listed below:

RISK FACTOR	QUALITY
Who is he?	Income
Can he pay promptly?	Employment
Will he pay promptly?	Residence
Can he be made to pay	Marital status
promptly?	Age
	References
	Reserve assets
	Payment record
	Reputation

Explain Carefully.   A second important step toward avoiding slow accounts is a clear explanation—both verbally and in writing—of the credit terms to the customer. The store should have a definite understanding with the new customer as to the amount of business he expects to charge in any one month or pay period. Establishing this credit limit helps to prevent overbuying and consequent slowness in payment.

Follow Up Promptly.   Promptly following up the accounts of all customers who do not pay their bills when due is the third step of a controlled credit and collection policy. When the monthly statement to the customer does not result in payment according to terms, the merchant must follow up promptly and consistently. This may be done with a set of printed reminders or notices, impersonal in nature, as shown below, so that the customer will understand that the treatment accorded him is similar to that given every other customer.

Telephone calls sometimes bring quicker results and some customers respond to telephone follow-up much better than they do to other methods. If the non-payment is the result of a grievance, this method of collecting will tend to remove the customer's objections to payment.

Suspend Slow-Pay Customers. A fourth step in an effective credit policy is to suspend temporarily further credit to all *slow-pay* customers—those who have not paid by the end of the credit period. Uniform and impartial suspension is absolutely necessary for making prompt-pay customers out of slow accounts. Unless this is done, customers will come to believe that the merchant does not mean what he says; and they will not take seriously future efforts to collect. Even though a few customers may be lost, this result is preferable to large losses because of failure to pay.

Help Delinquents. The fifth step in an effective credit policy is to help delinquents, by showing them how they can pay immediately, instead of merely dunning and threatening them. The retailer should telephone or write the delinquent, suggesting that he call at the store to talk over the matter of the past-due account.

When the customer comes in, a definite plan should be suggested to help him in paying the debt. If the amount is small, it can be settled, perhaps at one time; if it is large, monthly installments may have to be arranged. If, in addition, the customer also owes other merchants, it may be possible for him to refinance his total obligation through the help of a consumer credit agency. By doing this, he can pay all merchants in full and maintain his credit reputation.

Act Decisively. The sixth and final principle of an effective credit policy is to act decisively by promptly using collection pressure, collection agencies, or legal services with those who are able but apparently unwilling to pay. Immediate action is the only logical thing for the merchant to do with delinquents. Collection agencies and attorneys are usually willing to perform this service on a percentage basis. If they are successful in collecting the debt from the debtor, they are entitled to retain a portion of the amount collected.

Courtesy Ever Ready
Label Corp.,
Belleville, N.J.

Trade Talk

retail budget   expense budget
sales budget   controlled
average   credit
   inventory

Can You Answer These?

1. Give several causes of slow turnover in a store.
2. How can a merchant obtain more rapid turnover of stock?
3. Why is it important for the merchant to select credit risks carefully?
4. What personal characteristics or traits should the merchant consider before granting credit to anyone?
5. What are the six principles of controlled credit given in this part?
6. Why should the merchant explain his credit terms clearly and follow up delinquent accounts promptly?
7. In what different ways can the merchant help customers who have become delinquent in their payments?
8. In what ways does inventory control prevent inventory difficulties?
9. What purposes are served by (a) the sales budget and (b) the expense budget?

Problems and Projects

1. You have been asked by your employer, the owner of a well-regarded and successful men's clothing store, to assist him with his credit and collection problems. Your first assignment is to prepare a series of three or four collection letters to be sent to persons who have failed to make payments to the store when they were due. Prepare such a series, keeping them brief.

2. From as many sources as possible, obtain copies of collection letters and credit forms. Study these carefully from the standpoint of their effectiveness.
3. In the text on page 473 are listed four questions concerning the risk in extending credit and nine qualities of a credit applicant. Explain the advantages and disadvantages of each method.
4. Prepare a list of methods by which a retailer can deal with slow-pay or delinquent credit customers. Explain the advantages and disadvantages of each method.
5. Calculate the turnover rate in each of the following instances: (a) 150 cases of paint are sold and the average number in stock is 6; (b) a dress department sales were $125,000 last year. The average inventory at selling price was $10,-000; (c) purchases were $40,000; beginning inventory, $5,000; closing inventory, $9,000; average stock, $4,000 (all figures at cost).

Learning Your Job

1. If possible, ask your supervisor to show and explain the types of retail budgets kept by the firm. Bring sample budget forms to class and explain what goes in them and how they are used for control purposes. Keep these samples in your store manual.
2. Secure sample forms used by your store to control inventories and credit. Explain the nature and purpose of each. Include the forms in your store manual.
3. List the six principles of controlled credit. Find out how each is applied in your store. Prepare a brief written statement of your findings.

Personnel 20. Management

the costume

...s a rich girl. Go...ing goil to deny herself high fashion, whe... to the rescue with smart clothes at ...es. If you're loaded with taste, but not wit...'s and walk out looking like a mi...

NEW RONA

Unit 20 Part 68

The Employment Function

A well-known retail executive said that if he were to lose his building, equipment, and all his stock, he could rebuild his business provided he still had his store personnel. Most modern retailers will agree that an experienced, loyal, and congenial staff is the most important asset any business can possess.

The attitude of management toward the importance of personnel has changed greatly in recent years. Not too many years ago, less thought was given by the typical retailer to the selection of personnel than to the selection of merchandise. The progressive retail-store manager of today, however, knows that he cannot run a successful business without competent people. The best merchandise and the most modern building and equipment are of little value to the retailer if he does not have capable people who know how to make the most of these assets.

Today's manager, therefore, gives much thought to selecting the best people, training them, placing them in the jobs for which they are best suited, and providing them with healthful and pleasant working conditions.

The word "personnel," as you know, is derived from "person." In most stores of any size, there is a continuous need for persons to perform the various tasks that keep the store humming. Store expansion, promotions, transfers, and dismissals create demands for additional employees. These new employees must be located, interviewed, trained, and placed in the right jobs And the needs of all personnel must be looked after—compensation, morale, grievances, safety, and the like.

In a small retail operation, it is possible for the owner or manager to assume the entire personnel responsibility. In larger stores, however, it is not possible for him to do so; and a special department—the personnel department—is created for this purpose. This department is under the direction of a personnel manager. Depending on the size of the store, the personnel manager may have from two to twenty people assisting him.

477

The Job of the Personnel Manager

The personnel manager's job is a highly important one in a large department store or chain. In addition to recruiting new people to fill vacancies created by store expansion, promotions, and resignations, he sets up and runs training programs (discussed in Part 69); sets up standards for each job; establishes wage-and-hour standards in co-operation with management; helps to originate, then interprets and carries out, store personnel policy; and in general acts as the "go-between" for employees and management on grievance matters. If a union is involved, this latter duty is often a highly technical and complicated one.

The personnel manager's job in retailing is complicated by two additional factors:

1. The volume of retail business is not steady; it reaches a peak during certain periods of the day, certain days of the week, and on special occasions throughout the year. Most stores, therefore, not only maintain a regular staff but must also employ considerable extra help during peak periods.

2. Retail stores have a high labor turnover in many types of jobs, and the personnel manager must constantly be on the lookout for replacements. These replacements must usually be trained by the store.

Some personnel managers are promoted to their jobs from another position in the store. Many store executives feel that the personnel manager should have had experience "on the firing line"—as a general employee, as a supervisor, and as a department manager, before he can fully understand the problems of all employment levels of the business. Usually, when a person is promoted to this position from within the ranks, he is encouraged to take special courses in personnel administration at a nearby university or college.

Other personnel managers are selected primarily because of their comprehensive education in personnel work. Many colleges and universities offer undergraduate and graduate degrees in personnel management and labor relations. These programs are excellent sources for personnel employees. The person who aspires to the position of personnel manager will almost surely be required to have specialized training on the college level; at least the route to advancement will be considerably shortened by such preparation.

The personnel department is a service department; that is, it interprets personnel policy and advises managers and supervisors on personnel matters. Ex-

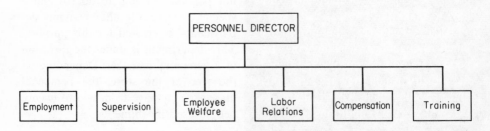

cept for those employees who work in the personnel department, it has no direct supervision over store personnel. Employee supervision is the responsibility of the various department heads, supervisors, and managers. Requests for new personnel and recommendations for training, promotion, transfer, and dismissal originate with the various department managers.

The personnel department performs six major functions in the typical large store.

1. Recruiting and employment
2. Training
3. Promotion, transfer, and dismissal
4. Employee compensation
5. Employee services
6. Employee relations

Recruiting, Selection, and Promotion

Requests for new personnel, as mentioned, do not originate with the personnel department. Let us assume that Mr. Burton, manager of the Men's Wear Department, has need for an additional salesperson. He makes out a personnel requisition, describing fully the qualifications needed to fill the position. After approval by management, this request is sent to the personnel department, which has the authority to locate suitable applicants. Usually the first thing the personnel department does is to look around the store to see if there is a qualified person in another department for whom this position would represent a promotion. If there is not, they will search their file of applicants. If this search does not turn up any likely candidates, they will undertake active recruiting outside the organization. They may run newspaper ads, put in requests with school and college placement offices, or make their needs known to various public and private employment agencies. They may do all these at the same time, in an effort to get as many applicants as possible—the more applicants interviewed, the better the chances are of getting the right person.

When applicants begin to come in, they are interviewed by a member of the personnel-department staff. The interviewer weeds out the undesirable candidates and sends to the manager of the Men's Wear Department only those whom he considers desirable prospects. He may make recommendations to the manager of the Men's Wear Department, but the final choice is up to the manager, since it is he who must supervise, train, and assume responsibility for the new employee. In recruiting employees, therefore, the personnel department performs a valuable screening service for the department managers, saving them much time that can be used to better advantage in running their own departments.

Selection of Employees

The cost of hiring and training store personnel is extremely high. Before an employee is ready to make a contribution to the store's progress and profits,

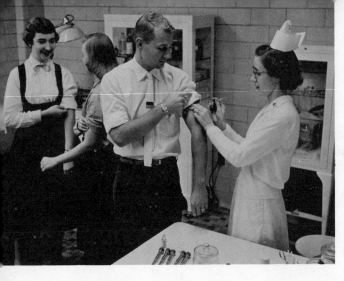

Many large stores have medical departments to protect the health of their employees.

hundreds—perhaps thousands—of dollars will be invested in him. Besides the actual cost of hiring and training, the store must also consider whether a new employee will fit in with the other members of the organization and whether he will contribute to the store's "personality." Employee selection, therefore, is serious business; and it must be approached as scientifically as possible.

Job Analysis and Specifications. The first step in the employment process is to find out the exact requirements of a position, so that the personnel recruiter will have a clear idea as to what requirements are necessary for the applicants. A job analysis includes:

1. A breakdown of the job—what the worker does and his various duties and responsibilities
2. Location of work and equipment used
3. Working conditions and special hazards
4. Education and training necessary to fill the job
5. Pay, hours of work, and opportunities for promotion

After the job analysis is completed, a brief summary—called a *job specification*—is made. This summary quickly gives the employment manager or interviewer a handy reference when he has a prospective worker before him. Often the worker is given a copy of this job specification, so that he may know what he is expected to do, and the nature of the working conditions.

Appraising an Applicant's Abilities. Information about an applicant's character and abilities may be obtained from several sources:

1. Application blank
2. References from schools and colleges
3. References from former employers
4. Personal references
5. Personal interview
6. Aptitude tests

The personnel department gathers as much information as possible from several or all of these sources. This material is valuable in the screening process.

Transfer and Promotion

On the recommendation of supervisors and department managers, the personnel department arranges for transfer of employees from one type of work to another and from one department to another. Promotions of employees are made only on the recommendation of supervisors and department heads; but the personnel department, through its training programs (discussed in Part 69) and rating systems, helps to encourage job growth and advancement and assists managers in evaluating job performance.

Employee rating may be done by supervisors on a monthly, semiannual, or annual basis. Of course, each employee is being constantly rated every day, but a formal rating report is required only periodically.

One means of rating salespeople is the shopping report. Many stores consider that the most effective shopping reports can be obtained by an outside agency, such as the Willmark Service System. This company employs sales analysts (shoppers) who make purchases of merchandise from salespeople, and while doing so carefully observe the salesperson's language and merchandise presentation. Information is recorded on a *shopping-report* form (see page 482). The shopping services rendered by the company are described as follows:

> Willmark's S.Q.B. (Selling Quotient Builder) is used by Willmark shopping analysts in reporting point-of-sale conditions. The S.Q.B. report reproduces, fact by fact, the manner in which the salesperson tested has served a typical customer; indicates exactly where the sales presentation was weak or strong; and enables the retail executive to correct selling weaknesses and commend efficient selling.
>
> This selling-performance report, graded on a percentage basis, provides salespeople with an incentive and stimulates their selling interest and enthusiasm. Many organizations increase this incentive by running contests and offering prizes to the salespeople achieving the highest grades. Experience has proved that such a program builds an overwhelming amount of employee good will, which in turn is reflected in improved customer service and increased customer good will.

Other Factors in Rating Employees. Most employee ratings, inside the store or by outside specialists, include personal factors such as dress, grooming, ability to get along with co-workers, willingness to accept criticism, and initiative. In establishing a rating scale, the qualities that have a direct relation to success in the employee's work are considered. Also, insofar as it is possible, ratings must be independent, impersonal, and based on unbiased judgments of these qualities. If an employee is rated fairly by two or more persons who are familiar with his work, the rating sheet may be a useful supplement to his other records.

Employee Welfare

The owners and managers of many stores want to make a genuine contribution

Form 20
Copyright, 1947, Willmark Service System, Inc.

S.Q.B.
(Selling-Quotient-Builder)

S.Q. [85] %

Company Name **Blank Bros.**
Address **33½ St. and Broadway**
City **New York**   State **New York**

Date **July 31, 1947**   Time **2:15** P.M.
Dept. **Sportwear**   Floor **3rd**

Quan.	Mdse. Purchased	Amt. Sale	Amt. Tend.
2	Sport Blouses	3.00	
	Tax	.06	
		3.06	3.06

Sample Copy

DESCRIPTION OF SALESPERSON

Man ○ Woman ⊗ Sp's. No. or letter **42 AI**

Approximate Age .... Build: Slender ○
Height .... Medium ○
Color of hair .... Heavy ○
Style of hair .... Wearing glasses ○
Description of clothes ....
....
Special marks of identification ....

A—APPROACH TO CUSTOMER
	Yes	No
1—Department Busy?	☐	⊠
2—Prompt Approach?	⊠	☐
3—If not prompt—		
a. did sp. recognize you as waiting customer?	☐	☐3
b. You waited aprox. min.		
c. Reasonable delay	☐	☐3
4—Sp's expression pleasant on approaching	⊠	☐2
5—Quote greeting "May I show you something?"		

VALUE 8

B—SECURING ATTENTION
	Yes	No
1—Was requested mdse. in stock?	⊠	☐
2—If not, did sp. attempt to fill your requirements?	☐	☐10
a. Suggested a substitute	○	
b. Offered to order item	○	
c. Directed you to another dept.	○	
3—Name item not in stock		
....		

VALUE 10

Did you voluntarily select all mdse. from a display   ☐ | ⊠
(If "Yes" do not answer Section "C")

C—ESTABLISHING INTEREST
	Yes	No
1—Was sp. familiar with location of stock?	⊠	☐2
a. Familiar with prices?	☐	⊠2
2—Showed wide enough assortment of mdse.	⊠	☐3
3—Showed mdse. pleasingly	⊠	☐3

VALUE 10

Was there any need to create desire or induce decision on purchased mdse.?   ⊠ | ☐
(If "No" do not answer Section "D")

D—CREATING DESIRE FOR MDSE.
	Yes	No
1—Gave details on good qualities of mdse.?	⊠	☐3
2—Stressed benefits you would enjoy from mdse. in use	⊠	☐3
3—Justified price of mdse.?	☐	⊠2
4—Answered questions satisfactorily	⊠	☐3

VALUE 11

E—TRADING UP
No opportunity to trade up   ○
	Yes	No
1—Made effort to trade up on requested mdse.?	⊠	☐12
a. Offered larger size unit	○	
b. Better quality mdse.	○	
c. More than one of item	○	
2—Actually showed this mdse.	⊠	☐2
3—Stressed benefits to be enjoyed from more or better mdse.	☐	⊠2

VALUE 12

F—SUGGESTION SELLING
No opportunity to suggest   ○
	Yes	No
1—Suggested additional mdse. other than that requested	⊠	☐12
2—Did sp. show this mdse.?	☐	⊠2
3—Did sp. stress benefits of buying suggested mdse.?	☐	⊠2
4—Quote suggestion "Would you be interested in shorts or slacks?"		

VALUE 12

G—APPEARANCE OF SALESPERSON
	Yes	No
1—Hair neat?	⊠	☐1
2—Clothing neat?	⊠	☐1
3—Fingernails clean?	⊠	☐1
4—Was salesperson—chewing gum— smoking on duty?—		○1
		○1

VALUE 5

H—APPEARANCE OF DEPARTMENT
	Yes	No
1—Floor clean?	⊠	☐
2—Mdse. neatly arranged?	☐	⊠1
3—Dept. well lighted?	⊠	☐
4—Mdse. clean and fresh?	⊠	☐

VALUE 1

I—COMPLIANCE WITH STORE SYSTEM
1—System used—Register ⊗	Book ○	Cert. ○
2—If register used, was drawer Closed ⊗	Could not observe ○	Open ○3
3—If system calls for receipt to customer— Was receipt given on above purchase?	⊠	☐8
4—Was merchandise given to you— After you paid ⊗		Before you paid ○6
5—Did salesperson call back—		

	Yes	No
Amt. sale	☐	⊠2
Amt. tend.	☐	⊠2
Change	☐	☐2
No change required	⊗	
6—Did sp. give you mdse. and change without unusual delay?	⊠	☐2

VALUE 25

J—CLOSING OF SALE
1—What did sp. say at close?
"Thank You."

Said nothing at close   ○6

VALUE 6

ADD NUMBERS LISTED BESIDE "NO" SQUARES AND CIRCLES IN WHICH X MARKS APPEAR. SUBTRACT TOTAL FROM 100, GIVING YOU THE S.Q. PERCENTAGE.

Remarks..
....

Performance rating of the employee by Willmark shopping analysts helps the employee as well as the store.

Courtesy Willmark Service System

to the welfare and happiness of their employees, and in a concrete way, give evidence of their interest in them. Moreover, most store managers feel that the men and women in their employ will be more productive if they lead well-balanced lives and have sufficient recreation and diversion.

The following employee services and activities are provided in many stores, and are usually under the supervision of the personnel department:

A job applicant is interviewed by a member of the personnel department.

1. *Cafeterias* where employees can obtain good food at reasonable prices.

2. *Employee Discounts* on store merchandise of from 10 to 20 per cent.

3. *Employee Mutual Benefit Associations.* These associations are formed for several purposes—entertainment, education, credit-union privileges, and betterment of employer-employee relationships.

4. *Retirement Plans.* These plans, whereby the store contributes to a monthly income upon retirement, are an inducement to experienced employees to remain in the store's employ.

5. *Group Life Insurance.* Under a group insurance policy, insurance protection is available at a lower cost than the employee could obtain in a regular policy.

6. *Employee Newspapers and Magazines.* These publications, containing news about promotions, social events, store policies, coming events, and so on, are good morale boosters and help to develop a "family image" about the store.

7. *Employee Organizations.* Musical, dramatic, social, and athletic organizations enable store workers to mingle in an informal atmosphere and help to keep morale high.

8. *Hospital, Dental, and Visiting-Nurse Service.* These services provide simple medical, dental, and general health care.

9. *Library for Employees.* Many large stores provide a modern library of books for recreational reading, as well as books and magazines for professional study and advancement.

10. *Vacations.* Most stores offer paid vacations to full-time employees.

Labor Relations

Maintaining harmonious employer-employee relationships is a relatively easy task in the small store, where the employee and the store owner or manager enjoy close, often very friendly, relations. In the large department and specialty stores, however, it is difficult, if not impossible, for the owner to keep in touch with his employees personally. The personnel department, therefore, is often charged with responsibility for handling employee grievances. Often, the grievance is just a misunderstanding that clears up when the employee finds a sympathetic ear or when a rule or policy is explained carefully.

Where a union is certified as a bargaining agent, the personnel manager is often the store's representative in its relations with the labor union.

Trade Talk

employee rating   personnel
job analysis   requisition
job specification   recruiting
personnel   shopping report
   director   S.Q.B.

Can You Answer These?

1. What are some of the duties of the personnel manager in a large department store?

2. What two factors, peculiar to retailing, complicate the personnel manager's job?

3. What are some of the ways in which personnel managers advance to their positions?

4. What is meant by the statement, "The personnel department is a service department"?

5. What six major functions are performed by the personnel department in the typical large store?

6. What are some of the ways used by the personnel department to locate applicants?

7. Why is proper selection of personnel so important in retailing?

8. From what sources may information be obtained about an applicant's character and abilities?

9. List and discuss briefly some of the ways in which store management contributes to the welfare of the employees.

Problems and Projects

1. Make a chart showing the duties and responsibilities of the person(s) responsible for personnel activities in one of the large stores of your community.

2. What do stores in your community do to create good will between employee and employer? What welfare programs do they carry on?

3. Find out and report to the class on the number and kind of labor unions operating in the retail stores of your community. Find out from what types of occupations they accept members. Try to obtain a copy of a union bargaining contract.

4. Ask a representative of the local office of the state employment service to speak to your class about the abilities and aptitudes needed in retailing and how they are tested.

5. If you were a personnel manager, how much value would you give to the personal interview as a means of selecting employees? Which would be more important in an applicant—experience or good character and personality coupled with the ability to learn?

Learning Your Job

1. Bring to class any shopping reports or other employee-rating forms used in your store. Describe how each is used.

2. Make a list of the employee welfare benefits your store offers.

Which of the benefits is most valuable to you personally? Why?

3. Describe how employee grievances are handled in your store. If a union is involved, describe its part in bringing grievances and other matters to the attention of management.

69 Training a Merchandise Team

Training is an important personnel function—a continuous part of every retail supervisor's job, regardless of department. The continuous responsibility for training store personnel may be illustrated in the buyer's job. All salespeople, experienced and beginners alike, need information and education about new merchandise; and they need to know about new uses, new features, and new values for merchandise the store has carried for some time. The buyer has intimate merchandise knowledge, acquired in the central market. He is in the best position to inform the sales staff regarding the features of the goods that motivated him to make the purchase, so that this information can be passed along to customers. Special "classes" are, therefore, held for all employees who are to sell this merchandise.

In the small store, training is carried on by the store manager. In the medium-sized store, responsibility for training may rest with the manager or be delegated to the experienced employee who has an interest and ability in this kind of work. In large stores, the personnel department co-operates with the various departmental supervisors in training and carries on certain phases of initial training.

Types of Training

In nearly all stores, at least two basic types of training are given: (1) initial training for new employees that will enable them to start on the job and (2) continuous training for workers already employed, to keep them informed concerning changes in store policies and regulations, new store plans, new merchandise, and promotion of this merchandise. In addition, stores often offer training for persons who have the potential to be promoted and for the store's executives.

Initial Training

The first training given to new employees is called *initial training* or *induction training*. This training usually deals with the sales-check and cash-register system, store policies, and basic salesmanship. The instruction is usually given in a store classroom, followed by a brief orientation period on the sales floor.

Typical of large-store programs is that of L. S. Ayres & Co., Indianapolis. The required initial training includes the following:

Store rules, organization, history, policies, and employee activities
Store tour
Store directory (for main-floor and downstairs salespeople)
Selling system
Cash register (for salespeople in departments using a cash register)
Salesmanship

Following initial sessions, the new person's training is continued on the job. This additional training may be given by a special training supervisor, but more commonly it is given by the assistant department manager or by an experienced employee who has been appointed sponsor in the department.

The sponsor takes charge of the new employee, introduces him to the other members of the department, takes him to lunch the first day, and in other ways helps to make him feel at ease in his new job. It is also the sponsor's job to observe the newcomer's work, to continue showing him the best ways to do the job, and to correct him when he makes errors.

In most large establishments, *store manuals* or handbooks are furnished to all new employees. The contents of these manuals vary, but the material in them is often grouped according to three main headings: store rules, general information, and employee benefits and activities. General handbooks and the various types of manuals fill an important place in store training. New employees can hardly be expected to remember all the information given to them during the initial training period, and the handbooks supplement the personal or class-room instruction.

Continuous Training

Continuous training is carried on in stores to supply salespeople and nonselling workers with information that will enable them to perform efficiently the work of the store. Continuous training for salespeople generally takes the form of instruction in the techniques of selling and of giving merchandise information. Merchandise information includes a general background of materials used, manufacturing processes, and selling points that will interest customers. In addition to this, information is given regarding the selling points of new and attractive articles of merchandise that are received in the store.

Continuous training of nonselling employees is also very important. Delivery-men, elevator operators, and office personnel all have contact with customers.

SPONSOR'S SLIP

Name of new salesperson . . . .

Number of new person . . . .

Dept. . . . . Date entered . . . .

Did you go over stock with new person, using attached sheet as guide? . . . .

Did you look over checks made by new person? . . . . (Checks should be written by new person but supervised by sponsor. Remember it is new person who needs practice.)

Did you introduce new person to

Floor Supt. . . . .

Aisle Supts. . . . .

Buyer . . . .

Asst. . . . .

Head of stock . . . .

Other salespeople . . . .

How many? . . . .

How much did new person sell on first day? . . . .
(Remember new person sells in your book only one day.)

Remarks . . . .

Signature of sponsor . . . .

Number of sponsor . . . .

Hand This Slip to Floor Supt.

To Floor Supt.:

Do you feel that a satisfactory sponsoring job was done? . . . .

Was new person shown the stock carefully and thoroughly? . . . .

Was new person helped with checks? . . .

Did you O.K. new person's timecard for nonselling? . . . .

Signature of Floor Supt. . . . .

Courtesy Mandel Bros., Chicago

Unless they reflect in their attitudes and actions the policies of the store, they can undo much of the good work done by salespeople and cancel the favorable impressions created by store advertising and other public-relations media.

Whatever the type of training, the work should be conducted in as interesting a fashion as possible; that is, training should be made pleasurable. Many stores, realizing the importance of this factor, have tried to give their training in an informal, interesting atmosphere. It is also necessary to supply some means of encouraging or motivating employees—of giving them reasons for studying and improving themselves. A department store in Louisville, Kentucky, by an employee-rating plan, rewards employees who have made an effort to study and whose performance on the job shows a resulting improvement. A detailed record is kept of each person's performance in the store and of the training work completed. Periodically, all employees whose records warrant it are then given increases in pay. A Seattle store introduced the element of novelty and at the same time made a game of the training effort. A "Mystery Shopper" contest was staged, in which salespeople were tested daily by an unknown shopper for skill in selling approach and suggestion selling. Cash prizes were awarded to the winners of this contest, and their names were listed on an honor roll in the store's employee newspaper.

Training for Promotion

Many stores fill responsible positions by promotion from within the store and,

Training classes are conducted by stores to keep their staff up to date on the best methods of selling.

Courtesy E. I. du Pont de Nemours and Co., Inc.

to make this policy really effective, offer definite help in preparing promising employees for promotion. Retail stores are increasingly employing capable, ambitious high school and college graduates, considering them excellent timber for future supervisory and executive positions. Such young people can profitably be given additional training and recognition by the store.

Executive Training

More advanced courses, somewhat resembling the promotional training courses, are often given to help store executives, both new and old. Such courses cover marketing problems, accounting, and sales promotion. To help executives teach others, courses are given in management problems, executive control, leadership, and training methods—for example, methods of training new section managers and buyers. Through a discussion of training needs and the problems that often arise in buyers' meetings and section managers' meetings, an attempt is made to develop skill in executives in leading group meetings and in training new employees.

The type of retail institution that generally carries on the training programs just described is the department store. A most important question in department-store training is whether this work should be carried on by centralized training departments or in a decentralized way; that is, directly by the heads of departments for the employees under them. Both systems of training are used.

Training in Chain Stores

The methods used in chain-store training are somewhat different from those employed in a department store or a smaller store. Methods are used that will permit the use in local stores of training material prepared in the main offices of the company and adapted to the needs of all stores in the system.

The training done by Sears, Roebuck and Company is a good example of chain-store training. The training materials prepared in the home office are used in the several hundred company-owned retail stores. In the larger stores, training is part of the work of the personnel department. In smaller stores, in which employees may number fifty or less, the educational work is conducted by the store manager or his assistant. Similar to the practice followed in department stores, training sponsors are used to relieve store executives of part of the training responsibility, particularly to give on-the-job training to individual employees.

The Sears general sales-training handbook, or manual, explaining the fundamental principles of selling, is provided for the use of all selling employees. Specific application of these principles is made through the special courses covering the principal kinds of merchandise sold in the company stores. In a hardware course, for example, much time is spent on sales training in hardware; in the paint course, on the selling of paint.

Many large food chains, national and regional, also have developed lengthy training programs. A typical training program puts the trainee through the various store activities. As he completes each phase of his training, he is given an opportunity to review his progress with the branch manager and personnel manager. On completion of this course, the trainee is made an assistant manager and is given further refresher training periodically.

Chains and many large independent stores also select bright young employees for college training. Sometimes, the firm pays the employee's tuition for night-school courses in adult evening schools or colleges. In other cases, the firm will pay all or a part of a retailing education in a college or university for those it picks as future executives.

Training in Public Schools

Public schools are taking an increasing interest in training for retailing and can be of much help to stores of all sizes. *Distributive education* is a vocational education program for persons in retailing, wholesaling, and other distributive occupations, which is sponsored by local boards of education. Local programs are aided by Federal and state vocational funds. These programs have been a substantial help to retailers.

Adult Distributive Education

Thousands of retail-store buyers, department heads, and junior executives have received instruction in supervisory training courses in such subjects as Job Instruction Training and Human-Relations Training. Salespeople and nonselling employees may enroll in their own communities in a wide variety of courses intended to improve their performance on the job and to fit them for promotion.

Co-operative Part-Time Programs

One of the greatest contributions made to retail stores and other distributive busi-

nesses by the public schools is the distributive education high school and post
high school co-operative part-time work-experience program. This program provides stores with the services of well-trained, intelligent high school students on a
half-time basis, the remaining time of the students being spent in school. A large
percentage of the students so employed become permanent employees of the
store upon graduation.

Distributive Education Clubs of America (DECA)

DECA refers to the program of youth activity operated by the Distributive Education Clubs of America. This youth activity program is designed for boys and
girls enrolled in part-time co-operative distributive education classes. It is organized on local, state, and national levels to provide incentives and recognition
for distributive education students. It encourages group participation, leadership
development, and career study and is recognized as a vital part of the total distributive education program.

The majority of local clubs plan activities that include social, civic, benevolent, fund-raising, and professional activities. The very nature of the distributive education instructional program and of DECA activities constantly emphasizes America's system of private enterprise and individual opportunity. Consequently, many merchants favor hiring these students because of their interest in the job and their related school study of that particular business.

Trade Talk

continuous training
executive training
induction training
DECA
initial training
distributive education
sponsor
store manual

Can You Answer These?

1. Why is training so important to the success of a retail business?
2. What kinds of skills and information are usually taught in initial training programs?
3. What are the duties of a training sponsor?
4. What kinds of skills and information are usually included in a continuous training program for sales personnel? for nonselling employees?
5. What is the purpose of promotional training? Who attends such classes?
6. What subjects are usually treated in executive training classes?
7. In what ways does chain-store training usually differ from that conducted by department stores?
8. Through what programs do the public schools aid retailers and those preparing for distributive occupations?
9. What is the purpose of the Distributive Education Clubs of America? What kinds of activities do local clubs carry on?

Problems and Projects

1. If a young person works in a store that offers little organized training, where can he go for training that will prepare him for advancement?
2. Name and describe the topics you would include in a continuous training program for each of the following: (a) a young salesperson in a department store whom you were considering as a potential assistant buyer; (b) a stockman in a chain-store supermarket who you thought could be a management trainee within a year; (c) a part-time high school student who works half-days in your hardware store and who wants to work for you after graduation; (d) a new salesperson with no experience who has just completed his first month in your store.
3. By yourself or as a member of a committee, find out what types of training are given by stores in your community. Prepare a report showing the training offered by various types and sizes of stores.
4. Visit the office of the person in charge of adult distributive education in your community. Let the director explain to you the various kinds of courses offered and report the information to your class.
5. Prepare a report on the purposes, organization, and activities of the Distributive Education Clubs of America. If material is not available locally, write to Distributive Education Clubs of America, 1010 Vermont Avenue, NW, Washington 5, D.C.

Learning Your Job

1. Describe the types of training your store offers. Which of them is given only to selected personnel and how are class members selected?

2. Write a report describing as completely as possible the initial training you received for your present work. Report to your class and compare your training with that of fellow class members.

3. Interview the person in charge of training in your store, covering what he considers to be the most important problems of training retail employees. Ask him for advice that he might give concerning the planning of a training program for yourself.

70 Advancing Your Career in Distribution

The Creed of Life

Isn't it strange that princes and kings,
And clowns that caper in sawdust rings,
And common folks like you and me,
Are builders for eternity?

To each is given a bag of tools,
A shapeless mass and a book of rules,
And each must make 'ere life has flown,
A stumbling block or a steppingstone.

Courtesy The Scott Paper Company

In pursuing a career in distribution, you are faced with the challenge of avoiding the "stumbling blocks" and locating the "steppingstones" that lead to a succession of positions in your career goal. Very likely, you have wondered just where the best career opportunities for you lie among the multitude of distributive occupations and how you may progress rapidly in a retail career. Through your study of retailing, you have formed some ideas regarding its organization and methods of operation. You are aware of the importance of retail distribution to your country's welfare and realize that there are many opportunities for employment in the field.

In this final part of this book, you will learn how retailers compensate employees. In addition, you will be challenged by some questions concerning yourself—questions that should help you in making plans for a career in distribution.

Compensation of Employees

The constant effort to reduce the costs of distribution has stimulated the interest of merchants in selling costs of every kind. Thus, stores are making earnest attempts to compensate employees in a manner that will bring forth their best efforts and yet keep selling expenses at the lowest possible percentage of sales.

It is difficult to find a method of compensation that is fair both to employer and to employees over a long period of time. The management of a store may have to experiment with a number of plans in order to find those that are best suited to its purpose and that are also satisfactory to its employees. The general types of compensation plans now in use in stores are described in the following paragraphs:

Straight Salary. Store workers, especially nonselling employees, are usually paid by the straight salary method. The advantages of this method are:

1. Salespeople and others know in advance exactly what they are to receive.
2. Only a small amount of clerical work is necessary to calculate the payments to be made.
3. The system is particularly suited to small stores where employees are frequently called upon to do a variety of work.
4. It encourages salespeople to spend the time necessary to render extra service to customers.

The disadvantages are:

1. It offers no additional reward for extra effort.
2. It penalizes the ambitious worker to the advantage of the lazy one.

Salary and Commission on Sales. A *commission* is a percentage of the money taken in on sales that is given to an employee. The method of paying a salary plus commission on sales is often used as an incentive to the salesperson to sell more goods. The advantages of this method are:

1. It rewards salespersons for additional selling effort.
2. It serves as a definite incentive to salespersons to put forth this effort.

The disadvantage is that it is difficult to adjust the rate of commission equitably for employees selling goods that differ widely in price.

Straight Salary Plus Bonus Based on a Quota. A *quota* is a sales-volume figure a salesperson is expected to reach. A *bonus* is compensation given in addition to the regular salary or wages. Sometimes a straight salary is paid, plus a bonus based on some quota. The bonus may depend on such things as the amount of sales, the amount of salary received, and the length of service. The advantages of this plan are:

1. It gives the employees something to look forward to in addition to the regular salary.
2. The quota serves as a sales goal.

The disadvantages are:

1. A bonus is often paid at such infrequent intervals that employees lose interest.
2. Employees often regard the bonus as a gift that they will receive regardless of the quality of their work.

Salary and Commission Based on Varying Quotas Adjusted According to Selling Costs. The amount of commission paid is sometimes adjusted in accordance with the department's *selling cost*—the ratio expressed as a percentage that exists between the total net sales of any department and the total salaries of the salespeople in the department over a given period. The advantages are:

1. A definite and scientific relationship between selling costs and volume of sales is obtained.
2. It tends to hold selling costs down.

The disadvantages are:

1. It is difficult to establish a fair quota satisfactory to both employer and employees.
2. A considerable amount of clerical work is involved in computing the total compensation due each selling employee.

Premium Money (P.M.'s). Salespeople are sometimes paid an extra amount for selling a particular piece of merchandise that is hard to sell. This extra amount is called *premium money* and is in addition to other kinds of compensation. "P.M. tickets," as they are called, are usually attached to the individual pieces of merchandise. The amount of the premium for each sale varies—usually it is from 10 cents to $1. The advantage of premium money is that it gives salespeople an extra incentive to sell slow-moving merchandise.

The disadvantages are:

1. The customer is frequently sold something she does not really want.
2. The amount of returned merchandise, the number of complaints, the loss of good will involved—all have helped to discourage the use of the premium system.

Know Your Temperament

Many a person has dropped out of the retail field because he did not understand his responsibilities as an employee. Many were not temperamentally suited to their jobs. Because there are many kinds of retail occupations and an almost unlimited variety of positions, it is important for the young retailer to examine carefully his abilities and temperament. Only after this self-analysis, can a person arrive at the answers to the basic questions leading to suitable career goals.

Security Versus the Venturesome Position. Do you prefer a position where you can show your worth through faithfulness, steadiness, patience, and persistence? Or do you enjoy work that requires imagination, ingenuity, and continuous creativity as well as the risk of failure? Nearly all of us lean one way or the other. Distribution has many occupations of both types. Positions, such as those in store-operations, finance and control, and personnel divisions tend to the security side, while those in merchandising and sales promotion are in the venturesome category.

Large or Small Establishment? Will you be happier in a large or small establishment? Do personal contacts and the fact that you see the results of your work and decisions immediately appeal to you? Or do you favor a large firm with well-defined channels of organization and specific policies? Does being a cog in the wheel bother you?

Specialist Versus Generalist. The specialist understands one field very well and deals primarily with practices and procedures. The generalist is concerned with people, leadership, and co-ordination. He must be able to see a wide area at a glance and make long-term decisions. Your understanding of yourself should give you the answer to the question of whether you want to be a specialist or a generalist.

Should You Go Into Business for Yourself?

Although hundreds of new businesses are started each day, the total number increases slowly, because almost every day the same number ceases operating. One reason so many fail is that the people who start them are poorly prepared by training and by character or are poorly financed. On the other hand, the very factors that make a business venture such a risk for some people multiply the chances of success for the educated, ambitious young person with the proper experience.

Why People Go Into Business for Themselves. A study of why people go into business for themselves was made by a large insurance company. It revealed the following answers:

> Even a big salary can't compensate for the satisfaction of being your own boss.

> There's a great security in knowing that you can't be fired, that your destiny is largely in your own hands.

> In your own business, you have the opportunity to use your own ideas and make your own decisions.

> Your success is your own. Whatever you build belongs to you. If you have the ability to make money, why not make it for yourself?

From these statements, it will be seen that the lure of owning and operating one's own business is rooted in motives that influence our whole economic system.

Disadvantages of Being a Small-Business Owner. Small-business

Department Store Sales

FOR CASH

56%

44%

ON CREDIT

1939

43%

57%

1960

PICTOGRAPH CORPORATION

It is interesting to note the increase in credit buying between 1939 and 1960.

men and women all over the country tell the same story about the disadvantages of their occupation,

> I work harder than I ever did in my life and have little time to myself. I've been so discouraged at times that I felt like giving up, and almost did. There's some new headache nearly every day and likely will be as long as I'll be in business. Competitors are always "hot on your trail" and sometimes scoop the market. Customers are moody. Economic conditions are frequently unstable. Taxes have a way of dampening one's incentive, and employees sometimes quit just when they become profitable producers.

The strange thing is that the small-business owner, when asked why he puts up with these conditions rather than pursue other lines of work, usually answers, "I like it."

The First Few Difficult Years. The longer you remain in business, the better become the chances for success. Statistics show that two out of three business failures occur before the business is five years old. It does not take long to find out whether or not the business succeeds.

Taking Time to Get Ready. Unlike the professions, such as law and medicine, deciding whether or not to go into business for oneself need not be done when one is very young—one can go into business at any age. This permits the prospective business owner to get a good education and the necessary experience in the business of his choice. It allows time for him to raise the required capital and to develop personality and character traits that are necessary to success. Capital is very essential to the young person who aspires to business ownership, because lack of it ranks with incompetent management as one of the two chief obstacles to business success.

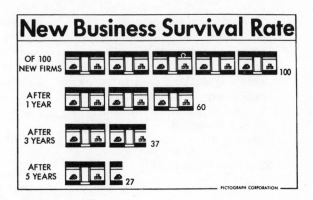

Final Tips to Young Workers

Having read this textbook up to this point, you undoubtedly have an interest in retailing, recognizing it as an important economic institution in every community or as a career for yourself. Whether or not you intend to pursue a retailing career, the authors wish to impart some final advice that may help to make "steppingstones" out of "stumbling blocks."

1. Select an occupation in line with your abilities and real interests, then locate a suitable position.
2. Don't discard an occupation solely because of an unpleasant experience in a particular position.
3. Terminate your employment when an objective analysis reveals that you are not suited to the work.
4. Don't be a job jumper. Changing jobs often causes people to become suspicious of your ability to hold a job.
5. Learn to do your present job well before concentrating on the one ahead.
6. Don't wait for breaks; make them.
7. Don't "win the battle and lose a war."
8. Never stop using good salesmanship, even for a minute.

The authors wish you success in your career.

Trade Talk

bonus   selling cost
commission   premium money
quota

Can You Answer These?

1. What are the two objectives of a good compensation plan?
2. Under what conditions is straight salary the best method of compensating retail employees?
3. What are the advantages and disadvantages of the salary and commission-on-sales plan?
4. On what basis are bonuses paid in retailing? What are the disadvantages of the salary plus bonus based on a quota plan?
5. How does the plan of compensating by a salary and commission based on varying quotas operate?
6. What is the trend regarding the payment of P.M.'s?

7. What questions concerning temperament should a person planning a retailing career ask himself?

8. What factors should be considered in deciding on a career as owner-manager of a business?

9. What suggestions do the authors give for success in a business career?

Problems and Projects

1. Using examples, explain why it is necessary for a company to experiment with a number of compensation plans.

2. Which of the compensation plans discussed in the text is most to your liking? Why?

3. For each of the following types of retailing jobs, recommend the method of compensation that would be best and defend your decision. (*a*) part-time salesperson in a chain shoe store; (*b*) cashier-checker in a supermarket; (*c*) salesperson in a high-fashion shop; (*d*) an assistant buyer who spends about half-time in actual sales work; (*e*) a salesperson who is also a training sponsor.

4. Choose between the alternatives described in the text under the heading of "Know Your Temperament" and between going into business for yourself vs. working for someone else. Give your reasons for your choice.

5. Ask your parents or someone else whom you respect to express opinions on each of the suggestions for job success given on page 497. Ask for additional items to be added to the list based on their experiences. Report your findings to the class.

Learning Your Job

1. Describe the methods of compensation used in your store. Using your wages, time worked, and sales record (if you sell) for one week, figure out what you would earn under two of the plans discussed in the text.

2. Categorize the occupations in the store for which you work according to whether they tend toward offering security or being venturesome, and as to whether they require specialists or generalists. Observe the people in each of the occupations under consideration to see whether they appear temperamentally suited to their occupations. Number the positions in order of your personal preference.

3. Interview at least three persons who work at the store where you are employed on the question, "Would you like to go into business for yourself? Why or why not?" Compare the results of your interviews with those of fellow class members and tabulate the results on the chalkboard.

Index